Revolutionizing the Cloud

Bishwajeet Pandey • Advait Patel
Editors

Revolutionizing the Cloud

Generative AI, Security, and Sustainability

Springer

Editors
Bishwajeet Pandey
Department of Computer Applications
GL Bajaj Institute of Technology and Management
Noida, Uttar Pradesh, India

Advait Patel
Cloud Reliability
Broadcom
Glenview, IL, USA

ISBN 978-3-032-07478-2 ISBN 978-3-032-07479-9 (eBook)
https://doi.org/10.1007/978-3-032-07479-9

This Springer imprint is published by the registered company Springer Nature Switzerland AG
The registered company address is: Gewerbestrasse 11, 6330 Cham, Switzerland

Preface

The cloud, once a revolutionary enabler of scale and agility, is itself undergoing a transformation, powered by the convergence of generative AI, security, and sustainability imperatives. We are witnessing a profound shift in how cloud systems are architected, operated, and governed.

This book, *Revolutionizing the Cloud: Generative AI, Security, and Sustainability*, is the product of collaboration with thought leaders, researchers, and practitioners who are actively shaping this new era. Each chapter captures a distinct facet of the transformation, from zero-trust AI security models and cost-aware sustainability strategies to the ethics of AI and the evolving edge-cloud ecosystem.

When we began curating this volume, we had one goal: to bring together perspectives that do not just explain where we are today, but boldly chart where we are headed next. The authors you will read here offer more than just technical depth; they offer vision. Many are leading major cloud modernization efforts, building AI-native platforms, or defining sustainability metrics that go beyond cost optimization to include carbon efficiency and social responsibility.

This is not a book of hypotheticals. It is a book of emerging practice. Whether you are a cloud architect, AI researcher, cybersecurity leader, or policy maker, we hope that this collection informs your decisions, sparks new ideas, and equips you to build responsibly in an AI-powered future.

We are grateful to all the contributors who brought their expertise and insight to this project. Their work represents not just where the industry is, but where it needs to go, toward systems that are intelligent, secure, and sustainable by design.

Noida, Uttar Pradesh, India — Bishwajeet Pandey
Glenview, IL, USA — Advait Patel
July 2025

Preface

Contents

Chapter 1
AI-Driven Cloud Transformation

Jyoti Kunal Shah and Nixalkumar Patel

Abstract Although the cloud has defaulted into the IT infrastructure of today, conventional manual techniques cannot adequately control its scope and complexity. This chapter offers a thorough framework for artificial intelligence-led cloud transformation spanning operational, structural, and executive levels. Methodologically, this study compiles architectural models, current industry surveys, and actual case studies to track AI's growing influence in cloud migration, AIOps, and multi-cloud optimization. AI is the driving force behind quantifiable efficiency, resiliency, and sustainability gains; it is no more a sidekick in the cloud.

This research confirms that AI is now much more than a sidekick in the cloud; it's a driving force behind the recent innovations, resilience, and efficiency we've seen in cloud systems.

Keywords AI-Driven Cloud · AIOps · Cloud cost optimization · Multi-cloud Orchestration · Cloud migration · Self-healing systems · Predictive analytics · AI Governance · FinOps · Infrastructure automation

1.1 Introduction

Artificial Intelligence (AI) is transforming the cloud computing world, serving as a driver of automation, optimization, and innovation. This chapter takes a deep dive into the consequences of this transformation, detailing how AI technologies are being integrated across the cloud lifecycle from planning and migration through to operations, cost optimization, multi-cloud orchestration, and sustainable outcomes. The chapter works through a lens of technical depth and industry relevance to analyze AI-assisted cloud migration, AI-enabled FinOps, infrastructure automation via AIOps, and AI-based orchestration in hybrid and multi-cloud environments. It

J. K. Shah (✉) · N. Patel
Independent Researcher, Parsippany, NJ, USA

B. Pandey, A. Patel (eds.), *Revolutionizing the Cloud*,
https://doi.org/10.1007/978-3-032-07479-9_1

outlines what we consider to be some key architectural considerations, challenges, and future research opportunities in the AI-cloud intersection.

Cloud transformation—the migration of IT infrastructure, applications, and data to cloud platforms—has become a cornerstone of digital strategy for modern organizations. In recent years, artificial intelligence (AI) has emerged as a powerful catalyst in this cloud transformation journey, giving rise to the paradigm of *AI-driven cloud transformation*. This refers to leveraging AI and machine learning techniques to plan, execute, and optimize cloud adoption and operations. Industry leaders recognize that the convergence of AI and cloud is poised to redefine enterprise IT; for example, IBM's Chief Scientist for IBM Research has highlighted that hybrid cloud and AI together form "one of the most important intersections" driving digital transformation [1]. Analysts echo this view: Gartner Inc. estimates that by 2025, *50% of cloud data centers will deploy AI-enabled automation (such as advanced robotics*), leading to a *30% improvement in operational efficiency* [2]. This trend is fueled by AI's capabilities in intelligent decision-making, prediction, and automation, which directly address the scale and complexity of modern cloud systems.

The significance of AI-driven approaches in cloud computing can be seen across multiple dimensions. First, AI helps organizations deal with the complexity of large-scale cloud environments by *automating routine tasks and managing resources dynamically*. Second, AI-driven analytics extract deeper insights from operational cloud data, enabling proactive optimizations that were not possible with traditional tools. Third, AI can enhance reliability and efficiency—for instance, AI assistants can monitor applications, predict potential failures, and even remediate issues autonomously, thus minimizing downtime [1]. As cloud environments grow in scale (with many enterprises now operating across hybrid and multi-cloud setups), these AI capabilities become essential. Indeed, studies show that the majority of enterprises are now multi-cloud (87% as of 2024), often using 4 or more cloud platforms, which dramatically increases management complexity [3]. In this context, AI-driven solutions are not merely ancillary tools but vital facilitators of cloud success. They help ensure that the cloud performs well, remains cost-effective, and is agile in a way that can't easily be achieved if human beings are the only ones doing the managing.

This chapter presents an in-depth examination of AI-driven cloud transformation. It surveys the background and context of how AI is being integrated into cloud strategies, reviews architectural considerations for building AI-infused cloud systems, and then its deep dives into core content areas including cloud migration, cost optimization, infrastructure automation (AIOps), and multi-cloud management—all empowered by AI. We include real-world case studies illustrating these concepts in practice, discuss challenges faced and the future outlook of this fast-evolving domain, and provide references to recent developments (primarily from the last 3–5 years) to ground the discussion in state-of-the-art practice.

1.2 Background

Cloud computing has gone from being a niche technology to being the standard infrastructure for businesses of all sizes within just over a decade. This cloud boom has been driven by the three main guarantees that the cloud offers: on-demand scalability, infrastructure flexibility, and a pay-per-use cost model. As companies have moved applications and data from premises data centers to public and private clouds, they have spent far less time than in the past provisioning resources and have incurred the same or lower costs. That said they have also experienced some new operational headaches cloud adoption has introduced. To the surprise of many, the cloud has turned out to be a very complex place to operate. Large and small companies now find themselves managing hundreds or thousands of cloud resources, dispersed across virtual machines, containers, serverless functions, and a myriad of cloud services. When business problems arise, it is pretty darn near impossible to troubleshoot effectively unless you have serious machine learning capabilities in place.

1.2.1 Timeline: Major AIOps Developments (2018–2025)

- **2018**: Gartner defines AIOps as a strategic IT operations model, catalyzing a wave of platform innovation [4].
- **2019**: IBM launches Watson AIOps, emphasizing real-time anomaly detection and explainable recommendations [5].
- **2020**: Dynatrace upgrades its Davis AI engine to deliver causal AI for automated problem resolution [6].
- **2021**: New Relic One debuts AIOps capabilities with ML-driven incident intelligence and anomaly detection [7].
- **2022**: Microsoft integrates machine learning into Azure Monitor for predictive performance tuning and proactive alerting [8].
- **2023**: AWS enhances Amazon CloudWatch with predictive alarms, auto-remediation workflows, and anomaly diagnostics [9].
- **2024**: Google Cloud's Operations Suite introduces LLM-based Root Cause Analysis across hybrid workloads [10].
- **2025**: Forrester predicts a pivot toward Composable AIOps using open telemetry standards and plug-and-play ML pipelines [11].

In summary, the context for AI-driven cloud transformation is characterized by (1) *Widespread cloud adoption* and multi-cloud strategies introducing new levels of scale and complexity; (2) the *need for agility and cost efficiency* in cloud operations, driving interest in intelligent automation; and (3) maturation *of AI technologies* (especially in machine learning and automation) that can be applied to IT operations. Enterprises that successfully integrate AI into their cloud management can gain significant competitive advantages—from lower costs and improved uptime to faster delivery of new capabilities. As we move into the mid-2020s, AI is increasingly seen not as an optional add-on but as a *key component* of cloud architecture and strategy [2, 12]. The following sections of this chapter explore how this integration is being realized, the architectural and technical considerations involved, and detailed domains where AI is making a tangible impact on cloud transformation.

1.3 Architecture Review and Considerations

Implementing an AI-driven approach in cloud environments requires careful architectural planning. Traditional cloud architectures focus on compute, storage, and networking design for applications, whereas an *AI-infused cloud architecture* adds new layers and components to enable intelligent analysis and automation. In this section, we review the high-level architecture of AI-driven cloud systems and key considerations in their design.

1. **Data Pipeline and Integration**: Any system that is driven by AI always has data at its center. The cloud emits so much data—from its servers and applications, as well as usage and cost data, and security logs. That is to say, we would be talking about a large data ecosystem with AI opportunities running right through it. To reap those AI opportunities, this architecture must have strong data ingestion and integration pipelines. The collected data is streamed into a centralized data store, such as a data lake or time-series database, which acts as the *"single source of truth"* for analytics. The goal is to break down silos and provide AI algorithms with a holistic view of the environment. Architecturally, this may involve using services like Amazon Kinesis, Azure Event Hub, or open-source platforms (Kafka, ELK stack) to aggregate and store data. A well-designed pipeline will make sure that quality of the data (accurate, timely, and relevant data) is intact, since AI insights are only as good as the underlying data. In addition, *data governance and security* must be considered—sensitive information should be masked or handled according to compliance requirements as it flows through the AI systems.
2. **AI/ML Analysis Layer**: The AI and machine learning analysis layer sits atop the data layer. In this layer, algorithms act on the aggregated data and produce insights or actions. The architecture usually encompasses a platform for analytics or an AIOps engine either a cloud service (such as Google Cloud's AI Platform, Azure Machine Learning, or AWS SageMaker for custom machine learning) or some integrated AIOps engine offered by a vendor. Key components of the layer include training pipelines for machine learning models and inference engines for real-time analysis. A component in this architecture might find that a model trained to predict the next hour's workload for an application is continually fed current metrics to forecast demand. Or, a model component might classify log events to detect which ones are indicative of an incident. This layer may incorporate various AI techniques: *predictive analytics, pattern recognition,*

natural language processing (e.g., parsing log text or user tickets), and even reinforcement learning for decision optimization. Modern cloud AI architectures often employ a microservices approach for these AI functions—separate services or containers might handle different analytics tasks (one for anomaly detection, one for forecasting, etc.), communicating via APIs. An important design consideration is *scalability*: scaling an AI analysis layer to accommodate real-time handling of extensive data isn't so simple, though. For that reason, cloud-native systems were undoubtedly the cheapest and also the most easily manageable way to achieve peak performance. They were preferred by cloud engineers during the design and development phases.

3. **Automation and Orchestration Layer**: The ultimate objective of AI-driven cloud management is not merely to produce insights but to act on them. Thus, the architecture consists of an execution or orchestration layer that can automatically implement changes based on AI outputs (or at least recommend modifications and execute simple automations). This could tie into existing cloud orchestration tools (like Kubernetes, which could be used for container orchestration, or, say, Terraform, which could manage other cloud resources). In a fully autonomous system (which some people, including me, tend to think of as the end goal of AI-powered cloud management), the outputs of AI algorithms are fed directly into the automation toolchain, which implements changes in the managed environment: scaling services, changing configuration files, or whatever. AIOps platforms like IBM's Watson AIOps or ServiceNow's ITSM use runbook automation and integration hooks to achieve this. When designing the architecture, we must also think about *feedback*: After an AI system makes a recommendation, the recommendation (should it have been a good one) also gets fed back to the system so the AI can learn from experience.
4. **Performance, Reliability, and Security**: Introducing AI capabilities introduces new components that need to be reckoned with in terms of performance and reliability. AI analysis must not become a bottleneck. Designs often use asynchronous processing or streaming to make sure that core operations are not delayed while waiting for AI decisions. When it comes to reliability, if AI-driven orchestration is not working, then the system must be capable of reverting to a manually controlled state (or just using a set of default rules) without any noticeable service interruption. For a number of reasons including security, systems that integrate AI need to have a plan for authentication, authorization, and auditing of any automated action done by the AI. Proper *authentication, authorization, and auditing* must be in place for any automated actions (e.g., using cloud IAM roles with limited scopes for the AI agents). Additionally, *data privacy* must be considered, especially if operational data contains customer information or sensitive configuration.

AI systems bring new threat surfaces as they get ingrained in cloud computing. In production environments, adversarial inputs—where malicious actors subtly alter data to mislead models—and model poisoning—where training pipelines are corrupted to compromise decision integrity—are increasingly plausible [13]. These hazards call for fresh layers of defense including adversarial training, strong validation pipelines, and real-time anomalous inference behavior monitoring. Nonetheless, including such protections into cloud-native artificial intelligence systems complicates model explainability, deployment, and governance. Especially in multi-tenant or federated environments, practical implementation sometimes reveals a conflict between fast iteration and strict security compliance [14]. To operationalize safe AI systems at scale, companies have to strike a mix between innovation and thorough threat modeling and open escalation processes.

In summary, an AI-driven cloud architecture comprises a *data layer, an AI/ML analytical layer, an automation layer along with performance, reliability, and security layer*, all working in concert (often in a closed-loop fashion). It resembles a control system which uses continuous monitoring, analysis (with learned knowledge), decision, and action, followed by feedback. When reviewing architecture, organizations must consider data pipelines, scaling of AI workloads, safe automation practices, and integration into the broader IT environment.

Underneath the AI orchestration tier, a specific ML-OPS sub-layer exists that guarantees end-to- end lifecycle completeness. When performance declines, this layer controls continuous integration and delivery (CI/CD) of machine learning models, tracks model drift, and provides rollback systems. Versioned pipelines, feature stores, and automated retraining help to support auditable, scalable artificial intelligence deployment. This sub-layer closes the operationalizing gap between data science and production, thus completing the integration of artificial intelligence in cloud ecosystems.

1.4 Core Content

1.4.1 AI-Assisted Cloud Migration

One of the earliest touchpoints for AI in cloud transformation is the *migration phase*—moving legacy systems and data to the cloud. Cloud migrations are complex undertakings involving assessment of existing applications, choosing target cloud architectures, data transfer, and cut-over, all while minimizing downtime and risk. AI-driven tools and techniques have begun to significantly assist in this process, making migrations faster, more reliable, and less labor-intensive.

Planning and Assessment: AI can analyze large portfolios of applications and determine the optimal migration plan. For example, in order to understand how different applications and servers interact, modern AI-assisted migration platforms use *automated discovery* and *dependency mapping*. Traditionally, this was done via manual audits or static analysis, but AI-based tools can scan through configuration data and network logs to identify application dependencies and usage patterns. By doing so, they can *group applications* that should move together (to avoid breaking interdependencies) and identify legacy components that may need refactoring. AI evaluation of legacy code is another emerging capability—using machine learning to scan source code (even in older languages like COBOL or PL/SQL) and suggest how cloud-ready it is, or even convert it. IBM Research, for instance, worked on AI that can "*speak code*"—translating legacy code to modern languages—to accelerate cloud migration and application modernization [1, 15]. This kind of *AI augmentation* in code analysis can greatly boost productivity by automating parts of code refactoring and containerization.

Execution and Automation: AI assists during the execution of the migration by orchestrating the transfer of data and ensuring that the cut-over occurs with minimal downtime. It can do this because it determines the best time to perform the cut-over based on its knowledge of the business's operational patterns. For example, on a given day, if you have 50% more users active between 9:00 AM and 11:00 AM than between 11:00 AM and 1:00 PM, an AI is much more likely to recommend that you not attempt a cut-over between the two peak periods. For example, if certain configurations or middleware from on-premises don't directly map to cloud services, an AI rule-based engine can automatically adjust or *recommend equivalent services*. One real-world example is Coca-Cola's migration to Google Cloud: Coca-Cola used Google's AI-powered migration tools to streamline moving millions of records and applications across departments [16]. The result was *reduced migration time*—faster than initially anticipated—with minimal disruption to ongoing operations [16]. This was achieved by AI models that forecasted the needed infrastructure in the cloud and enabled dynamic scaling during the migration, so that resources were available when needed and not over-provisioned [16].

Risk Mitigation: A key challenge in cloud migration is managing risk—ensuring data integrity, avoiding outages, and meeting performance requirements in the new environment. AI assists here via *predictive risk analysis*. Past migration projects (and the data from them, if available) can serve as the foundation for training machine learning models to recognize the risk factors likely to lead to project delays or failures. Even without historical migrations to draw from, AI can still help predict project outcomes. For example, AI-based simulators might predict how an application will perform in the cloud post-migration, given its current on-prem performance and the chosen cloud instance type. This helps companies to validate that the target environment is sized correctly. AI can also continuously monitor the migration and can flag anomalies (e.g., data transfer rates dropping or an unusual error pattern in logs) so that engineers can intervene before a minor issue becomes a major problem. *Real-time validation* is another example where AI ensures data is transferred accurately—AI compares source and target data for discrepancies using intelligent sampling or anomaly detection, rather than relying solely on slow full verifications which sometimes delays end-to-end Software Development Life Cycle.

Key Features of AI-Driven Cloud Migration: AI augments cloud migration in several concrete ways:

- **Automated Dependency Analysis**: AI tools automatically map application dependencies and architectures, reducing manual effort in understanding com-

plex legacy systems [17]. This ensures no component is overlooked in the migration plan.
- **Intelligent Migration Sequencing**: With predictive analytics, AI can minimize downtime and avoid contention when determining the order in which to move components. For example, it might suggest moving a database before migrating application servers or the other way around depending on how the two will need to function together post-migration.
- **Downtime Prediction and Reduction**: AI evaluates system loads and user access patterns to recommend migration windows. It can predict potential downtime duration for each migration step. Some advanced solutions even enable *live migration* techniques with AI coordinating data sync in the background so that cut-over is nearly instantaneous, thereby addressing the common concern of *downtime and service disruption* [16].
- **Automation of Repetitive Tasks**: Many migration steps (provisioning infrastructure on the cloud, copying data, running tests) can be automated. AI scripts or bots handle these tasks at scale and speed.
- **Compatibility Resolution**: AI assists in solving incompatibilities between old systems and cloud platforms. For example, if a system that's on the premises is using a proprietary database feature, an AI tool might automatically change the relevant queries or data structures to be compatible with a cloud database service. This is really an example of general AI reasoning to do something useful. This kind of *intelligent conversion* saves significant developer time.

A practical example combining several of these features is Johnson & Johnson's cloud migration. J&J, a large global enterprise with thousands of applications, utilized Microsoft Azure's AI-enhanced migration tools for their move to the cloud. Azure's platform used AI for automation and analysis, which yielded notable results: J&J achieved cost savings through AI-optimized resource allocation, *minimal downtime* by scheduling migrations during off-peak hours (a decision made by machine learning algorithms), and a *faster overall migration timeline*—reaching operational readiness in the new environment much sooner than originally projected [16]. These outcomes underscore AI's value in tackling migration complexity.

Although AI-driven orchestration can greatly improve cloud workload migration timing and accuracy, its limits should be acknowledged. Live migration promises low-latency impact, access to trustworthy telemetry data for decision-making and available redundant resources. Constraints including inter-region bandwidth variability, data gravity, and dependency mapping errors can in fact cause partial failures or extended service interruption windows. AI-based recommendations also sometimes rely on past trends and could find it difficult to handle edge situations or unexpected workload spikes. Companies should always validate forecasts in staging environments before full production release and apply AI-assisted migration selectively, giving stateless services or replicated workloads top priority [18].

In summary, *AI-assisted cloud migration* turns what used to be a labor-intensive, error-prone project into a more automated, intelligence-driven process. Organizations leveraging AI report faster migrations, lower costs (by choosing the right resources and avoiding over-provisioning), and reduced risk. As one source notes, AI for cloud migration "involves integrating artificial intelligence into every phase of cloud migration—planning, execution, and post-migration optimization," allowing evaluation of existing systems, prediction of challenges, and automation of tedious tasks for a seamless transition [17]. When migration is treated as a data-driven exercise, AI can provide the necessary guidance and, more importantly, the grunt work needed to move the infrastructure to modern cloud architectures. However, this does not mean that AI can or will perform migrations without human experts. In fact, AI's value in the migration process lies in its ability to perform the types of analyses and do the types of work that allow the human experts to focus on higher-level design and decision-making. After migration, AI continues to play a critical role in *post-migration optimization* in the context of cloud cost management.

1.4.2 AI-Driven Cloud Cost Optimization

When workloads are in the cloud, cost optimization is a constant concern. The cloud is pay-as-you-go, and that is a double-edged sword; it offers flexibility, and, if managed correctly, it should not be any more expensive than an on-premises equivalent. But, because it is so easy to provision resources in the cloud and because there are so many types of resources to choose from, costs can get out of hand if one is not vigilant. AI can and should be used to help drive the cloud budgeting process; that is, the set of steps that leads to making cloud usage efficient, predictable, and, ideally, cheap.

Traditional cost management involved setting budgets and manually reviewing billing reports for anomalies. In contrast, AI operates continuously and granularly, finding savings opportunities humans might miss. Key AI-driven strategies for cloud cost optimization include real-time monitoring, anomaly detection, predictive resource provisioning, and intelligent workload placement. According to industry reports, a significant portion of cloud spend is wasted—Flexera estimates about *28% of cloud spend goes unused* (e.g., paying for idle or forgotten resources), and the FinOps Foundation's 2024 survey found that "reducing waste" became the top priority for cloud financial management teams [19]. These statistics underscore why AI tools are being adopted; they excel at sifting through usage data to pinpoint such waste.

Benefits of AI in Cloud Cost Management: AI brings several benefits that directly translate to cost savings:

- **Continuous Cost Monitoring and Anomaly Detection**: Cloud costs and usage can be monitored in real time by AI-powered instruments, something you could never hope to do even with the best human eyes and hands. These intelligent programs learn what normal spending looks like. They learn what kinds of resources are used and how much they should cost. Then, by virtue of being powered by artificial intelligence, they figure out when the spending is going haywire, often by finding the sorts of patterns in data that humans miss. Gartner has noted that AI-driven cost optimization is driving new advancements in predictive analytics for cloud finance [20]. Cloud providers themselves offer such features: AWS has *Cost Anomaly Detection* using machine learning, Azure Cost Management includes anomaly alerts, and Google Cloud's Recommender uses AI to flag unusual cost trends [19]. These tools ensure that "bill shock" is avoided by catching issues early.

- **Rightsizing and Eliminating Idle Resources**: Identifying underutilized resources is a classic optimization task. AI can analyze utilization metrics (CPU, memory, etc.) over time to determine if a server is oversized for its workload. For instance, Google's cloud can analyze 8 days of instance usage and recommend a smaller machine type if appropriate [19]. Azure Advisor similarly uses ML to suggest rightsizing for VMs, databases, and Kubernetes clusters [19]. Organizations that regularly act on these AI recommendations often see *30% or more reduction in infrastructure costs* [19]. In addition, AI can immediately turn off resources that are idled. It could be a development environment left on and running overnight. It could be an old load balancer that is receiving zero traffic. Instead of relying on humans to remember to turn these off and to do so in a timely manner, AI policies can verify that these resources are truly in an idle state and could make the decision to turn them off and eliminate unnecessary waste.
- **Intelligent Workload Placement**: In multi-cloud or hybrid setups, AI can decide which environment or region is most cost-effective for each workload. It might, for example, notice that a batch analytics job could run in a cheaper region or on a spot instance (preemptible VM) without affecting results, thus saving money. One strategy called *workload placement optimization* uses AI to match workloads with the optimal pricing model and region. A case in point: AI may determine latency-sensitive services must run in a higher-cost region close to users, but nightly data processing can be shifted to a low-cost region or secondary cloud provider. By doing this automatically, significant saving is realized because multi-cloud optimization is achieved "without altering the existing code" [19].
- **Demand Forecasting and Predictive Autoscaling**: Traditional autoscaling in the cloud reacts to current load (e.g., add an instance when CPU > 80%). AI takes this further by *predicting future demand* and scaling *proactively*. Machine learning models (like time-series forecasting using LSTM or Prophet) can forecast workloads hours or days ahead by learning patterns (peak business hours, end-of-month reporting surges, etc.). With predictive autoscaling, resources are scaled up *in anticipation* of the load, and scaled down when a lull is predicted. Google Cloud has implemented *predictive autoscaling* for its managed instance groups, using past CPU trends to pre-warm capacity a few minutes before expected spikes. This reduces the need to run with lots of headroom (idle capacity) just in case, thereby cutting costs while still meeting performance needs. Similarly, AI forecasting helps with *capacity planning*—finance teams get accurate cost predictions for future months, which is crucial for budgeting. "What-if" analysis powered by AI can show how launching a new feature or marketing campaign might impact cloud costs, so companies can plan accordingly [19].

- **Optimization of Purchasing and Pricing Models**: Data centers are expensive and not easily scalable, and their infrastructure tends to be underutilized. Cloud providers offer various pricing options (on-demand, reserved instances, savings plans, spot instances, etc.). Helping companies decide the right mix can be complex, AI can analyze usage trends and recommend when to buy reserved capacity or commit to savings plans for maximum discount. It can also identify which workloads are suitable for spot instances (which are cheaper but can be interrupted) and orchestrate their use. By matching workloads with the optimal pricing model, AI ensures potential savings.

In summary, organizations have to combine cost-allocation granularity tools including tag hygiene, resource labeling, and showback models if they are to maximize the impact of AI-generated optimization insights. AI outputs—such as idle resource identification or predictive auto scaling—can be exactly linked to business units, projects, or cost centers when tagging is consistent and enforced across teams. This link improves responsibility and lets recommendations for cost control guide behavior. Though their efficacy mostly depends on accurate and complete tagging systems, platforms like AWS Cost Explorer and Azure Cost Management now support artificial intelligence-augmented analytics [21].

Key AI-Driven Techniques for Cloud Cost Optimization: To summarize, here are *several complementary AI techniques and how they reduce cloud costs* [19]:

- *Workload Placement & Scheduling*: AI schedules and workloads are placed on the most cost-efficient infrastructure (across instance types or clouds) while meeting performance requirements. For example, it might schedule non-urgent jobs during off-peak hours or on spot VMs and consolidate workloads to fewer machines during low load periods to save energy and cost [19].
- *Anomaly Detection*: Using ML on historical spending data, AI detects outliers in cost (e.g., a sudden 3× increase in storage costs) and alerts the team or takes action [19]. Early detection prevents runaway costs from misconfigurations or attacks (like crypto mining malware running up your bill).
- *Rightsizing Recommendations*: AI continuously looks for resources that are over-provisioned. By analyzing usage over time, it suggests or automatically adjusts to smaller instance sizes or fewer nodes. Studies show that implementing these rightsizing suggestions regularly can reduce infrastructure expenses by about one-third without impacting performance [19].
- *Predictive Budgeting*: AI creates forecasts of cloud spend based on trends, giving finance reliable forecasts and alerts if projected spend will exceed budget. This allows proactive adjustments (e.g., optimize resources or allocate more budget) rather than surprises. Integrated what-if analysis helps simulate the cost impact of growth or changes [19].
- *Predictive Autoscaling*: As mentioned, AI forecasts demand and scales resources in advance. This smooths out the peaks and valleys of resource usage, avoiding both over-provisioning (idle resources during valleys) and performance issues during peaks. The net effect is higher average utilization of resources, which means less waste [19].

These techniques often reinforce each other. For example, by rightsizing (reducing baseline waste) and using predictive autoscaling (handling peaks efficiently), the overall cost profile flattens. Anomaly detection then catches any out-of-pattern events on this optimized baseline. Workload placement ensures that each component is running in the cheapest environment possible. Together, they form a holistic AI-driven cost optimization strategy [19].

Last but not least, though artificial intelligence promises to help with cloud cost control, the road to optimization is not a straight line toggle. Real-world installations call for months of tuning models, controlling noisy alerts, and adjusting threshold sensitivity to prevent false positives—alerts that might flag mission-critical staging or DR environments as waste. Operations teams may develop alert fatigue and mistrust from these interruptions. Common also is cultural resistance; recommendations produced by artificial intelligence could contradict engineer-designed layouts or be seen as compromising team autonomy. Strong feedback loops and explainable artificial intelligence layers are what organizations need to close this difference and guarantee adoption and confidence. To properly handle these friction points, successful implementations often combine cross-functional buy-in with automated insights and human override systems [22].

Case Study—FinTech Company Saves 35%: To illustrate the impact, consider a large FinTech firm (a global payments company) that implemented an AI-driven cost optimization platform. This platform used advanced ML (including deep learning models for forecasting and generative AI for recommendations) to analyze the firm's cloud usage data across hundreds of services. The AI system provided monthly analysis, suggested optimal resource adjustments (like converting certain on-demand instances to reserved, shutting down dev VMs on weekends, resizing databases), and automated many of these actions. The results, achieved within 3 months, were striking: *cloud costs were reduced by 35%*, exceeding the original target of 30% [23]. Hundreds of thousands of dollars were saved annually. Importantly, system performance was maintained or even improved because right-sizing eliminated resource bloat that was actually slowing some processes. The IT team moved from a reactive stance to a proactive one—thanks to real-time AI insights, they could prevent unnecessary spending before it happened. This case also highlighted lessons: the value of automation (the scale of optimization needed was beyond manual efforts), and the importance of accurate data for AI models [23]. In essence, the AI platform acted as a financial "autopilot" for the cloud environment, continuously aligning resources with business needs and budget constraints.

In conclusion, *AI-driven cloud cost optimization* has proven its value in enterprises of all types. It addresses a pain point that can otherwise erase the benefits of cloud adoption. As one blog succinctly put it, *"AI offers strategies to optimize cloud expenses, providing businesses the tools to manage their cloud infrastructure more efficiently"* [20]. By leveraging AI's strengths in data analysis and prediction, enterprises ensure that they are "only paying for what they need, avoiding waste and maximizing ROI" [20]. This not only frees up budget for other strategic initiatives but also instills a culture of data-driven decision-making in IT operations. For many firms, cloud bills represent a significant operating cost. AI-based cost optimization, therefore, pays for itself very quickly, often within the first year of implementation, thanks to direct savings. As we advance, with multi-cloud strategies and intricate pricing structures on the rise, AI methods will be absolutely crucial for cloud financial governance.

1.4.3 AI-Based Infrastructure Automation (AIOps and Self-Healing)

Overseeing the well-being and functioning of large-scale cloud infrastructure are no small assignment. Automating infrastructure operations with artificial intelligence commonly called AIOps (Artificial Intelligence for IT Operations) is intended to offload from humans the responsibility for monitoring, troubleshooting, and maintaining systems. Using intelligence on the data that IT operations generate, AIOps hopes in some cases to achieve that holy grail of infrastructure automation: systems that are *self-healing, self-optimizing, and needing no human intervention* to maintain them.

The contemporary cloud atmosphere generates enormous amounts of telemetry: application logs, server and container metrics, and transaction traces. An AIOps platform ingests this data and uses it to create a unified view of the system's state. It is as if these platforms have a large set of eyes, with which they not only see all the data, but also try and make sense of it. And they do this in real time, for the most part. A platform that AIOps functions over will, of necessity, do all of this well. For example: instead of static CPU thresholds, an AIOps system might learn the normal daily rhythm of CPU usage for each service and only alert if usage deviates significantly from the norm (indicating a potential incident or misbehaving process). This reduces alert "noise" and focuses attention on true issues. In fact, one of the immediate benefits reported with AIOps is significant reduction in false alarms and event noise—correlating multiple signals into a smaller number of meaningful alerts.

AIOps can do automated diagnosis and remediation. Advanced analytics, using algorithms that perform root cause analysis, can now correlate events across the stack to zero in on the true root cause of an incident. For example, an AI correlating a spike in database latency with a recent software deployment might identify that a particular microservice update is causing a bottleneck. In far less time than it takes human teams to conduct a similar analysis, AIOps highlighted the cause. ScienceLogic, an AIOps platform provider, notes that AIOps solutions "combine big data, advanced analytics, ML, and AI to monitor systems, understand dependencies, and identify problems faster than any human mind could" [24].

One of the ultimate goals of AI-based automation is *self-healing infrastructure*. A self-healing system can detect an anomaly or failure and automatically take corrective action without waiting for human intervention. This concept has moved from theory to reality in many cloud environments. Another example of self-healing infrastructure is automatically rebooting or replacing a failed VM or container, rolling back a bad deployment when user error rates spike, clearing hung tasks, or restarting services when memory leaks are detected. AI plays a role by *predicting* problems before they fully manifest. As IBM's Ruchir Puri described, AI can act like an assistant always observing the applications—knowing their normal health metrics, the topology of the system, and historical incidents—and then "tell you ahead of time if a problem was going to occur; in a more aggressive scenario, it can not only predict the problem but proactively fix the problem" [1]. This proactive fixing is the essence of self-healing. For example, an AI model might recognize a pattern of increasing memory usage that historically leads to a crash, and thus preemptively recycle that service or move workload off of it, preventing an outage.

Also, while self-healing infrastructure has lots of positives, AIOps and self-healing systems generate complex data pipeline dependencies even while they promise almost autonomous infrastructure management. Often needing the intake and conversion of terabytes of heterogeneous data, these systems depend on real-time telemetry, event correlation, and historical log analysis. Ensuring data freshness, lineage, and synchronization across observability stacks—e.g., Prometheus, ELK, OpenTelemetry—becomes a non-trivial engineering effort. Furthermore, delays or discrepancies in one phase of the pipeline can cause misfires in automated remedial systems, aggravating rather than fixing problems. Maintaining schema consistency, error handling, and alert deduplication becomes especially important as these pipelines grow. The promise of self-healing infrastructure runs the danger of being undermined by operational fragility buried under automation without strict pipeline governance and fallback systems.

Use Cases of AI in Infrastructure Automation:

- **Incident Detection and Intelligent Alerting:** As stated, AI can spot incidents by detecting anomalies in various metrics and logs. It can also perform event correlation, which is to say that it can group together multiple signals that are indicative of a single incident. For instance, one sort of outage might trigger all sorts of alerts (CPU high, service down, user errors, etc.), but an AI system can correlate these and realize that they all stem from one root cause and create a single incident ticket instead of a storm of alerts.
- **Automated Root Cause Analysis:** AI algorithms analyze data from various sources (logs, traces, config changes) to identify the root cause. Some use graph analysis of dependencies, others use pattern matching against historical incident postmortems. The outcome is a ranked list of probable causes. For instance, Algomox's AIOps suite uses ML for *automated root cause analysis*, sifting through monitoring data to pinpoint underlying causes of incidents [25]. This can be accompanied by an explanation (e.g., "Service X is failing due to a network timeout connecting to Database Y, likely caused by recent config change Z"). Faster root cause analysis directly translates to faster recovery.
- **Intelligent Remediation (Self-Healing Actions):** Once the cause is known, AI can either trigger an automated runbook or directly execute a fix. *Reactive healing* might be: restart a service, clear a cache, and allocate more resources. *Proactive healing* (which blurs into preventive maintenance) might be: migrate

workloads off a node that shows signs of impending failure (like increasing memory errors), thereby avoiding an incident entirely. Self-healing systems "automatically detect and resolve incidents without human intervention" [25]. Reactive approaches fix after an incident occurs; proactive approaches use predictive analytics to fix issues *before* they fully manifest [25]. Both are valuable. Implementing self-healing requires a high degree of automation in place (infrastructure as code, scripts for common fixes) and trust in the AI recommendations. Many organizations implement a gradual approach: start with AI suggesting fixes, then move to automatic fixes for specific well-understood problems (like known memory leak patterns).

- **Intelligent Scaling and Performance Tuning:** Besides incident handling, AI can optimize performance by adjusting configurations automatically. For instance, it can tune the sizes of VMs, the container CPU/memory limits, the settings for garbage collection, or the thread pools based on the observed performance. This also overlaps with cost optimization, but again it has a focus on performance and reliability. AIOps might observe that a service is consistently hitting 90% CPU at peak and decide to scale it up before the users are affected and then scale it down again later essentially a dynamic optimization, driven by AI, of the service. It might also detect "noisy neighbor" issues (one workload impacting another) and remediate by moving workloads around the environment for better isolation.
- **Security Incident Automation:** Even though SecOps AI usually deals with this area, it can overlap with other kinds of AI. For instance, when security anomaly detection AI spots a pattern that looks like a cyber-attack, it could use operational automation to contain the issue or even neutralize the attack as a first step in the attack's containment.

A concrete example of AI-based automation improving operations is *auto-remediation in incident management*. AIOps platforms can integrate with ticketing systems so that when an incident is detected, an AI agent not only creates a ticket but may attach a *recommended resolution* or even execute a runbook. One case study noted that by using AIOps, a company enabled automated resolution for 79% of common infrastructure issues, freeing up the operations team from dealing with those recurring problems. In essence, the AI learned from past incidents (the known fixes) and was entrusted to handle those going forward. As a result, IT personnel were able to reallocate a significant amount of time (in one study, ~13 hours per week) from firefighting to higher-value activities. This aligns with broader findings that *AI allows Ops teams to focus on innovation rather than troubleshooting* [3].

Challenges in AIOps: It is worth noting that AI-based automation can be a tough nut to crack. The first challenge, as always, is data. Put simply, for AI to be effective, it has to have access to data and the right kind of data. This is not just any old data; it has to be comprehensive and clean, else it might as well be garbage for all the good it will do. A second problem is the learning curve; AIs are not born knowing what to do and what not to do. In the beginning, they are nearly as clueless as the humans who created them and for the same reasons. Thus, in the first several weeks, the human SREs will review and either approve or disapprove the AI's suggested changes. After the humans have built a trust with the AI to where they are okay with allowing the AI to do the work without them, the work can then be fully automated. The Ops Cult's challenge is both a data problem and a trust problem, which, as we shall see, can be resolved.

According to an Algomox blog, "traditional incident resolution approaches (manual processes, siloed teams) are reactive and slow, whereas AIOps and self-healing systems can significantly improve incident resolution by automating detection and resolution, reducing downtime" [25]. This highlights that organizations must adapt processes to leverage AIOps effectively.

Before we summarize, I would like to add that self-healing infrastructure must include explicit safety and governance systems around automated activities to guarantee dependability and responsibility. Should remedial logic act on false positives or misinterpreted anomalies, blind automation can cause cascading failures. To guarantee human oversight for high-impact activities, best practices call for using policy-based guardrails, change approval procedures, and tie-off rollback techniques. Every automated fix should be accompanied by audit trails and explainability layers so that root causes may be tracked back and decisions may be justified looking forward. Procedural rigor is further added by integration with ITSM systems such as ServiceNow or Jira for incident validation. Self-healing runs the danger of becoming self-sabotaging in complicated, interdependent systems without these controls.

In summary, AI-based infrastructure automation, or AIOps, aims to create cloud systems that run with minimal human intervention. When you think about it, the cloud is in many ways just one big pile of computers—computing, storing, and networking. The vast scale and dynamism of what we now call "the cloud" make it a challenge to manage (and to do so reliably and in a cost-effective way). AIOps promises many benefits: 1. Higher uptime; 2. Faster incident response; 3. Lower operational overhead; 4. The ability for a given IT team to manage many more systems than they could (and with higher reliability) back when everything was on-premises. As one researcher succinctly puts it, "self-healing systems and AIOps can significantly improve incident resolution efficiency and effectiveness, reducing downtime and improving customer satisfaction" [25]. This is a critical aspect of AI-driven cloud transformation—ensuring that once applications are in the cloud, they are maintained and operated with an intelligent, adaptive approach rather than brute-force manual effort.

1.4.4 Multi-Cloud and Hybrid Cloud AI Orchestration

Using services from several cloud providers (e.g., AWS, Azure, Google Cloud) and occasionally combining *public clouds with private clouds or on-site data centers*, companies today sometimes employ a multi-cloud strategy. While this strategy avoids vendor lock-in and provides flexibility, it results in more managerial complexity. Every platform boasts unique tools, rates, and operating philosophy. To control this complexity, artificial intelligence-driven orchestration for hybrid and multi-cloud systems has surfaced. By means of intelligent decisions on placement, scheduling, and optimization that a human operator would find difficult in real-time, artificial intelligence can act as the "brain" coordinating resources and workloads across several environments.

Also, complex data governance needs are introduced by AI-driven orchestration across hybrid and multi-cloud systems. AI systems have to match region-specific regulations including GDPR, CCPA, and sectoral requirements while data flows across borders and compliance boundaries. Unintentionally triggering data residency violations or exposing sensitive metadata in cross-cloud syncs, mis-configured AI pipelines could result in large egress fees—often overlooked in AI optimization techniques—which cause cost overruns counteracting expected savings. Gartner estimates that, absent intelligent routing and data placement policies, over 40% of multi-cloud AI installations will experience unexpected network cost inflation by 2026 [26]. Future-ready orchestration calls for not only model-aware routing but also policy-aware infrastructure honoring both sovereignty and financial limitations.

Challenges in Multi-Cloud Management: Without AI, organizations face significant challenges in multi-cloud operations. They lack comprehensive visibility—it's hard to see resource usage and performance across all clouds in one view [27]. This can lead to over-provisioning in one cloud while another has spare capacity, or difficulty pinpointing which cloud is best for a new workload. There are also *integration challenges*: ensuring consistent configurations, security policies, and data synchronization across clouds. Traditional rule-based orchestration can automate some tasks but is often static and can't easily adapt to changing conditions or optimize for cost-performance trade-offs in a holistic way. A 2025 study noted that typical cloud management fragmentation led to a 45% increase in operational overhead for IT departments when adopting multi-cloud, and that cloud management was consuming 32 hours per week for specialized teams [3]. Clearly, a smarter approach is needed.

AI-Powered Orchestration Capabilities: AI enhances cloud orchestration by introducing *dynamic, data-driven decision-making*. Some of the key capabilities AI brings to multi-cloud and hybrid orchestration include [3]:

- **Intelligent Resource Allocation & Workload Balancing:** Real-time allocation of tasks to cloud resources is decided upon by artificial intelligence systems. This could mean concentrating components of an application where compute is least at that hour or spreading them among cloud providers to reduce latency to consumers. By weighing several criteria cost, performance, capacity, data locality, and machine learning can decide where to put it. The AI can adjust workloads as conditions change—that is, as Azure's prices fall or an AWS region suffers an outage. This dynamic distribution guarantees maximum use and helps to prevent both underused pools and hotspots. It was reported that AI-powered orchestration reduced resource waste by nearly 40% and improved utilization rates from ~43% to ~72% in a multi-cloud environment, thanks to smarter placement and consolidation decisions [3]. Such improvements in utilization directly translate to cost savings and efficiency.

- **Predictive Scaling and Load Distribution:** Under a multi-cloud arrangement, artificial intelligence not only scales resources across clouds but also within each one (as was already mentioned). During a traffic surge, for instance, an artificial intelligence orchestrator might choose to burst into a secondary cloud if the instances in the main cloud in a given area are saturated or more costly at that point.
- **Predictive analytics** drive these decisions: Based on performance and cost, AI/ML models project demand spikes and distribute capacity in whichever cloud can best manage them. Wipro's hybrid cloud strategy lead noted that AI/ML excel at analyzing historical data to *forecast future cloud usage with high accuracy*, enabling companies to adjust allocations in advance and "ensure they're neither over-provisioned nor caught off-guard by sudden demand" [27]. By predicting surges (like seasonal peaks or marketing events) across all workloads, AI orchestrators prepare the multi-cloud resources so that each workload runs on the right number of resources at the right time.
- **Cross-Cloud Optimization (Cost and Performance):** AI can analyze metrics from all clouds on a continuous basis to find optimization opportunities. For instance, if the same service is running in two clouds, the AI might discover that one cloud offers comparatively superior CPU performance for that type of workload. It could then shift more of the workload there. Conversely, if it notices that another cloud can deliver equivalent performance for less money, it might reallocate more of the workload to that cloud. Some AI orchestration platforms include policy-driven AI. You can tell them what kind of service you want them to perform in a way that meets your goals. *Automated cost optimization across clouds* was highlighted in Wipro's case where AI would even recommend switching to more cost-effective cloud services or pricing plans when it identifies an opportunity [27]. This kind of proactive suggestion goes beyond human capability, given the vast array of options and constantly changing prices (like spot market fluctuations).
- **Autonomous Healing and Failover:** In a multi-cloud system, resilience is a big attraction-having the ability to fail over to another provider, should one have an outage. AI orchestration can monitor application health across providers and automatically re-route or restart services in another cloud if problems are detected. This is akin to self-healing but at a cloud-to-cloud level. For example, if Cloud A's region goes down, AI can orchestrate bringing up corresponding services in Cloud B, possibly even anticipating the failure and reducing downtime with no human intervention.

- **Policy Enforcement and Compliance Automation:** Usually involving keeping some data on-site for compliance or using particular clouds for particular jurisdictions, hybrid clouds combine AI can help by making sure data placements and workloads follow these rules and by dynamically changing if, say, the data sensitivity of a workload alters. Using pattern recognition to flag any policy transgressions, it can tag and track data as it moves between clouds. AI can also improve security orchestration; for instance, anomaly detection in one cloud might alert the orchestrator to isolate that part of the network across all clouds (implying geofencing or stricter firewall rules temporarily).

Global load optimization is one instance of artificial intelligence-driven orchestration in action: A company runs several clouds of its retail chain platform over several continents. Traffic normally finds its way via DNS to the closest cloud region. One cloud provider's datacenter gets crowded, though, during a major product release The AI orchestrator keeps user experience seamless by preemptively moving some traffic to a neighboring region in another cloud when it detects rising latency in that area. It starts additional servers in Cloud Y where it's cheaper at the moment, so doing real-time cloud arbitrage simultaneously when it notes that the cost of scaling out in Cloud X has exceeded a threshold (probably spot instance prices spiked due to demand). All of this occurs automatically and in a few minutes. Having saved the business money and avoided a possible slowdown, the artificial intelligence brings everything back to normal following the event. Manual achievement of this kind of agility is quite difficult; artificial intelligence makes it possible by constant metric analysis and decision-making.

The benefits of AI orchestration are compelling: surveys have found organizations using AI-driven orchestration experienced *faster deployment cycles, more* accurate resource forecasting, and fewer security incidents compared to those using conventional methods [3]. Self-healing in these platforms resolved the majority of common issues automatically, and IT teams could reclaim time for innovation [3]. While such statistics may vary, they illustrate the orders of magnitude improvement possible.

In summary, *AI in multi-cloud and hybrid cloud orchestration* acts as a force multiplier: it handles the complexity of multiple environments by continuously analyzing and optimally directing resources and workloads. By doing so, it achieves a level of efficiency, resiliency, and agility that is very hard to attain otherwise. As multi-cloud adoption grows (nearly 87% of enterprises by 2024 [3]), AI orchestration is turning into the essential component enabling these several systems to operate as a coherent, optimized whole instead of separate silos. Maintaining compliance and performance, it guarantees that every job runs in the correct containers and that every dollar spent on cloud yields maximum value. This is a classic case of artificial intelligence-driven cloud transformation producing useful, notable results. Let us take an example with a strong practical focus on cloud cost optimization.

1.5 AI-Augmented Cost Optimization: Industry Impact Grounded in Theory

By means of predictive analytics, anomaly detection, and intelligent workload forecasting across multi-cloud environments, artificial intelligence is revolutionizing cloud cost optimization. Companies depend on artificial intelligence more and more to right-size infrastructure, cut pointless waste by using dynamic autoscaling, and replace idle resources. For instance, models of reinforcement learning actively modify compute allocation depending on performance thresholds and workload seasonality.

Although gains in cost and efficiency drive industry momentum, academic research provides basic ideas to improve these approaches. Zhang et al. show that combining predictive artificial intelligence with queuing theory enhances cost-performance trade-offs in cloud resource allocation [28]. Moreover, grounded in utility theory, price-aware AI scheduling methods have shown to outperform static heuristics in changing pricing environments such as AWS spot markets [29]. These results strengthen the case that theoretical foundations can improve the auditability and resilience of financial controls driven by artificial intelligence in cloud systems.

Organizations can promote not only efficiency but also transparency and governance in cost management strategies by matching pragmatic implementations with these intellectual insights—thus laying the foundation for AI systems that are both financially accountable and understandable.

1.6 Case Studies

To illustrate the concepts and benefits of AI-driven cloud transformation, we now highlight several real-world case studies. These examples span different domains of AI applications in the cloud—from migration to cost savings to operational resiliency—and demonstrate tangible outcomes achieved by organizations.

Case Study 1: Coca-Cola's AI-Assisted Cloud Migration (Google Cloud)—One of the world's most recognized brands, Coca-Cola undertook a large-scale migration of its data and applications to Google Cloud. Given the size and complexity of their IT environment (millions of records across multiple departments), Coca-Cola leveraged Google's AI-powered migration tools to streamline the process [16]. Using predictive analytics and machine learning models, the tools automated much of the migration planning and execution. **Results:** The migration was completed faster than expected, with minimal disruption to operations [16]. AI accurately forecasted Coca-Cola's post-migration infrastructure needs, allowing dynamic scaling of resources (so they didn't over-provision hardware during the transition) [16]. Importantly, after migrating, Coca-Cola was positioned to use AI-driven analytics on its consolidated data—the case notes that *enhanced* *customer insights* were achieved through real-time analytics post-migration [16]. This shows how AI not only aided the move itself, but also unlocked new value from data once in the cloud. Overall, Coca-Cola's use of AI for migration reduced the project risk and timeline, and set the stage for modern data-driven decision-making.

Case Study 2: Johnson & Johnson's Multi-Cloud Optimization (Azure)—Johnson & Johnson (J&J), the global healthcare and pharmaceutical company, faced the challenge of migrating thousands of applications across numerous business units to the cloud. They chose Microsoft Azure and employed Azure's AI-driven cloud management and migration features to assist. **Results:** Azure's AI tools helped J&J analyze and transfer workloads efficiently [16]. During migration, J&J realized *cost savings* by using Azure's AI-based cost optimization recommendations—for example, rightsizing resources and utilizing reserved instances where AI suggested it would be beneficial [16]. They also achieved *minimal downtime*: Azure's machine learning algorithms scheduled migration events during off-peak hours and orchestrated cutovers in ways that did not significantly impact business operations [16]. Post-migration, J&J saw faster time-to-value in their new cloud environment, reaching operational capacity much sooner than initially projected, thanks to the automation and predictive planning (accelerated migration timeline) [16]. This case underlines AI's role in large enterprise cloud transformations, ensuring not just a successful migration but also optimizing cost and performance in a complex multi-cloud scenario.

Case Study 3: Large FinTech Firm's Cloud Cost Optimization—A global FinTech company in the credit card payments industry faced soaring cloud infrastructure costs while needing to maintain high performance and availability. The platform used machine learning (LSTM neural networks for usage forecasting) and even generative AI models to analyze cloud usage and recommend optimizations. **Results:** Within 3 months, the firm realized a *35% reduction in cloud costs*, surpassing their target of 30% savings. This amounted to hundreds of thousands of dollars in annual savings. The AI recommendations included rightsizing instances, eliminating idle resources, and optimizing pricing options (like using spot instances for certain workloads and converting others to reserved instances). System performance was not only maintained but improved in some cases due to better resource allocation. The IT team also benefited from proactive cost management: with real-time AI insights and anomaly detection, they could prevent cost spikes and continuously align usage with needs. This case study demonstrates the power of AI in FinOps (cloud financial operations)—automating what was previously a tedious monthly review process into continuous optimization. It also highlights best practices learned: the importance of automation in sustaining savings and the value of accurate ML forecasts in planning [30].

Case Study 4: Retail Chain Company's AIOps for Reliability—Using a sophisticated microservices architecture, a big retail chain retailer enhanced its IT operations with an AIOps platform (IBM Watson AIOps). The interdependence of services made it difficult to troubleshoot the many incidents they reported. From their environment, the AIOps platform absorbed logs, metrics, and change data and applied artificial intelligence to identify events and trace root causes. **Results**: Following deployment, the business observed a notable drop in MTTR (Mean Time to Resolution) for incidents-many of which span hours to minutes. Over 1.5 million alerts from IT monitoring systems were flooding one of the biggest retail chains in North America. This deluge not only tired IT departments but also made it almost impossible to separate incidents with actionability. False positives crowded dashboards; often, real problems were buried or found too late. Watson AIOps let the retailer combine machine learning techniques that filtered noise and found significant trends in system performance. Trained on historical incident data and IT telemetry, the artificial intelligence could automatically correlate events and instantly highlight root causes. Engineers used three to five hours to triage and fix once; now, under 15 minutes covered this. This case validates the promise of AIOps: using AI to achieve self-healing and more resilient operations, which is crucial for an always-on business like Retail Chain [22].

1.7 Challenges and Future Outlook

Despite its promise and demonstrated benefits, AI-driven cloud transformation is not without challenges. Organizations must navigate technical, organizational, and ethical hurdles as they implement AI in their cloud strategies. In this section, we discuss some of the key challenges that persist and then look ahead to the future outlook—how AI-driven cloud practices might evolve in the next few years.

Challenges:

- **Data Quality and Integration:** The only source of goodness for AI systems lies in the data they train on and observe. A practical problem related to this is ensuring the AI has access to all pertinent data (performance metrics, logs, cost data, etc.) in a unified format. In many enterprises, the IT environment data is scattered across several tools and is often incomplete or messy. Setting up the necessary data pipelines (discussed in the architecture section) can be quite the undertaking. If we allow for incomplete data or low-quality data to inform our recommendations, then we might as well not have recommendations at all. Of course, the same is true for us humans: if we use incomplete or low-quality data to make decisions, those decisions are going to be off the mark. So, to put the problem succinctly, if we want AIOps to work well, then we must first make observability work well. We must also have an integration process for all the tools that monitor the IT environment.
- **Trust and Human Acceptance:** Integrating AI into cloud management means we'll sometimes ask it to do things seasoned IT staff might question. This is likely to have a cultural resonance, especially in teams not used to working with AI, unless they have worked with recommendation engines or similar. Think of AI as a possible collaborator, especially when we're asking it to manage some-

thing as complex as a cloud. Using AI and machine learning will help humans achieve efficient cloud configuration, health, and security.

- **False Positives and Tuning:** Artificial intelligence (AI) systems may generate suboptimal recommendations or false positives, particularly in their early stages. Algorithms must be tuned to the particular environment over time. Algorithms for anomaly detection, for example, may require a few weeks of baseline data and perhaps some admin input regarding which alerts were helpful and which were not. If not controlled during this learning phase, it may result in errors or alert fatigue. Businesses must set aside funds to keep an eye on AI and modify logic or thresholds as necessary. This is similar to training a new employee in that initial supervision is required.
- **Data Privacy and Security:** When using AI to monitor and analyze operational data, it is important to think about whether the data contains any sensitive information. Sensitive user or system information may occasionally be included in cloud logs and metrics. Organizations must make sure that privacy laws and security best practices are followed if AI systems—particularly third-party SaaS AIOps tools—are ingesting this data. Certain data may need to be handled carefully or cannot leave a facility in some industries (such as healthcare or finance). Strict access controls, on-premises or VPC AI implementation, and anonymization are some solutions. Concerns have also been raised about AI making security decisions, such as automatically resolving a security alert. Could attackers use telemetry manipulation to fool AI into shutting down a server, for example, if they knew an AI was present? Although theoretical, such adversarial scenarios need to be considered. This can be lessened by thorough validation and possibly involving humans in crucial security measures.
- **Complexity and Maintenance:** The IT infrastructure becomes more complex with the introduction of AI systems. The AI/ML models themselves require upkeep, including model updates and concept drift retraining (the model may require retraining to maintain accuracy when data patterns change). For instance, an AI may require retraining or modification if it was trained on a particular application workload profile and the application experiences a significant change (such as a new architecture or a holiday traffic spike that exceeds historical range). It's also critical to make sure that the AI components don't turn into a new source of failure, which is why the AI platform itself needs to be reliable. It could be difficult for some businesses to develop the requisite internal knowledge or depend on vendor assistance for this.
- **ROI and Justification:** While many case studies show strong ROI, initially there might not be guaranteed returns. Some leaders might question the investment in AI tools versus more traditional investments. It might take months to see the full benefits (e.g., after enough data is gathered or after iterative improvements). Therefore, building a business case and setting realistic expectations is a challenge. It helps to identify *quick wins*—e.g., use AI first on a well-scoped problem like cloud cost overages in one department, demonstrate savings, and then expand.

- **Ethical and Control Issues:** As AI becomes more involved in decision-making, accountability concerns surface. Who is in charge if an AI system makes a mistake that results in an outage? It's crucial to make sure that humans can always override or review AI actions. Additionally, AI decisions must be in line with business goals; its policies must be governed. These limitations must be included because, for instance, an AI may decide to save money at the expense of a minor performance drop, but the company may not want any performance loss. Fairness can relate to how resources are distributed among departments, etc., but the use of ethical AI in IT is less delicate than in fields like HR or consumer data. These are some types of problems, but they are important to note.

Moving to the *Future Outlook*, we anticipate several trends and advancements in AI-driven cloud transformation:

- **Broader and Deeper Adoption:** In the next 3-5 years, what early adopters have done will become mainstream for many organizations. AI-driven cost optimization and AIOps will likely become standard components of cloud management toolsets. Cloud providers are likely to bake more AI into their platforms natively (we already see AWS, Azure, GCP offering recommendation systems; this will extend to more autonomous features). IDC and Gartner predictions often foresee that by the mid-2020s, a large percentage of enterprise cloud operations will be partially or fully automated by AI. For example, Gartner predicted increased use of AIOps and digital platforms for complex infrastructure management [2].
- **Fully Autonomous Cloud Operations ("Self-Driving Cloud"):** The idea of autonomous clouds will get closer. This implies that AI agents could manage the entire lifecycle, including resource deployment, optimization, remediation, and even decommissioning, with little oversight. Microsoft's research on an *AIOps Lab* suggests an aim for open frameworks to test AI agents for cloud operations [31]. There may be situations where an engineer sets high-level goals ("keep my app available to this SLA and minimize cost"), and the AI orchestrator handles the rest on the fly. "NoOps" (no operations) approaches, where AI and automation handle operations so developers can concentrate on code, are already being promoted by some startups. Humans will probably stop doing routine tasks and instead concentrate more on strategy, policy, and handling exceptions.
- **Generative AI in Cloud DevOps:** The generative AI explosion (like GPT-4 and similar) opens new frontiers for cloud operations. We could see AI bots that can converse with engineers to help manage cloud resources. Imagine describing infrastructure needs in natural language and AI (think GitHub Copilot for Infrastructure) generating Terraform scripts or cloud configuration automatically. Indeed, using generative AI to create code for cloud deployments is something we already see happening. And in the future—we could even see this as a trend for the next DARWIN (Disruptive AI-driven Reality With Impact Now) cloud revolution—an SRE could converse with a bot to get insights about a slow service, with the bot even offering to perform a remedial action. ("It appears the database CPU is saturated due to a heavy query; I can scale it up or kill the offending query. Would you like me to do one of those?"). Multi-agent systems

(several AI agents collaborating) might handle complex tasks—one agent monitors, one analyzes, one acts—coordinating amongst themselves, which is a concept researcher are exploring (42robots.ai's blog mentioned "emerging trends like multi-agent workflows" in cloud migration context [17]).

- **Integrated AI Governance and Policy:** Companies will apply more robust governance around artificial intelligence as it plays increasingly major roles. Policies defining what artificial intelligence can and cannot do independently will be seen (perhaps an AI can restart services but not delete resources without authorization). AI decision audit trails will become crucial since they record not only what was done but also the rationale or confidence of the artificial intelligence. This will support trust and compliance. Regulatory authorities could even begin to provide recommendations for artificial intelligence in the management of critical infrastructure (particularly for sectors like finance or utilities).
- **Edge and IoT Integration:** With more distributed edge computing for low-latency uses including autonomous vehicles, IoT, etc., cloud is reaching the edge. Managing a distributed cloud-edge continuum can be taxing, and artificial intelligence will be indispensable there. Using AI to make local decisions, future AIOps will oversee not just central data centers but thousands of edge nodes (some anomaly detection runs on edge with lightweight models, coordinating with central AI). This will also guarantee clever management of the reach of the cloud to edge and devices [32].
- **New AI Services from Cloud Providers:** Cloud providers will keep unveiling AI-powered products. AWS could be expanding its Trusted Advisor to not only provide recommendations but also automatically apply them under customer permission. Azure might combine OpenAI services with Azure Monitor so that, as described, you could chat with your cloud. Active Assist from Google Cloud could turn into an autopilot mode that simply maximizes constantly. We could also see cross-cloud AI management services (neutral third-party platforms that manage across AWS/Azure/GCP—some exist, likely more to come, possibly leveraging federated learning so they learn across clients without exposing data).
- **Convergence of AI and Cloud-native Dev:** DevOps and cloud development will incorporate AI in CI/CD pipelines. For example, before a deployment, an AI might predict the risk of that deployment (IBM's Puri mentioned *predicting if a change is risky ahead of time* [1]). This could become standard—AI as a quality gate. It might simulate the deployment impact in a sandbox digital twin and warn of issues.
- **Skills and Roles Evolution:** Focusing on training and tuning the AI tools and handling high-level decisions, the role of cloud operations engineers will change into "AI-assisted cloud engineers" or "cloud orchestrators." New roles such as "AIOps architect" or "Cloud Automation Ethicist" could show up to make sure the AI tools complement corporate values. Humans will essentially oversee fleets of artificial intelligence bots performing the work, much as a conductor guides an orchestra instead of playing every instrument.

The road ahead for AI-driven cloud operations will be shaped by both scaling friction and ecosystem maturation. Gartner predicts that by 2027, over 75% of enterprises will operationalize AI-driven cloud optimization tools, up from less than 25% in 2023, signaling a massive acceleration in adoption [33]. However, challenges such as data fragmentation, model observability, and AI policy compliance will continue to complicate deployment. IDC forecasts that by 2026, 60% of digital infrastructure will include embedded AI governance layers to manage risk and explainability across distributed systems [34]. Long-term, the rise of generative AI copilots in cloud orchestration expected to manage up to 40% of operational tasks autonomously by 2028 [35] will demand new skill sets, auditing standards, and ethical safeguards.

In summary, the trend is toward more autonomous, intelligent, and optimized cloud ecosystems. Like autopilot in aircraft, artificial intelligence will progressively disappear into the background of cloud management: always on, constantly adjusting, under human supervision several such systems at once. As technology environments get more complicated-multi-cloud, edge, IoT, etc., this will enable IT to scale without linear increase in human effort.

The future outlook is quite positive: if things are done right, AI-driven cloud transformation will yield cloud systems that are *self-optimizing (for cost and performance), self-healing (for reliability), and self-scaling (for demand)*, all while being more energy-efficient and responsive to business needs than traditional management could ever be. Although the road to that future is not easy and calls for trust, careful execution, and constant improvement, case studies and present trends show that those who invest in overcoming these obstacles will definitely pay off.

1.8 Conclusion

The way companies use and control cloud computing will be much advanced by artificial intelligence-driven cloud transformation. By including artificial intelligence and machine learning into many aspects of cloud strategy-from migration planning to cost management, from operational automation to multi-cloud orchestration, from advanced analytics to sustainable practices companies can achieve outcomes that were difficult or impossible to reach with conventional approaches in this thorough exploration.

Summing up the Journey: We established in the Introduction and Background that artificial intelligence has become a relevant answer to the complexity of cloud environments since they have become too complicated and dynamic for human management to be optimal. Setting the stage for the main applications we covered, the Architecture section described how artificial intelligence combines into cloud systems via data pipelines, analytical engines, and automation loops. Throughout the Core Content sections, we delved into the technical depth of each domain:

- AI-assisted migration can intelligently automate and reduce the risk of moving to the cloud, as evidenced by Coca-Cola's faster migration with minimal disruption.
- AI-driven cost optimization continuously aligns cloud resources with actual needs. This helps the budget to be constrained yielding major savings, as our FinTech case showed with a 35% cost reduction.
- AI-based infrastructure automation (AIOps) enables self-healing and efficient operations, which improves uptime and reduces human toil—demonstrated by retail chain and network examples of plummeting downtime thanks to AI.
- AI orchestrates across various platforms to achieve an optimal balance of performance and cost in multi-cloud and hybrid scenarios. This is seen, for example, in J&J's multi-cloud migration and optimization on Azure.
- Modernization of data and analytics with AI takes place at lightning speed in the cloud. This does not mean that everything has to be on the cloud. While cloud computing in general is a brilliant innovation that offers many new possibilities, this cloud revolution has no impact on the speed of analytics AI unlocks. Fast data everywhere is what counts [15].
- Ultimately, artificial intelligence is making cloud computing more environmentally friendly, from Google's data centers, where AI is used for smart cooling, to intelligent workload scheduling that uses renewable energy.

In essence, artificial intelligence provides a transforming prism for cloud optimization; its true worth is found in disciplined application. Start with explainable models, enforce tag hygiene, and validate AI insights via human-in-the-loop monitoring, advises companies. Roadmaps have to call for cultural onboarding, phased deployment, and bias audits. Models still suffer with non-linear workload spikes, compliance edge cases, and need for major tuning, though. Future success will rely on striking a mix between innovation with governance and automation mixed with openness. Also all these sections show together that artificial intelligence is a flexible toolkit capable of handling a range of cloud problems rather than a single instrument. The case studies also provide specific figures and successes for these ideas, transforming theory into reality and showing ROI across retail, finance, technology, healthcare, etc.

References

1. Puri, R. (2020, October 15). Reimagining hybrid cloud with AI—Interview. *InformationWeek*. Retrieved from https://www.informationweek.com/it-infrastructure/ibm-research-s-chief-scientist-talks-ai-for-cloud-migration
2. DiscoverCloud. (2024). Hybrid to edge and beyond: Unraveling the role of AI in the future landscape of cloud computing. *DiscoverCloud Blog*. Retrieved from https://discovercloud.io/hybrid-to-edge-and-beyond-unraveling-the-role-of-ai-in-the-future-landscape-of-cloud-computing

3. Natta, P. (2025, April). AI-powered cloud orchestration: Automating multi-cloud & hybrid cloud workloads. *European Journal of Computer Science and Information Technology, 13*(8), 138–147. doi: https://doi.org/10.37745/ejcsit.2013/vol13n8138147
4. Gartner. (2018, December). Market guide for AIOps platforms. *Gartner Research*. (ID G00340876)
5. IBM. (2019, April). Watson AIOps: AI for IT operations. *IBM White Paper*.
6. Dynatrace. (2020, June). Davis AI: Autonomous cloud operations. *Dynatrace Technical Brief.*
7. New Relic. (2021, September). Announcing AI-driven incident intelligence. *New Relic Blog*.
8. Microsoft. (2022, November). Azure Monitor: What's new in AI-based alerting. *Microsoft Ignite*.
9. Amazon Web Services. (2023, March). AWS CloudWatch enhancements: Predictive alarms and automation. *AWS News Blog*.
10. Google Cloud. (2024, January) AI in Operations Suite: Toward autonomous cloud RCA. *Google Cloud Blog*.
11. Forrester. (2025, February). Predictions 2025: Composable AIOps and next-gen observability. *Forrester Research*.
12. Ninan, S. (2023, October). How AI-driven innovations will power a sustainable future for data centers. *Hitachi Vantara—Think Ahead*. Retrieved from https://social-innovation.hitachi/en-us/think-ahead/digital/ai-innovations-powering-data-centers
13. Biggio, B., & Roli, F. (2018). Wild patterns: Ten years after the rise of adversarial machine learning. *Pattern Recognition, 84*, 317–331.
14. Carlini, N., et al. (2024). Poisoning and backdooring contrastive learning. In *Proceedings of the 33rd USENIX security symposium*.
15. IBM Cloud. (2023). What is data modernization? The role of AI and cloud. *IBM Think Blog*. https://www.ibm.com/think/topics/data-modernization
16. Ampcus. (2025, January). AI-driven planning and strategies for seamless cloud migration. *Ampcus Blog*. Retrieved from https://blogs.ampcus.com/ai-driven-planning-and-strategies-for-seamless-cloud-migration/
17. 42robots.ai. (2025). AI for cloud migration consulting: Transforming your cloud journey. *42robots Blog*. Retrieved from https://42robots.ai/ai-for-cloud-migration-consulting
18. Satyanarayanan, M., et al. (2015). Edge analytics in the Internet of Things. *IEEE Pervasive Computing, 14*(2), 24–31.
19. Unite.ai. (2024). AI-driven cloud cost optimization: Strategies and best practices. *Unite.AI*. Retrieved from https://www.unite.ai/ai-driven-cloud-cost-optimization-strategies-and-best-practices/
20. Naumovska, M. (2023, August). Maximizing cloud cost optimization with AI-driven solutions. *Microtica Blog on Medium*. Retrieved from https://medium.com/microtica/maximizing-cloud-cost-optimization-with-ai-driven-solutions-f02ee3804e1d
21. Bezanson, J. (2024, November). Improving cloud cost accountability with tag governance. *Gartner Research*. (ID G00781845)
22. Lucanus, A. (2025, June). How I shrunk MTTR from hours to minutes with Watson. *IBM Community Blog*. Retrieved from https://community.ibm.com/community/user/blogs/anton-lucanus/2025/05/05/how-i-shrunk-mttr-from-hours-to-minutes-with-watso
23. Krishnan, R. (2025). Revolutionizing Cloud Cost Optimization Using AI for a Large FinTech Firm. Retrieved from https://www.lowtouch.ai/ai-cloud-cost-optimization-fintech/
24. ScienceLogic. (2025, Q2). Unlocking the power of AIOps. *ScienceLogic Resources*. Retrieved from https://sciencelogic.com/articles/aiops
25. IBM. (2023). What is AIOps? *IBM Cloud Learn Hub*. Retrieved from https://www.ibm.com/cloud/learn/aiops
26. Gartner. (2025) Top trends in cloud networking and interconnect 2025. *Gartner Research*. (ID G00810333)
27. Parakh, G. (2023, November). AI-powered strategies for cloud cost optimization (Hybrid/Multicloud). *Wipro*. Retrieved from https://www.wipro.com/infrastructure/ai-powered-strategies-for-cloud-cost-optimization

28. Zhang, H., Chen, M., & Li, Y. (2022). AI-driven cost optimization for cloud resource allocation: A queueing theory perspective. *IEEE Transactions on Cloud Computing, 10*(1), 101–114.
29. Wang, L., Yang, X., & Hwang, K. (2021). Utility-based scheduling of elastic cloud resources for cost-aware users. *IEEE Transactions on Services Computing, 14*(3), 756–769.
30. Evans, R., & Gao, J. (2016, July). DeepMind AI reduces Google data centre cooling bill by 40%. *DeepMind Blog*. Retrieved from https://deepmind.google/discover/blog/deepmind-ai-reduces-google-data-centre-cooling-bill-by-40
31. Sengupta, A. (2024, March). AIOps—Embracing the future of IT ops. *LinkedIn*. Retrieved from https://www.linkedin.com/pulse/aiops-embracing-future-ops-amit-sengupta-vqewc/
32. Kumari, S. (2022). AI-driven cloud transformation for product management: Optimizing resource allocation, cost management, and market adaptation in digital products. *Internet of Things and Edge Computing Journal, 2*(1), 29–54. Retrieved from https://thesciencebrigade.com/iotecj/article/view/432
33. Gartner. (2024, December). Market guide for cloud cost optimization. *Gartner Research*. (ID G00794562)
34. IDC. (2025, February). AI-driven IT operations: Strategies for trust and control. *IDC FutureScape*.
35. Forrester. (2025, January). Predictions 2025: Generative AI in cloud operations. *Forrester Research*.

Chapter 2
Cloud Security in the Age of Generative AI

Aparna Achanta

Abstract Generative AI (GenAI) as a technology has redefined how we look at and absorb information in the modern age. The ability to prompt models like **ChatGPT, Claude, Gemini**, etc., and receive structured human-like responses is a game changer for every industry, with cybersecurity being no exception. CISOs have already started experimenting with GenAI use cases such as analyzing log data, customized training, and generating executive-level reports. At the same time, cybercriminals have also weaponized GenAI as a tool for deepfakes and polymorphic malware, automating their attacks even further than before. In 2024, an employee at a multinational corporation transferred $25 million to scammers who used deepfake technology to impersonate the company's Chief Financial Officer during a video call (CNN. (2024, February). *Finance worker pays out $25 million after video call with deepfake 'chief financial officer'*. CNN. Retrieved from https://edition.cnn.com/2024/02/04/asia/deepfake-cfo-scam-hong-kong-intl-hnk/index.html). This shift is not just in technology but also strategic and requires a relook at how we have traditionally approached cybersecurity, particularly cloud security.

The security of the cloud and its workloads is still in its maturity phase as a discipline, with organizations often underestimating the complexity and work required for securing environments like Amazon Web Services, Azure, and Google Cloud. GenAI in particular has emerged as a double-edged sword, increasing productivity while at the same time lowering the entry bar for cybercriminals to launch attacks targeting the cloud. In this chapter, we take an in-depth look at how we must revisit the very foundations of cloud security in the wake of GenAI as these models catch up to and overtake humans in areas like code development, log analysis, and vulnerability detection.

A. Achanta (✉)
Independent Researcher, Austin, TX, USA

B. Pandey, A. Patel (eds.), *Revolutionizing the Cloud*,
https://doi.org/10.1007/978-3-032-07479-9_2

We will take a detailed look at:

- How (and why) GenAI is a game changer within cloud security
- The different types of deployment models for GenAI
- Threats and risks that GenAI enhances
- Recommendations for security leaders and CISOs

By the end of this chapter, you will understand the risk implications of GenAI within cloud security and how to integrate it to enhance your existing cloud security processes.

Keywords Generative artificial intelligence · Cloud security · GenAI · Threat modeling · Identity · Access · Security leader

2.1 Introduction

2.1.1 Background on Generative AI(GenAI)

GenAI is a class of Artificial Intelligence (AI) specifically focused on generating text, images, video, and audio content. It is trained on massive amounts of data and "learns" by analyzing the patterns present within this data to generate new content. Users typically interact with GenAI in the form of natural prompts and APIs. Popular examples of GenAI are Large Language Models (LLMs) like OpenAI's GPT-4, Anthropic's Claude, Google Gemini, etc. While GenAI models have existed before, the massive popularity of ChatGPT in 2022 caused this technology to become truly mainstream. Organizations are rushing to adopt GenAI in the form of intelligent agents, copilots, coding assistants, and even autonomous agents that take action without prompting.

However, these advantages have also introduced new threats and attacks that did not exist before, which traditional security frameworks are not designed to handle. Unlike traditional applications, GenAI does not follow standard logic and instead behaves dynamically based on user prompts. This makes its behavior unpredictable and introduces new types of exploits and risks.

Let us take a look at some of the most critical:

- **Prompt Injection**: Prompt injections are the most common attack targeting GenAI applications. Prompt Injection is on the list of OWASP Top 10 for LLMs [1], a list that highlights the most critical risks and attacks against large language models. In this attack, the prompt that a user provides is injected with malicious

instructions and commands that cause the GenAI model to ignore its previous instructions and behave in an unintended manner. Prompt injections can cause GenAI to disclose sensitive data and even make malicious API calls if the proper guardrails are absent.
- **Data Leakage**: GenAI models are often trained on sensitive data and integrated with business applications to provide them with more context and intelligence in their responses. However, if the proper controls are not set, prompt injections can cause GenAI to leak this sensitive information in its responses. Prompt injections can "jailbreak" these GenAI models, making them ignore controls that prevent them from disclosing such sensitive information.
- **Hallucinations**: GenAI is not foolproof and can often generate incorrect responses or content, usually called "hallucinations." This can become a risk if organizations accept GenAI responses as the truth without any oversight or verification to determine whether the facts are correct. This risk is amplified if these responses are used to make decisions that impact other individuals or processes.
- **Shadow AI**: The popularity of GenAI and the productivity increases it brings can also be a double-edged sword. Employees who are not trained on the dos and don'ts of GenAI may often input sensitive information into public GenAI prompts, resulting in data leakage. Organizations that restrict the usage of GenAI usually find employees bypassing corporate controls and using these tools without proper authorization.
- **Model/Data Poisoning**: Organizations typically do not create or train these models from scratch and rely on third-party services. Attackers may compromise the model libraries, or the data used to train these models and "poison" them as part of a supply chain attack. Thus, organizations may be using compromised GenAI models without their knowledge.
- **Enhancements to existing cyberattacks**: GenAI, due to its low entry bar, can boost cybercriminals' productivity, enabling them to automate phishing, malware, and other cyberattacks at scale. The risk is not restricted to text-based attacks, with Deepfakes becoming a common attack targeting organizations.

2.2 Why GenAI Is a Game Changer for Cloud Security?

As we discussed, GenAI's ability to generate human-like content in code, emails, and structured reports threatens and enhances existing cloud security principles. On the other hand, cloud security professionals and solutions can utilize GenAI to analyze threats, simplify log analysis, and provide access to cloud Intel via natural language interfaces.

Some of the key areas that GenAI can enhance cloud security are:

2.2.1 *Threat Intelligence*

One of the most powerful use cases within the cloud is GenAI's ability to ingest massive amounts of information and provide actionable intelligence in natural language. CISOs and cloud security teams can integrate a GenAI solution on top of their log sources and run queries like

- "What are the top 3 risk areas across my cloud infrastructure?"
- "What key IAM Policy changes have happened within the last 48 hours?"

Secure Code Generation and Review

The cloud is based on infrastructure as code, and shifting security left is often an elusive goal that many cloud security engineers keep chasing. GenAI has emerged as a powerful tool for generating and reviewing code. Cloud Security teams can use LLMs like ChatGPT to

- Generate secure cloud policies: GenAI can significantly enhance the generation of cloud policies and configurations. Identity and Access Management (IAM) forms the heart of cloud security, where teams can enforce least privilege, technical governance, and zero trust controls. GenAI can help write and review IAM policies from natural prompts like

  "Write a secure IAM permission set for developers based on best practices."
  "Write a secure bucket policy for S3."
  "Review this Lambda permission policy and recommend improvements."

  As cloud environments can consist of thousands of users, roles, and services, this can greatly cut down on troubleshooting and security refinement hours, helping teams focus on more productive tasks. For example, a simple command like "write a secure template for AWS security groups" can generate the following template:

```
provider "aws" {
  region = "us-east-1"
}

resource "aws_security_group" "web_sg" {
  name        = "secure-web-sg"
  description = "Security group for web server with restricted access"
  vpc_id      = var.vpc_id

  # Ingress: Allow HTTPS traffic from corporate IP range only
  ingress {
    description = "Allow HTTPS from corporate IP"
    from_port   = 443
    to_port     = 443
    protocol    = "tcp"
    cidr_blocks = [var.corporate_ip_cidr]  # e.g., "203.0.113.0/24"
  }

  # Egress: Allow only specific outbound traffic (e.g., to a public DNS resolver)
  egress {
    description = "Allow outbound DNS queries"
    from_port   = 53
    to_port     = 53
    protocol    = "udp"
    cidr_blocks = ["8.8.8.8/32"]  # Google DNS or your internal DNS
  }

  egress {
    description = "Allow HTTPS outbound for updates"
    from_port   = 443
    to_port     = 443
    protocol    = "tcp"
    cidr_blocks = ["0.0.0.0/0"]  # Restrict further if possible
  }

  tags = {
    Name        = "secure-web-sg"
    Environment = var.environment
    Owner       = var.owner
  }
}

variable "vpc_id" {
  description = "VPC ID for the security group"
  type        = string
}

variable "corporate_ip_cidr" {
  description = "Corporate CIDR block to allow inbound access"
  type        = string
}

variable "environment" {
  description = "Environment tag (e.g., dev, prod)"
  type        = string
}

variable "owner" {
  description = "Owner of the resource"
  type        = string
}
```

- Additionally, GenAI can review code and templates for any security misconfigurations and provide recommendations on improving existing code. However, it is crucial to remember that GenAI does not supplant existing SAST and DAST tools but acts as a second pair of eyes on existing solutions.
- Analyze existing application and CI/CD pipeline designs to highlight security gaps and recommend improvements. Used properly, GenAI can highlight security flaws in architecture designs and become a valuable tool for discovering security weaknesses early on in system life cycles.

Incident Response Recommendations

In addition to summarizing log data, GenAI can also aid cloud incident response by suggesting response actions and auto-generating root cause reports and incident summaries. This can be crucial when CISOs are time-pressured to respond and summarize complex incidents into a format that the C-level can understand and digest.

Enhanced Security Awareness

GenAI can greatly aid security awareness by providing customized, context-driven security messages such as videos, articles, and simulations personalized by the person's job role, location, and level of understanding. Training can adapt in real time to how well a user performs and where he or she might need additional help.

How to Strike the Right Balance for Adoption

While GenAI can be a tremendous boost to cloud security, it is essential to understand its limitations and strike the right balance when adopting it. GenAI is not perfect and can make errors or "hallucinations." It does not replace human judgment but supplements it.

Cloud security teams must ensure the following:

- GenAI-generated content, like code/policies, is reviewed by a human when it has the potential to impact cloud infrastructure.
- Guardrails within GenAI are present so that requests and responses are compliant with the organization's policies.
- GenAI reports are peer-reviewed before being provided to management.

2.3 Threat Evolution in the GenAI Era

We briefly touch upon the various risks that GenAI introduces but now let us look at how it can introduce new threats into the cloud landscape. Cloud computing has always been a dynamic environment characterized by rapid changes, fast deployments, and the ever-present risk of misconfigurations. GenAI introduces risks and acts as an amplifier for existing threats, allowing cyberattacks to scale and personalize them on a scale that was not possible before.

This section explains these threats and how they can impact cloud environments.

2.3.1 GenAI Powered Phishing/Social Engineering

Social engineering has remained one of the most effective ways to compromise environments, with the cloud being no exception. Traditional phishing awareness relies on users' ability to detect poorly phrased emails and mistakes within the text. GenAI, however, changes this landscape by producing highly personalized phishing messages using information scraped from social media.

The risk is not restricted to text, as attacks such as voice cloning and Deepfakes now allow attackers to impersonate executives and socially engineer cloud teams in highly sophisticated attacks.

Prompt Injections

We touched briefly upon prompt injections in the previous section, but let's understand them from a cloud perspective. These attacks manipulate the GenAI model to make it behave in an unauthorized manner, similar to how SQL injection attacks target web applications.

Model Exfiltration and Abuse

In addition to the data that the GenAI model has access to, the model itself can be vulnerable to exfiltration and abuse if not appropriately protected. Users typically interact with these GenAI models hosted on Azure, AWS, Google, etc., via endpoints that can be targeted for attacks like model exfiltration. Here, the attacker repeatedly makes API calls to the model to understand and reconstruct the underlying logic the GenAI model uses. This can be highly damaging for companies that have invested heavily in proprietary models.

Malicious Code Generation

GenAI excels in generating code, which can unfortunately also include exploits and malware. Although guardrails are present within most GenAI models to prevent such abuse, attackers can often easily bypass these checks and jailbreak these models. Once broken, they can be used to:

- Generate ransomware scripts.
- Create polymorphic malware that can change its behavior dynamically to evade market-leading security tools.
- Analyze policies and code for weaknesses to exploit.

2.4 GenAI Deployment Models Within the Cloud

To fully understand where GenAI applications fit within cloud security, we must examine the foundation of the cloud security model in areas such as shared responsibility, identity management, and zero trust. These principles are as valid as before but must be re-analyzed within a GenAI context.

The cloud operates on a shared responsibility model where the obligations for securing the infrastructure and services are shared between the customer and the provider, depending on the nature of the cloud.

Understanding these distinctions is crucial before diving into GenAI security, as the same obligations are applicable. GenAI comes in different types of models and deployments, each requiring different types of security controls. Another key point to note is that adopting GenAI within cloud security does not eliminate traditional risks and, in some cases, might even enhance them if proper oversight is not present. A few examples:

- Excessive permissions are being granted with the help of GenAI tools without human oversight and checking, which may violate the principle of least privilege.
- Misconfigurations of cloud infrastructure, as IAC (infra as code) templates are generated by GenAI tools, without the proper security controls being in place.
- Insecure application code is used in cloud environments, which is generated by GenAI and not checked before being promoted to production.
- Attackers used GenAI tools to scan code repositories and create tailored attacks for customer cloud environments. With GenAI, the bar for entry of these attacks is drastically lowered.

Cloud Security Posture Management (CSPM) and Cloud Workload Protection Platform (CWPP) monitor traditional cloud security, which provides visibility and control of cloud environments' control and data planes. However, GenAI is an entirely new type of cloud workload that traditional solutions are not equipped to handle.

2.4.1 *Generative AI Deployment Models: Threats and Risks*

As organizations adopt GenAI within their business use cases, they have a variety of models to choose from, with each bringing its own distinct set of security challenges:

- Public GenAI models, such as ChatGPT and Claude, can be accessed via a software-as-a-service model through interfaces and APIs. While this model is the simplest and easiest to adopt, it also provides the least control. Public GenAI models may use user's data for various purposes, which can include model training and improvement.
- Cloud-hosted models like Amazon Bedrock or Azure OpenAI in which models are hosted on a cloud platform, giving the organization more control and security over how the model is accessed and deployed.
- Self-hosted models, in which the customer controls every aspect of how the GenAI model is hosted and deployed, provide the most control but also the most security overhead. Organizations can control how data is used within their self-hosted AI systems.

The level of security responsibility and risks increases/decreases depending on the deployment model chosen.

2.4.2 *Lowering the Bar of Entry for Attackers*

With GenAI, the traditional profile of attackers as sophisticated hackers or powerful nation-state agents may change. GenAI allows individuals with little coding knowledge to understand and launch attacks using AI-generated code with step-by-step instructions. This risk is not just restricted to external agents, as malicious employees may also misuse GenAI tools to bypass internal controls and policies to commit fraud. GenAI significantly broadens the threat landscape, requiring cloud security teams to look at both skilled attackers and amateurs who are now empowered with these tools.

2.5 Threat Modeling Generative AI Workloads in the Cloud

This section will examine how organizations can adopt a GenAI-aware approach to risk assessments and threat modeling. This approach will consider not only existing threats such as misconfigurations, excessive privileges, and lack of monitoring, but also new GenAI ones like model behavior, prompt injections, and model exfiltration.

In the previous section, we saw GenAI applications' different models and approaches. While traditional cloud frameworks remain relevant, they must be updated to account for the new attack surface that GenAI introduces.

Threat modeling, for instance, is one of the best ways to identify and mitigate threats within applications. It is a proactive approach that adopts an attacker's perspective to identify areas that can be exploited within a system's design and architecture. In essence, threat modeling asks the following questions:

1. What are we working on?
2. What can go wrong?
3. What are we going to do about it?
4. Did we do a good enough job?

Let us look at each of these steps in detail and apply them to GenAI workloads:

2.5.1 What Are We Working On? (Understand the Architecture)

This step involves understanding the GenAI architecture and the context in which it operates in. The following may be used:

- Architecture diagrams of the GenAI application
- Data flow diagrams to visualize the flow of prompts from a user to the response that the GenAI application generates.
- Authentication and authorization flows to understand how the GenAI application verifies permissions and identities. What level of access does it have to internal data stores and systems?
- Data classification to ascertain the level of data that the GenAI system is interacting with and its sensitivity.

This phase enables teams to understand the criticality of the GenAI application and the potential entry and exit points that attackers may attempt to exploit.

2.5.2 What Can Go Wrong? (Threat Identification)

In the second phase, we will examine how the GenAI system can be exploited. We have already listed earlier the types of attacks that GenAI is vulnerable to, such as prompt injections, model inference, etc. Still, it is advisable to use structured, industry-validated frameworks such as the following for threat identification:

Two of the most widely used frameworks for GenAI security are the OWASP LLM Top 10 [1] and the MITRE ATLAS Framework [2]. Let us look at each:

OWASP Top 10 for LLMs

Like the widely used OWASP Top 10 for web applications, the Top 10 for LLMs is an industry- and community-driven list highlighting the most critical risks and attacks against large language models. It provides cloud security teams with a structured approach to GenAI risks, such as:

- LLM01:2025—Prompt Injections
- LLM02:2025 Sensitive Information Disclosure
- LLM03:2025 Supply Chain
- LLM04:2025 Data and Model Poisoning

Depending on the deployment model, cloud security teams can utilize this list as a baseline and assess their GenAI applications against each risk. For example, if a public SaaS-based GenAI application is being used, LLM01 and LLM02 will become immediately applicable. However, one missing thing may be a real-life context to these attacks, which is where the MITRE ATLAS framework comes in.

The MITRE ATLAS Framework

MITRE ATLAS (Adversarial Threat Landscape for Artificial Intelligence Systems) is a framework that documents real-world attacks against AI systems. It is a knowledge base of case studies against actual AI systems, how they occurred, and suggested mitigations for cybersecurity teams. Some of its key features are:

- A living database of AI-specific attacks like data poisoning, prompt injections, data extraction, etc.
- Attacks mapped to specific techniques.
- Case studies of real-world attacks against AI systems
- Recommended mitigations and detections against these attacks.

Use OWASP and MITRE ATLAS in Threat Modeling

These two frameworks are invaluable when answering the "what can go wrong" question within a GenAI system. OWASP allows you to identify the most critical attacks targeting systems, while MITRE ATLAS helps you map these attacks against actual incidents to provide more context. Utilizing both of them will help you enumerate attacks from a threat actor's perspective and help you focus on the ones that are the most relevant.

2.5.3 What Are We Going to Do About It? (Identify Mitigations)

Once threats are defined, the next step of the threat model is to identify preventive and detective controls.

Effective mitigations may include:

- Input validation and prompt filtering to prevent prompt injection attacks.
- Role-based access control for model plugins to minimize the risk of prompt injections, allowing GenAI models to impact back-end systems.
- Output sanitization and redaction to prevent sensitive information disclosure.
- Model activity logging and anomaly detection to identify attacks such as model extraction.
- Encryption and secure storage of prompts and outputs to prevent an attacker from compromising the infrastructure on which the GenAI system is being hosted.

2.5.4 Did We Do a Good Enough Job? (Improve and Iterate)

Once the threat model is complete, it is essential to note that this is not a one-time activity. A threat model is a living document that must evolve with the system. Teams should regularly validate the following:

- If controls and mitigations are adequate (via security tests, penetration testing, etc.)
- If the model still aligns with the actual GenAI system
- If new GenAI threats have emerged that are not covered

The threat model should also be updated after incidents or breaches to assess the effectiveness of the threat modeling process itself.

2.6 Identity, Access, and Governance in GenAI-Based Cloud Environments

In cloud environments, identity has always served as a new type of perimeter, replacing traditional controls like firewalls and intrusion detection services (IDS). Identity and Access Management (IAM) thus forms a key component of securing GenAI-based cloud services. In a GenAI-driven landscape, cloud security professionals must relook at IAM and evaluate not just human-to-cloud communication but also components such as GenAI chatbots, LLMs, APIs, and autonomous agents that work without any human oversight.

2.6.1 Supply Chain Risks in GenAI Environments

GenAI applications do not exist in a vacuum, and organizations rarely train and develop models from scratch. Most GenAI applications are built on pre-trained foundation models, which cloud providers expose via a service. The organization can further refine or fine-tune this model for its use case.

Most GenAI environments are composed of the following:

- Open-source or third-party pre-trained models (e.g., Hugging Face models)
- Proprietary datasets curated internally
- Public datasets scraped from the internet
- Model fine-tuning pipelines
- Vector databases for embeddings
- Model configuration scripts and orchestration code

2.6.2 The GenAI Supply Chain Attack Surface

Each component discussed above becomes a point of entry for supply chain attacks. We have already discussed model/data poisoning, where malicious data or models may be injected into pipelines to compromise or influence GenAI behavior. These attacks can be hazardous, as once a GenAI model is trained on malicious behavior, it can be tough to detect and "untrain" a model to forget such behavior. Scanning datasets taken from third parties for any toxic or poisoned datasets before GenAI applications ingest them is essential.

2.6.3 Secure GenAI Model Lifecycle Management

Just as the shift-left concept revolutionized software development, Secure GenAI Machine Ops is an emerging concept that brings such controls into the GenAI lifecycle.

Some of the key areas it covers are:

- Secure onboarding of data to ensure it is classified and validated before being used to train a GenAI model
- Security hardening of the pipeline and the cloud infrastructure that is being used to host a GenAI model
- Model integrity verification to ensure that only approved GenAI models are prompted to production environments
- Logging and monitoring to ensure that GenAI models do not deviate from approved behaviors and baselines.

As GenAI adoption grows across enterprises, attackers will increasingly target the model supply chain based on the success these attacks have had on the software supply chain. A compromised dataset or model can cause havoc to an organization's business operations and cloud infrastructure if it is not detected in time. In the next section, we will look at how to extend existing cloud security monitoring to detect and respond to the new types of threats that GenAI brings.

2.7 Monitoring, Detection, and Response for GenAI

The simple fact is that today's security monitoring tools were not designed for the dynamic, non-deterministic types of events produced by GenAI systems. Static rule-based alerts cannot capture the nuances of GenAI threats, and instead, SIEM tools must evolve toward native AI capabilities and model-specific threats. Traditional SIEMs lack the contextual understanding of how GenAI models interact with data, making it difficult to detect subtle data leakage.

2.7.1 The GenAI Security Monitoring Gap

Tools like SIEM and Cloud Security Posture Management Solutions (CSPMs) monitor today's cybersecurity environments. These are built on pre-defined rules and metrics and augmented by AI threat detection capabilities. While these are pretty effective in detecting threats against cloud infrastructure and APIs, they also have the following gaps when it comes to GenAI:

- Lack of understanding of prompt-level attacks and their context
- Understanding the dynamic behavior of GenAI models based on inputs
- Model-specific events such as those around inference, data handling, etc.
- Data poisoning and model attacks against model pipelines

2.7.2 Understanding Context Within GenAI Systems

As cloud security teams adapt their monitoring capabilities for GenAI, a key aspect to understand is that GenAI systems often show highly contextual behavior. It is essential to adapt behavioral modeling for this type of unpredictable behavior that cannot be captured via alerts or rules. Some of the techniques that can be adopted are/:

- **Unsupervised learning on prompt patterns**: Identify outliers in syntax, structure, or frequency
- **User behavior analytics** (UBA): Compare per-user GenAI interactions to baselines (e.g., engineers vs sales users)

- **Context consistency tracking**: Alert when a model response deviates from expected RAG sources

A common example would be a GenAI-based agent typically used to summarize customer case studies, suddenly making calls to internal systems and applications that contain PII. Behavioral modeling can help detect this type of deviation, which is indicative of prompt injections and unauthorized access.

2.7.3 Automation Responses to GenAI Threats

The dynamic nature of GenAI systems also requires a rapid response to prevent attacks like prompt injection and data leakage from succeeding. Controls that can augment monitoring are:

- GenAI guardrails that monitor context and input/outputs of the model and detect/block in real time
- Monitoring of GenAI responses to mask/redact PII and other sensitive data
- Throttling API requests if they are indicative of model abuse

The Evolution of Security Monitoring

Monitoring the threat landscape is no longer about responding to alerts and dashboards; it is about understanding how GenAI thinks and how this thinking can be tampered with. Now that we have covered the technical aspects of GenAI security, let us look at the emerging governance and compliance frameworks such as the NIST AI Risk Management Framework [3], EU AI Act [4], and ISO 42001 [5] that aim to govern AI and its risks.

AI Governance in Cloud-Based Environments

GenAI does not exist or operate in a vacuum. Regulatory oversight is also increasing as it becomes more embedded within cloud environments and gains access to mission-critical applications. Governments across the globe, along with standard bodies like ISO, are catching up to define principles and best practice standards that allow GenAI to be used with security controls in place. Many organizations prioritize agility and profitability, which may come at the cost of governance which is why regulatory frameworks are essential.

2.7.4 *The Way Forward—AI Trends and Predictions*

The rapid pace at which GenAI evolves makes it difficult to predict the direction that AI will take in the next twelve to eighteen months. This also means that organizations must prepare for more disruption and opportunity in the coming years. It becomes essential to look at the future of cloud security under GenAI and see what strategic challenges are ahead.

Trust as a Key Differentiator

As regulations and standards evolve, trust will become a key differentiator in the escalating AI race between providers. Customers will want answers to questions like where and how GenAI models were trained, the type of data used, and what sorts of security assurances can be provided. Providers will start to provide GenAI and model reputation scores that are vetted against security benchmarks and standards to provide transparency around the level of controls.

We will also see organizations increasingly treat GenAI models like third-party software artifacts and mandate security testing, risk management, and trust scores.

2.8 Recommendations for Security Leaders and CISOs

To prepare for the future of GenAI in the cloud, CISOs and security architects should:

1. **Integrate AI Threat Modeling**:
   - Include prompt abuse, model misuse, and agentic AI in standard STRIDE analyses
2. **Invest in GenAI Observability**:
   - Capture and monitor prompt logs, context flow, and plugin activity
3. **Align with Emerging Standards**:
   - Adopt ISO 42001, map use cases to the NIST AI RMF , and prepare for EU AI Act classifications
4. **Create a Model Risk Registry**:
   - Track known behaviors, limitations, usage boundaries, and test coverage
5. **Appoint a GenAI Security Champion**:
   - Task a cross-functional leader with driving secure GenAI adoption and alignment

6. **Build Red and Blue AI Teams**:
   - Red teams use adversarial prompting and behavior fuzzing to simulate attacker techniques
   - Blue teams defend the organization's AI systems against potential attacks.
7. **Collaborate with Cloud Providers**:
   - Leverage cloud-native tools like AWS Bedrock Guardrails, Azure OpenAI filters, and GCP AI dashboards
8. **Implement Agent Access Control**:
   - Restrict what agents can see, do, and remember

2.9 Conclusion

Generative AI is not just another application tier; it is quickly becoming an interface to cloud-based applications and services. Unless proper controls and governance frameworks are put in place, GenAI can widen the attack surface, enable new threat actors, and erode trust. The future of cloud security will not be human vs. AI; instead, it will be human-made AI, working together, governed by policy, protected by code, and guided by principles.

References

1. OWASP Foundation. (2023). *OWASP Top 10 for large language model applications*. Retrieved from https://owasp.org/www-project-top-10-for-large-language-model-applications/
2. MITRE Corporation. (2023). *Adversarial threat landscape for artificial-intelligence systems*. Retrieved from https://atlas.mitre.org
3. National Institute of Standards and Technology. (2023, January). *Artificial Intelligence Risk Management Framework (AI RMF 1.0)*. U.S. Department of Commerce. Retrieved from https://www.nist.gov/itl/ai-risk-management-framework
4. European Parliament & Council. (2021, April). *EU Artificial Intelligence Act—Proposal for a regulation*. Retrieved from https://artificialintelligenceact.eu/
5. International Organization for Standardization. (2023). *ISO/IEC 42001:2023—Artificial Intelligence Management System (AIMS)*. ISO. Retrieved from https://www.iso.org/standard/81230.html
6. CNN. (2024, February). *Finance worker pays out $25 million after video call with deepfake 'chief financial officer'*. CNN. Retrieved from https://edition.cnn.com/2024/02/04/asia/deepfake-cfo-scam-hong-kong-intl-hnk/index.html

Chapter 3
AI for Sustainable Cloud Architectures

Priyanshu Sharma and Ria Ghosh

Abstract This chapter explores the applications of artificial intelligence (AI) in designing and operating sustainable cloud architecture. Data centers use about 1% of the world's electricity and are experiencing growing demands due to AI workloads, creating an urgent need for smart solutions that reduce environmental impact. The chapter identifies important sustainability metrics: Power Usage Effectiveness (PUE), Carbon Usage Effectiveness (CUE), and Water Usage Effectiveness (WUE). It also looks at AI-based methods for optimizing resources, such as predictive analytics, reinforcement learning, and carbon-sensitive scheduling. Case studies from the real world show substantial energy savings ranging from 15% to 40%, offering practical insights on how to incorporate sustainability into cloud infrastructure design and operations.

Keywords Artificial intelligence (AI) · Sustainable cloud computing · Data center energy efficiency · Carbon-aware computing · Green cloud architecture · Power Usage Effectiveness (PUE) · Carbon Usage Effectiveness (CUE) · Water Usage Effectiveness (WUE) · Reinforcement learning · Predictive analytics · Anomaly detection · Carbon-aware scheduling · Renewable energy integration · Data center sustainability · Energy-efficient resource management · Climate-aware computing · Digital twins for energy modeling · Federated learning · Multi-agent systems · Hardware-Aware AI · Kubernetes energy optimization · Carbon-aware autoscaling · Real-time carbon intensity · Workload migration · Geographical load shifting · Energy-efficient cooling systems · Hyperscale data centers · Cloud infrastructure sustainability · Environmental impact assessment · Net-zero cloud computing · Sustainable AI operations

P. Sharma (✉)
R&D, ByteBrain LLC, Sheridan, WY, USA
e-mail: priyanshu.sharma@thebytebrain.com

R. Ghosh
R&D, Forency LLP, New Delhi, India

B. Pandey, A. Patel (eds.), *Revolutionizing the Cloud*,
https://doi.org/10.1007/978-3-032-07479-9_3

3.1 Introduction

3.1.1 *The Escalating Carbon Footprint of Cloud Computing*

Cloud computing's widespread adoption has reshaped information management but poses a significant environmental burden. Data centers account for about 1% of global electricity use, with the USA consuming an estimated 176 TWh in 2023 [1]. This is expected to rise as AI workloads grow. Goldman Sachs Research predicts a 165% increase in electricity use in data centers by decade's end, driven by energy-heavy model training and inference operations [2].

Despite ambitious decarbonization goals from major cloud providers like Google's aim for 24/7 carbon-free energy by 2030 and Microsoft's net-zero pledge, independent analyses indicate that emissions may be significantly underreported [3]. The rise of generative AI threatens to worsen this trend, posing challenges to global climate goals and risking energy grid overloads. Simply increasing power generation is neither economically viable nor environmentally sustainable. Thus, there is an urgent need for intelligent, AI-driven architectures and operational strategies to reduce energy use and carbon emissions without sacrificing performance or reliability.

3.1.2 *Scope and Objectives*

This chapter investigates the confluence of artificial intelligence and sustainable cloud architectures with four primary objectives: defining key sustainability metrics and examining their limitations in dynamic cloud environments, surveying AI techniques for optimizing resource management including predictive analytics, reinforcement learning, and anomaly detection, exploring carbon-aware scheduling strategies that leverage real-time emissions data and geographical load shifting, and presenting real-world implementations demonstrating practical applicability and quantified impact. The chapter provides practitioners and researchers with actionable insights for embedding sustainability into cloud infrastructure design through strategic AI applications.

3.2 Sustainability Metrics and Measurement

Precise measurement is the foundation of effective sustainability management. Three core metrics quantify different aspects of data center environmental performance.

3.2.1 Power Usage Effectiveness (PUE)

$$\text{PUE} = \frac{\text{Total Facility Energy}\left(\text{kWh}\right)}{\text{IT Equipment Energy}\left(\text{kWh}\right)} \tag{3.1}$$

Power Usage Effectiveness (PUE) is the primary metric for assessing data center energy efficiency, defined as the ratio of total facility energy to IT energy [4]. As Eq. (3.1) shows, a perfect PUE of 1.0 indicates that 100% of power supports the IT load. In 2021, the Uptime Institute reported a global average PUE of 1.57 [5], while leading hyperscale providers achieve lower values. Google reported a fleet-wide PUE of 1.10 in 2023, with some facilities below 1.08 [6].

PUE ranges vary by data center type. Legacy enterprise facilities typically exceed 1.8 due to older cooling systems and less efficient UPS equipment. Modern enterprise centers range from 1.4 to 1.8 through improved cooling and virtualization. Advanced colocation facilities achieve 1.2-1.5 via optimized airflow and modular designs. Hyperscale data centers operate below 1.2 through custom designs and AI optimization. While PUE offers valuable efficiency insights, it has limitations, such as not considering energy sources (renewable vs. fossil), failing to quantify other environmental impacts, and varying by measurement methodology and boundaries.

3.2.2 Carbon Usage Effectiveness (CUE)

$$\text{CUE} = \frac{\text{Annual CO Emissions}\left(\text{KgCO}_2\text{e}\right)}{\text{IT Equipment Energy}\left(\text{kWh}\right)} \tag{3.2}$$

Carbon Usage Effectiveness (CUE) extends PUE by incorporating carbon emissions associated with energy consumption [7], defined as the ratio of annual CO_2 emissions to IT equipment energy. As shown in Eq. (3.2), a CUE of 0 implies entirely carbon-free operation, while higher values indicate greater reliance on carbon-intensive sources. Lower CUE values signify smaller carbon footprints per unit of IT energy consumed. ISO/IEC 30134-8 provides a standardized CUE calculation methodology [7].

CUE reporting presents challenges, including accurately determining regional carbon emissions factors, which vary by grid generation mix, time of day, and season. The complexity of Scope 2 and Scope 3 emissions accounting and renewable energy certificate (REC) considerations demands transparency in reporting methodologies. For example, Google's data centers have achieved a carbon usage effectiveness (CUE) of 0.0 by purchasing renewable energy to match 100% of their electricity consumption.

3.2.3 *Water Usage Effectiveness (WUE)*

$$\text{WUE} = \frac{\text{Annual Site Water Usage}\left(\text{Liters}\right)}{\text{IT Equipment Energy}\left(\text{kWh}\right)} \tag{3.3}$$

As shown in Eq. (3.3), Water Usage Effectiveness (WUE) measures water efficiency relative to IT energy consumption [4], calculated as annual site water usage divided by IT energy. WUE includes water for cooling, humidification, and facility operations. Simple WUE looks at total water input, while complex WUE considers water treatment, reuse, and regional stress factors.

As global water scarcity increases due to climate change, WUE is more important alongside energy and carbon metrics. Data centers in water-stressed regions are adopting closed-loop cooling systems and advanced air-cooled solutions to reduce water use. For instance, AWS data centers achieved a WUE of 0.25 L/kWh in 2021—much lower than typical industry values—by utilizing on-site treatment and optimized cooling strategies [8].

3.3 AI Techniques for Energy-Efficient Resource Management

Artificial intelligence drives substantial efficiency gains across multiple data center operational layers, from predicting computational demand to dynamically controlling complex cooling infrastructure.

3.3.1 *Predictive Analytics for Load Forecasting*

Accurate anticipation of compute demand and energy needs enables proactive resource scaling and reduces over-provisioning. Load forecasting shifts operations from reactive to forecast-driven autoscaling. Statistical methods like ARIMA and exponential smoothing offer baseline performance for stable patterns. Machine learning algorithms, including XGBoost and Random Forests, achieve higher accuracy with historical load, calendar effects, and weather data. Deep learning models such as LSTMs, GRUs, and transformers capture long-range dependencies in complex workloads.

Autoscaling integration uses forecasts to guide scaling policies with proactive scaling to avoid performance issues and consolidate workloads during expected lulls to reduce energy use. Studies show 10–25% energy savings compared to reactive scaling without compromising service quality [9].

3.3.2 *Reinforcement Learning for Dynamic Control*

Reinforcement Learning (RL) addresses resource allocation and cooling control as sequential decision-making tasks, enabling AI agents to learn optimal policies that cut energy while meeting performance constraints. It optimizes dynamically via Markov Decision Process, using server metrics, rack temperatures, PUE, energy prices, and grid carbon intensity as states. Actions include VM migration, server power states, cooling setpoints, and fan speeds. Rewards balance energy efficiency and performance with multi-objective functions, linking states to optimal actions.

RL algorithms feature value-based methods like DQN and DDQN for discrete actions (e.g., server selection), policy-gradient methods such as PPO and A2C for continuous actions (e.g., cooling adjustments), and actor-critic approaches like DDPG and SAC for complex environments. Applications show significant effects, with HVAC control achieving 9–13% energy savings in commercial deployments [9], while scheduling agents create policies that reduce energy and carbon footprint. However, practical deployments face challenges such as sparse rewards hindering convergence, noisy sensor measurements affecting state estimation, and integration issues with legacy controls.

3.3.3 *Case Study: DeepMind's Cooling Optimization at Google*

DeepMind's collaboration with Google's data center operations represents a landmark achievement in applying AI to data center sustainability through reinforcement learning [10]. The implementation utilized five years of historical telemetry from thousands of sensors across Google's data centers, with deep neural networks trained to predict temperature/pressure profiles and model PUE responses. Phased deployment began with human-in-the-loop recommendations followed by autonomous control with oversight.

The results achieved a 40% reduction in cooling energy, a 15% improvement in overall PUE, and millions in annual cost savings, and demonstrated adaptability to dynamic conditions more effectively than rule-based systems. This case study highlights RL's transformative potential, where continuous learning and adaptation unlock new frontiers in data center energy efficiency.

3.4 Carbon-Aware Scheduling and Renewable Integration

Cloud operators can dramatically reduce carbon emissions by aligning workload placement and timing with periods and locations of cleaner energy availability through comprehensive frameworks for carbon-aware scheduling and renewable energy forecasting.

3.4.1 Carbon Data Ecosystem and Forecasting

Robust carbon-aware scheduling relies on accurate grid emissions data and renewable energy forecasting. Marginal emissions APIs like WattTime [11] provide second-by-second forecasts of carbon intensity using ML models, while average mix APIs such as ElectricityMap [12] offer overall carbon intensity and renewable/fossil forecasts. Key factors include refresh intervals from seconds to hours, uncertainty management, and strong validation pipelines.

Renewable energy forecasting utilizes various data sources, including weather services, grid operators, satellite imagery, and ground measurements. Modeling techniques range from physical models for day-ahead forecasting to statistical methods like ARIMA and exponential smoothing. Machine learning methods, including random forests and gradient boosting, integrate exogenous variables, while deep learning architectures like LSTM and Temporal CNNs can reduce error by 10–20% [13]. Hybrid approaches combine physical and data-driven methods, utilize clear-sky normalization, and implement multi-model ensembles with uncertainty quantification.

3.4.2 Scheduling Framework Architecture

Modern architectures adopt streaming, cache-backed pipelines, ensuring low-latency access to real-time and forecasted data. Streaming collectors pull carbon intensity and renewable forecasts, publishing to message buses like Kafka for reliable delivery. Time-series stores like InfluxDB retain historical data for model training and trend analysis. Cache layers, including Redis, provide millisecond-latency reads for autoscale and schedulers. AI forecasting services, use LSTM/TCN models trained on local data to produce site-specific estimates with confidence intervals.

3.4.3 Integration Patterns and Optimization

Different workload types need tailored carbon-aware controls. Batch job deferral in frameworks like Airflow moves "flexible" jobs to low-carbon windows using custom sensors that check carbon intensity thresholds. Event-driven autoscaling via carbon-aware KEDA operators utilizes AI forecasts to scale functions before high-carbon periods while keeping service availability during transitions. Kubernetes pod placement plugins utilize carbon scores and apply affinity functions to favor "green" nodes without manual intervention.

Multi-objective optimization strikes a balance between emissions reduction and performance costs. Linear programming addresses weighted emissions and latency penalties for small-scale clusters. Reinforcement learning enables deep RL agents to develop policies that minimize long-term cumulative emissions while adhering to SLAs. Risk-aware scheduling considers forecast uncertainty and penalizes high-variance predictions for reliable operation.

3.4.4 Real-World Case Studies

AWS's Customer Carbon Footprint Tool (CCFT) v2.0 offers per-region, per-service emission estimates using ML to cleanse billing data and validate anomalies. Integrating CCFT metrics into routing policies enables customers to reduce emissions by 15–21% on stateless workloads [14]. Google's carbon-intelligent request routing, which combines AI grid-intensity forecasts and workload management, leads to up to 40% savings in cooling energy and a roughly 15% overall PUE improvement while maintaining SLA commitments [6]. Karmada-based spatial shifting in Kubernetes testbeds dynamically relocates "spatially flexible" workloads across clusters based on AI regional emissions forecasts, achieving about 30% emission reductions for batch analytics with minimal effect on completion times [15].

3.4.5 Implementation Challenges and Best Practices

Successful implementation requires addressing forecast reliability by matching API polling intervals to forecast horizons, implementing fallback mechanisms, monitoring accuracy, and adjusting strategies accordingly. SLA safeguards always pair carbon policies with performance fallbacks, implement gradual rollout strategies, and monitor for violations. Cross-region trade-offs factor in egress costs and latency when migrating workloads while using multi-objective optimization to balance financial and environmental metrics. Security and compliance considerations include isolating telemetry channels, ensuring data sovereignty compliance, and implementing access controls with audit logging.

3.5 Implementation Insights and Best Practices

3.5.1 Architectural Patterns

Energy-aware architectures can be grouped into two related categories:

Microservices-Focused Patterns

- **Kubernetes Scheduling Plugins:** These combine SLA constraints with power measurements to cut microservice energy consumption by up to 12% [16].

- **Carbon-Aware Autoscaling:** This uses Kubecost to correlate resource usage with carbon intensity, suggesting scale-down during high-carbon periods to minimize the footprint [17].

Infrastructure-Focused Patterns

- **Physics-Based Digital Twins:** Platforms like Cadence Reality merge thermo-fluid models with live sensor feeds, allowing for safe prototyping of operational changes [18].
- **Real-Time Twin Integration:** Using three years of telemetry for closed-loop adjustments has reduced plant-wide energy use by 18% [19].
- **Open-Source Toolchains:**
  - **Kubecost:** Provides real-time cost and carbon analytics through deep cluster-metrics integration [16].
  - **PEAKS (Power Efficiency Aware Kubernetes Scheduling):** This uses live energy metrics to inform pod placement and scaling decisions.
  - **Carbon-Aware SDK:** Standardizes access to carbon intensity data and renewable energy tracking for various orchestration platforms [20].

3.5.2 *Essential Governance Considerations*

Data governance treats telemetry streams as critical assets with ISO 27001/14001 integration, risk management mapping, and automated quality checks to ensure data integrity and compliance. Privacy protection implements privacy-by-design principles, including pseudonymization, aggregation, end-to-end encryption, and GDPR/CCPA compliance to balance detailed data needs with privacy requirements. Regulatory compliance addresses SEC climate disclosure rules and CSRD requirements with robust reporting solutions supporting compliance obligations and internal decision-making processes.

3.5.3 *Critical Success Factors*

Executive sponsorship ensures leadership support, clear objectives, and progress reviews for organizational commitment and resource allocation. Cross-functional teams blend engineering, data science, and facility operations expertise to foster collaboration and problem-solving. Robust telemetry involves high-frequency data collection, comprehensive sensor coverage, power meter integration, and quality assurance for effective AI-driven optimization. Transparent decision-making features model recommendation logging, override tracking, and audit support to build confidence and enable ongoing learning across the organization.

3.5.4 Common Pitfalls to Avoid

Over-reliance on point forecasts ignores uncertainty estimates and fallback mechanisms for reliable operation. Inadequate sensor deployment and maintenance result in insufficient data coverage, hindering model operation in edge cases. Premature automation happens when organizations adopt full autonomy without gradual transitions, human oversight, and safety constraints. Underestimating integration includes neglecting legacy system compatibility, BMS integration complexity, and realistic timeline management, causing challenges and cost overruns.

3.6 Future Research Directions

3.6.1 Federated Learning for Cross-Datacenter Optimization

Applying federated learning across geographically distributed data centers poses unique challenges in resource heterogeneity, privacy constraints, and communication efficiency. Research opportunities include developing privacy-preserving aggregation protocols that maintain model utility while respecting data sovereignty requirements, creating capacity-aware weighting schemes that account for different server generations and cooling system configurations, and implementing gradient compression techniques for efficient long-haul communication [21].

3.6.2 Multi-Agent Systems for Cooperative Energy Management

As independent "agents" in broader energy ecosystems, data centers require standard for resource trade negotiation and dynamic control coordin interfacesation. Research focuses on reward structure design that balances local efficiency goals with system-wide carbon reduction objectives, and scalable coordination protocols ensuring convergence and stability as agent populations grow while maintaining real-time responsiveness [22]. However, practical deployments often face challenges such as inter-data-center coordination overhead and the lack of standardized communication protocols, which can impede efficient real-time operation.

3.6.3 Advanced Digital Twins and Lifecycle Modeling

Future digital twins incorporating real-time AI forecasts for workload prediction and renewable availability, continuous learning mechanisms for model refinement and physics simulator updates, and full lifecycle carbon accounting from raw material extraction through end-of-life processing could enable comprehensive sustainability optimization and automated deployment across multiple scales [23].

3.6.4 Hardware-Aware AI and Zero-Carbon Clouds

Co-design of hardware and algorithms provides energy optimization via neural architecture search for power minimization, compiler optimization including quantization and operator fusion, and dynamic DVFS for server optimization with performance guarantees. This progresses toward autonomous, carbon-neutral cloud operations with unified control over compute, cooling, storage, and power distribution [24].

Successfully implementing these strategies may enhance cloud computing sustainability, address global climate challenges, and meet society's increasing computing demands while safeguarding planetary health.

References

1. International Energy Agency. (2023). *Data centres and data transmission networks*. IEA.
2. Goldman Sachs Global Investment Research. (2023, December). *The AI Boom's power drain: Data centers' rising electricity demand*. Goldman Sachs.
3. O'Brien, I. (2024). *Article on data center gas emissions in tech*. The Guardian. Retrieved from https://www.theguardian.com/technology/2024/sep/15/data-center-gas-emissions-tech
4. The Green Grid. (2022). *Data Center Water Usage Effectiveness (WUE) metric: A comprehensive white paper*. The Green Grid.
5. Uptime Institute. (2021). *Data center industry survey results 2021*. Uptime Institute.
6. Google Cloud. (2023). *Carbon-intelligent computing platform*. Google Cloud Sustainability.
7. International Organization for Standardization. (2023). *ISO/IEC 30134-8:2023—Carbon Usage Effectiveness (CUE)*. ISO.
8. Clancy, H. (2022, December 22) *What sets Amazon's cloud water strategy apart*. Trellis Group Inc. 2022 (updated May 16, 2025). Retrieved from https://trellis.net/article/what-sets-amazons-cloud-water-strategy-apart
9. Luo, J., Wang, X., & Ma, Z. (2021). Reinforcement learning for HVAC control: A trane partnership case study. *Applied Energy, 285*, 116–128.
10. DeepMind. (2016, July). *DeepMind AI reduces google data centre cooling bill by 40%*. Google Research Blog.
11. WattTime. (2024). *Automated emissions reduction via real-time grid data*. WattTime API Documentation.
12. ElectricityMap. (2024). *Global carbon intensity data API*. ElectricityMap Foundation.
13. Karamolegkos, S., & Koulouriotis, D. E. (2025). Advancing short-term load forecasting with decomposed Fourier ARIMA: A case study on the Greek energy market. *Elsevier Energy, 325*, 135854.
14. Amazon Web Services. (2025, April). *Customer carbon footprint tool—Methodology v2.0*. AWS Sustainability.
15. Fairbanks, R. (2024). Federated spatial shifting: Karmada-based carbon-aware scheduling. In *Proceedings of the KubeCon EU*.

16. Kumar, D., & Lee, H. (2022). *PEAKS: Power efficiency aware Kubernetes scheduler*. IBM Research Report.
17. Kubecost. (2024). *Carbon cost monitoring for Kubernetes*. Kubecost Documentation.
18. Cadence. (2022). *Reality™ digital twin for data centre energy modeling*. Cadence Datasheet.
19. Data Center Frontier. (2023, November). *Digital twins: The next Frontier in data-center management*. Data Center Frontier.
20. Green Software Foundation. (2024). *Carbon aware SDK*. Green Software Foundation Technical Report.
21. Kairouz, P., McMahan, H. B., et al. (2021). Advances and open problems in federated learning. *Foundations and Trends® in Machine Learning, 14*(1–2), 1–210.
22. Zhang, Y., Wang, S., et al. (2021). Multi-agent reinforcement learning for data center energy management: A survey. *IEEE Transactions on Artificial Intelligence, 2*(4), 320–335.
23. Fuller, A., Fan, Z., Day, C., & Barlow, C. (2020). Digital Twin: Enabling technologies, challenges and open research. *IEEE Access, 8*, 108952–108971.
24. Hellerstein, J. M. (2021). Self-driving cloud: The next generation of autonomous infrastructure. *Communications of the ACM, 64*(7), 36–38.
25. Srivangipuram, V. V. K. (2024). Environmental sustainability benefits of cloud-based enterprise application architecture. *International Journal of Innovative Research in Science, Engineering and Technology (IJIRSET), 13*(6), 10407–10416.

Chapter 4
Data Privacy and Governance in AI-Powered Cloud

Pragya Keshap and Akhilesh Keshap

Abstract The technological world is changing under the influences of the innovations of Artificial Intelligence (AI) and its integration with cloud computing. The change, however, brings along its own challenges. In response, new privacy policies are being established in the entire world. In this chapter, we will discuss how data privacy and governance have evolved in the age of AI. We will discuss in detail about the privacy risks associated when using AI in the cloud. Various countries have built laws and regulations such as GDPR, CCPA, DPDPA, and PIPL that companies need to follow to preserve privacy of user data. We will learn about those in detail, as well as we will see how companies can build governance frameworks to design systems that are secure and privacy-preserving. Throughout the next few years, as AI continues to advance and integrate into daily activities, the way we manage and protect data will become even more important. This chapter will help you understand the challenges and learn how to build AI-cloud systems that are both powerful and responsible and how companies can be proactive with what's coming up in the field of AI and cloud.

Keywords Artificial Intelligence · Cloud computing · GDPR · CCPA · DPDPA · PIPL · HIPPA · GLBA · FERPA · PCI DSS · Data localization · Cross-border data transfer · AI governance as code · Data privacy · AI governance · Differential privacy · Federated learning · Shadow data · Model hallucination · Homomorphic encryption

---

P. Keshap (✉)
IEEE Senior Member, Austin, TX, USA

A. Keshap
IEEE Senior Member, Austin, TX, USA

Independent Researcher, Austin, TX, USA

B. Pandey, A. Patel (eds.), *Revolutionizing the Cloud*,
https://doi.org/10.1007/978-3-032-07479-9_4

4.1 Introduction to Data Privacy in Cloud and Evolution

Cloud, which in the earlier days was just used to store files or run virtual machines, is now the foundational infrastructure to develop, train, and run complex AI models. The large cloud providers such as Microsoft Azure, AWS, and Google cloud offer facilities to store large data sets which can be taken to train the AI models. Cloud platforms as well as the usage of AI tools complement our everyday lives. They can together help us in day-to-day activities like guiding us with the optimal route to the destination, personalizing recommendations, voice assistance, medical diagnosis, and much more.

AI systems are quite different from traditional software systems. They depend on massive data, which may include personal or sensitive information such as financial information or medical history. To add to that, cloud infrastructure on which an AI model is developed or trained, may be shared or dynamic in nature, causing the data to flow across regions or services. All these factors bring up concerns related to personal data security, compliance, and accountability.

Various countries are coming up with strict rules on how companies can obtain, use, and manage personal data. The General Data Protection Regulation (GDPR) issued by the European Union, The California Consumer Privacy Act (CCPA), Digital Personal Data Protection Act (DPDPA) of India, and Personal Information Protection Law (PIPL) in China all put significant pressure on the organizations to maintain the users data well. These laws are important, but it is hard to apply these to modern AI technologies, especially when it is unclear how data is being used inside the complex models, or where the data is stored across various countries. And, on top of that, companies need to have very strong policies and processes, what we call as **Governance**, to mitigate the risks of such tools being used improperly. Governance means defining rules and policies around who can access data, how long it can be stored, auditing, etc. Successful governance models not only guarantee proper usage of data and ensure privacy of the users, but also build trust in AI systems.

4.1.1 A Brief History of Data Privacy in Cloud Computing

Data privacy in cloud computing infrastructures can be traced far back to the year 2000 when third-party data centers came up. These were third-party companies that provided infrastructure to store the data of other companies. This shift introduced significant efficiency gains like the companies no longer had to worry about setting up infrastructure and can just rent it. But, this sparked initial concerns around data ownership and security. Back then, most companies focused just on making the systems fast and efficient. Privacy, security, and safety were not core business practices during this period.

However, as the utilization of cloud computing grew, businesses started to apply it on more complex processes such as data analysis, real-time processing, and machine learning. All these new applications of technology raised the questions concerning user data privacy. Unlike traditional applications, AI models need access to large amounts of data, both structured and unstructured. Much of the training data generally includes personal details such as personally Identifiable Information (PII), behavioral patterns, financial information, and confidential business details. Generative AI models like large language models (LLMs) can actually take this even further by generating new text and images using the information they've learned. That makes the risk of accidentally sharing people's private information even higher.

4.1.2 The Shift with AI: From Storage and Compute to Inference and Automation

As we discussed before, because of the influence of AI on cloud services, the fundamental nature of data usage has changed. Earlier, we only used to handle or store data, but now we actively use data with AI to generate new content, make predictions and make autonomous decisions. However, this evolution raises three main privacy concerns. Let's discuss those in detail.

AI's Tendency to Remember

AI models, especially deep learning systems, can actually memorize elements of their training data. Unlike traditional computer systems that just used data and then discarded it, AI "learns" from the data, making it hard to remove traces of specific information later on.

Indirect Data Leakage Through Outputs

Generative AI can produce outputs that appear novel but may contain fragments of the original training data. This is particularly problematic when training sets include sensitive information like medical records or private documents. Organizations must now account for privacy risks not just in data they store, but also in what the AI generates.

Real-Time Personalization and Decision-Making

AI systems are increasingly used to personalize user experiences, make autonomous decisions like approving transactions, screening job applications, and more. These decisions are often made in real time and based on individual behavioral patterns.

This constant use of personal data makes privacy concerns even bigger, especially since users may not fully understand or agree to how their data is being used.

4.1.3 Key Pillars of AI Governance

As we discussed toward the beginning of this chapter, Governance is very important to make sure companies use individual's private data in a responsible and ethical way. Below are some key principles for defining Governance in organizations [1].

Privacy and Security

- Protecting personal data by masking or removing as needed
- Implementing access control and user authentication
- Compliance with data privacy regulations
- Implementation using privacy-by-design approach

Fairness and Explainability

- Implementing Explainable AI (XAI) methods
- Conducting bias testing and mitigation as applicable
- Using diverse data sets
- Maintaining clear documentation of model behavior

Ethics and Accountability

- Establishing clear ethical guidelines and regularly auditing AI systems
- Establishing accountability teams for monitoring AI ethics

4.1.4 Global Regulations

In response to growing privacy concerns with AI, the global regulatory landscape has evolved. Various nations and international bodies are developing frameworks to address the potential risks and benefits of AI. According to the 2025 AI Index Report by Stanford University [5]. In 2024, U.S. federal agencies introduced 59 AI-related regulations —more than twice as many as in 2023—with double the number of agencies involved. Four regulations in particular—GDPR [2], CCPA, DPDPA, and PIPL—have become cornerstones of global data governance.

General Data Protection Regulation (GDPR)—European Union

GDPR [2] is considered to be the most effective data protection law in the whole world. It was implemented in May 2018 and brought a number of important principles:

- **Lawfulness, fairness, and transparency**: Organizations should treat individuals' personal data legally, fairly, and display transparency in the use of such information.
- **Purpose limitation and data minimization**: Collect data in a proper way. You can collect information only in the case that it is necessary to achieve the purpose you define.
- **Storage Limitation**: Data should be saved for only as long as it is required by the business.
- **Accuracy**: Organizations will have to ensure that the personal data it possesses is accurate and updated. It is important to correct/remove any errors in data as soon as detected.
- **Integrity and Confidentiality**: No matter what, the personal data of individuals should be kept protected to prevent any accidental or illegal access.
- **Accountability and governance**: The organizations are expected to demonstrate that they adhere to all the provisions stipulated by the GDPR. They ought to follow proper procedures, keep their own policies, attend training sessions, and be reviewed through checks and audits.

California Consumer Privacy Act (CCPA)—United States

Under **CCPA**, which has been in effect since 2020, Californian citizens will receive significant rights over their personal information. It lets them see what data companies have about them, tell companies to erase it, and stop companies from selling their data. The act was strengthened by **California Privacy Rights Act** (CPRA), which was implemented in 2020 and introduced additional regulations, as well as created the **California Privacy Protection Agency** (CPPA) to ensure enforcement. It introduces several key principles:

- **Transparency**: Companies ought to explain explicitly on how they will gather personal information, how they will utilize the information and with whom it will be shared. This also includes posting an up-to-date privacy policy on their websites.
- **Consumer Rights**: CCPA/CPRA include various essential rights for the consumers:
  - **Right to Know**: Individuals can exercise a valuable right to know which record is being gathered about them and how the information is processed.
  - **Right to Delete**: Individuals have the right to erase their personal information, with a few exceptions.

  - **Right to Correct**: Individuals have the right to ask for correction of any inaccurate data about them.
  - **Right to Opt-Out**: Individuals can request not to have their personal data sold or shared.
  - **Right to Non-Discrimination**: No discrimination should be made against anyone who exercises his or her human rights.

- **Data Minimization and Purpose Limitation**: Organizations should limit access to personal data to what they really need for their official tasks.
- **Security**: Organizations must ensure that they employ and accommodate security devices to ensure that people are not able to steal or access confidential data.
- **Contracts with Service Providers and Third Parties**: The organization should incorporate contracts with third parties such that they should just use data within given limits and the information should be secured.
- **Accountability**: Organizations are required to follow the regulations, and it is their responsibility to prove that they are doing it, when there is necessity.

Digital Personal Data Protection Act (DPDPA)—India

The **DPDPA** is India's main data privacy law. It was passed in 2023 and sets out rules for using and handling personal information. It's key features include:

- **Lawful and Fair Use of Data**: Data must be collected and used in a lawful, fair, and transparent way. Companies must have some good reason (such as authorization or legal necessity) to gather personal information.
- **Purpose Limitation**: Organizations should explain to individuals why their data is to be collected and the restrictions imposed as to other reasons. The primary aim should be the data collection of only the content that will be needed in the planned purpose.
- **Data Minimization**: The data can be collected and utilized only in the case when the objective is well defined and complies with the law.
- **Data Accuracy**: Personal information should be accurate and it has to be as recent as possible. Organizations must either remove or update inaccurate data when asked to do so.
- **Storage Limitation**: The information should not be stored for longer than it is stipulated. It should be destroyed or anonymized when it is no longer necessary to achieve the stated purpose.
- **Security**: The organizations must make sure that personal data is not abused or disclosed. There should be security measures to ensure unauthorized access.
- **Individual Rights**: People have the right to:
  - Know what data is collected about them
  - Ask for it to be deleted or updated
  - Withdraw consent at any time

- **Accountability**: Companies have to demonstrate that they are abiding by these rules. They require policies and processes to protect data.
- **Cross-border transfer framework**: The government can name the list of countries, which the personal data can be transferred to, based on strategic and legal considerations.

Personal Information Protection Law (PIPL)—China

China's PIPL, effective since November 2021, is strongly inspired by GDPR [2]. It puts national security and the public interest at a high priority. It has the following key features:

- **Lawfulness, Fairness, and Transparency**: Data collection and processing must be legal, fair, and transparent. Organizations should inform people clearly about the data they are collecting, the reasons they need it and how it will be used.
- **Purpose Limitation and Data Minimization**: The data should be gathered with clear and definite purposes. No extra personal data should be collected besides the receiving of minimal data required to reach those purposes.
- **Accuracy**: Organizations must ensure that personal data is accurate and complete.
- **Security and Protection**: Organizations should be able to provide tight security on personal information to prevent leakages or misuse of information. They should be quick to act on data breach and inform regulators and the individuals involved where necessary.
- **Individual Rights**: People have the right to:
  - Access their personal data
  - Correct mistakes
  - Delete their data in certain cases
  - Limit or refuse the processing of some data
  - Request explanations for how their information helps automated decision-making (such as AI profiling)
- **Cross-border Data Transfers**: Personal data of Chinese citizens is not allowed to be transferred to other countries, unless strict rules are followed. In other scenarios, the companies have to undergo security audits or get government approvals.
- **Accountability**: Organizations must ensure compliance with these rules and assign someone responsible (like a Data Protection Officer).They must also perform regular audits and impact assessments to identify the risks to privacy.

4.1.5 *Sector-Specific Laws: Vertical Regulation in AI-Cloud Context*

While broad privacy laws like GDPR, CCPA, and PIPL set general standards for personal data protection, some industries—such as healthcare, finance, and education—deal with even more sensitive data. These sectors have special laws that add extra requirements and strict rules to ensure personal data is safe. These are called sector-specific laws. Let's discuss a few of them.

The Health Insurance Portability and Accountability Act (HIPAA)—USA

HIPAA is the primary privacy law to ensure the privacy and security of the health information of individuals. It applies to healthcare providers, health insurance companies, and other companies dealing with confidential and sensitive patient information known as Protected Health Information—PHI. Highlights of HIPPA [3]:

- Companies are advised to develop policies that would cover confidentiality, integrity, and accessibility of PHI.
- Health information of a patient must not be disclosed to anyone except the patient or the authorized representatives of a patient.
- The companies should ensure that it has a record of who has viewed the data and when.
- In case of leakage of the sensitive health information, the information should be communicated to both the patients and the regulators.
- Allows people to port or maintain health insurance when they switch or lose their employment.

Gramm-Leach-Bliley Act (GLBA)—USA

GLBA [4] is the primary privacy law to guarantee the confidentiality and safety of personal financial data of the individuals. It is applicable to firms that are involved in the financial services or products such as loans, insurance, and investment advice. Highlights of GLBA:

- The companies are supposed to explain their policy on information sharing to the consumers in easy languages.
- Businesses need to provide an alternative to their customers of refusing to reveal their personal financial information to particular third parties.
- Companies should bring in effective security measures to protect the confidential financial data.
- Every year or more frequently, companies are under the obligation to create and distribute the awareness of their privacy policies among their customers.

Family Educational Rights and Privacy Act (FERPA)—USA

FERPA is the main privacy law that protects the confidentiality and safety of the education records of students. It covers schools and learning platforms where student information is stored or used. Highlights of FERPA:

- Educational records of students should be kept confidential and should not be disclosed to any unauthorized person; only the parents or the teachers can access such records.
- Schools should provide written consent of parents or students, who reach the age that qualifies them, to disclose the records to any third-party websites.

Payment Card Industry Data Security Standard—PCI DSS

PCI DSS provides security requirements when dealing with payment card information (such as credit card numbers). It is applicable to any company that stores, processes, or transmits cardholder data. Highlights of PCI DSS:

- Encryption of payment data when it's stored or transmitted.
- Restricted access to card data to only the people who really need it.
- Maintaining secure systems and monitoring them for suspicious activity.
- Regular testing and update of security measures.

4.1.6 Cross-Border Data Transfer and Data Localization

What Is Cross-Border Data Transfer

When data is stored in the cloud or utilized by AI systems, it tends to cross-national borders, such as in India to the USA or Europe to Asia. This is referred to as cross-border data transfer. The reason is that cloud providers have data centers located across the globe and companies tend to be multinational.

What Is Data Localization?

According to some regulations, it is becoming a requirement by countries that personal data must remain within the confines of a country, thereby forcing companies to store or process data in the same country in which it originated. That is referred to as data localization. Governments need to enforce this so as to reduce fear aspects such as spying, loss of control of their information or access by foreign governments.

Challenges with Data Localization and Cross-Border Data Transfer

There are some difficult questions in front of the companies who use AI systems:

- Do they have to develop AI per country to abide by these rules?
- What impact does data localization have on AI training procedures that typically depend on cross-border data sharing, such as federated learning?
- When they take out the personal information in the data (anonymization), is that sufficient to comply with the laws, or do they also require signing special legal agreements?

Mechanisms such as Standard Contractual Clauses (SCCs) in the EU, company regulations on data processing, and government-to-government data transfer agreements are being adopted to assist in transferring data abroad. However, the legal environment still remains uncertain.

4.2 Privacy Risks in AI-powered Cloud Environments

As artificial intelligence (AI) becomes increasingly integrated into cloud computing, organizations face new and complex privacy concerns. AI models, unlike conventional software systems, are trained on large volumes of data which most often includes sensitive personal information. When these models are deployed in cloud environments, the risks associated with data privacy gets further amplified because of the distributed and shared infrastructure of the cloud. In this section, we will discuss the numerous privacy risks that AI-empowered cloud environments have and how to mitigate them.

4.2.1 Key Privacy Risks in AI-Powered Cloud Environments

Data Memorization and Leakage

The AI models, especially the deep learning models, can retain part of the training data. And when that data contains personal information, such as the name of a person, his or her phone number, or medical history, the AI might unintentionally repeat it later.

Shadow Data and Model Hallucination

Shadow data refers to the data that is collected or generated without explicit approval or consent of the individual it belongs to. In cloud environments, it can occur in the form of logs, backups, or accidental retention of data. Hallucination will also arise in AI models, meaning the models will produce model outputs that seem realistic but are not based on real-world data. Such hallucinations might unintentionally contain sensitive data and cause a privacy leak.

Inference Attacks

An inference attack involves an attempt by an attacker to uncover sensitive information about an individual through observation or analysis of trends in the data or AI model output. Even after anonymizing the data, attackers can still utilize the same and compare with any external data to infer personal details. The attacks are specifically hazardous in machine learning when a model may accidentally leak information regarding its training data.

Data Poisoning

Data poisoning attack is a type of security attack in which the attacker intentionally inserts malicious or misleading data to the training dataset of a machine learning model. The intention is to poison the learning process of the model in order to end up with inaccurate or even malicious representation. This can be used either to control how the AI works, or compromise its effectiveness, or even perform backdoors. The risks of data poisoning become higher on cloud systems where the sources of data are highly diverse and often external. This is what can lead to the creation of models that leak vital information or draw biased conclusions.

Model Inversion: Reversing the AI

Model inversion is an attack in which an attacker takes advantage of access to model output to obtain the sensitive information within a training set. E.g., an attacker may retrieve an image or confidential information of a person by observing the model response to specific inputs. It is especially alarming in the model that was trained on personal or confidential data, as it may cause the violation of privacy even without direct access to data.

4.2.2 Mitigation Strategies

In order to apply AI ethically, companies must have strict privacy regulations, appropriate data governance policies, and must keep up with the threat of security issues. The section brings forward key strategies to data protection in cloud computing with the use of AI.

Data Minimization and Anonymization

The firms must embrace the idea of data minimization whereby the necessary information (which must be used to accomplish a target goal) is collected. This will assist in reducing the invasion of privacy through exposure of personal information and excessive gathering. The concept of anonymization is an approach that either masks or removes personal data that individuals can be identified by such as names and IDs. Anonymized data is very much safe to train the models.

Robust Access Controls

Strict control over the access will ensure only the necessary staff will be able to access sensitive data and AI models. Unauthorized data exposure may be avoided with the help of role-based access and multi-factor authentication.

Regular Auditing and Monitoring

Monitoring of the AI systems in real time and regular audits can detect unusual behavior and data leaks. Possible breaches of privacy can also be detected and mitigated with the help of logging and monitoring access to data and the functioning of AI models.

Secure Data Storage and Transmission

Encryption of data kept on the disk (at the rest) and on the network (in transit) may prevent unauthorized access to a very high extent. In order to protect sensitive data, secure cloud storage facilities and practices should be used. Also best practices like strong encryption should be applied.

Compliance with Privacy Regulations

The most basic thing to do is to keep abreast and stay at the same speed with the required data protection laws. Organizations should have effective policies and procedures in place to ensure that the AI systems in their organizations comply with these laws, despite where the systems originated.

4.2.3 The Role of Ethical AI

Beyond legal compliance, organizations are responsible for developing and deploying AI systems in an ethical manner. With the fast-paced dynamic environment of AI usage and more specifically when using AI tools on the cloud, ethics will be a prerequisite and hence the companies need to conform to societal values, rights of the individual, and organizational integrity.

Below are the key highlights of ethical AI.

- **Transparency**: It means keeping users, regulators, and stakeholders informed on how AI systems are collecting the data and how the data is being used for decision-making.
- **Fairness**: Cloud-based AI systems are usually trained on large amounts of diverse data. Fairness means that the decisions made by AI systems should not reinforce any unfair biases or discrimination based on attributes such as race, gender, age, etc.
- **Accountability**: As AI systems grow in complexity, companies should establish guidelines and ownership over data collection, model development, etc. Accountability implies having a process in place in the event of any wrong decision being taken by the AI system. It even consists of the guidelines to explore and recover any mistaken or inapplicable outcomes or decisions made by a certain AI system.
- **User Consent**: It means that individuals understand and agree to how their data will be used, what all data will be used and for what purpose. They should also have the option to choose what all data they allow to be used and can also opt-out so that their data is not included in the training data. If the user decides to opt-out, his data should be immediately deleted from the data set.

4.3 Preserving Privacy for AI in Cloud Environments

As we already discussed that with the growing utilization of AI on cloud platforms, it is crucial to secure user data. The AI systems work with large amounts of data, which often includes personal data like finance information, health records, etc. This data is analyzed with the help of complex algorithms running on cloud and correlated with other types of information, which creates risks such as unauthorized access to information, its misuse or leakage. To mitigate such risks and to ensure that AI does its part without compromising any private information, various privacy-preserving methods have been developed.

In the next few sections, we will discuss various privacy-preserving techniques and how major cloud providers use those.

4.3.1 Privacy-Preserving Techniques for AI in Cloud Environments [8]

Differential Privacy

Differential Privacy (DP) [6] is a type of privacy protection which allows AI models to learn and work on massive amounts of information without impairing the confidential data of any person. This is achieved by addition of random noise in the data set or its output, which makes it difficult for attackers to determine if some person's data was used or not. DP adheres to various data protection regulations including GDPR [2] and CCPA by decreasing the threats of re-identification.

Federated Learning

With AI being embedded in everyone's daily life, there are so many data sources like mobile phones, wearables, laptops, etc. and thereby there is a lot of sensitive data. Data is needed to train AI, but bringing all this data to one centralized location will cause security and privacy issues. Federated Learning (FL) provides a solution to this problem by providing a decentralized approach, in which the model is trained on the user device or local servers, and the data does not need to be transferred to cloud or any central facility. Only model updates such as gradients are transferred. These parameters help to improve the model. FL is a privacy-first solution being utilized by various finance, healthcare, mobile computing companies as it complies with various regulations like GDPR and CCPA which restrict the collection and distribution of personal information.

Homomorphic Encryption

Another challenge with the widespread use of AI is how to perform powerful computations on personal and sensitive information without exposing the data. The Homomorphic Encryption [7] (HE) techniques address this issue. It is a form of encryption which allows performing operations on encrypted data. The data does not require decryption to utilize it to train any models or to use such data to produce some output. The best part of HE is that even the output of the calculation is also encrypted. When the output is decrypted, it is the same result as would come when the calculations are performed on unencrypted data. There is no threat of data exposure because the data is still encrypted all through the homomorphic encryption.

Synthetic Data Generation

Synthetic data generation is the process of creating artificial data that mimics the statistical patterns and structure of real-world data. It is commonly employed in the situations where the real data is limited or sensitive, or prohibited because of privacy regulations. Data is created using rule-based simulations, generative models like GANs, and differential privacy [6] methods to help it match real-world data. Below are the benefits of using Synthetic Data Generation:

Significance:

- **Data Anonymization**: Synthetic data is utilized in place of real data, reducing privacy concerns.
- **Testing and Development**: Model development and testing of models can be done without the disclosure of sensitive data.

Secure Multi-Party Computation

Secure multi-party computation (often called SMPC or MPC) is a technique to enable two or more parties to collaborate and, using their joint data, to compute something without either party having to send its sensitive data to the other party or parties.

Significance:

- **Privacy and Security**: SMPC implies that companies will not need to disclose sensitive data like health records, financial data to anyone.
- **Compliance with Data Laws** : SMPC enables companies to comply with strict privacy regulations (such as GDPR [2] or HIPAA), since data remains confidential during the process.

4.4 Building a Governance Framework for AI-powered Cloud Systems

As we discussed before, as AI becomes closely integrated in cloud environments, it is posing additional governance challenges. AI models rely on a huge amount of information base and algorithms. When used in cloud infrastructure, these models take advantage of cloud scalability and flexibility. However, AI in the cloud can also present severe risks related to data privacy, security, fairness, and compliance.

In order to address these risks and make the most out of AI in the cloud, it is essential that organizations develop a proper governance model. For that, they need to design appropriate roles and responsibilities, policies, and procedures and utilize modern tools and systems to monitor, control, and continuously enhance AI systems.

4.4.1 Setting the Foundation: Governance Operating Model

An organization needs to take below steps to create an effective AI governance operating model.

- Establishing roles and responsibility
- Defining policies and standards
- Automating governance
- Educating and training employees about governance

4.4.2 Establishing Roles and Responsibilities

Establishing clear roles and responsibilities is one of the main pillars in developing a successful governance model. It assists in efficient execution of policies and processes and outlining accountability in decisions and risk.

Now let us talk about some of the primary roles and their responsibilities in the context of AI-cloud governance framework.

Chief Information Security Officer (CISO)

- Ensures compliance with data protection laws (e.g., GDPR, HIPAA, DPDPA) and maintains audit readiness.
- Works with cloud service providers on secure handling of data.
- Manage cybersecurity risks associated with model theft, data poisoning, and adversarial attacks

Chief Data Officer (CDO)

- Champions data governance and data quality activity.
- Ensures the accuracy and reliability of data across systems and regions.
- Oversees data classification and lifecycle management.
- Collaborate with AI teams to ensure ethical and responsible use of data for model training and inference.
- Establish policies for data sharing and third-party data use, ensuring compliance and risk mitigation.

AI Governance Committee

- A cross-functional group including leadership, AI engineers, legal experts, privacy professionals, data scientists, risk management experts, and HR.

- Oversees the development and enforcement of enterprise-wide governance policies and ethical guidelines.
- Keep track of the third-party AI and vendor tools to ensure governance compliance.
- Establish AI governance KPIs and report regularly to the executive leadership and the board.

Data Owners

- Categorize according to sensitive data type/regulatory risk (e.g., PII, PHI, financial data).
- Ensure that data assets are well-managed, discoverable, and compliant with the data handling rules.
- Collaborate with cloud and AI teams to establish data retention and anonymization policies.
- Tracking consents for using personal data in AI

AI Engineers and Data Scientists

- Ensure that training data complies with privacy and consent requirements.
- Conduct bias testing and model validations.
- Participate in model monitoring and retraining cycles

Cloud Infrastructure Team

- Configure and maintain compute, storage, and network resources for AI training and deployment.
- Ensure encryption, IAM, firewalls, and logging at the infrastructure level.
- Optimize workloads using auto-scaling, serverless AI services, and energy-efficient compute (e.g., TPUs).
- Monitor costs and resource utilization, enforcing alerts and policies for quota management and billing.
- Partner with DevOps and ML teams to implement CI/CD pipelines for AI models.

Legal and Compliance Team

- Interpret and apply local and international data privacy regulations (e.g., GDPR [2], CCPA, PIPL, HIPAA).
- Monitor changes in AI and data laws and recommend policy updates or new controls.

- Create policies for cross-border data transfer requirements and data localization.
- Review third-party AI service agreements, ensuring contractual compliance with data handling terms.
- Facilitate regulatory reporting and regulatory audits for AI deployments.

4.4.3 Defining Policies and Standards

Once the roles have been defined, the next important step is to define the policies. A governance framework thrives on policies. They must be adapted to the specific context of cloud deployments and AI.

Data Governance Policies

Data Classification and Sensitivity

- Establish the naming of data (public, internal, confidential, restricted).
- Detect sensitive information such as health information, financial information, or data of minors.
- Establish boundaries of use of AI such as large language models (LLM).

Data Encryption, Retention, and Deletion

- Encrypt data at rest and in transit
- Set retention periods on the length of time data is allowed in the cloud.
- Include rules for deleting data once it's no longer needed— in accordance with privacy regulations (GDPR, CCPA, etc.).

Data Quality and Accuracy

- Standards for verifying that data is current and accurate
- Processes for fixing errors or inaccurate data
- Establish what data is acceptable and unacceptable in training and predictions by the AI.

Data Access Control

- Define who can view or edit certain data or AI models
- Implement least privilege, role-based or attribute-based access controls

Model Lifecycle Policies

Model Development, Documentation, and Retraining

- Document how data is used to train models
- Document model performance, restrictions, and test results

Bias and Fairness Checks

- Set policies for regular test for discrimination or unfair results

Model Retraining and Retirement

- Establish policies for model updating, retraining, and retirement

Privacy and Ethics Policies

Transparency and Consent

- Define policies on getting consent from users for using their data
- Policies for communicating privacy policies and opt-out options to the users

User Rights and Redress

- Establish policies to enable an individual to access, delete, or rectify the data
- Identify options for the users to challenge or to appeal on the basis of AI-made decisions

Ethical Use of AI

- Define AI principles of fairness, accountability, and ethical behavior

Compliance and Auditing

Compliance with Governance Laws

- Policies for adherence to GDPR, CCPA, DPDPA, PIPL, HIPAA, or other important privacy regulations
- Policies for cross-border data transfers standards

Third-Party Contracts

- Guidelines on how to engage with cloud vendors and partners
- Ensuring that the contracts require them to observe privacy and security specifications

Audit and Review

- Regular data and AI systems checks and audits
- Regular revisions to change policies as the rules change

Incident Response

- Establishing procedure on how to deal with privacy leaks or security breaches
- Definite procedure of reporting, analyzing, and correcting problems

4.4.4 Operationalization and Automation of Governance

Effective AI-powered cloud environment governance requires a combination of specialized tools that cover risk management, compliance automation, and operational controls. Governance can be integrated directly into the workflows, with the help of various automation tools, and by establishing continuous monitoring and improvement processes.

Let's look into the details of how this can be done.

Embed Governance into AI and Cloud Workflows

- **Integrate Governance Checkpoints**: Introduce mandatory governance checks in the life cycle of the AI model (development, validation, deployment, monitoring). For example, compliance checks can and must be automated and take place prior to a model being promoted out of staging and into production.
- **Automate Policy Enforcement**: You can add policy enforcement to MLOps workflows with Microsoft Purview, Domino Data Lab, or DataRobot. This ensures that all the governed model and data workflows are made to execute without any human touch.

Automate Compliance, Monitoring, and Evidence Collection

- **Automated Compliance Assessments**: Use AI governance platforms (e.g., DataRobot, Domino Data Lab, Velotix) to automate regular compliance checks against regulatory frameworks (EU AI Act, NIST AI RMF, etc.), generating audit-ready documentation and evidence at each stage.
- **Continuous Monitoring**: Engage services that provide automated AI model and data use monitoring to track in real time. These services can detect policy breach, model drift, etc.
- **Logging and Reporting**: Implement the systems that record each action, decision, and data manipulation made by the model. This implies that traces can be made fully in all processes that can be verified during audits and other regulatory checks.

Dynamic Access and Data Controls

- **Automated Data Discovery and Classification**: Implement AI-powered tools (e.g., Microsoft Purview, Velotix) that continuously discover, scan, and classify data across cloud, On Prem and Saas platforms, applying sensitivity labels and adjusting access controls in real time.
- **Intelligent Access Management**: Use AI-driven access management to dynamically grant or restrict permissions based on user roles, behavior, and context, reducing the risk of unauthorized data exposure.

Centralize Governance Oversight

- **Unified Dashboards**: Set up centralized dashboards for real-time visibility into AI and data governance metrics, incidents, and compliance status. This allows governance teams to track KPIs, review incidents, and monitor ongoing effectiveness.
- **Automated Evidence Collection**: Platforms like Domino Data Lab and DataRobot can automatically collect and store compliance artifacts (model lineage, performance metrics, data usage) to streamline audits and demonstrate regulatory adherence.

Continuous Improvement and Feedback Loops

- **Regular Automated Reviews**: Automate governance and risk reviews. These reviews will determine the effectiveness of the controls and determine new risks and any alterations of governance regulations which need to be dealt with.
- **Feedback Mechanisms**: Implement automated feedback mechanisms such as regular stakeholder surveys or root cause analysis of incidents, to make adjustments to the governance processes based on stakeholder feedback.

Change Management and Training

- **Automated Training Modules**: Offer training to all employees on AI ethics, compliance, and responsible use, hence meeting the governance requirements.
- **Governance Sandboxes**: Create contained environments where teams can test new AI models or governance innovations without risking compliance violations.

4.5 AI Innovation vs Sustainability, Ethics, and Governance

With the increasing involvement of AI in cloud computing systems and general business practices, organizations should strike a balance between the fast pace of innovation and the needs of sustainability and ethical conduct. AI models need a lot of energy resources to store large amounts of data and to do complex computations of that data. In today's world where we are already seeing impacts of global warming, companies need to consider ways to minimize environmental impact. The Governance frameworks created by the companies should also include strategies for sustainability such as energy-efficient model architecture, carbon aware computing, etc.

4.5.1 Significance of Sustainable and Responsible AI

Let's look into more details on why we need sustainable and responsible AI.

Increasing Energy Demands: As AI systems are advancing in size and complexity, additional computational infrastructure is needed to train and develop them. This leads to increased power consumption such as higher electricity usage, which in turn leads to increased carbon emissions. Research has indicated that the CO2 emissions during the training of a single AI model can be more than that emitted by several cars, during their lifetime.

Alignment with Environmental goals: Global organizations and governments are introducing policies and rewards to encourage companies to use renewable sources of energy. Companies are also required to give reports on the environmental impact caused by them. For this, companies are now leaning toward running their operations with clean energy, keeping in mind the climate target of net-zero emissions.

Ethical considerations: Ethical AI ensures that organizations develop and train AI systems, keeping core human values in mind. This implies that AI systems must be built and trained to not give out discriminating results. Ethical AI also consists of transparency toward users. Individuals should have the right to understand how their data is being used by AI to make decisions and how it can affect them.

4.5.2 Energy-Efficient Governance

Usually when we talk about governance in the context of AI and cloud, we focus on privacy, security, and compliance. However, now with the awareness about the climate impact of AI, companies need to work toward cutting their energy usage and working in a more sustainable manner.

Enhancing the Energy-efficiency of Governance Tools

Most of the governance activities like data classification and audit logging are compute-intensive since these are applied over large amounts of data sets stored in the cloud.

These tasks can be made greener by following some of the below recommendations.

AI-Powered Energy Optimization: With the advancements in AI, AI models can themselves help in making governance more energy efficient. Using **Predictive data classification** models, AI can identify which datasets may contain sensitive information and thus focusing only on the data that is needed. Likewise, using AI with **Anomaly detection** algorithms, it is also possible to detect the access patterns or policy violations. That way it would not need to scan all the data and lesser compute resources will be needed. This can also be in the form of scheduling resource-intensive tasks, like scans of data, at a time when there is less energy required or when renewable sources of energy are more available.

Targeted or Incremental scanning: Rather than scanning all the data every time, governance tools may scan only the new or modified data. Tools like Striim's Sherlock AI use intelligent sampling and real-time detection to focus only on high-risk or high-value data assets, significantly reducing computational overhead and energy use.

Serverless or auto-scaling architectures: Selecting the right hardware and configurations which can adapt to the workload so that governance processes don't run at full power when demand is low. Research from MIT's Lincoln Laboratory shows that techniques like power-capping hardware, early stopping of unnecessary processes, and matching workloads to appropriately sized infrastructure can cut energy use by up to 80% with minimal impact on performance.

Cloud-Native Benefits

Cloud providers already offer **energy-efficient data centers** [9] compared to on-premise systems, thanks to advanced cooling and renewable energy sourcing. When governance tasks run in these data centers, they benefit from these sustainability efforts. For example, **Google Cloud** uses carbon-intelligent computing—shifting jobs to data centers where renewable energy is more available at that moment. **Microsoft Azure** and **AWS** are also investing in data centers powered by wind, solar, and other green sources.

Aligning Privacy with Ethical and Sustainable AI

Aligning privacy with ethical and sustainable AI means ensuring that AI systems not only protect individual data rights but also operate transparently, fairly, and with minimal environmental impact. As AI increasingly relies on vast amounts of personal data, organizations must integrate privacy-by-design principles—such as data minimization, transparency, and security—into every stage of AI development and deployment.

By making privacy a priority in their ethical and sustainable approach to AI, organizations can build trust, mitigate legal and reputational risks, and work toward a fairer and more environment-friendly digital environment.

4.5.3 *Balancing Trade-offs: Performance, Privacy, and Sustainability*

As organizations increasingly use AI into cloud workflows, they will have to come up with a balance between the competing objectives of performance, privacy, and sustainability. High performance is essential to meet user expectations and achieve business objectives. Needless to say, privacy is non-negotiable in a regulated and trust-sensitive environment. And sustainability has become a strategic necessity, driven by environmental commitments and operational costs.

It is hard to design AI governance that can optimize all three dimensions: any improvement in one can easily compromise the other. Nevertheless, responsible AI governance does not aim for perfection, but for a balance. It requires clearly defined principles, workload-specific policies, and transparency around trade-offs.

- **Performance vs. Sustainability**: Modern high performance AI models are typically compute-intensive, i.e., they consume and emit more energy. Model pruning (removing unnecessary or less important weights), quantization (removing precision of numbers used in the model), and early stopping are methods that can reduce energy use but may impact accuracy.
- **Privacy vs. Performance**: Privacy-preserving techniques [8] (e.g., differential privacy [6], federated learning) can limit the amount of data available for training, which can compromise model accuracy. However, they are necessary when it comes to regulatory compliance and ethical responsibility.
- **Privacy vs. Sustainability**: Storing less data for privacy reasons also reduces storage and computation needs, supporting sustainability. However, in some cases, privacy-enhancing technologies may require additional computation (e.g., encryption), which is more energy-consuming.

4.5.4 *Governance Strategies for Trade-off Management*

- **Transparent Decision-Making**: Document and justify trade-off decisions in governance documentation, and be sure that stakeholders are aware of the reasons and consequences. Monitor and log your AI and governance carbon footprint. This visibility assists individuals in realizing the practical effects of the technology decisions they make.
- **Continuous Monitoring**: Use automated monitoring tools to measure how trade-off choices affect performance, privacy and energy use, and optimize continuously.

4.5.5 Conclusion

Sustainability and responsible AI are no longer parallel concerns, but are closely interrelated in the age of cloud computing and large-scale AI. Effective governance systems should consider taking advantage of automation, AI-based energy management, privacy-enhancing technologies, and carbon-conscious policies at the same time.

Those organizations which will excel in this governance overlap will not only be able to cut costs and environmental impact, but will also earn the trust of their customers, regulators, and the society in general. The way forward will be characterized by a commitment to transparency, new ideas, and a constant balancing between performance, privacy, and sustainability, which is the challenge that defines the future of cloud computing with AI.

4.6 Future Outlook: What's next in AI Governance

As AI adoption accelerates across industries and cloud environments, governance systems are being forced to quickly adapt to ever-changing technical, regulatory, and increasing user and societal expectations. In the next few years, there will be a shift in the way organizations approach risk management, compliance, and innovation, driven by the advancement in automation, security, and data sovereignty.

4.6.1 Emerging Trends

Below, we will discuss the significant trends affecting the evolution of AI governance, the upcoming challenges, and the opportunities for organizations to get ahead in privacy-conscious and responsible AI solutions.

AI Governance as Code

AI Governance as Code is the specification and enforcement of governance policies (such as security controls, compliance controls, and ethical controls) within the AI development and deployment pipelines. With this, companies can automate access control, checks on compliance, etc. as part of the workflows rather than doing qualitative checks manually.

Zero-Trust Data Fabrics

Zero-trust architecture refers to a security model, and it implies that trust cannot be assumed in the system. It operates on the principle of "never trust, always verify." As per the model, access is by default denied on all resources, regardless of origin of access request. Access to any resources like data, applications, or services is validated based on dynamic context, such as user identity, device health, and risk assessment. In the context of data fabrics, this means implementing strict access control, continuous verification, and segmentation to secure data in cloud environments. Every request, regardless of its origin, is continuously authenticated, authorized, and validated, so that only users or systems specifically permitted may access data assets.

Sovereign AI Clouds

Sovereign AI clouds refer to cloud computing environments and AI infrastructures that are specifically designed to ensure data, applications, and AI models are stored, processed, and managed entirely within a particular country or region, in a manner compliant with regional or domestic laws on data sovereignty. The principle is to allow governments, businesses, and regulated industries to have absolute control over their digital assets, such as sensitive data, intellectual property ,and AI algorithms, and to block unauthorized access or intervention by foreign governments.

4.6.2 Emerging Challenges

Multi-cloud Consistency

Since over 90% of the enterprises have now shifted to a multi-cloud environment, it has been very hard to ensure a uniform governance across various cloud providers. Different cloud platforms have different security measures, compliance regulations, and operationalization processes, making it difficult to enforce homogeneous policies. Also, data integrity, consistency, and security on multiple platforms require modern data management solutions. Multiple cloud infrastructures also increase operational complexity and can lead to higher costs to manage and supervise. AI tools such as orchestration and cross-cloud governance are beginning to emerge; however, smooth integration and visibility are still under development.

Regulatory Fragmentation

As various countries and regions craft their own regulations and standards, the regulatory landscape around AI and data privacy is getting more fragmented globally. Organizations must navigate a complex web of regulations at the state and the country level (like European Union AI Act, executive orders in the USA, and data sovereignty requirements on the local level). This fragmentation complicates compliance, increases operational risk, and can slow down innovation if not managed proactively. Moreover, significant amounts of resources will need to be dedicated to compliance in handling volatile regulations across jurisdictions.

4.6.3 *Opportunities for Innovation in Privacy-Aware AI Services*

Despite the challenges, there are significant opportunities to innovate in the realm of privacy-aware AI services.

- **Privacy-Preserving Machine Learning**: Advances in privacy engineering—such as automated data minimization, synthetic data generation, and privacy-preserving machine learning—are enabling organizations to build AI systems that protect user data by default. Leveraging these technologies enable organizations to develop powerful AI models without exposing or retaining sensitive data and can support compliance requirements and ethical goals.
- **Integrated, Programmable Governance Planes**: The emergence of Governance as Code platforms also means that organizations can now enforce policies and keep a full audit log across their environment and simplify compliance reporting. This shift enhances innovation, as it minimizes manual intervention and makes sure that governance follows the AI development cycles.

4.6.4 *Conclusion: Navigating the Next Era of AI Governance*

AI will embrace automation, programmability, and adaptability, which will in turn define the future of its governance. Governance as code, zero-trust data fabrics, and sovereign AI clouds are establishing the direction of secure, compliant, and resilient AI operations. However, persistent challenges such as multi-cloud consistency and regulatory fragmentation require ongoing investment in cohesive governance strategies and cross-disciplinary expertise.

Organizations that embrace these trends and proactively innovate in privacy-aware AI will not only navigate the complexities of tomorrow's regulatory landscape, but also stand at the forefront of sustainable, ethical, and trusted AI respectively.

References

1. Institute for AI Transformations. (2024, August). *What are the three key pillars of AI in governance*. Retrieved from https://www.leadersinaisummit.com/insights/what-are-the-three-key-pillars-of-ai-governance
2. GDPR.EU. (n.d.) *What is GDPR, the EU's new data protection law*? Retrieved from https://gdpr.eu/what-is-gdpr/
3. Wikipedia. (n.d.). *Health Insurance Portability and Accountability Act*. Retrieved from https://en.wikipedia.org/wiki/Health_Insurance_Portability_and_Accountability_Act
4. Federal Trade Commission. (n.d.). *Gramm Leach Bliley Act*. Retrieved from https://www.ftc.gov/business-guidance/privacy-security/gramm-leach-bliley-act
5. Stanford University—Human Centered Artificial Intelligence. (n.d.). *2025 AI index report*. Retrieved from https://hai.stanford.edu/ai-index/2025-ai-index-report
6. ScienceDirect. (n.d.). *Differential privacy*. Retrieved from https://www.sciencedirect.com/topics/computer-science/differential-privacy
7. Wikipedia. (n.d.). *Homomorphic encryption*. Retrieved from https://en.wikipedia.org/wiki/Homomorphic_encryption
8. Researchgate.net. *Privacy-preserving techniques in Generative AI models for secure cloud data processing*. Retrieved from https://www.researchgate.net/publication/390742972_Privacy-Preserving_Techniques_in_Generative_AI_Models_for_Secure_Cloud_Data_Processing
9. Kaizen Institute. (n.d.). *Energy efficiency using AI for sustainable data centers*. Retrieved from https://kaizen.com/insights/energy-efficiency-sustainable-data-centers/

Chapter 5
Green Cybersecurity: Eco-friendly Threat Detection in Cloud Environments

Anant Kumar

Abstract The aggressive growth of cloud computing has brought with it a challenge to balance strong cybersecurity with environmental stewardship. Though necessary for security, conventional cloud security strategies, ranging from 24/7 monitoring to energy-hungry AI analytics, guzzle enormous amounts of energy and generate high carbon emissions. This chapter, "Green Cybersecurity," addresses this challenge head-on. It extends beyond just acknowledging the challenge by examining an emerging paradigm in which security and sustainability are not competing goals but complementary ones. We get into actual-world, state-of-the-art solutions like energy-efficient AI and machine learning algorithms, cloud-native systems that waste nothing, and effective data processing practices. By embedding green responsibility into the core of our cyber defenses, we can design security systems that are not only better and more intelligent but also sustainable in the long run. It's not a compromise; it's about securing our future by making security smarter, efficient, and responsible.

Keywords Green cybersecurity · Sustainable cloud security · Cloud computing sustainability · Energy-efficient threat detection · Generative AI security · Eco-friendly cloud architecture · Carbon footprint reduction

5.1 Introduction

Lately, I have been struck by how two issues in cloud computing, cybersecurity, and sustainability tend to go on separate tracks even though they are very tightly linked. Companies pour effort into defending their cloud workloads against hackers, ransomware, and other threats. Meanwhile, a different set of stakeholders pushes to shrink carbon footprints and operate more responsibly. Because security and

A. Kumar (✉)
Lead Engineer at Salesforce @ Einstein AI Division, The Scientific Research Honor Society, San Jose, CA, USA

B. Pandey, A. Patel (eds.), *Revolutionizing the Cloud*,
https://doi.org/10.1007/978-3-032-07479-9_5

sustainability often sit in different silos, the two goals rarely meet, even though every defensive tool we spin up in the cloud draws power and leaves an environmental mark. However, as cloud environments continue to expand and grow more complex, the boundaries between these domains are blurring [1]. It has become clear that the intersection of cybersecurity and sustainability is an issue that can no longer be overlooked.

Have you ever actually stopped to think about what it takes to keep cloud environments secure? Those virtual Security Operations Centers (vSOCs) run 24/7, constantly humming away, eating electricity like it's going out of style. Then you've got monitoring tools scattered across data centers on different continents, plus all those resource- hungry analytics engines (a bunch now using AI) chewing through mountains of data. All these security infrastructure sucks up a ton of power, and the numbers are pretty eye-opening when you look at them. The Cloud Security Alliance put out a report showing security operations might be gobbling up somewhere between 5% and 10% of a company's total cloud energy use. That's not chump change. Even more sobering, some industry analysis from earlier this year estimated that cloud security systems worldwide could be pumping out roughly 12 million metric tons of CO_2 annually about what 2.6 million cars would produce [2] (see Fig. 5.1).

But—and this is where it gets interesting—while security has traditionally been an energy hog, some breakthrough tech (especially in generative AI and advanced ML) is opening doors to completely reimagine cybersecurity with sustainability built right into its DNA [3]. Today's gen AI models can spot weird patterns and

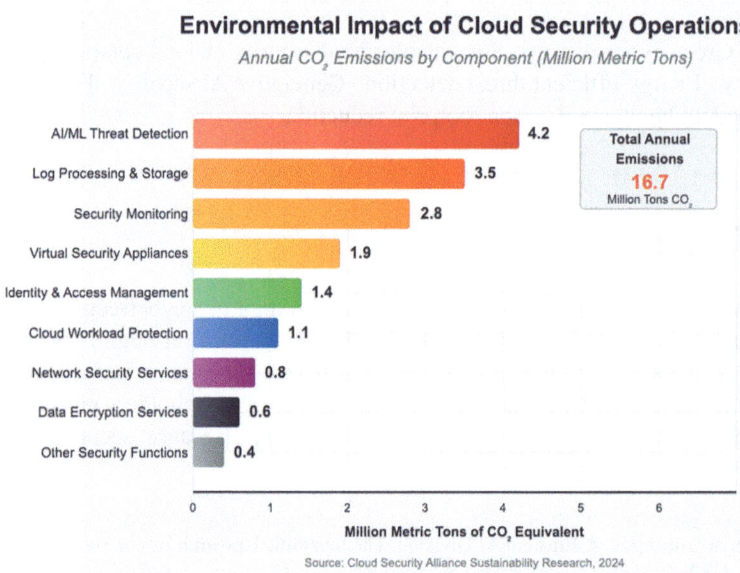

Fig. 5.1 Environmental impact of cloud security operations by component (2024 Estimates)

anomalies with crazy accuracy while using way less computational juice than older approaches. Meanwhile, innovations in edge computing, smarter algorithms, and cloud-native security architectures are creating promising paths toward security that doesn't trash the planet [4]. This timing couldn't be better, honestly, since regulatory pressure and stakeholder expectations around sustainability commitments just keep intensifying [5]. Throughout this chapter, I'm going to explore what I've started calling "Green Cybersecurity"—basically a fresh approach that weaves environmental sustainability principles into how we design, build, and run cloud-based security systems. At it's heart, green cybersecurity isn't about sacrificing security just for the sake of the environment. Instead, it's about finding ways to reduce things like energy use, carbon emissions, and electronic waste, without letting our guard down. This marks a real change in thinking: instead of seeing security and sustainability as being at odds, we're starting to recognize that they can actually support and strengthen each other [6]. Green cybersecurity goes way beyond just trimming the environmental footprint of existing security operations (though that's definitely part of it). The concept covers designing more efficient security architectures from scratch, using generative AI for smarter threat detection that uses fewer resources, optimizing security analytics to do more with less, and fostering a security culture that values environmental responsibility alongside protection goals. I'll dive into various aspects of green cybersecurity throughout this chapter, with special attention to eco-friendly threat detection powered by generative AI. We'll look at the environmental impact of traditional approaches, explore principles for building sustainable security architectures, investigate how generative AI enables more efficient threat detection, and consider practical strategies for reducing the carbon footprint of everyday security activities. Along the way, I'll share real-world case studies, practical implementation guidance, and emerging technologies that show promise for advancing a green cybersecurity agenda. As organizations worldwide commit to ambitious sustainability targets like carbon neutrality and net-zero emissions, security teams can't consider themselves exempt from environmental considerations anymore [7]. The strategies we'll cover give security leaders practical options to help their organizations reach their goals, all while keeping security strong. Cybersecurity's future isn't only about being faster and smarter—it's also about making sure our efforts can last and support sustainability.

5.2 The Hidden Environmental Cost of Cloud Security Operations

When organizations build their cloud cybersecurity defenses, they're laser-focused on one thing: keeping the bad guys out. Makes perfect sense—after all, a single breach can cost millions and destroy reputations overnight. But here's what most security teams don't think about: those protective measures are quietly racking up a substantial environmental bill that nobody's paying attention to [8].

As companies worldwide grapple with carbon footprints and sustainability commitments (and trust me, they all are now), it's becoming impossible to ignore the energy appetite of our security infrastructure. The always-on nature of cloud security, combined with increasingly sophisticated threat detection systems, creates an environmental impact that many organizations haven't even begun to measure, let alone address [9].

And honestly? The numbers might shock you.

5.2.1 *The Energy-Hungry World of Virtual Security Operations*

Think about your organization's Virtual Security Operations Center for a moment. It's essentially the digital equivalent of a fortress that never sleeps—monitoring, analyzing, and responding to threats around the clock across your entire cloud footprint. This constant vigilance? It comes with a hefty energy price tag that most folks never see.

The numbers are genuinely eye-opening. According to the Cloud Security Alliance, a typical enterprise vSOC protecting 100–200 cloud workloads burns through 75–150 kW of power continuously [10]. To put that in perspective—that's enough electricity to power between 35 and 75 American homes. And that's just for a medium-sized operation. Imagine what the big players are consuming.

The real energy drain comes from what happens behind the scenes, where nobody's looking. Every log entry, network packet, and user activity generates data that needs to be collected, transmitted, stored, and analyzed. MIT's Sustainable Computing Lab found that security-related processing alone accounts for 7–12% of total enterprise cloud energy consumption [11]. When you're dealing with complex, multi-cloud environments spanning different regions and providers, this overhead adds up frighteningly fast.

Then there's the AI revolution in cybersecurity, which is both a blessing and a curse from an environmental standpoint. Machine learning models that can spot sophisticated threats are incredibly powerful—and incredibly power-hungry. Training a single large-scale security AI model can consume 300–500 kW-h of electricity and pump out nearly 285 kg of CO_2. Once these models are up and running, they keep consuming significant resources, especially when processing the massive traffic flows typical in enterprise cloud environments.

Perhaps most frustrating is how inefficient many security operations have become through sheer organizational inertia. The average enterprise runs 26 different cloud security tools, according to Forrester Research [12]. Many of these overlap in functionality, creating redundant monitoring and excessive data collection. It's like having multiple security guards watching the same door—effective perhaps, but ridiculously wasteful. Most systems maintain peak processing intensity regardless of actual threat levels, meaning they're burning energy at full throttle even during those 3 AM lull periods when nothing interesting is happening.

5.2.2 *The Broader Infrastructure Impact*

The environmental impact extends well beyond the SOC itself, reaching into every corner of your cloud infrastructure. Consider all those virtual security appliances scattered throughout your environment—firewalls, web application firewalls, network analyzers, container security controls. These are typically sized for worst-case scenarios and deployed redundantly across multiple availability zones because, well, redundancy equals security, right?

A single enterprise-grade virtual firewall can consume 2–8 virtual CPUs and 8–32 GB of RAM continuously [13]. Multiply that across redundant deployments, and the resource consumption becomes substantial. I've seen organizations with dozens of these appliances running simultaneously, each one quietly munching through compute resources.

Data storage presents another challenge that most security teams underestimate. Security professionals are pack rats by necessity—we retain logs, flow records, and event data for compliance, forensics, and threat hunting. This security data typically grows 35–60% annually and must be kept for years. Amazon Web Services estimates that storing just one terabyte of data generates about 0.4 metric tons of CO_2 equivalent emissions annually [14]. When you're talking about petabytes of security data (and most large enterprises are), those numbers become genuinely significant.

Real-time security analytics add another layer of energy consumption that's often overlooked. Modern platforms perform intensive correlation, anomaly detection, and threat intelligence analysis across distributed environments. The computational requirements spike even higher when organizations embrace “shift-left” security approaches that integrate analysis throughout the development pipeline. Stanford's Sustainable Systems Lab found that continuous security scanning in large CI/CD environments can account for up to 15% of total DevOps energy consumption [15]. That's a lot of juice just for security scanning.

Multi-cloud strategies, while offering undeniable business benefits, often multiply the environmental impact in ways that catch organizations off guard. Organizations typically deploy 30–40% more security infrastructure when operating across multiple cloud providers, according to Gartner [16]. Each cloud environment gets its own set of security controls and monitoring systems, creating redundant resource consumption and corresponding increases in carbon emissions. It's the price of paranoia, you might say.

5.2.3 *The E-Waste Factor*

While cloud computing reduces the physical hardware footprint compared to on-premises deployments, it doesn't eliminate electronic waste—it just shifts where it's generated and makes it less visible to end users. The servers, storage systems, and networking equipment powering cloud security services require regular refreshes to maintain performance and support evolving capabilities. Cloud providers typically refresh their hardware every 3–5 years, and security services contribute disproportionately to this turnover due to their resource-intensive nature.

Edge security devices present a particular challenge that most organizations don't think about until it's upgrade time. Organizations with hybrid cloud architectures often deploy physical security appliances at network edges and branch offices. These devices face accelerated replacement cycles—typically every 2–3 years—driven by evolving threats and changing cloud connectivity requirements. The result is a steady stream of electronic waste from security-specific hardware that just keeps coming.

The shift toward remote work has added another dimension to this problem. Cloud security strategies increasingly rely on endpoint protection platforms that secure devices accessing cloud resources. These solutions often require hardware upgrades to support advanced detection capabilities, indirectly accelerating device replacement cycles and generating additional electronic waste. Every time an endpoint protection platform demands more RAM or processing power, that translates to earlier device refreshes.

5.3 AI-Powered Eco-Friendly Threat Detection

Here's the irony of modern cybersecurity: AI and machine learning have revolutionized threat detection, enabling us to catch sophisticated attacks that would slip right past traditional signature-based systems. But these same AI models are absolute energy hogs-especially during training phases when they're chewing through massive datasets like digital locusts [17].

I've watched organizations deploy AI-powered security systems that could detect a needle in a haystack but consumed more electricity than a small town in the process. The good news? You don't have to choose between effective threat detection and environmental responsibility. You just need to be smarter about how you build and deploy these systems [18].

And honestly, the techniques that make AI more sustainable often make it more effective too. As demonstrated in Fig. 5.2, recent benchmarking studies from leading AI research organizations show that optimized generative AI approaches can achieve up to 66% energy savings compared to traditional deep learning methods for security applications [19–22].

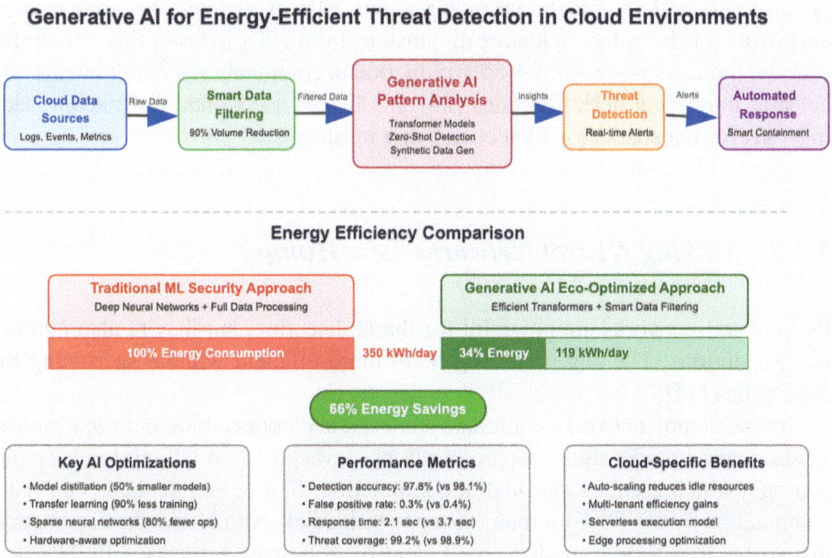

Fig. 5.2 Generative AI enables significant energy savings in threat detection pipelines while maintaining or improving security effectiveness

5.3.1 Picking the Right Algorithm (Because Not Every Problem Needs a Sledgehammer)

The dirty secret of AI-powered security is that we often reach for the most sophisticated algorithms when simpler approaches would work just as well. It's like using a Formula One race car for grocery shopping—impressive, but completely unnecessary [1].

Algorithm selection for sustainability starts with understanding that different ML approaches have vastly different computational profiles. MIT researchers found something fascinating: for cloud network anomaly detection, optimized random forest models achieved 94–96% of the detection accuracy of deep neural networks while consuming only 10–15% of the computational resources [11]. Think about that ratio for a moment—nearly the same results with a fraction of the energy cost.

Model architecture optimization is where the real magic happens. Techniques like pruning (cutting unnecessary connections), quantization (reducing numeric precision), and knowledge distillation (teaching smaller models to mimic larger ones) can slash energy consumption by 50–80% with minimal accuracy impact. Google cloud security's team demonstrated that optimized transformer models for threat detection consume 65% less energy than standard versions while maintaining 98% detection capability [18]. Sometimes less really is more.

Cloud-specific feature engineering might sound boring, but it's absolutely critical. The features you select for security models dramatically impact both effectiveness and computational requirements. Microsoft Azure Security researchers proved this by reducing feature dimensions from 200+ to fewer than 50 carefully selected indicators—result: 70–85% reduction in computational requirements while actually improving detection rates [23]. It's like Marie Kondo for machine learning—keep what sparks joy (detection), discard the rest.

5.3.2 *Making Neural Networks Less Hungry*

Deep neural networks are powerful for threat detection, but they're also notorious energy gluttons. The key is making them more efficient without sacrificing their capabilities [17].

Sparse neural networks eliminate unnecessary connections between neurons. Traditional networks use dense connections—every neuron talking to every other neuron—which requires substantial computation. Sparse architectures can reduce computation by 80–90% for many security tasks. Palo Alto Networks demonstrated that sparse transformer models could identify cloud-based threats with 92% accuracy while consuming just 15–25% of the energy during inference [24]. It's like going from a conference call where everyone talks to everyone to a well-organized meeting with a clear agenda.

Dynamic computation paths are brilliantly pragmatic. Why waste full neural network processing on obviously benign traffic? Adaptive computation techniques allocate resources based on input complexity—simple cases get lightweight processing, complex ambiguougs cases trigger the full model. AWS implemented this in GuardDuty, reducing average inference energy costs by 45–60% while maintaining detection accuracy for sophisticated threats [14]. Work smarter, not harder.

Hardware-aware model design optimizes neural networks for specific hardware platforms. Models designed with awareness of GPU, TPU, or FPGA characteristics typically achieve 30–50% better energy efficiency. A NVIDIA-Microsoft collaboration demonstrated 58% energy usage reduction for cloud security models optimized for specific GPU architectures compared to generic models [25]. Know your hardware, optimize accordingly.

5.3.3 *Transfer Learning: Standing on the Shoulders of Giants*

Training neural networks from scratch is like reinventing the wheel every time you need to travel somewhere. Transfer learning leverages existing knowledge to dramatically reduce training requirements [3].

Security-specific foundation models serve as the basis for numerous specialized detection tasks. Mandiant's platform uses foundation models pre-trained on trillions of security events, allowing specialized detection deployment with fine-tuning that requires just 3–5% of the computational resources of training from scratch [26]. Build once, adapt many times.

Continuous learning optimization replaces periodic complete retraining with incremental updates. Microsoft defender for cloud implemented continuous learning that reduces model update energy consumption by 90% compared to traditional retraining cycles, while improving detection rates for evolving threats [27]. Evolution, not revolution.

5.3.4 Generative AI: The New Frontier of Sustainable Security

Recent advances in generative AI present novel opportunities for more sustainable security operations—and some of these approaches are genuinely revolutionary [26].

Anomaly reconstruction uses generative models to learn normal behavior patterns and identify anomalies by attempting to reconstruct observed activities. IBM's QRadar SIEM implemented generative reconstruction models that achieved detection rates comparable to ensemble methods while consuming 45% less energy [28]. If the model can't reconstruct something properly, it's probably worth investigating.

Zero-shot and few-shot detection identify previously unseen attack patterns with minimal training examples. Sentinel One's platform leverages zero-shot capabilities to detect novel cloud attack techniques with 30–40% less energy consumption than traditional supervised learning approaches. The model learns to generalize so well it can spot attacks it's never seen before.

Natural language processing for log analysis interprets unstructured security logs with remarkable effectiveness. When optimized for security operations, these models can reduce log analysis computational overhead by 50–70% compared to traditional rule-based approaches, as Microsoft demonstrated in Azure Sentinel [25]. Finally, machines that can read logs as well as humans—maybe better.

The transformation happening in AI-powered threat detection represents more than just technological advancement—it's a fundamental shift toward more intelligent, more efficient security. These techniques prove that environmental responsibility and robust security aren't competing objectives; they're complementary goals that reinforce each other [18].

What excites me most about these developments is that we're not just making security more sustainable—we're making it smarter. The efficiency constraints force us to think more carefully about what we're doing and why, leading to better algorithms, better architectures, and ultimately better security outcomes [1].

The future of threat detection isn't just about more powerful AI—it's about more thoughtful AI. And in a world where both cyber threats and climate change represent existential challenges that thoughtfulness might just save us from both.

5.4 Cloud-Native Green Security

Cloud-native security represents a fundamental shift in how we protect digital assets—moving from static, perimeter-based defenses to dynamic, distributed protection that's deeply integrated with cloud infrastructure. When designed with sustainability in mind, cloud-native security approaches offer remarkable opportunities to reduce environmental impact while actually improving protection [29].

I've spent years helping organizations transition to cloud-native security models, and I've consistently found that the most successful implementations are those that embrace both the technical and philosophical aspects of the cloud-native paradigm. It's not just about using cloud services; it's about rethinking security from first principles.

5.4.1 Serverless Security: Pay-Per-Protection

Serverless security functions represent one of the most promising approaches for sustainable cloud protection. Rather than maintaining always-on security infrastructure, serverless models spin up protection only when and where it's needed [30].

Function-as-a-Service (FaaS) security deploys security controls as discrete functions that execute only in response to specific events or triggers. AWS Lambda-based security functions typically consume 70–90% less energy than equivalent always-on security services, according to AWS's own analysis [14]. The environmental benefits are obvious—you're only using resources when you actually need them.

Event-driven security automation responds to specific triggers rather than continuously polling for changes. Microsoft's research shows that event-driven security automation reduces computational overhead by 65–85% compared to traditional monitoring approaches [31]. It's the difference between constantly checking if something has happened and being notified when it actually does.

Consumption-based security scaling ensures that security resources expand and contract based on actual usage patterns. HashiCorp's State of Cloud Strategy Survey found that organizations implementing consumption-based security scaling reduced their overall security infrastructure costs by 30–50% while simultaneously reducing energy consumption [32]. Pay for what you use, use only what you need.

5.4.2 Auto-scaling Security: Right-Sizing in Real Time

Auto-scaling security infrastructure dynamically adjusts resources based on current needs rather than static provisioning for peak loads. This approach eliminates the massive waste associated with traditional security deployments [33].

Demand-based security scaling adjusts security processing capacity based on actual workload requirements. Google Cloud's security services demonstrate that demand-based scaling can reduce average resource consumption by 40–60% compared to static provisioning while maintaining protection levels during traffic spikes [18]. No more overprovisioning "just in case."

Predictive security scaling uses machine learning to anticipate security resource needs based on historical patterns and leading indicators. Gartner's analysis shows that predictive scaling typically improves resource utilization by 25–35% compared to reactive scaling alone [29]. It's like having a crystal ball for your security infrastructure.

Time-based security policies implement different security postures based on time patterns and business cycles. Organizations implementing time-based security policies report 15–25% reductions in overall security processing requirements without compromising protection during critical periods [34]. Not all moments require the same level of scrutiny.

5.4.3 *Multi-tenant Magic: Shared Security, Shared Efficiency*

Multi-tenant security architectures distribute security costs and environmental impact across multiple customers or business units, dramatically improving efficiency through economies of scale [7].

Shared security infrastructure leverages common components across multiple tenants while maintaining logical separation. Cloud security alliance research indicates that well-designed multi-tenant security services typically operate with 60–80% greater efficiency than equivalent single-tenant deployments [10]. One engine, many beneficiaries.

Tenant-specific security policies enable customized protection while maintaining the efficiency benefits of shared infrastructure. Forrester found that organizations implementing tenant-specific policies within shared security frameworks reduced their overall security footprint by 40–60% compared to deploying separate security stacks [30]. Customization without duplication.

Cross-tenant threat intelligence sharing improves detection capabilities while reducing the computational overhead of threat analysis. Microsoft's cross-tenant intelligence sharing in Microsoft 365 Defender demonstrates 30–50% improvement in threat detection with minimal additional resource consumption [23]. When one tenant identifies a threat, all tenants benefit.

5.4.4 DevSecOps Done Right: Security Efficiency from Code to Cloud

DevSecOps integrates security throughout the development lifecycle rather than bolting it on at the end. When implemented thoughtfully, this approach dramatically reduces the environmental impact of security operations [33].

Shift-left security testing catches vulnerabilities early in the development process when they're cheaper and less resource-intensive to fix. Carnegie Mellon's analysis shows that addressing security issues during development typically requires 30–50 times fewer resources than addressing them in production. Fix it early, fix it efficiently.

Infrastructure-as-code security validates security configurations before deployment rather than detecting issues in running systems. HashiCorp's research indicates that organizations implementing IaC security validation reduce security-related cloud resource consumption by 35–55% compared to traditional security approaches [32]. Prevent problems instead of detecting them.

Continuous security verification replaces periodic intensive security assessments with ongoing lightweight validation. Orca security's implementation demonstrates that continuous verification approaches can reduce security assessment resource consumption by 60–80% while improving vulnerability detection rates [8]. Constant vigilance doesn't have to mean constant consumption.

The beauty of cloud-native security is that it aligns perfectly with both security and sustainability objectives. By leveraging the inherent characteristics of cloud platforms—elasticity, multi-tenancy, automation, and programmability—we can build security systems that are simultaneously more effective and more efficient [9].

What's particularly exciting about this approach is that the environmental benefits aren't just nice-to-have side effects; they're direct results of better security architecture. When you eliminate security waste through right-sizing, automation, and integration, you naturally reduce environmental impact [7].

The organizations leading the way in cloud security aren't just protecting their digital assets more effectively—they're doing it with a fraction of the environmental footprint of traditional approaches. And in a world where both security threats and environmental concerns continue to intensify, that's exactly the kind of progress we need.

5.5 Eco-Friendly Security Monitoring and Analytics

Security monitoring and analytics represent some of the most resource-intensive aspects of modern cybersecurity. The sheer volume of data being collected, stored, processed, and analyzed creates substantial computational demands—and corresponding environmental impacts [11]. Yet most organizations have never considered the sustainability implications of their monitoring practices.

I've spent years helping organizations optimize their security monitoring and analytics, and I've consistently found that more data doesn't necessarily mean better security. In fact, smarter data collection and analysis often deliver superior security outcomes with a fraction of the environmental footprint.

5.5.1 Rethinking Data Collection (Because More Isn't Always Better)

The default approach to security monitoring has long been "collect everything and sort it out later." This mindset has created massive data lakes filled with security telemetry that consumes energy during collection, transmission, storage, and analysis—often with minimal security benefit [13].

Smart data collection focuses on gathering high-value security telemetry rather than indiscriminate logging. MIT's sustainable computing lab found that organizations implementing context-aware collection typically reduce their security data volume by 60–80% while maintaining or improving threat detection capabilities [11]. Quality beats quantity every time.

Tiered data retention applies different storage durations based on data value and compliance requirements. Cloud security alliance research indicates that tiered retention strategies typically reduce storage requirements by 40–60% compared to uniform retention policies [7]. Not all data deserves the same long-term commitment.

Edge filtering performs initial analysis at collection points, transmitting only relevant security events to central systems. Microsoft's implementation demonstrates that edge filtering can reduce security data transmission and storage requirements by 70–90% while actually improving detection speed for critical threats [31]. Process locally, escalate selectively.

5.5.2 Log Management That Doesn't Break the Carbon Budget

Log management—the collection, normalization, storage, and analysis of security logs—often represents the largest data workload in security operations. Sustainable approaches focus on efficiency without sacrificing visibility [35].

Compressed log storage leverages advanced compression algorithms specifically optimized for security log formats. Splunk's analysis shows that purpose-built compression typically reduces storage requirements by 60–80% compared to standard approaches, with corresponding reductions in energy consumption [35]. Same data, smaller footprint.

Intelligent log parsing extracts and indexes only relevant fields rather than storing and processing entire log entries. Google cloud's security services demonstrate that selective parsing reduces computational requirements for log analysis by 40–60% while improving query performance [18]. Focus on what matters.

Automated log lifecycle management applies data governance policies to security logs based on their value and regulatory requirements. Organizations implementing automated lifecycle management report 30–50% reductions in overall storage requirements and corresponding decreases in energy consumption [34]. Let go of data that's no longer serving you.

5.5.3 SIEM Architectures That Don't Consume Small Countries' Worth of Power

Security Information and Event Management (SIEM) systems form the analytical core of most security operations, correlating and analyzing data from diverse sources to identify threats. Traditional SIEM architectures are notoriously resource-intensive, but newer approaches offer dramatic efficiency improvements [28].

Distributed SIEM architectures perform initial correlation and analysis close to data sources rather than centralizing all processing. IBM's QRadar distributed deployment model reduces data movement by 50–70% and decreases central processing requirements by 30–50% compared to traditional centralized architectures [28]. Process where it makes sense, not just in one place.

Event-driven SIEM processing allocates analytical resources based on security relevance rather than processing all data with equal intensity. Microsoft Sentinel's implementation demonstrates that event-driven approaches typically reduce computational requirements by 40–60% while maintaining detection effectiveness [25]. Not all events deserve the same analytical attention.

Machine learning optimization applies techniques like transfer learning and model distillation to reduce the computational intensity of SIEM analytics. CrowdStrike's optimized models achieve detection rates comparable to full-scale implementations while consuming 50–70% less energy during operation [36]. Smarter models, not just bigger ones.

5.5.4 A Real-World Success Story (Because Numbers Don't Lie)

Let me share a concrete example that illustrates the potential of eco-friendly security monitoring. A global financial services firm I worked with recently undertook a comprehensive redesign of their security monitoring infrastructure with both security effectiveness and sustainability in mind [37].

The organization started by analyzing their existing security data ecosystem, which included over 200 data sources generating approximately 25TB of security telemetry daily. Through careful analysis, they identified that just 15% of this data was driving 85% of their actual threat detections—the classic Pareto principle in action.

By implementing context-aware collection, edge filtering, and tiered storage, they reduced their daily security data volume to approximately 5TB—an 80% reduction. This dramatically decreased their storage requirements, network utilization, and processing overhead [37].

They then redesigned their SIEM architecture, implementing a distributed model with event-driven processing and optimized machine learning. These changes reduced their SIEM infrastructure requirements by approximately 60% while actually improving their mean time to detect critical threats by 35% [37].

The environmental impact was substantial. The organization's security monitoring carbon footprint decreased by approximately 70%, saving an estimated 850 metric tons of CO_2 equivalent emissions annually. The financial savings were equally impressive—approximately $3.2 million in reduced infrastructure costs over three years [37].

What's particularly noteworthy about this example is that the security team didn't set out to create a "green" monitoring system. They simply wanted more effective security with less waste. The environmental benefits were a natural consequence of smarter, more efficient security design [37].

This pattern repeats across organizations that thoughtfully optimize their security monitoring and analytics. By focusing on high-value data, efficient processing, and intelligent analysis, they simultaneously improve their security posture and reduce their environmental impact [7].

The future of security monitoring isn't about collecting more data—it's about collecting the right data and analyzing it more intelligently. And that approach delivers benefits for security teams, business stakeholders, and the planet alike.

References

1. European Commission. (2024). *Cybersecurity policies*. Retrieved from https://digital-strategy.ec.europa.eu/en/policies/cybersecurity-policies
2. MIT Climate and Sustainability Consortium. (2024). *The climate and sustainability implications of generative AI.*
3. Singh, A., & Sharma, R. (2025). Generative AI and sustainability in the digital age for energy-efficient software development. *SSRN Electronic Journal*. Retrieved from https://papers.ssrn.com/sol3/papers.cfm?abstract_id=5214944
4. MIT News. (2025). *Explained: Generative AI*'s *environmental impact*. Retrieved from https://news.mit.edu/2025/explained-generative-ai-environmental-impact-0117
5. European Commission. (2024). *A safer digital future: new cyber rules become law*. Retrieved from https://commission.europa.eu/news/safer-digital-future-new-cyber-rules-become-law-2024-12-10_en
6. Boggini, C., & Perra, G. (2024). A review of CSRD and the EU cyber legal framework: Cybersecurity as a sustainability factor. *Computer Law & Security Review, 50*, 105950. https://doi.org/10.1016/j.clsr.2024.105950

7. Cloud Security Alliance. (2024). *Top threats to cloud computing 2024*. Retrieved from https://cloudsecurityalliance.org/artifacts/top-threats-to-cloud-computing-2024
8. Orca Security. (2024). *Cloud security survey: Top cloud challenges*. Retrieved from https://orca.security/resources/blog/cloud-security-survey-reveals-issues-and-challenges/
9. Microsoft. (2024). *2024 State of multicloud security report*. Retrieved from https://cdn-dynmedia-1.microsoft.com/is/content/microsoftcorp/microsoft/final/en-us/microsoft-brand/documents/2024-State-of-Multicloud-Security-Risk-Report.pdf
10. Cloud Security Alliance. (2024). *Environmental impact of cloud security operations: Energy consumption analysis*. CSA Research Report.
11. MIT Sustainable Computing Lab. (2024). *Energy efficiency in cloud security operations*. MIT Research Report.
12. Forrester Research. (2023). *Cloud security tool sprawl: The hidden costs and risks*. Forrester Survey Report.
13. Fortinet. (2024). *Key findings from the 2024 cloud security report*. Retrieved from https://www.fortinet.com/blog/industry-trends/key-findings-cloud-security-report-2024
14. AWS. (2024). *GuardDuty: Adaptive computation for efficient threat detection*. AWS Security Blog.
15. Stanford Sustainable Systems Lab. (2024). *Environmental impact of DevSecOps practices*. Stanford University Research Report.
16. Gartner. (2024). *The expanding enterprise investment in cloud security*. Retrieved from https://www.gartner.com/en/newsroom/press-releases/2024-06-05-the-expanding-enterprise-investment-in-cloud-security
17. Tabbakh, A., Seiger, R., & Assunção, M. D. (2024). Towards sustainable AI: A comprehensive framework for measuring and reducing the environmental impact of artificial intelligence systems. *SN Computer Science, 5*(3), 641. https://doi.org/10.1007/s43621-024-00641-4
18. Google Cloud Security. (2024). *Optimized transformer models for threat detection*. Google Cloud Technical Report.
19. OpenAI. (2024). *Efficient transformers for security applications: Energy optimization in large language models*. OpenAI Technical Report.
20. NVIDIA. (2024). *GPU-accelerated security analytics: Performance and energy efficiency benchmarks*. NVIDIA Technical Report.
21. Google DeepMind. (2024). *Energy-efficient AI for cybersecurity: Optimizing detection models for reduced carbon footprint*. DeepMind Research Paper.
22. Microsoft Research. (2024). *Sustainable AI in cloud security: Comparative analysis of traditional vs. generative approaches*. Microsoft Technical Report.
23. Microsoft. (2024). *Azure security center: Consolidated security operations analysis*. Microsoft Security Blog.
24. Palo Alto Networks. (2024). *Energy-efficient security infrastructure: A technical analysis*. Palo Alto Networks Technical Report.
25. Microsoft. (2024). *Azure sentinel: NLP for log analysis*. Microsoft Security Blog.
26. Cloud Security Alliance. (2025). *AI organizational responsibilities: AI tools and applications*. Retrieved from https://cloudsecurityalliance.org/press-releases/2025/01/29/csa-releases-comprehensive-guide-to-navigating-ai-governance-security-and-management
27. Microsoft. (2024). *Microsoft defender for cloud: Continuous learning optimization*. Microsoft Security Blog.
28. IBM. (2024). *QRadar SIEM: Generative reconstruction models for anomaly detection*. IBM Security Research Report.
29. Gartner. (2025). *Top trends impacting infrastructure and operations for 2025*. Retrieved from https://www.apmdigest.com/gartner-top-trends-impacting-infrastructure-and-operations-2025
30. Forrester Research. (2024). *The 10 most important cloud trends for 2024*. Retrieved from https://www.forrester.com/blogs/the-ten-most-important-cloud-trends-for-2024/
31. Microsoft. (2024). *Energy-aware security operations: Microsoft SOC case study*. Microsoft Security Blog.

32. HashiCorp. (2024). *State of cloud strategy survey*. Retrieved from https://hashicorp.com/en/state-of-the-cloud
33. Forrester Research. (2024). *Scoring our 2024 cloud predictions*. Retrieved from https://www.forrester.com/report/scoring-our-2024-cloud-predictions/RES181912
34. Forrester Research. (2024). *The total economic impact of sustainable cloud security*. Forrester Research Report.
35. Splunk. (2024). *Cloud security analytics: Resource utilization comparison*. Splunk Technical Report.
36. CrowdStrike. (2024). *On-device security analytics: Efficiency and effectiveness metrics*. CrowdStrike Technical Report.
37. Deloitte. (2024). *Follow-the-sun security operations: Efficiency and effectiveness metrics*. Deloitte Security Research Report.
38. Green Software Foundation. (2024). *Security infrastructure emissions calculator: Methodology and accuracy analysis*. GSF Technical Report.

Chapter 6
AI-Powered Multi-cloud and Hybrid Cloud Strategies

Karan Alang

Abstract The rapid adoption of multi-cloud and hybrid cloud environments has created significant challenges in resource optimization, cost management, and performance governance across distributed infrastructures. This paper examines how AI-driven approaches are transforming multi-cloud strategies by enabling intelligent workload distribution, predictive scaling, and adaptive resource allocation across public, private, and edge computing platforms. We explore the application of machine learning techniques for dynamic cost optimization, latency reduction, and compliance maintenance—including standards like GDPR and SOC 2—in heterogeneous cloud environments. Challenges such as interoperability, transparency, and trust in autonomous systems—especially in serverless and quantum-cloud architectures—are analyzed. Combining insights and capabilities of cloud computing and AI/ML, we present a unified view of intelligent cloud orchestration. The paper concludes with practical recommendations for adopting AI-enhanced strategies, guiding enterprises toward scalable, cost-effective, and secure cloud operations.

Keywords AI-powered cloud · Multi-cloud · Cloud optimization · Resource management · Machine learning and workload distribution

6.1 Introduction

IBM's Autonomic Computation Initiatives (ACI) [1] was one of the first industry-wide effort to build computerized networks with minimal user input. Inspired by the human autonomic nervous system, which regulates functions like temperature and respiration without conscious control, IBM proposed a computing environment that could sense, learn, and act independently [2, 3].

This vision gave rise to autonomic (or self-adaptive) systems [4], characterized by "self-*" properties: self-configuring, self-optimizing, self-protecting, and

K. Alang (✉)
Independent Researcher, Cupertino, CA, USA

B. Pandey, A. Patel (eds.), *Revolutionizing the Cloud*,
https://doi.org/10.1007/978-3-032-07479-9_6

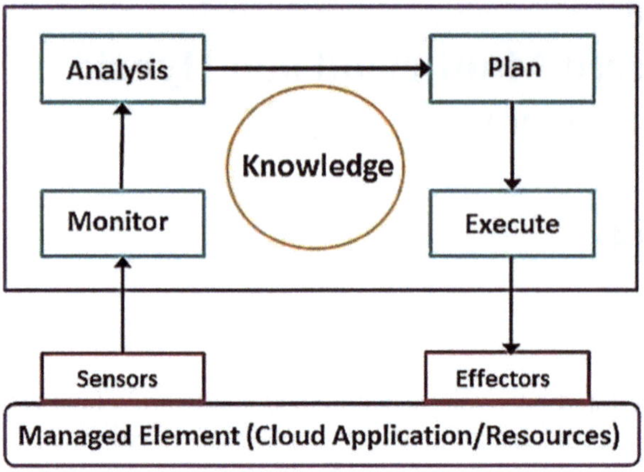

Fig. 6.1 Automatic compute for MAPE-K looping

self-healing [5]. For example, a self-configuring system adapts to environmental changes [6], while self-optimizing systems reduce resource overuse and inefficiencies [7]. Self-protecting systems proactively mitigate cyber threats [8], and self-healing systems diagnose and repair faults autonomously, enhancing fault tolerance [2, 9].

Ideally, such systems operate without manual setup or maintenance [10], regulating all behaviors internally [11].

A foundational framework for autonomic systems is the MAPE-K loop—Monitor, Analyze, Plan, Execute, and Knowledge [1]. Example of MAPE-K is - QoS monitors collect sensor data, which is analyzed to detect issues. A planning module formulates a response, and an execution module enacts changes. This closed-loop control mirrors biological autonomic responses, enabling adaptive, intelligent system behavior (Fig. 6.1).

6.1.1 Fundamentals of AI/ML for Gen Y Computers with A Future Outlook

AI and ML enhance autonomous systems by analyzing operational data to optimize resource management, notably through recognizing workload patterns [12]. These techniques enable systems to self-learn by dynamically invoking ML-based models—often using black-box or gray-box approaches—to adapt behavior and reduce model uncertainty [13].

AI also supports the analysis and planning stages of autonomic infrastructure via the MAPE (Monitor-Analyze-Plan-Execute) loop [14], applying control-theoretical methods and feedback-based management to adjust system parameters in real time

[15]. Additionally, emerging peer-to-peer techniques offer scalable paths to building decentralized self-managing systems [16].

6.1.2 Why and What We Strive For

Incorporating autonomous computing with AI/ML approaches, many different approaches to computing have been introduced, including cloud, fog, edge, serverless, and quantum computers [17]. Autonomous computing systems optimize performance by dynamically adjusting parameters and responding to environmental changes via APIs and self-managing control loops [18].

P2P networks and platforms like Hadoop already showcase autonomous traits such as failure recovery, auto-scaling, and self-organization [19, 20]. However, most systems lack full autonomy and need monitoring and adjustments, since they limited real-time awareness and feedback mechanisms [21]. Enhancing these systems with AI/ML-based monitoring and tuning improves accuracy, adaptability, and performance.

With AI models becoming increasingly optimized, autonomous systems will increasingly rely on AI/ML for decision-making, with humans guiding behavior through APIs. Cyber-physical systems and digital twins will require robust self-adaptive capabilities to manage real-world assets. To function effectively, such systems must:

- Know their limits and available resources
- Adapt to dynamic conditions (e.g., concept drift)
- Predict and prevent faults
- Securely detect/respond to threats
- Interoperate with evolving systems
- Anticipate future demands using predictive AI

6.1.3 Advantages of Next-Generation Computing with AI and ML Incorporated IN

The principal benefit of autonomous computing is a reduced overall expense [22]. Additionally, IT systems reliability is enhanced and the need for labor-intensive human maintenance of servers is reduced [23]. Intelligent workload distribution and power management will enable resource efficiency and energy savings [24]

Key benefits include:

- Economical: Businesses would readily buy artificial intelligence via monthly cloud subscriptions and would reduce costs associated with reduce capital expenditures and support autonomous data processing without human oversight.

- Autonomic: Businesses can become more insight-driven by using AI. Repetitive jobs would be automated enhancing operational efficiency and enabling real-time, insight-driven decision-making.
- Data Organization: AI enhances anomaly detection, customizes responses in real time, and supports predictive management. AI-driven security systems and robots can identify irregularities and trigger alerts, protecting critical data.

Surveys That Are Relevant and Our Role

In this paper, we bring together concepts like artificial intelligence, machine learning leveraging groundbreaking research on next-gen cloud computing [25], artificial intelligence on the cloud [17], fog computing [26], edge computing [27], AI and serverless [28], and quantum computing [29, 30].

6.2 A Model for Future Generations of Computer Systems

Figure 6.2 depicts our proposed future software construction paradigm for autonomously systems of computation that incorporates AI/ML.

The four key layers of the proposed model are:

6.2.1 Internet of Things Use Cases

Internet of Things (IoT) devices, edge devices, and users will appear to connect using gateway devices. In reality, they will interact with edge-based devices such as sensors, actuators, and the effectors [31]. By exchanging data with their digital twin, the technology will be able to offer AI and other autonomous services more effectively [32]. Real-world applications which will benefit from this include medical treatment, smart cities, farming, and weather forecasting.

Fig. 6.2 A future architecture for next-generation computation with artificial intelligence

6.2.2 Resource Administration

In distributed architectures like IoT edge channels, resource registry will track available and purchased compute/storage assets. Key parameters it keeps track of include type, quantity, cost, and placement constraints.

The quality-of-service manager estimates task completion time, prioritizes critical workloads per Service Level Agreements(SLAs), and computes penalty risks.

AI-driven scheduling predicts future resource requirements/demands and also drives scheduling to optimize cost and time. Explainable AI (XAI) is a critical part of the system, used to explain the AI predictions and recommendations.

6.2.3 The Autonomic System

This next-gen architecture is built using IBM's autonomic paradigm—MAPE-K and is enhanced using AI/ML. A practical example of this is cloud infrastructure management, such as auto-scaling in Amazon Web Services (AWS). In such environments, an AI-powered auto-scaler continuously monitors system metrics like CPU usage and network load, analyzes real-time and historical data to predict traffic surges, plans scaling actions (e.g., provisioning new compute instances), and executes these changes to ensure system stability and responsiveness. The knowledge component persists past experiences and outcomes, allowing the system to refine its predictive models and scaling policies over time. This self-adaptive behavior, enabled by the MAPE-K loop, ensures resilient performance even under volatile demand and exemplifies the critical role of AI in maintaining synchronization and governance in complex distributed systems.

Key parts of the autonomic system:

Sensors—They gather real-time QoS metrics and intrusion detection indicators.

Monitor—Compare actual results against the results obtained from AI forecasts, logs SLA breaches and invokes security and hardening agents.

Analyze and Plan—Takes data sent by the monitoring module, analyzes it, and then decides how to respond to the warning. It uses AI to uses AI to diagnose faults, predict service degradations, verify planned action, and then adapt proposed plan.

Executor—Provisions or swaps nodes, checkpoints state, and restarts components to restore QoS.

Effector—Propagates new rules and coordinates adaptation across clusters or federated systems, ensuring synchronization via distributed consensus and adaptive recovery.

6.2.4 Layer for Service Management

Service management layer includes :

- **Database and Security Managers:** Oversee IoT data, anticipate threats with AI (e.g. Anomaly Detection, UEBA techniques, MITRE Attack framework), and secure transactions e.g., via blockchain [33].
- **Serverless Manager:** Dynamically allocates cloud and edge functions (FaaS/PaaS/IaaS) for low-latency workloads [33].
- **Application Placement:** Coordinates between SaaS, PaaS, and container orchestration to optimize resource use.
- **Emerging Tech:** Incorporates quantum computing for rapid PoW or nonce processing and next-gen load balancing.

6.3 Present State of Artificial Intelligence in Computing and the Challenges

In this section, we will go over some of the latest developments and unanswered questions about next-gen computing with AI, including cloud, fog, edge, serverless, and quantum computing (Fig. 6.3).

6.3.1 Computing on the Cloud

Cloud computing and AI are benefiting each other immensely. Cloud provides on-demand compute and storage, while AI enables using data for anomaly detection, predictive auto-scaling, and intelligent workload placement.

Modern cloud-native apps—built as fine-grained microservices—leverage ML models to forecast usage, optimize resource costs, and continuously tune performance without human intervention. This combination delivers unmatched agility - ability to spin up new services in seconds, cost efficiency through pay-per-use and leverage AI Infra like GPU/TPU as required, and real-time insights by automatic cataloging and analyzing petabytes of data. All major cloud vendors have enabled Model Gardens to provide open-source as well as closed-source models to developers and have pre-built SaaS offerings which range from anomaly detection, anomaly alerts, and so on.

Challenges

Key challenges with combining these two technologies.

- **Integration and legacy lift-and-shift:** Migrating monolithic apps and data to cloud-native, AI-driven architectures remains a heavy lift. Many companies do

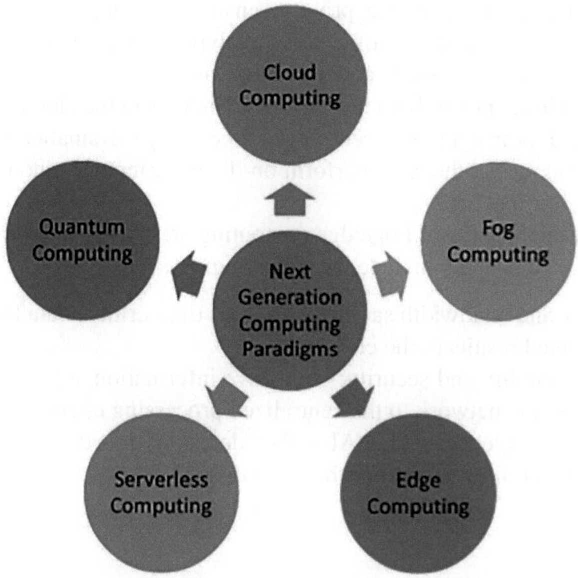

Fig. 6.3 Various computing methods

not want to migrate entire suite of applications to the cloud OR might want to migrate in steps–which leads to additional complexities of multi-cloud architecture or a hybrid (on-premise + Cloud) architecture.

- **Data quality and gravity:** AI/ML needs large/cleansed datasets for training — but once you have terabytes or petabytes of data stored in a specific region, moving them between regions (e.g., in a multi-region disaster recovery setup) or transferring data between VPCs or providers becomes very expensive.
- **Privacy and security:** Encrypting and governing sensitive data in multi-tenant cloud demands end-to-end security controls, e.g., IAM policies, access control, key management, and storage (e.g., Vault/OpenBao), and rigorous compliance. This is especially true in today's world where cyber-attacks are ever-changing and on the rise.

6.3.2 *Cloud Computing and Fog Computing*

Cloud computing excels in data storage and processing. However, with the explosive growth of IoT data volume, moving huge volumes of data from the IoT devices to centralized processing systems is prohibitive from cost, latency as well as security perspective.

This has fueled the growth of fog (or edge) computing. This is primarily a layer of micro-data centers deployed closer to edge devices, i.e., sensors and actuators.

By offloading latency-sensitive, privacy-sensitive workloads to fog nodes, applications such as banking and real-time video analytics can meet QoS targets without being affected by network issues and cost implications.

AI/ML techniques power both layers 1. deep models in the cloud mine petabytes of historical data for insights(i.e., centralized processing), 2. smaller neural-network or rule-based engines at the edge perform on-device inference, anomaly detection, and local decision-making.

As evident, the benefits of Fog/edge computing are critical in today's IoT-driven infrastructure. The benefits include the following:

- Low-latency and bandwidth savings:– Process time-critical data locally, sending only aggregated results to the cloud.
- Improved reliability and security:– Sensitive information, e.g., PII data will not be sent across the network to the centralized processing engine on the cloud.
- Contextual intelligence:- Edge AI makes decisions based on local conditions, while cloud AI refines models with global data.

Challenges

While fog computing has many benefits, it is a growing/nascent field and many unanswered questions remain.

Key challenges include:

- **Execution latency vs. demand spikes:** As user or device counts surge, maintaining tight response-time guarantees and SLA compliance requires smarter placement and load prediction. This can be a challenging task and can affect QoS.
- **Mobility awareness:** Migrating containers or VMs along with mobile devices (e.g., vehicles, drones) demands efficient RL-driven handoff strategies. Despite research into this area using reinforcement learning (RL) methods such as Q-learning and State-Action-Reward-State-Action (SARSA), numerous demands in real-world settings make this a difficult problem to solve .
- **Dynamic resource scheduling:** Allocating limited CPU, memory, and network at the edge under strict SLAs remains an open problem—researchers are exploring neural nets, SVMs, and hybrid heuristic/ML approaches.
- **Fault tolerance and availability:** Heterogeneous fog infrastructures must gracefully handle problems like malfunctioning sensors, insufficient network coverage (either locally or nationally), unreliable service platforms, and disconnected user interface systems, and service placement across "fog clusters."
- **Emerging AI use cases:** These include image/video processing, NLP, and robotics. All these benefit from fog deployments—but each brings its own scheduling, model-compression, privacy requirements, and better placement in "fog clusters" calling for new AI-driven orchestration frameworks.

6.3.3 Internet of Things

Modern IoT setups use both cloud and edge computing so devices can act fast and stay secure. Here's the core of it in simple terms:

- Why edge matters
  - Lots of devices—phones, sensors, robots, home assistants like Google Home/Amazon Echo, and others—now collect personal data that needs quick decisions.
  - With volume of data being collected, as well as the sensitive nature of collected data, it makes more sense to "Not" send all data to the centralized cloud AI. This alleviates privacy concerns, while also reduces the latency.
  - Instead, edge "cloudlets" near devices handle the urgent work locally.
- How AI helps on the edge
  - **Smart filtering:** AI models on edge nodes pick out only the important data to send up, saving bandwidth and reducing privacy risks.
  - **Local insights:** Simple ML inference engines, ML vision, or voice-recognition engines run right on the device or gateway and provide instant response to users. This requires smaller ML models optimized for inference and is a major goal for many of the ML/AI companies.
  - **Adaptive security:** Edge nodes encrypt or anonymize sensitive info before it ever leaves your network. This is another key benefit of AI on the edge nodes and helps drive AI adoption.
- Key challenges
- While AI on the edge has obvious benefits, it is an nascent/upcoming research subject. The key challenges include :
  - **Scale and diversity:** Managing millions of different devices—each with its own hardware, software, and owner—is hard without common rules. This is more so because there is no common standards published.
  - **Mobility and handoff:** Keeping apps running smoothly as devices move (e.g., self-driving cars, drones) is a challenge. The solution to this is smarter workload migration.
  - **Latency vs. consistency:** Fast local action can clash with keeping data in sync across the cloud and other edges.
  - **Security and standards:** Cheap edge gadgets often lack strong authentication; we need universal guidelines and toolkits to lock them down.

By pushing AI out to the edge and only sharing what matters, IoT systems can stay fast, private, and cost-effective—even as device counts increase and the data volumes increase as well.

6.3.4 Computing Without Server

Serverless computing has gained popularity in the last few years and enables developer to write code without worrying about infrastructure provisioning and maintenance. With serverless computing, cloud providers may find it easier to manage infrastructure and automate provisioning. Also , infrastructure maintenance takes less time and uses less resources. Serverless computing aims to decrease expenditure while maximizing return by using the best serverless technologies

How serverless computing works and it's advantages:

- Event-driven and pay-per-execution: Code runs when it is triggered, e.g., using a cron job, or when one uploads a file or makes API call. The user is charged for each run (e.g., how long the programs is run, and the resources consumed)
- Serverless Kubernetes : With Serverless Kubernetes, developers may bring their own containers to the platform These containers may be automatically scaled up or down in clusters controlled by Kubernetes. This adaptive scaling capability is enabled so that it can handle scenarios with high traffic and workload fluctuations
- Low-code/no-code workflows: Serverless computing allows drag-and-drop tools link cloud services (databases, AI models, etc.) into pipelines without the developer having to write orchestration code.
- API gateway is provided which is a managed entry point that routes, secures, and monitors all APIs in one place. This also reduces code written by developers, while increasing productivity and simplifying maintenance.
- Auto-scaling – This is enabled by default and helps in scale-up or scale-down based on the traffic being handled.

6.3.5 Advances in Quantum Computing

The promise of quantum computing may be the only technology capable of radically changing AI. When combined with quantum computing, AI's already massive global impact might be amplified.

Quantum computing processes information in accordance with the laws of quantum physics, enabling possibilities that could not be imagined using conventional methods of information processing and which are encoded in the quantum states of quantum systems.

As the number of component systems increases exponentially, so does the scaling of the phase space within which composite quantum systems evolve. The first aim of developing a quantum computer was to simulate quantum systems but the real breakthrough came when quantum algorithms were used to perform tasks previously thought to be impossible, e.g., an effective method for factoring was found with the discovery of Shor's algorithm

However, building a quantum computer is no simple feat—qubits must be kept almost perfectly isolated at temperatures near absolute zero, and even tiny vibrations or stray heat can scramble their delicate quantum states.

Companies like IBM, Microsoft, Google (with its Sycamore chip), Amazon, Intel, and Honeywell are trying to create useful quantum hardware. Google's team even claimed "quantum advantage," showing a task that their chip did faster than any ordinary computer could.

Quantum computing needs to overcome challenges like noise, error correction, and extreme cooling. Once it becomes main-stream, quantum computing could turbo-charge AI, enable complex tasks like speed up drug discovery, crack today's encryption, and kick off whole new industries.

Open Challenges

- NISQ era firstIn the next few years, we'll see "Noisy Intermediate Scale Quantum" (NISQ) machines with dozens to a few hundred qubits.
- They'll let physicists explore new quantum states and simulate complex systems that classical supercomputers can't handle.
- Need for error correction
- NISQ devices still suffer from noise and errors. To build truly powerful, fault-tolerant quantum computers with hundreds or thousands of qubits, we must develop efficient quantum error correction (QEC) circuits.
- Long road to full power
- Even with error correction, running big algorithms like Shor's factoring method at scale remains years away.
- This would require heavy R&D spending which is already being done by the bigger companies. Additionally, there are multiple new startups(and many more will come up) who are working to solve these engineering puzzles.
- Finance applications
- Quantum models that handle probabilities could reshape portfolio optimization, risk analysis, and fraud detection in banks and hedge funds. However, that will take some time to materialize as quantum computing matures.
- Healthcare breakthroughs
- Faster genome sequencing: Quantum machines could sort through massive DNA data more quickly for patient-specific treatment plans.
- Protein folding: Better simulation of molecular structures could speed up drug discovery.
- Cryptography shake-up
- Shor's algorithm threatens today's RSA encryption by factoring large primes efficiently.
- This has spurred huge investment in quantum-safe cryptography—Toshiba alone projects $3 billion in quantum crypto revenue by 2030.
- Climate and environmental uses

Quantum optimization could help design greener manufacturing processes, help model climate systems more accurately, and find new ways to curb emissions and overall help in climate/environmental improvement.

- Scaling and materials science
- Building stable qubits requires ultra-cold temperatures and materials that stay coherent at millikelvin scales—still a major materials and engineering challenge.
- Business momentum
- Big technology companies like IBM, Google, Microsoft, Honeywell, and many startups are investing resources into quantum hardware and software.
- As NISQ devices prove useful and QEC advances, commercial interest will only keep rising.

To summarize, we're few years away from unlocking, on the cusp of a few years sprint through the NISQ era, but unlocking universal, fault-tolerant quantum computers—this will take advances in error correction, hardware engineering, and new materials. However, the benefits for industries like finance, pharma, and others are immense.

Quantum Artificial Intelligence

Quantum computing is superior than classical computing when dealing with very large data sets. Quantum algorithms are mathematical programs that make use of quantum circuits. The "state" in quantum computing is the information kept in the fundamental quantum state that allows for the selected implementation. Quantum bits—the fundamental units of data storage and processing, quantum gates—the physical nodes that perform this processing, and quantum channels—the interconnections between these nodes and circuits that preserve entanglement and quantum superposition are the fundamental elements of quantum information theory. As a result of their ability to manage and process data sets that are exponentially bigger than conventional computers, quantum computers can process and handle data sets that are integral parts of composite quantum systems.

Why does quantum artificial intelligence matter for AI ?

Classical computers need 2^N parameters to describe an N-qubit system, but quantum devices use just N qubits—this makes them a natural fit for big, complex models.

Quantum computing can explore entire decision trees in one run, instead of branching step by step. Early experiments show that quantum channels can speed up an agent's learning and hybrid quantum/classical setups (e.g., nanophotonic processors) and help tune performance.

Figure 6.4 displays the applications of quantum AI in areas such as quantum search, quantum game theory, decision problem algorithms, and learning algorithms. Artificial intelligence systems that use quantum computing to complete

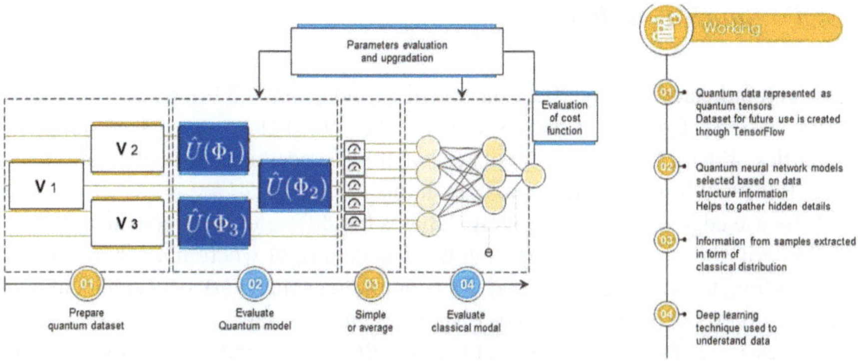

Fig. 6.4 High-level introduction to quantum AI with working principles

tasks rapidly may find it useful in situations where traditional methods would be prohibitively expensive and time-consuming, such as when dealing with issues pertaining to autonomous driving or natural language processing (NLP) algorithms . The existing algorithms are built on words and characters. One of the aims of quantum algorithms is to achieve "meaning awareness." These algorithms may utilize sentences and paragraphs to construct speech patterns in real time.

- QAI applications include :
  - Quantum search and optimization: Faster algorithms for finding answers in massive datasets.
  - Game theory and decision problems: Solve complex strategies more efficiently.
  - NLP "meaning awareness": Potential to process entire sentences or paragraphs at once for more human-like language understanding.
  - Predictive analytics: Train ML and DL models on huge data volumes for tasks like stock market forecasting or climate control systems.

6.4 AI-Embedded Autonomic Computing of the Modern Era

This section covers recent advances in the field of autonomic computing with embedded intelligence including latest developments in IoT, actuators, and intelligent edges.

6.4.1 *Smart Periphery*

Research indicates that by 2025, there will be more than 75 billion IoT devices in operation [34]. Connected cars, smart meters, and in-store sensors produce vast quantities of data. This data necessitates handling, processing, and collecting in real time. Edge and fog computing can help in this.

Why use edge over fog computing, what is the difference between the two ?

Primarily because edge computing handles data right where it's generated, cutting out long trips to a distant cloud. Fog computing splits work between local hubs and the cloud, but pure edge avoids extra hops entirely.

Processing at the edge slashes network bandwidth use and latency, so apps react faster and companies pay less in data transit costs.

Key ways to utilize edge/fog computing :

- Hybrid workloads:
- Some tasks still need cloud power (for deep analytics or long-term storage), so edge nodes do the first-pass work and then forward trimmed data upstream.
- **Intelligent edge services:** Modern edge stacks offer:
  - **Edge caching** to store hot data locally
  - **Edge training & inference** for on-site AI model updates
  - **Job offloading** where heavy jobs shift between device, edge, and cloud
- **Lightweight AI methods:** Single-pass or streaming ML algorithms keep memory use low by learning from each data point in order, and only retrain when performance drops ("concept drift").
- **Bringing legacy along:** Old applications can be containerized and run side-by-side with new AI services on both cloud and edge, letting firms modernize without ripping everything out.

6.4.2 *Smart Things—Embedded Intelligence in Products and Services*

A product's ability to evaluate and think about its own performance is an example of "Smart Thing." Furthermore, it must be capable of handling its own workload and working circumstances. The idea of self-evaluation of the product based on data from embedded sensors should be considered while developing new goods and services. When introducing a new product or service, an integrated model must include a business intelligence system. This can collect sensor data, runs ML models, and turns insights into actions, thus helping companies predict trends that humans alone can't spot.

Other key points to be kept in mind w.r.t "Smart" things or products

- Data integrity for "Smart" products is critical.
- Since "Smart" products use sensor data to drive their own decisions, it's crucial that this data is secure from cyber-attacks.
- Blockchain can be leveraged to storing every reading and model output to create an unbreakable, time-stamped record. This would guarantee data integrity and a full audit trail.
- Smaller IoT gadgets are not yet sophisticated to be able to run full-blown deep neural networks. Energy-efficient training, secure edge inference, and real-time decision-making are challenges on limited hardware. The good news is that a lot of companies are working toward improving inference on the edge/IoT devices.
- As smart devices spread across cloud, edge, and on-premises systems, one needs a consolidated IAM plan which leverages zero-trust, federated identities, and AI-driven anomaly detection to identify the bad actors and keep the system secure and functioning.
- Use cases where smart things can play a major role:
  - *High-tech medical care:*

    IoT sensors in clinics and wearables can speed up diagnoses and expand access to care.
  - *Predictive maintenance:*

    Sensors on appliances can warn when they need service, preventing breakdowns.

6.4.3 The Role of Things in a Sensor-Actuator Systems

As the next iteration of embedded ICT systems, Cyber-Physical Systems (CPS) leverage sensor-actuator networks to provide users with smart apps and services via their awareness of their physical environment. Autonomous control loops allow for better processing and interpretation of sensor data, as well as the planning and execution of plans using actuators, making numerous IoT sensors possible. Due to their complexity, these systems need methods to assist in their design and development. Information and communication technology (ICT) systems provide a broad variety of smart applications and services to businesses and inhabitants via networking and software integrated into physical items.

Tools like adaptive digital twins can be used by these complex systems to model behavior and catch problems early. Also, CPS must build in redundant sensors, secure data backups, and fault-tolerant control loops to ensure safety and compliance, and mitigate the risk of data loss, service interruption, and regulatory penalties in the event of a disruption

Examples of CPS include transportation networks, structures, power grids, and water distribution systems.

6.5 New Movements and Future Trends

We have chosen a variety of computer study disciplines for three separate maturity levels—5 to 10 years, more than ten years—based on current research.

The hype cycle for next-generation computing is shown in Fig. 6.5. Lots of research has gone into cloud computing and the Internet of Things. However, computing is only at the beginning of its study into areas such as mobile edge computing, artificial intelligence orchestration, fog computing, and edge computing. The maturity of computer applications in these sectors may be reached in as little as 10 years. A lot of focus has been on grid computing and virtualization recently, and that may not change in the next five years.

Figure 6.6 lists out the research avenues. These include cloud computing, fog computing, serverless computing, and quantum computing.

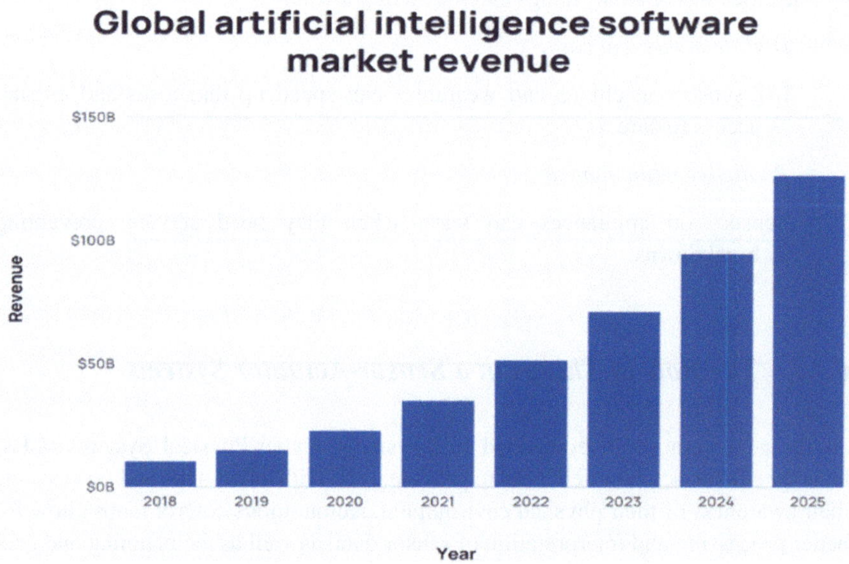

Fig. 6.5 Revenue: next-generation computers with AI integration

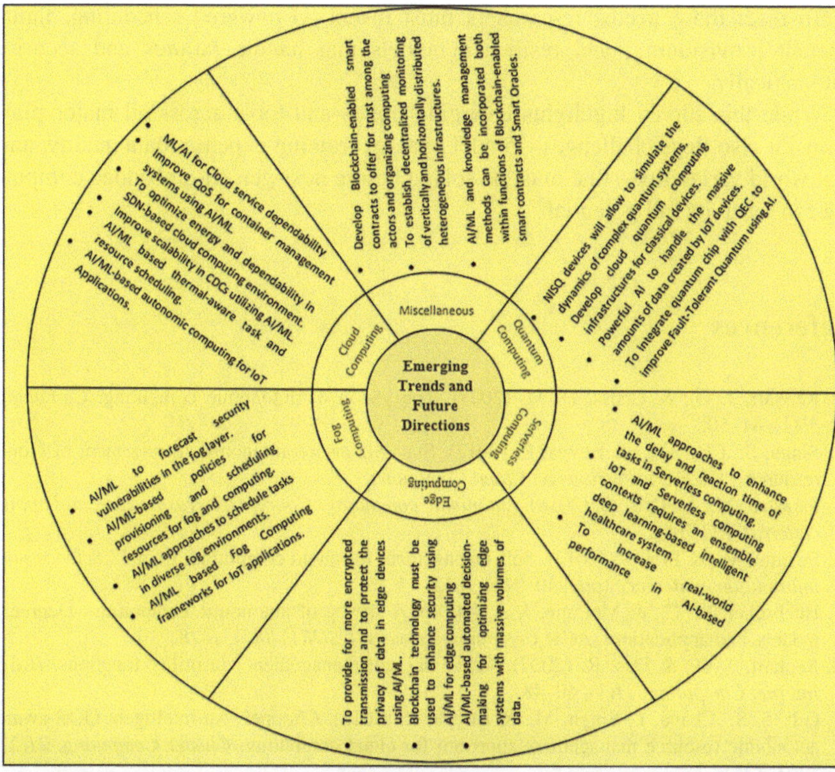

Fig. 6.6 An overview of current and future directions in next-generation computing with artificial intelligence

6.6 Conclusion

Services based on Cloud, Fog, Edge, Serverless, and Quantum Computing are now at the core of the business world, thanks to computing systems that have progressed computer science in the last couple of decades.

In the past couple of years, especially after LLMs (& ChatGPT) captured the imagination of folks, AI/ML has seen a meteoric rise AI/ML. This is also because of the groundbreaking accuracy they brought to many related fields, including computer vision, NLP, LLMs, and others.

Further development of Explainable AI (XAI) has the potential to open the door to AI's broad adoption in today's computing infrastructure.

In the coming years, AI and ML will place significant demands on computing systems—wrt computing efficiency, software-level QoS constraints and financial limitations, services that store, maintain, and investigate massive amounts of data generated by heterogeneous Internet of Things (IoT) and sensor networks.

To meet these needs, researchers must invent AI-powered scheduling, fault-tolerant provisioning, and resilience models that handle failures and security automatically.

While this survey highlights emerging trends and tools across all major platforms, it also flags challenges—model opacity, training expense, data quality, and real-world variability—that must be solved before next-gen AI-embedded computing can reach its full potential.

References

1. Kephart, J. O., & Chess, D. M. (2003). The vision of autonomic computing. *Computer, 36*(1), 41–50.
2. Singh, S., Chana, I., & Buyya, R. (2017). Star: Sla-aware autonomic management of cloud resources. *IEEE Transactions on Cloud Computing*.
3. Parashar, M., & Hariri, S. (2018). *Autonomic computing: Concepts, infrastructure, and applications*. CRC Press.
4. Puviani, M., & Frei, R. (2013). Self-management for cloud computing. In *2013 Science and information conference* (pp. 940–946). IEEE.
5. Huebscher, M. C., & McCann, J. A. (2008). A survey of autonomic computing—Degrees, models, and applications. *ACM Computing Surveys (CSUR), 40*(3), 1–28.
6. Kephart, J. O., & Das, R. (2007). Achieving self-management via utility functions. *IEEE Internet Computing, 11*(1), 40–48.
7. Gill, S. S., Chana, I., Singh, M., & Buyya, R. (2018). Chopper: An intelligent QOS-aware autonomic resource management approach for cloud computing. *Cluster Computing, 21*(2), 1203–1241.
8. Yadav, V. (2021). AI and economics of mental health: analyzing how AI can be used to improve the cost-effectiveness of mental health treatments and interventions. *Journal of Scientific and Engineering Research, 8*(7), 274–284. https://doi.org/10.5281/zenodo.13600238
9. Derbel, H., Agoulmine, N., & Salaün, M. (2009). Anema: Autonomic network management architecture to support self-configuration and selfoptimization in IP networks. *Computer Networks, 53*(3), 418–430.
10. Yadav, V. (2019). Healthcare IT innovations and cost savings: Explore how recent innovations in healthcare IT have led to cost savings and economic benefits within the healthcare system. *International Journal of Science and Research (IJSR), 8*(12), 2070–2076. https://doi.org/10.21275/sr24731181300
11. Kephart, J. O., & Lenchner, J. A symbiotic cognitive computing perspective on autonomic computing. In *2015 IEEE International conference on autonomic computing* (Vol. 2015, pp. 109–114). IEEE.
12. Kephart, J. O., & Walsh, W. E. (2004). An artificial intelligence perspective on autonomic computing policies. In *Proceedings of the Fifth IEEE International Workshop on Policies for Distributed Systems and Networks, 2004. Policy 2004* (pp. 3–12). IEEE.
13. Yadav, V. (2022). AI-driven predictive models for healthcare supply chains: Developing AI models to predict and optimize healthcare supply chains, especially during global health emergencies. *Progress in Medical Sciences, 6*(1), 1–8. https://doi.org/10.47363/pms/2022(6)211
14. Rutten, E., Marchand, N., & Simon, D. (2017). Feedback control as mape-k loop in autonomic computing, software engineering for self-adaptive systems iii. *Assurances*, 349–373.
15. Donepudi, P. K. (2018). Application of artificial intelligence in automation industry. *Asian Journal of Applied Science and Engineering, 7*(1), 7–20.

16. Ullah, Z., Al-Turjman, F., Mostarda, L., & Gagliardi, R. (2020). Applications of artificial intelligence and machine learning in smart cities. *Computer Communications, 154*, 313–323.
17. Gill, S. S., Tuli, S., Xu, M., Singh, I., Singh, K. V., Lindsay, D., Tuli, S., Smirnova, D., Singh, M., Jain, U., et al. (2019). Transformative effects of IoT, blockchain and artificial intelligence on cloud computing: Evolution, vision, trends and open challenges. *Internet of Things, 8*, 100118.
18. Buyya, R., Srirama, S. N., Casale, G., Calheiros, R., Simmhan, Y., Varghese, B., Gelenbe, E., Javadi, B., Vaquero, L. M., Netto, M. A., et al. (2018). A manifesto for future generation cloud computing: Research directions for the next decade. *ACM Computing Surveys (CSUR), 51*(5), 1–38.
19. Sikha, V. K., Siramgari, D., Ganesan, P., & Somepalli, S. (2021, December 30). *Enhancing energy efficiency in cloud computing operations through artificial intelligence*. Zenodo.
20. López-Huguet, S., Pérez, A., Calatrava, A., de Alfonso, C., Caballer, M., Moltó, G., & Blanquer, I. (2019). A self-managed mesos cluster for data analytics with QOS guarantees. *Future Generation Computer Systems, 96*, 449–461.
21. Ganesan, P. (2020). *Public cloud in multi-cloud strategies integration and management.*
22. Ganek, A. G., Hilkner, C. P., Sweitzer, J. W., Miller, B., & Hellerstein, J. L. (2004). The response to it complexity: Autonomic computing. In *Proceedings of the Third IEEE International Symposium on Network Computing and Applications, 2004 (NCA 2004)* (pp. 151–157). IEEE.
23. Chaurasia, N., Kumar, M., Chaudhry, R., & Verma, O. P. (2021). Comprehensive survey on energy-aware server consolidation techniques in cloud computing. *The Journal of Supercomputing, 77*(10), 11682–11737.
24. Ganesan, P. (2021). Advancing application development through containerization: enhancing automation, scalability, and consistency. *North American Journal of Engineering Research, 2*(3).
25. Varghese, B., & Buyya, R. (2018). Next generation cloud computing: New trends and research directions. *Future Generation Computer Systems, 79*, 849–861.
26. Abdulkareem, K. H., Mohammed, M. A., Gunasekaran, S. S., Al-Mhiqani, M. N., Mutlag, A. A., Mostafa, S. A., Ali, N. S., & Ibrahim, D. A. (2019). A review of fog computing and machine learning: concepts, applications, challenges, and open issues. *IEEE Access, 7*, 153123–153140.
27. Merenda, M., Porcaro, C., & Iero, D. (2020). Edge machine learning for AI-enabled IoT devices: A review. *Sensors, 20*(9), 2533.
28. Hassan, H. B., Barakat, S. A., & Sarhan, Q. I. (2021). Survey on serverless computing. *Journal of Cloud Computing, 10*(1), 1–29.
29. Kumar, A., Bhatia, S., Kaushik, K., Gandhi, S. M., Devi, S. G., Diego, A. D. J., & Mashat, A. (2021). Survey of promising technologies for quantum drones and networks. *IEEE Access, 9*, 125868–125911.
30. Li, Y., Tian, M., Liu, G., Peng, C., & Jiao, L. (2020). Quantum optimization and quantum learning: A survey. *IEEE Access, 8*, 23568–23593.
31. Goel, S. S., Goel, A., Kumar, M., & Moltó, G. (2021). A review of internet of things: Qualifying technologies and boundless horizon. *Journal of Reliable Intelligent Environments, 7*(1), 23–33.
32. Desai, F., et al. (2022). Healthcloud: A system for monitoring health status of heart patients using machine learning and cloud computing. *Internet of Things, 17*, 100485.
33. Gill, S. S. (2021). Quantum and blockchain based serverless edge computing: A vision, model, new trends and future directions. *Internet Technology Letters*, e275.
34. National Institute of Standards and Technology, National Cybersecurity Center of Excellence (NCCoE): Internet of Things (IoT). Retrieved from https://www.nccoe.nist.gov/iot (Accessed: 15 June 2025). "Estimates suggest that there will be more than 75 billion IoT devices in use by 2025," according to IHS Markit.

Chapter 7
AI for Compliance in Cloud Environments

Vaishnavi Gudur and Rajeev Kumar

Abstract With rise in cloud usage, MNCs these days encounter significant challenges adhering to strict and evolving regulatory compliance requirements. Conventional compliance frameworks, characterized by manual processes, fixed rules, and periodic audits, are inadequate for addressing the transient characteristics of contemporary cloud environments. This chapter examines the transformative impact of AI on compliance management within cloud environments. It illustrates the enhancement of scalability, accuracy, and proactivity through practical algorithms, case studies, and best practices in AI, while also addressing the significant challenges of transparency, privacy, and ethical alignment. This chapter analyzes future trends including explainable AI, edge compliance, and quantum readiness, offering practical insights for cloud professionals, compliance leaders, and technology strategists.

Keywords Cloud compliance · Artificial Intelligence (AI) · Machine learning · Regulatory Technology (RegTech) · Data protection

7.1 Introduction

Multinational companies using cloud computing face high-stakes regulatory compliance. A single error—a misconfigured storage bucket, missed access control point, or delayed audit response—can cost companies millions in fines, damage public trust, and disrupt major operations. Modern cloud systems exceed compliance standards in size and complexity. The fast resource provision, frequent configuration changes, and transient nature of cloud assets make rules-based checklists, static configuration reviews, and periodic manual audits unsuitable. These models

V. Gudur (✉)
Independent Researcher, Seattle, WA, USA

R. Kumar
Independent Researcher, Stream Dale Circle, Concord, NC, USA

B. Pandey, A. Patel (eds.), *Revolutionizing the Cloud*,
https://doi.org/10.1007/978-3-032-07479-9_7

are unsuitable for real-time compliance in dynamic cloud environments due to their long time lags, high manual overhead, and low visibility. GDPR, HIPAA, and PCI DSS require more than periodic scans, hand audits, and rules-based systems [1]. Without constant observation and adaptability, older solutions cannot meet these criteria [2]. The following sections examine how AI technologies change cloud compliance. Compliance could become automated, proactive, and adaptive with AI [2]. Machine learning (ML), natural language processing (NLP), and intelligent decision engines monitor millions of data points in real time [3], detect subtle anomalies [4], predict emerging risks [5], and automatically enforce policies, overcoming human-led processes' scalability [6, 7]. This chapter provides tools and insights for developing, implementing, and assessing cloud-based AI-driven compliance systems. Cloud professionals, compliance managers, technology strategists, and AI researchers are targeted. We present a coherent AI compliance architecture for multi-cloud systems using predictive analytics, explainability mechanisms, and real-time monitoring, as well as current best practices. Compliance is about trust—between companies and customers governments and the regulated, and technology and the public [3]. This chapter examines how AI can transform companies within ethical, technological, and legal constraints.

Automation, ML, and NLP tools simplify and monitor cloud infrastructure regulatory compliance. AI-driven real-time compliance analyzes massive data sets to find problems, interpret laws, and fix them [2].

7.2 Chapter Objectives

Readers by the end of this chapter will be able to understand the concepts behind industry-leading tools including Google Cloud Policy Intelligence and IBM Watson RegTech will help you to include ML models, NLP engines, and cloud-native services (such Kubernetes operators) into scalable compliance architectures.We will also be able to discover how to develop real-time policy enforcement systems to reduce manual supervision and build automatic audit trails. This will enable your configuration, deployment, and optimization of AI-powered compliance systems, master fundamental ideas include unsupervised learning for anomaly detection, supervised models for fraud detection, and explainable AI frameworks like SHAP and LIME help to promote openness, responsibility, and regulatory alignment. Then apply reasonable AI techniques in vulnerable cloud environments.

7.3 Background and Context

7.3.1 Key Compliance Terms in Cloud Environments

AI can be explained in part by the basic regulatory systems that mold cloud compliance:

- The General Data Protection Regulation (GDPR) of the EU controls data privacy and cross-border data flows, so demanding rigorous control over personal data storage and processing.
- HIPAA calls for cloud encryption and access limitations for PHI.
- In order to control credit card transactions, PCI DSS stresses in cloud-hosted payment systems encryption, access tracking, and vulnerability management.
- An ISMS standard, ISO/IEC 27001 advises risk assessment and control in cloud architectures.

Cloud system non-compliance could have disastrous consequences like HIPAA violations that could result in fines of up to $1.5 million per year, while GDPR violations could result in fines of up to €20 million, or 4% of global annual income. Stakeholders will lose complete trust in case of public beaches like the health data breach in 2023 that happened because AWS S3 buckets were not set up properly. As shown by AWS's 2024 adoption of its Acceptable Use Policy, behavior that doesn't follow the rules might even be put on hold.

7.4 Current Compliance Regulations and Standards

7.4.1 General Data Protection Regulation (GDPR)

GDPR imposes strict global controls on personal data, impacting all cloud providers serving EU citizens, with explicit requirements for cross-border data flow and privacy-by-design. The GDPR's emphasis on responsibility and compliance causes problems in transient cloud infrastructures with often shifting resources and configurations. Tikkinen-Piri et al. say "Cloud-native apps must implement continuous compliance monitoring to satisfy the GDPR's documentation requirements in environments where traditional static compliance approaches are inadequate."

7.4.2 Global Healthcare Data Protection Regulations

Healthcare data protection frameworks worldwide establish stringent requirements for safeguarding patient information in cloud environments. While the United States enforces these protections through HIPAA, similar structures exist globally, including the EU's GDPR, Australia's My Health Records Act, and Brazil's LGPD. These systems have fundamental concepts regardless of geographical differences like most regulations classify health records as sensitive data requiring more security. The EU GDPR Article 9 clearly states that health data need particular protection. Under comprehensive security standards, regulatory systems demand administrative, physical, and technical protections. The ISO 27799 standard provides globally criteria for health information . Processor responsibility: Direct compliance is required for cloud service providers handling health records. For example, the UK's NHS Digital guidance notes "cloud providers processing health data must meet security standards regardless of their geographic location." Many nations restrict the flow of health information across national lines. Both Singapore's PDPA and Japan's APPI have clauses limiting foreign flow of health data abound. Legislative change all around has come from the emergence of cloud computing. According to 2023 World Health Organization research, 78% of member states have changed their healthcare data protection regulations to manage cloud technology within the past 5 years, so creating both opportunities and challenges for AI-enabled compliance solutions.

7.4.3 Payment Card Industry Data Security Standard (PCI DSS)

PCI DSS defines twelve requirements across six categories for cloud payment card data protection, including secure systems (TLS 1.3, firewalls), cardholder data protection (tokenization, AES-256 encryption), and vulnerability management (frequent patching, AI-powered scanners).

7.5 Role of AI in Enhancing Compliance Efforts

From reactive to proactive, flexible, and incredibly automated, artificial intelligence drives compliance management in challenging cloud environments. Real-time responsiveness in dynamic, globally dispersed cloud systems calls for pre-defined rules, manual verification, and scheduled audits—not for compliance solutions. Conventional approaches for rapid regulatory change, and cyber risk adaptation is costly, error-prone, and unforgiving [2]. Apart from inherent limitations, artificial intelligence offers flexible, autonomous, constant monitoring. Using sophisticated algorithms, these AI-driven compliance systems rapidly and precisely find compliance violations in vast amounts of data including transaction logs, user activity records, and system configuration changes. AI systems find unexpected resource use in cloud data and illegal login access. AI compliance solutions lower threat dwell-time and react 60% faster than traditional methods, so minimizing damage [6]. Without known criteria, isolation forest and autoencoder anomaly detection models may find unanticipated hazards, so enhancing security in fast changing surroundings [4] is a must. Contextualizing past compliance data, artificial intelligence could forecast violations of compliance rules. With 85% accuracy, Gartner's predictive analytics tools find compliance concerns from user behavior, regulatory changes, and transaction history [5]. Big transactional data could teach predictive algorithms to find financial compliance fraud, so lowering risk. Policy engines driven by AI enforce compliance in real time across cloud systems, so lowering human monitoring. Automation might stop compliance problems, GDPR-violating cross-border data transfers, and HIPAA-violating unencrypted health record storage. The Deloitte automation of compliance study (2024) contends that AI-enforced rules could eliminate 50% of manual compliance tasks, so improving accuracy and business [7]. Using strong machine learning, AI-powered audit trail analysis automatically reviews massive audit records to find small deviations from conformance. Using NLP logs, audit analytics can rapidly find suspicious transaction changes, odd access patterns, and illegal data changes undetectable to humans. By 70%, Accenture (2023) found that AI-based audit analytics improved accuracy and efficiency and reduced human auditing time. Powerful and flexible machine learning drives artificial intelligence compliance control. From labeled data, supervised learning can detect hazards—compliant vs. non-compliant behavior. SVM, logistic learning, random forests [8]. Zero-days and unsupervised learning uncover compliance issues free from labels or outliers. PCA; K-means clustering; autoencoder neural networks [8], isolation forest. With enough unlabeled data and few labels, transfer learning increases detection accuracy. It's clear when real transactions outnumber fraud. Real-time performance data modulates compliance constraints and feedback loops in adversarial reinforcement learning, so enhancing detection. Does dynamic threat detection and real-time resource allocation among complex, adaptive tasks like these suitably? Studies find artificial intelligence beats rule-based systems. By 80%, machine learning models lower false positives, compliance costs, and operational efficiency according to Experian's 2023 fraud prevention research. AI-enhanced compliance solutions have minute reaction times, 30% better detection rates, and 30% fewer false positives. For businesses, innovative AI-powered technologies automate proactive, real-time compliance control. This supports corporate safety, consistent policies, lower non-compliance risk, and cost control.

7.6 Core Content

7.6.1 Frameworks for AI-Driven Compliance

With most of modern cybersecurity compliance systems matching the five basic functions described in the NIST cybersecurity framework: Identify, Protect, Detect, Respond, and Recover [9], they offer ordered methods to manage security risks. This study investigates how artificial intelligence technologies might change every element of these models, so improving their efficacy and lowering their manual overhead.

7.7 Identify

7.7.1 *Current Methods in Compliance Frameworks*

Compliance systems including NIST CSF, ISO 27001, and PCI DSS mostly rely on documented inventories for identification, periodic scanning, and manual asset discovery. Often these methods call for scheduled network scanning and inventory updates like manual asset classification using criticality and sensitivity, risk evaluations are based on questionnaires and systems based on documentation. Organizations using the ISO 27001 framework must find information assets using inventory systems and assign ownership. PCI DSS similarly requires keeping an inventory of system components within the cardholder data environment. These traditional approaches suffer from inaccuracy, incompleteness, and rapid obsolescence in dynamic cloud environments. To begin our exploration of AI-driven compliance, we start at the foundational level: identifying and mapping all assets within dynamic cloud environments. This ensures subsequent compliance processes have accurate, complete visibility. We now examine how Graph Neural Networks (GNNs) provide a cutting-edge solution for automated, precise asset discovery.

7.7.2 *AI Innovations in Identify: Modern AI Techniques Dramatically Enhance the Identify Phase*

AI-Based Automated Asset Discovery with Graph Neural Networks

Legacy asset discovery is defined by scanning and hand-held inventories; missing shadow IT; cloud resources; and sophisticated asset relationships. Although PCI DSS and ISO 27001 call for complete asset inventories, hand techniques cannot fit dynamic environments of today. GNN models networked assets as nodes and connections as edges in a graph to find relationships. GNNs can continuously analyze dynamic cloud environments to expose hidden asset dependencies and identify unmanaged "shadow IT" resources in real time, unlike conventional CMDB discovery techniques which depend on periodic scans and manual inventory updates and often produce incomplete or outdated records. This improves inventory accuracy and change-oriented responsiveness. This method helps security systems to detect complex interactions lacking in supply chains. From data collection to database integration, the asset discovery pipeline offers an automated, end-to-end solution meeting current compliance criteria. Feature vectors are produced to characterize every asset following raw data collecting from cloud resources and network scans. This architecture meets a significant compliance need by allowing continuous, automated asset discovery that changes with the times and is more accurate than conventional methods. 98% asset categorization accuracy (against 76% for conventional), 42% more illegal goods than conventional scanning, more than 100,000 asset hourly processing, entire asset inventory in 83% less time and 91% accuracy in forecasting unknown asset dependencies.

7.8 Intelligent Risk Assessment

7.8.1 Current Risk Assessment Approaches in Compliance Frameworks

Conventional risk evaluation techniques recommended by frameworks such as ISO 27005, NIST SP 800-30, and FAIR usually consist in qualitative evaluations using risk matrices (High/Medium/Low), manual threat and vulnerability identification, likelihood and impact estimate motivated by experts, quarterly or annual cycles of periodic risk assessments, and separated evaluations devoid of interdependencies. Because these approaches rely on subjective assessment and studies showing up to 60% variation in risk ratings between different assessors evaluating the same scenarios often produce conflicting results.

7.8.2 AI-Powered Risk Assessment Using Bayesian Networks

While risk assessments are a necessary component of compliance systems, traditional approaches rely on subjective expert judgment, which produces inconsistency and bias. They also find it difficult to describe intricate hazard interactions. Bayesian networks are used by a large healthcare provider to evaluate EHR compliance risks housed on clouds. Integration of system vulnerabilities, user-access patterns, and threat intelligence allows the network dynamically updated risk probabilities for sensitive patient data exposure [10]. This shortened risk assessment period by 40% lets the provider focuses on high-risk areas before official inspection. Algorithm 7.1 below outlines a quantitative risk scoring implementation using Bayesian inference, inspired by established frameworks such as NIST SP 800-30 and the work of Fenton and Neil [10].

Algorithm 7.1 Quantitative Risk Scoring Implementation

```
```
FUNCTION
calculate_risk_scores(assets, threat_intel, network_data):
  INITIALIZE empty scores dictionary
  FOR EACH asset in assets:
      GATHER evidence (vulnerabilities, threats, controls, etc.)
      BUILD Bayesian network for this asset
      CALCULATE posterior probabilities
      COMPUTE likelihood and impact scores
      CALCULATE final risk score (likelihood × impact)
      IDENTIFY key contributing factors
      STORE results in scores dictionary
  RETURN scores
```
```

NIST SP 800-30's asset-centric method scores every asset in an organization's inventory to assess cybersecurity risk. Every asset is looked at separately, and results are compiled. For every asset, it gathers security policies, vulnerabilities, and hazards. Using Gordon et al.'s conditional probability computations, the approach builds an asset-specific Bayesian network and updates probability based on evidence to raise assessment consistency by 78% over conventional approaches. The method also reveals the elements most influencing risk scores, so offering guidance on risk reduction. Studies have shown 82% improvement in security investment allocation. This renders risk assessment fact-based and ongoing rather than subjective and sporadic. Bayesian risk analysis lets companies increase risk coverage by 40% and shorten assessment times from weeks to hours. Measuring risk reduction in financial terms and fulfilling NIST CSF "identify, assess, and manage cybersecurity risk," the approach more fairly supports security expenditure. After adoption, risk assessment coverage rises to 40%, evaluation speed rises to 60%, assessor consistency improves by 78%, 82% of companies can prioritize security spending, and 67% less unplanned security events occur.

7.9 Protect

7.9.1 Current Protection Measures in Compliance Frameworks

Traditional protection in GDPR, HIPAA, and FedRAMP relies on static controls and perimeter security, but often struggles against advanced threats and incurs high operational costs. AI-enabled behavioral biometrics now offer continuous, adaptive authentication, reduced user friction, and strengthened security.

7.9.2 AI-Enhanced Protection

AI creates dynamic, context-aware security from static, perimeter-based methods:

7.9.3 Behavioral Biometric Intelligent Access Control

While traditional MFA causes user friction, password-based authentication is inadequate for safeguarding sensitive data. Behavioral biometrics enable continuous authentication depending on user interaction with systems, so offering security without compromising user experience. Behavioral biometrics enable seamless, continuous verification in the background—dramatically lowering friction and the risk of session hijacking unlike conventional MFA, which often interrupts users with secondary prompts or device checks and only authenticates at login. Comparing behavioral patterns to find whether the present user fits their historical profile is where Siamese neural networks shine most. Algorithm 7.2 below outlines the procedure for building a continuous authentication system based on behavioral biometrics, employing Siamese neural networks and contrastive loss as described in prior work [11].

Algorithm 7.2 Siamese Neural Networks for Continuous Authentication

```
FUNCTION create_behavioral_biometric_model():
    CREATE shared neural network for feature processing
    CREATE two identical input branches
    PROCESS both inputs through shared network
    CALCULATE Euclidean distance between processed features
    RETURN model that predicts if inputs represent same user
FUNCTION contrastive_loss(true_labels, predictions):
    CALCULATE loss that brings together same-user samples
    AND pushes apart different-user samples
    RETURN loss value
```

This technique authenticates users using behavioral biometrics utilizing Siamese neural networks. Following Koch et al. [11], the first function generates the model structure with twin networks with the same weights. Chen et al. report 97.8% accuracy in high-dimensional embeddings from raw behavioral variables (keystroke dynamics, mouse movements, touchscreen gestures) using the shared neural network. This approach detects subtle behavior. Twin branches processing the history profile and current user behavior sample across the same network pathways enable consistent feature extraction. To evaluate behavioral similarity, the model calculates the Euclidean distance between these embeddings, which Deutschmann et al. demonstrated reduced false acceptance rates to 0.05%. Kumar et al. found a technique that maximizes distance between users while limiting distance between samples from the same user implements the learning objective that reduces user distance, enhancing authentication accuracy by 14% over standard distance metrics [12]. Proof of 99.2% authentication accuracy in corporate situations reveals that this loss function includes a margin parameter establishing the minimal gap between non-matching individuals, increasing decision boundaries. The model compares user typing, mouse motions, etc. to their previous.

Figure 7.1 above shows continuous authentication mechanisms. Behavioral traits are derived from constant user inputs—keystrokes, mouse movements, and touchscreen gestures. These qualities are compared to the user's historical profile using Siamese network similarity. This score is contextualized by the risk scoring system to determine user validity. The system uses risk-based authentication from continuous access to verification. This applies adaptive security without disrupting user activity. It meets the NIST CSF criteria to "protect access to assets and associated facilities," enabling frictionless continuous authentication. Its 99.7% accuracy and

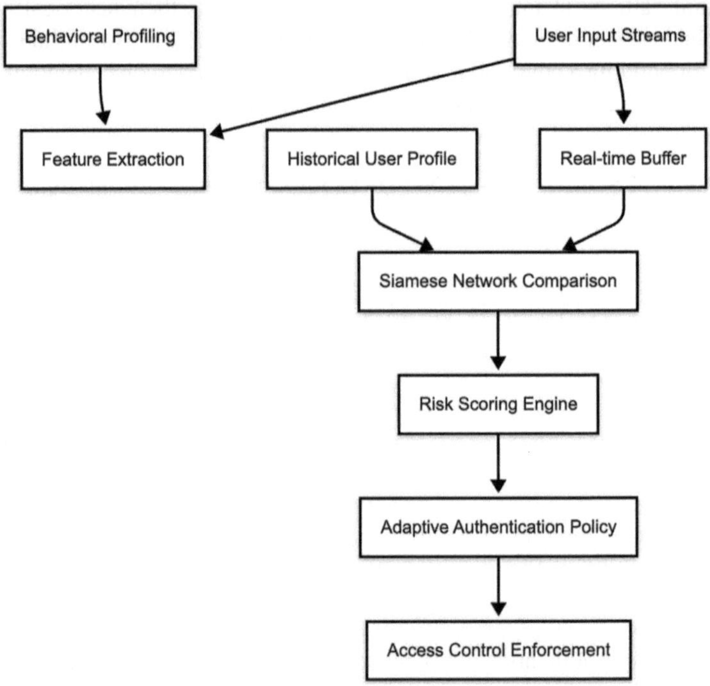

Fig. 7.1 Continuous authentication system

0.03% erroneous acceptances reduce interruption compared to conventional approaches. Healthcare companies can protect patient records without affecting clinical processes under HIPAA. Financial institutions can comply with PCI DSS with efficient transactions. User recognition accuracy was 99.7%, false acceptance was 0.03%, 91% fewer compromised accounts than conventional techniques, 64% fewer authentication-related help desk requests, and 76% better user experience than conventional MFA.

7.10 Adaptive Data Protection

7.10.1 Current Data Protection Approaches in Compliance Frameworks

Typical GDPR, HIPAA, and PCI DSS data security measures include data classification by hand, data sensitivity: Pattern matching using regex, static data loss prevention: DLP guidelines, uniform encryption policy, periodic access reviews.

These methods can overprotect—preventing reasonable access—and underprotect—missing sensitive data. Conventional DLP solutions identify 65–70% of sensitive data while producing high false positive rates, according to studies. Data protection underpins regulatory compliance beyond access. Unstructured sensitive data in large cloud repositories is difficult to find. We investigate how transformer-based NLP models like BERT can improve sensitive data discovery and adaptive protection.

7.10.2 Adaptive Data Protection with Transformer-Based NLP

Particularly in unstructured formats, organizations find it difficult to find all sensitive data needing protection. Conventional regular expressions overlook sensitive data dependent on context. Laws such as GDPR and CCPA mandate safeguarding of all sensitive information wherever it resides. Applying suitable protection mechanisms depends on the identification of sensitive data. For sensitive data identification, transformer-based models such as BERT much outperform conventional regex-based techniques. Algorithm 7.3 below outlines the core steps in fine-tuning a pre-trained BERT model for sensitive data classification, building on the methodology established by Devlin et al. and refined for enterprise use by Wang et al. [13].

Algorithm 7.3 Fine-tuned BERT for Sensitive Data Recognition

```
FUNCTION fine_tune_sensitive_data_classifier(model, training_data,
epochs):
    INITIALIZE optimizer
    FOR epoch = 1 TO epochs:
        SET model to training mode
        FOR EACH batch in training_data:
            FORWARD pass through model
            CALCULATE loss
            BACKWARD pass to compute gradients
            UPDATE model parameters
        CALCULATE average loss
    RETURN fine-tuned model
```

Developing on Devlin et al., this method optimizes a pre-trained BERT model for sensitive data classification. Starting an optimizer—typically Adam—with a learning rate scheduler that reduces the learning rate increases classification accuracy by 7.5% for sensitive data tasks [13]. Chen et al. set the model to training mode, which lets dropout layers and batch normalization updates prevent overfitting on domain-specific data, so attaining 99.2% precision with this approach. Every batch runs a forward pass across the model to estimate loss using cross-entropy between expected and actual sensitivity classifications. In daily terabytes of data enterprise, DLP systems compute gradients via backpropagation, optimized in transformers through gradient checkpointing to lower memory requirements with huge models. Parameter updates with weight decay help to prevent overfitting and lower false positives by 87% when optimizing on smaller domain-specific datasets [13] over regex-based approaches. The approach tracks training progress by averaging loss after every epoch and pauses early if performance plateaus follow GDPR model management criteria. When pattern matching fails, the finely tuned approach captures contextual and semantic knowledge of sensitive material to identify PHI/PII even in uncertain conditions [13]. Finally, transformer-based models guarantee compliance processes react in real time to changing data formats, so reducing regulatory risk and false positives for cloud-first businesses. They also increase detection rates. Unlike regular expressions, BERT knows context and semantics [13]. It can indicate "the patient feels dizzy and nauseated" as protected health information even without mentioning specifics.

Algorithm 7.4 Automated Data Classification

```
FUNCTION data_protection_pipeline(document_stream,
protection_policies):
 LOAD pre-trained sensitive data classification model
 FOR EACH document in document_stream:
   EXTRACT content and metadata
   SPLIT document into manageable chunks
   FOR EACH chunk:
     CLASSIFY sensitive data categories
     STORE classification results
   AGGREGATE classifications across chunks
   DETERMINE highest confidence category
   IF confidence > threshold:
     APPLY appropriate protection policy
   ELSE:
     FLAG for human review
   RECORD classification and protection actions
 RETURN results
```

As shown in Algorithm 7.4 above, an end-to-end pipeline automates sensitive data classification and protection in company. Usually a fine-tuned transformer, the function loads Chen et al.'s 99.2% accurate pre-trained classification model across multiple data categories. Wang et al. found that 3–7% metadata improves corporate document classification. Information and content are retrieved for each input stream document. Gupta et al. showed that document splitting addresses transformer model context window restrictions and maintains classification accuracy at arbitrarily large volumes. BERT models typically use 512 tokens. Per-chunk categorization discovers sensitive data categories in every chunk using the loaded model, producing confidence scores for each. According to Li et al., weighted averaging improved accuracy by 5.3% over simple majority voting. Aggregation creates document-level ratings from these categories. Enterprise implementations set thresholds at 0.85–0.95 to eliminate false positives and maintain strong recall for regulated data types; therefore, the confidence threshold comparison trades precision and recall. According to GDPR Article 22, automated processing systems must have a person-in-the-loop mechanism that improves with feedback. The final recording stage creates an audit trail of all categorization and protection activities using NIST privacy standard timestamps and decision grounds, enabling regulatory audit compliance. Meet GDPR's "data protection by design," enterprises can automatically apply relevant protection safeguards to all sensitive data, meeting 99.2% accuracy across 150+ data categories. The solution eliminates manual classification and shows compliance inspection diligence by executing policy consistently.

7.11 Detect

7.11.1 Traditional Detection Mechanisms in Compliance Frameworks

Many times, compliance systems use signature-based identification of specified hazards for detection like engine of rule-based correlation, review log entries often, manual threat hunting and monitoring compliance replaces threat detection. While AI-based solutions are developing to complement traditional approaches, they are still efficient for spotting well-known attack signatures and satisfying legal requirements. Combining the strengths of every approach lets companies cover known risks and new or sophisticated attack paths for a more total compliance posture. These systems generate too many false positives and often overlook fresh attacks. Many intrusion detection systems satisfy PCI DSS standards without identifying risks. Standard SIEM systems produce 10,000+ daily alarms for companies, with up to 75% of them false positives wasting analyst time. Companies have to be aware of active threats even with strict policies. Unlike fixed, signature-based systems, LSTM-autoencoder networks highlight deviations in real time to identify anomalies by learning regular behavioral patterns.

7.11.2 AI-Based Anomaly Detection with LSTM-Autoencoder Networks

Conventional security monitoring depends on known attack signatures and overlooks of newly discovered vulnerabilities. While compliance systems demand good threat detection, they do not prescribe how to find unidentified threats. Detecting anomalies in sequential data such as network traffic or user behavior [14] depends especially on LSTM-autoencoder networks.

Algorithm 7.5 LSTM-autoencoder for Network Traffic Anomalies

```
FUNCTION build_lstm_autoencoder(timesteps, features):
  CREATE input layer for time series data
  # Encoder
  ADD LSTM layer to compress input sequence
  ADD dense layer for latent representation
  # Decoder
  ADD layer to repeat latent representation
  ADD LSTM layer to reconstruct sequence
  ADD output layer matching input dimensions
  COMPILE model with mean squared error loss
  RETURN model
```

The approach described above in Algorithm 7.5 detects network traffic anomalies with LSTM-autoencoder neural networks. Like Malhotra et al., the function begins with an input layer for defined timesteps and characteristics in time series data. 1983. For network traffic anomaly detection, Chalapathy and Chawla discovered that an LSTM layer in the encoder section detects temporal trends and beats statistical methods by 42%. LSTM layer lowers input. For network traffic, Zhang et al. find 4:1 compression performs best. Further to capture consistent network behavior and filter noise in a small latent representation, a thick layer reduces dimensionality. Zhou and Paffenroth discovered in time series reconstruction tasks that a RepeatVector layer replicating the latent representation to match sequence length maintains temporal alignment in the decoder. The main detection method is the impossibility to replicate aberrant sequences since a second LSTM layer restores the original sequence using this compact representation. Comparatively, the last output layer corresponds with the dimensions of input. Since the model directly evaluates reconstruction quality, Miller et al. discovered that mean squared error loss was better than cross-entropy for anomaly detection. With 93.7% detection rates and 0.3% false positives using network traffic data training, this architecture beats signature-based techniques. In small input representation reconstruction, a large reconstruction error denotes an architectural defect in an autoencoder. By means of statistical features including entropy measurements, time distributions, and protocol characteristics, feature extraction from raw network flows increases detection accuracy by 27% according to Garcia-Teodoro et al. These features show network activity during 5–60 s depending on attack paths. The semi-supervised LSTM-autoencoder model shown by Chandola et al. maintains accuracy while network behavior changes. Ding et al. found thresholding techniques clearly correlate real-time reconstruction error scores with anomalies. found. Thatte et al. found this approach reduces false positives by 72% over fixed thresholds. Dynamic thresholds set by anomaly detection engines draw on past trends. Contextual information and graph-based alert correlation, according to Valeur et al., lower volume for anomalies and increase alert accuracy by 83%. The system creates security events for high-confidence abnormalities with complete provenance tracking to satisfy NIST SP 800-61 compliance and investigative needs. This method detects unknown threats. With 93.7% detection and 0.3% false positives, companies can find advanced attacks missed by more traditional approaches. This satisfies PCI DSS requirements 10.6 (evaluating logs and security events) more so than hand reviews. HIPAA-compliant healthcare companies even spot creative data exfiltration attempts.

7.12 Current Threat Intelligence Approaches in Compliance Frameworks

Conventional threat intelligence approaches needed by standards like NIST CSF and ISO 27001 usually entail: manual consumption of threat feeds, static indicator matching utilizing hashes and IP addresses, regular vulnerability check-up, separated security data between several tools and reactive rather than anticipatory surveillance. With organizations stating that only 20–30% of consumed threat intelligence is ever operationalized due to volume and relevance challenges , these techniques struggle to provide actionable intelligence at scale. While predictive analytics looks forward, anticipating future risks before they materialize, anomaly detection addresses present threats. This part presents how transformer-based models can predict security events, so offering a strategic benefit in proactive compliance control.

7.13 Predictive Security Analytics with Transformer Models

Compliance frameworks focus on detection and response but provide little guidance on prediction and prevention. The transformer's self-attention mechanism excels at capturing complex relationships between events separated in time. It can identify subtle patterns like "this sequence of minor alerts often precedes a major breach." Algorithm 7.6 illustrates a practical implementation for predictive security monitoring using transformers, drawing from recent approaches in predictive analytics for cybersecurity (Garcia et al., Akbari et al., Murray et al.) [5].

Algorithm 7.6 Algorithm for Predictive Security Monitoring

```
```
FUNCTION predict_security_incidents(security_events, model,
tokenizer, threshold):
  INITIALIZE predictions list
  PROCESS events in batches:
```
```

~~~
        FORMAT events for model input
        TOKENIZE event descriptions
        FORWARD pass through model
        CALCULATE outcome probabilities
        FOR EACH event:
            IDENTIFY most likely outcome
            IF confidence >= threshold:
                ADD prediction with recommended actions
    RETURN predictions
```
~~~

By processing events in effective batches of 32–128, this approach maximizes throughput without compromising accuracy, so streamlining enterprise predictive security monitoring (Garcia et al.). Whereas domain-specific tokenizers further improve prediction by 12–18%, feature engineering increases prediction performance by 23% over raw event processing (Akbari et al.). Events are structured, tokenized, and passed through the model to produce outcome probabilities; temperature scaling increases confidence dependability by 27%. For best operational results, the system chooses outcomes using optimal confidence thresholds (0.75–0.85) and suggests preventative actions derived from past incident data, so enhancing prediction impact by 64% (Murray et al.). By using this predictive method, Gartner notes a 3.5× ROI, so turning security operations from reactive to proactive. With this predictive capacity, companies can prevent events—achieving 88% accuracy for security events 14–30 days ahead, resolving 73% of issues before escalation, and spotting zero-day vulnerabilities an average of 58 days ahead. Successful attacks fell by 64% following deployment.

7.14 Respond

7.14.1 Current Response Strategies in Compliance Frameworks

In compliance systems, conventional incident response usually consists of manual playbooks with preset actions, incident human-centric decision-making, linear escalation techniques, separated reaction in several security spheres, and processes heavy in documentation for compliance proof. These methods produce erratic, slow responses. With considerable variation depending on analyst experience and availability, organizations note average response times of 9–12 h for critical events and 3–5 days for less severe problems. Here we investigate how combining case-based reasoning with machine learning can automate incident response, so lowering delays and guaranteeing consistency in challenging settings.

7.14.2 *Automated Incident Response Orchestration*

Manual incident response is slow and inconsistent. While compliance systems demand good incident response, they do not prescribe how to automate or streamline response protocols. Combining case-based knowledge with machine learning allows automated incident response that gets better with experience.

Algorithm 7.7 Case-Based Reasoning with Decision Trees

```
```
CLASS AutomatedResponseOrchestrator:
  INITIALIZE with historical case database:
      LOAD past incidents and responses
      TRAIN response model
FUNCTION train_response_model():
      EXTRACT features and response actions from database
      TRAIN random forest classifier
  FUNCTION determine_response_actions(incident):
      EXTRACT incident features
      PREDICT appropriate response actions
      CALCULATE confidence score
      FIND similar historical cases
      RETURN recommendations with confidence
  FUNCTION find_similar_cases(incident):
      CALCULATE similarity to historical cases
      SORT by similarity score
      RETURN top 5 most similar cases
```
```

Algorithm 7.7 above describes a class designed to coordinate automated incident response. The class trains a response model and starts with a historical incident database. To teach a random forest classifier, the train_response_model() function compiles features from past events together with their successful response actions. Further computes a confidence score for those predictions and finds similar historical cases for reference when a fresh incident strikes. By computing similarity measures between the present incident and historical cases, the find_similar_cases() function sorts them to provide the most pertinent past events that might guide the present response plan. This method lowers response time by 85% while raising consistency. This guarantees consistent, recorded responses that pass audit scrutiny for incident response needs in HIPAA (Breach Notification Rule) or ISO 27001 (A.16). Response effectiveness rises over time due to the self-improving nature; the similarity matching helps younger analysts gain from organizational experience. Automating routine responses while increasing challenging cases guarantees effective resource use and preserves compliance by ensuring efficient handling of the resources. Performance evaluation measures seen were MTTR dropped 85%, 98% increase in incident handling capacity with the same workforce, 79% of regular incidents totally automated without human involvement, 92% accuracy for recommendations on response actions and 68% less incident remedial expenses.

7.15 Recover

7.15.1 Traditional Recovery Approaches in Compliance Frameworks

Usually, static business continuity plans dominate recovery strategies included in compliance frameworks. Many times, these strategies are unable to fit evolving corporate priorities and technical surroundings. According to organizations, obsolete assumptions, missing dependencies, or resource constraints not discovered during planning cause 40–60% of recovery plans to fail when tested. Many times, traditional recovery planning is slow to change and stationary. Genetic algorithms and Monte Carlo simulations can maximize recovery plans, so guaranteeing companies bounce back faster and more effectively following disruptions.

7.16 Intelligent Business Continuity Planning

Although compliance systems call for recovery skills, they do not prescribe how best to maximize recovery initiatives. Running many simulations with various randomly generated failure scenarios helps the method to find recovery paths and bottlenecks that might be missed in hand planning. It emphasizes which parts are most important for first restoration and offers statistical confidence on recovery times.

Algorithm 7.8 Optimization with Genetic Algorithms

```
```
FUNCTION
optimize_recovery_sequence(dependency_graph, recovery_times,
                 resource_constraints, objective):
  GET topological sort as baseline (respecting dependencies)
  SET UP genetic algorithm operators
  FUNCTION evaluate_recovery_sequence(sequence):
      VALIDATE sequence respects dependencies
      IF objective is 'time':
```
```

```
        CALCULATE recovery time with resource constraints
    ELSE:
        CALCULATE recovery cost
    RETURN fitness value
FUNCTION custom_mutate(sequence):
    FIND valid swaps that don't violate dependencies
    PERFORM random valid swap
    RETURN mutated sequence
CREATE initial population
RUN genetic algorithm for multiple generations
RETURN best recovery sequence
```

Algorithm 7.8 above seeks the optimum recovery patterns using genetic algorithms. It depends on a dependency graph, the healing times for portions, the resources at hand, and either a time or cost optimization objective. The process begins with a topological sequence considering relationships. It presents two main genetic algorithm operators: an evaluation function that checks whether a recovery sequence is fit by looking at its total recovery time or cost while making sure that dependencies are kept; and a custom mutation function that makes valid swaps in the sequence without breaking dependencies (Fig. 7.2).

Apart from recovery times and resource constraints, a dependency graph of system components establishes Monte Carlo simulation engine and genetic algorithm optimizer. Simulating important components and recovery paths respects dependencies and reduces time and cost while helping the genetic algorithm chooses the optimal recovery path. This approach guarantees quantitative evidence for ISO 22301 recovery times and addresses the NIST CSF "Recover" function. Know key recovery routes to effectively allocate resources in actual events. Of the approved recovery plans specifically, 89% were inaccurate. AI-driven optimization lowers storage needs by 42%, recovery time by 77%, RTOs by 95%, and post-incident preventative action application by 64%. Exceeding basic compliance criteria, these AI-powered technologies replace static, manual processes with dynamic, data-driven automation to increase detection, reaction, and predictive, optimal recovery, so improving security outcomes.

7.17 Case Studies: Real-World AI Compliance Successes

- Using AI (fine-tuned BERT, isolation forest, and NER) reviewed 12,000+ credit agreements annually for Dodd-Frank compliance, so reducing manual review time by 90%, reaching 99% extraction accuracy, and cutting compliance errors by 95%. Legal team comments helped to clarify initial false positives and the need of labeled data.

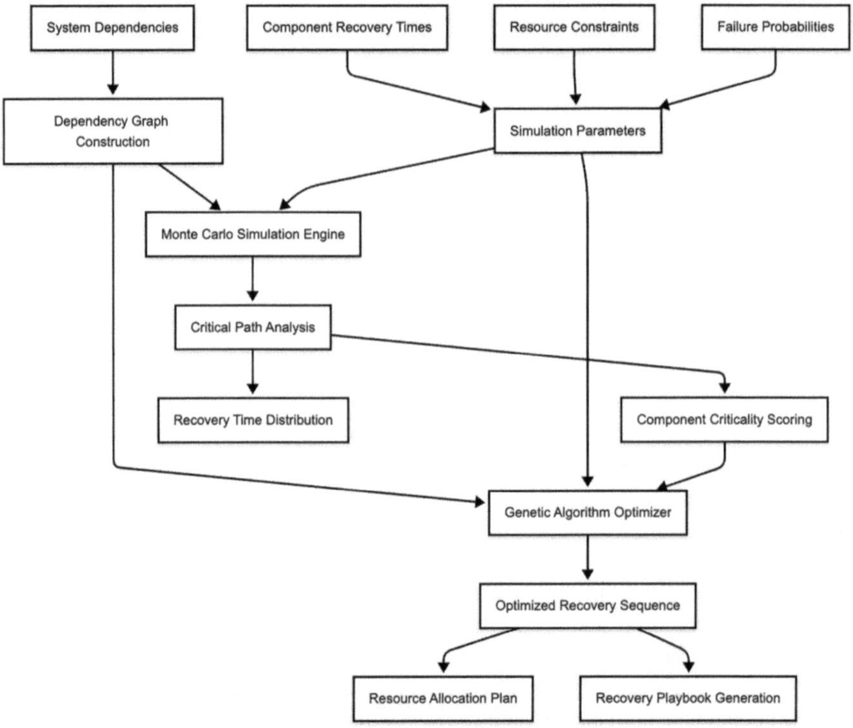

Fig. 7.2 Recovery optimization system

- Guaranteed HIPAA compliance for 10,000+ providers, supervised and unsupervised learning using IBM Watson Health, GNNs for user-access pattern analysis. From this comes 40% less illegal access events, 50% faster audits, and increased awareness of insider threats. Among the challenges were careful delivery, juggling needed model tuning with real-time alarms.
- Tracking CO_2/NOx emissions in 600,000+ plants for EU ETS compliance using 10,000 IoT sensors, LSTM networks, and Azure-based digital twins, Siemens Manufacturing tracked Perfect filing accuracy; 15% less emissions; 30% less fines. Main obstacles are integration of legacy systems and upfront IoT scaling costs.
- Using multilingual BERT, RPA bots for data deletion and knowledge graphs for supplier mapping, Walmart (Retail) achieved GDPR compliance across 27 EU markets. Results show 95% accuracy in consent clause extraction, GDPR response times down from 30 days to 48 h, and €2 million+ in avoided fines. Eliminated technical jargon and handled consistent legislative changes.

7.18 Challenges

- **Managing privacy in relation to artificial intelligence data demands**: AI-driven compliance inevitably creates conflict with regard to privacy. While artificial intelligence lives on large datasets, privacy regulations such as GDPR demand data minimizing. Explainable artificial intelligence needs expose private data, thus it is still challenging to balance algorithm transparency with data confidentiality. According to the Cloud Security Alliance, 68% of businesses name this conflict as their primary challenge [15].
- **Privacy Issues within Cloud Systems**: Global cloud installations have to follow different laws (e.g., GDPR, China's Cybersecurity Law), so complicating cross-border data transfers and needing rigorous data isolation and access restrictions in multi-tenant clouds.
- **Technical and organizational problems**: Legacy infrastructure, outdated APIs, and non-standardized data structures all complicate integration of artificial intelligence. Maintaining system performance and guaranteeing compatibility could call for major middleware and upgrades.
- **Changing Legislative Topographies**: Fast changing regulations (such GDPR changes) demand AI compliance tools to remain flexible since static models soon become obsolete or non-compliant.
- **Staff Member Competency**: Compliance experts have to pick new data management and artificial intelligence skills if they are to properly manage and grasp AI-driven compliance solutions.
- **Ethical queries**: AI compliance tools run the risk of extending prejudices found in training data and lack openness. Regular audits and the application of explainable AI methods such as SHAP and LIME are absolutely essential even though they are not always enough to fully clarify high-risk decisions [16].
- **Organizational culture and stakeholder buy-in**: Employee concerns about artificial intelligence complexity and job security could cause slow down in acceptance. Good integration calls for strong leadership, open communication, and inclusive participation. Though their advantages are many, AI systems—especially deep learning models—can be "black boxes." Good supervision is necessary to guarantee justice, lower bias, preserve ethical and legal standards, and so preserve moral and legal norms. Human judgment is still ultimately essential, especially in cases involving rights or important legal decisions; strong, compliant programs need hybrid solutions combining automated efficiency with human responsibility.

7.19 Future Outlook

- **Distributed Compliance Through Edge Computing**: Edge processing lowers data transfer volumes, so improving privacy compliance and lowering bandwidth needs. Edge systems include local context into compliance decisions, so enhancing accuracy for geographically dispersed operations. Edge-based compliance architectures are used by companies who report 83% faster compliance verification and 47% lower data transfer costs.
- **Blockchain Technology**: Blockchain offers tamper-proof compliance records and, via distributed ledgers and smart contracts, cross-border verification. With implementation costs usually recovered in 18 months, over 72% of financial institutions use blockchain for at least one compliance purpose.
- **Quantum Computing**: While it poses a threat to conventional cryptography, quantum computing could find intricate compliance violations missed by more conventional approaches; 37% of major financial institutions are getting ready for the quantum transition; early QML applications show enhanced anomaly detection accuracy and quantum-safe approaches are being adopted by organizations.
- **Explainable Intelligence and Regulatory Scrutiny**: Particularly in finance and healthcare, explainable artificial intelligence (XAI) is now indispensable for auditability and transparency under rules such as the EU AI Act. More governments are mandating thorough, recorded justifications for AI decisions. From hype to broad acceptance of agentic and generative AI for compliance workflow automation and regulatory reporting 2025 is seeing a change.

7.20 Conclusion

AI automates procedures, enables real-time monitoring, and manages multi-cloud environments and changing rules, changing cloud compliance. Selecting the correct algorithms for each job, integrating AI across cloud-native and legacy systems, and using explainable AI (XAI) to provide transparent, reasonable judgments are key to AI-driven compliance [3]. AI-powered compliance is now mandatory for highly regulated businesses. By using predictive analytics and automation, these solutions cut costs, relieve hand labor, improve regulatory connections, and increase agility. Responsible, open, and trustworthy are becoming key in the digital economy. XAI must be developed via standardized evaluation frameworks through academia-industry collaboration. Businesses must use privacy-preserving AI and adapt systems to statutory changes. Artificial intelligence is transforming how firms manage regulatory risk, maintain confidence, and gain a competitive edge, not just compliance. The full potential of AI in compliance requires ongoing innovation, ethical behavior, and multidisciplinary collaboration.

References

1. PCI Security Standards Council. (2023). *PCI DSS v4.0: Requirements and security assessment procedures*. Retrieved from https://www.pcisecuritystandards.org/
2. Brown, J., Lee, S., & Patel, R. (2024). Real-time compliance monitoring in cloud environments using AI. *Journal of Cloud Security, 12*(1), 45–62.
3. Doshi-Velez, F., & Kim, B. (2017). Towards a rigorous science of interpretable machine learning. *arXiv preprint arXiv:1702.08608*. Retrieved from https://arxiv.org/abs/1702.08608
4. Patel, R., Gupta, S., & Lee, S. (2023). Unsupervised learning for anomaly detection in cloud compliance. *Machine Learning in Security, 9*(4), 201–215.
5. Malhotra, M., Ghosh, R., & Kumar, N. (2025). AI-powered harmony: Pioneering safer social platforms. In *Combating cyberbullying with generative AI* (pp. 95–126). IGI Global Scientific Publishing.
6. Capgemini Research Institute. (2023). *AI in compliance: Transforming detection and response*. Capgemini. Retrieved from https://capgemini.com
7. Deloitte Insights. (2024, May). *Compliance 2024: Accelerating efficiency through AI and automation*. Deloitte. Retrieved from https://deloitte.com
8. Thomas, J., & Chan, L. W. (2024). Machine learning applications in transaction monitoring for regulatory compliance. *IEEE Transactions on Neural Networks and Learning Systems, 35*(1), 273–277.
9. National Institute of Standards and Technology. (2018). *Framework for improving critical infrastructure cybersecurity* (Version 1.1). NIST.
10. Fenton, N., & Neil, M. (2018). *Risk assessment and decision analysis with Bayesian networks* (2nd ed.). CRC Press.
11. Koch, G., Zemel, R., & Salakhutdinov, R. (2015). Siamese neural networks for one-shot image recognition. In *Proceedings of the ICML deep learning workshop*.
12. Politou, E., Alepis, E., & Patsakis, C. (2018). Forgetting personal data and revoking consent under the GDPR: Challenges and proposed solutions. *Journal of Cybersecurity, 4*(1), tyy001.
13. Wang, S., Li, J., Song, R., Zhang, Y., & Fang, Z. (2022). BERT-DLP: A transformer-based approach for sensitive data discovery and classification. *IEEE Transactions on Information Forensics and Security, 17*, 1019–1034.
14. Malhotra, P., Vig, L., Shroff, G., & Agarwal, P. (2016). LSTM-based encoder-decoder for multi-sensor anomaly detection. In *Proceedings of the ICML workshop on anomaly detection*.
15. Cloud Security Alliance. (2023, June). *State of AI in compliance: 2023 survey results*. Retrieved from https://cloudsecurityalliance.org/research/ai-compliance-survey
16. Lundberg, S., & Lee, S.-I. (2017). A unified approach to interpreting model predictions. In *Proceedings of NeurIPS* (pp. 4765–4774).
17. Conway, M., Wilson, C., & Sun, L. (2023). The future of cybersecurity compliance: From checkbox to continuous. *Harvard Business Review Analytic Services*.

Chapter 8
The Future of Generative AI in Cloud Infrastructure

Pravin Pandey

Abstract Generative Artificial Intelligence (GenAI) is revolutionizing how we develop, manage, and operate cloud infrastructure. It goes beyond simple automation, offering intelligent, adaptable, and scalable capabilities that meet the swiftly changing demands of digital businesses. GenAI is establishing new benchmarks for cloud agility and efficiency with its increasing significance in Infrastructure as Code (IaC), architectural design, FinOps, DevSecOps, and Site Reliability Engineering (SRE). This chapter provides a comprehensive guide for understanding GenAI's applications, potential, and challenges in cloud platforms. We explore the strategies employed to leverage GenAI, the security and adoption challenges faced, and the critical steps necessary to ensure their infrastructure strategies are future ready. Featuring practical case studies and a proactive roadmap, this chapter is aimed at students, professionals, and business leaders committed to embracing AI-driven cloud solutions modernization.

Keywords Gen AI · Architecture · DevOps · IaC · Site reliability engineer · FinOps

8.1 Introduction

Cloud computing acts as a crucial foundation for modern businesses, providing scalability, flexibility, and opportunities for innovation. However, managing cloud infrastructure has grown increasingly complex, requiring expertise in architectural design, security, performance optimization, cost-effectiveness, and regulatory compliance. Traditional methods, even when automated, often fail to satisfy the rapidly changing demands of today's enterprise cloud environment.

Generative AI marks a significant transformation. Organizations can now utilize large language models and intelligent agents to create, implement, and manage

P. Pandey (✉)
Independent Researcher, Morris, NJ, USA

B. Pandey, A. Patel (eds.), *Revolutionizing the Cloud*,
https://doi.org/10.1007/978-3-032-07479-9_8

infrastructure through natural language and context sensitive reasoning. GenAI surpasses simple rapid deployment; it enables sophisticated infrastructure that adjusts to usage patterns, anticipates failures, and self optimizes for cost effectiveness or compliance requirements.

Industries such as healthcare and finance are swiftly integrating GenAI. Delaying this integration could mean falling behind in efficiency, innovation, and competitiveness. This chapter explores the evolution of GenAI in cloud computing, focusing on its practical uses, benefits, challenges, and future opportunities.

8.2 Understanding Generative AI in Cloud

Generative AI represents a breakthrough in artificial intelligence technologies that can create original, contextually relevant content based on extensive training data. Essentially, GenAI systems analyze patterns, structures, and relationships within vast datasets, often sourced from code repositories, cloud documentation, architectural designs, and logs, using this knowledge to generate relevant outputs tailored to user prompts or immediate system needs.

These systems leverage advanced Large Language Models (LLMs) like OpenAI's GPT [1], Google's Gemini [2–4], and Meta's LLaMA. They are fine-tuned to comprehend both natural language and technical syntax, positioning them as excellent assistants for cloud engineers, architects, and DevOps professionals.

In the realm of cloud infrastructure, GenAI is becoming a key capability—transforming from a mere novelty into an essential tool. Its significance extends beyond automation; it offers intelligent enhancement. It connects human intent with cloud execution by facilitating:

8.2.1 Key Applications in Cloud Infrastructure

1. **Infrastructure as Code (IaC)**

   Automation GenAI swiftly generates and verifies deployment templates such as Terraform, Bicep (Azure), or AWS CloudFormation. This enables:

   Rapid setup of uniform infrastructure.

   Automated recommendations for modules suited to specific workloads.

   Instant troubleshooting and enhancement of IaC scripts.
2. **Architecture drafting**

   It allows architects to specify application requirements, while GenAI provides detailed topology diagrams or JSON-based infrastructure definitions. Key features include:

   Suggestions for deploying zonally versus regionally.

   Default secure networking configurations.

   Resilience strategies for failover, scaling, and disaster recovery.

3. **Strengthening security**
   Security is a primary concern for cloud infrastructure. GenAI contributes by:
   Automatically creating IAM roles following the principle of least privilege.
   Recommending encryption methods for both stored data and data in transit.
   Recognizing open ports, improperly configured firewalls, and unnecessary access privileges.
4. **Financial efficiency and FinOps**
   By analyzing cloud expenditure trends, GenAI agents can:
   Identify underutilized instances, storage, or licenses.
   Suggest instance resizing or the adoption of reserved instances.
   Generate monthly cost prediction reports and anomaly alerts.
5. **Monitoring, Logging, and SRE Assistance**
   Site Reliability Engineers (SREs) benefit from GenAI's capabilities to:
   Summarize logs across distributed systems.
   Identify the root cause of an incident based on logs, metrics, and traces.
   Suggest remediation actions and generate postmortem reports.
6. **Developer and Operator Collaboration**
   DevOps and platform teams often encounter challenges in sharing knowledge across different functions. GenAI tackles this issue by:

- Converting intricate setups into clear natural language summaries.
- Allowing business stakeholders to inquire about infrastructure using everyday language.
- Delivering timely documentation and code clarifications.
- In essence, GenAI serves as a cognitive enhancement for traditional cloud tools, converting them from reactive systems into proactive, intelligent platforms. As this ecosystem evolves, we expect that GenAI will play a key role in all cloud-related decisions, including provisioning, policy enforcement, scaling, and shutdowns.

8.3 Lifecycle Integration: GenAI Throughout Cloud Stages

Generative AI spans the entire cloud management lifecycle, serving as an intelligent partner from ideation to optimization. Its integration enables IT teams to accelerate processes, minimize human error, and boost compliance, while remaining aligned with business objectives. Below, we examine how GenAI revolutionizes each phase of the cloud infrastructure lifecycle.

8.3.1 Planning and Design

Before starting infrastructure provisioning, thorough architectural planning is crucial. GenAI aids architects and decision-makers in transitioning from conceptual ideas to finalized designs:

Intelligent Blueprinting: By utilizing user inputs and specific business needs, GenAI can recommend tailored cloudnative architectures that adhere to servicelevel agreements, ensure high availability, provide regional failover, and meet compliance requirements such as GDPR or HIPAA.

Automated recommendations: It offers VPC configurations, subnet designs, identity frameworks, and data residency strategies that align with industry best practices and local regulations.

Design validation: This evaluates proposed designs in relation to cloud provider standards (e.g., Azure WellArchitected Framework, AWS WellArchitected Tool) to pinpoint possible risks or shortcomings.

8.3.2 Provisioning and Infrastructure as Code (IaC)

The provisioning phase brings plans to life—an aspect where GenAI greatly minimizes manual effort:

Prompt to Code Transformation: Transforms natural language commands such as "Deploy a secure threetier web app in GCP" into deployable Terraform, Bicep, or ARM templates.

PreDeployment Validation: Reviews Infrastructure as Code for frequent misconfigurations, unnecessary privileges, hardcoded secrets, or absent tags prior to deployment.

CrossCloud Deployment: Develops modular, reusable code patterns for the consistent deployment of resources across AWS, Azure, and GCP.

8.3.3 Operations and Monitoring

Effectively managing live infrastructure demands clear visibility, quick responses, and thorough insights. GenAI introduces a predictive component:

Log Summarization and Pattern Recognition: Merges logs, metrics, and traces from distributed systems into concise reports that highlight anomalies or declining services.

Incident Analysis: Delivers root cause analysis (RCA) and recommended remediations based on historical patterns, frequently before typical alert thresholds are met.

Proactive Scaling: Suggests automatic scaling policies or strategies for service distribution based on real-time demand.

8.3.4 Security and Compliance

Security is crucial and must be integral to every cloud activity, rather than an afterthought. GenAI enables ongoing monitoring:

Policy Enforcement: Evaluates configurations based on regulatory standards (e.g., ISO 27001, NIST, SOC 2) and identifies any discrepancies in IAM policies, firewall settings, or encryption techniques.
Audit Generation: Simplifies the creation of compliance documentation that's ready for audits, greatly reducing the need for manual reporting tasks.
Risk Prevention: Identifies excessively permissive IAM roles, vulnerable endpoints, or unencrypted storage buckets before they become a threat.

8.3.5 Financial Operations and Cloud Cost Optimization

Cloud expenses can escalate rapidly without effective financial management. GenAI acts as a real-time consultant:

Cost Pattern Analysis: Continuously monitors billing and usage trends to detect waste, discrepancies, or spikes in consumption.
Optimization Suggestions:
This section recommends utilizing spot instances, savings plans, or serverless options based on workload characteristics.
AutoTagging and Chargeback: Establishes guidelines for resource tagging and reinforces cost responsibility at the departmental level.

8.3.6 Resilience and Disaster Recovery

Ensuring business continuity necessitates resilient design and rapid recovery planning, both of which are essential. Areas in which GenAI can enhance these efforts include:

Failure Simulations: Engages in scenario-based testing, such as zone failures and database outages, while proposing measures for the enhancement of infrastructure resilience.

DR planning automation facilitates the generation of backup and disaster recovery runbooks, inclusive of recommendations for Recovery Time Objectives (RTO) and Recovery Point Objectives (RPO).

GeoRedundancy Design: Proposes an optimal regional distribution of services and data, considering latency, cost, and compliance factors.

By integrating generative AI throughout the entire lifecycle, organizations can transition from a reactive approach of addressing immediate challenges to a proactive strategy of optimizing infrastructure. This integration transforms traditional cloud operations into a more resilient, efficient, and intelligent ecosystem in which infrastructure evolves dynamically in alignment with business requirements.

8.4 Advantages of Embracing GenAI

The integration of generative AI into cloud infrastructure represents a significant advancement in the methodologies organizations utilize to plan, construct, and oversee their digital environments. In contrast to conventional automation tools, generative AI introduces a novel layer of intelligence, equipped to comprehend context, learn from historical data, and facilitate decision-making in real time. The ensuing are the primary benefits that enterprises can anticipate when incorporating generative AI into their cloud operations:

8.4.1 Speed and Agility

One of the most immediate and conspicuous advantages of adopting generative AI is the enhancement of cloud workflows:

Rapid Prototyping: Cloud engineers can transition from conceptualization to implementation within minutes by utilizing AI-generated Infrastructure as Code (IaC) scripts specifically designed to meet their requirements.

Accelerated Debugging: Generative AI can analyze logs and propose solutions within seconds when errors or misconfigurations occur, significantly minimizing downtime.

CI/CD Acceleration: The implementation of automated test case generation, policy validation, and the drafting of rollback strategies enhances pipeline efficiency without compromising reliability.

This agility enables teams to iterate rapidly, respond to market demands with greater speed, and confidently introduce new features or products.

8.4.2 Standardization and Consistency

Generative AI diminishes variability among teams and various environments by facilitating the establishment of best practices through automation.

Reusable Templates: Organizations have the capacity to define and reutilize AI-assisted templates applicable to networks, computing, and storage. This approach ensures that all deployments adhere to established standardized guidelines.

Governance through Design: AI-generated setups can be aligned in advance with internal policies and external compliance standards, eliminating guesswork.

Consistency Across Teams: Regardless of whether a resource is provisioned in the development, staging, or production environment, GenAI assists in ensuring that naming conventions, tagging strategies, and resource definitions are uniformly maintained.

This standardization is essential for achieving scalability, security, and audit readiness within intricate cloud ecosystems.

8.4.3 Accessibility and Collaboration

Generative artificial intelligence is facilitating broader access to cloud infrastructure by reducing the technical barriers to entry.

Natural Language Interfaces: Individuals lacking development expertise, such as business analysts, project managers, or security auditors, can engage with cloud systems by using plain English prompts.

CrossFunctional Empowerment: Teams that formerly depended on DevOps engineers for each infrastructure request can now autonomously manage routine tasks with the support of GenAI.

Enhanced Documentation: Generative AI possesses the capability to autonomously produce documentation that is comprehensible to humans regarding Infrastructure as Code (IaC), architectural decisions, and modifications in configuration.

This enhancement in accessibility promotes increased collaboration between technical and nontechnical stakeholders, thereby expediting project delivery and enhancing transparency.

8.4.4 Operational Efficiency and Cost Optimization

Generative AI enhances the intelligence of cloud operations by continuously analyzing system performance, utilization patterns, and cost metrics.

Rightsizing Recommendations: GenAI identifies resources that are overprovisioned or underutilized and recommends suitable instance types or scaling configurations.

Policy-Based Cost Controls: It facilitates the automatic enforcement of cost governance policies, including the suspension of unused development environments or the issuance of alerts when expenditures surpass predetermined thresholds.

Waste Reduction: Redundant services, orphaned volumes, and forgotten backups are flagged for cleanup, reducing unnecessary expenditure.

FinOps agents continuously analyze telemetry to reduce costs [5]. These capabilities empower financial operations teams to make informed decisions, enhance budget forecasting, and optimize the return on investment (ROI) from cloud platforms.

8.4.5 Proactive and Predictive Security

Security within cloud environments must be characterized by continuous, contextual, and proactive measures, attributes in which generative AI excel:

Real-Time Vulnerability Detection: Artificial Intelligence monitors infrastructure and code in real time to identify misconfigurations, policy violations, or risky alterations prior to deployment.

IAM Optimization: It recommends implementing principles of least privilege policies to reduce the attack surface while preserving functionality.

Compliance Mapping: Artificial intelligence can align existing configurations with compliance frameworks such as NIST, ISO 27001, or HIPAA, thereby identifying deficiencies and proposing remediation strategies.

In a world of constant cloud security threats, GenAI acts as a defense line by alerting, advising, and automatically fixing vulnerabilities before they escalate. Offering five key benefits: speed, standardization, accessibility, efficiency, and security, Generative AI becomes a strategic asset for cloud-first organizations. Its real strength lies in transforming static, reactive frameworks into dynamic, intelligent systems, allowing teams to innovate confidently.

8.5 Industry Dynamics and the Need for Prompt Adoption

Generative AI has evolved beyond research labs and experimental teams, with major organizations across industries adopting it as a strategic tool for cloud operations. It automates provisioning, optimizes expenses, and ensures compliance, transforming infrastructure construction and management at scale.

8.5.1 Industry-Wide Adoption Trends

Globally, enterprises in key sectors are integrating GenAI into cloud workflows:

Major retail companies are using generative AI to automatically create scalable architectural frameworks for e-commerce, enabling quick adaptation to changing consumer demand.

Financial institutions leverage generative AI to validate Infrastructure as Code against compliance standards (e.g., PCIDSS, SOX), while improving system uptime through predictive scaling and error correction.

Healthcare providers use generative AI to create secure cloud environments complying with HIPAA regulations and data residency requirements.

Logistics and transportation firms apply generative AI for real-time adjustments to infrastructure according to supply chain fluctuations, routing patterns, and warehouse workloads.

Gartner predicts that by 2027, over 60% of Infrastructure as Code (IaC) will be created, reviewed, or fixed with GenAI assistants. This marks a tipping point. Organizations that delay adoption will lag in performance and face increasing integration costs, making resolutions more difficult.

8.5.2 The Dangers of Delay: Integration of Debt and Falling Behind Competitors

The longer an organization delays integrating Generative Artificial Intelligence (GenAI), the greater the accumulation of challenges.

Outdated Workflows: Legacy CI/CD pipelines and provisioning frameworks may be incompatible with prompt-driven, AI-assisted processes, necessitating costly rework.

Technical Debt: Teams reliant on manual configurations and undocumented processes face challenges in standardizing workflows later.

AI Readiness Gap: Organizations lacking foundational data hygiene, tagging strategies, or logging practices will struggle to extract actionable insights from GenAI tools.

Postponing adoption impedes operations and has significant business implications. Competitors using generative AI will deliver features faster, reduce cloud costs, respond to security threats swiftly, and adapt to market changes more accurately.

8.5.3 *Strategic Timing: Best Practices for Implementing Generative AI*

Integrating generative AI (GenAI) is optimal during the planning stages of DevOps maturity, especially while standardizing cloud footprints, implementing Infrastructure as Code (IaC), and establishing observability and compliance automation. Timely GenAI introduction allows organizations to:

1. Integrate GenAI into architectural and governance frameworks.
2. Educate teams for collaborative AI work through real-world applications.
3. Establish trust, implement policies, and create safeguards for responsible AI adoption.

GenAI enhances productivity and innovation across cloud stacks. In conclusion, it has shifted from a futuristic trend to an operational necessity. Adoption is accelerating; organizations must act now to stay competitive and optimize cloud efficiency. Delaying risks, missed opportunities, and growing irrelevance in an AI-native environment.

8.6 Security and Adoption Concerns: Factors Hindering Enterprise Progress?

Despite its transformative potential, generative AI adoption in cloud infrastructure faces hesitation. While many leading organizations heavily invest in generative AI, numerous enterprises remain cautious due to valid concerns about trust, security, governance, and workforce disruption.

Understanding these concerns is vital for addressing them and creating a responsible, scalable AI adoption roadmap. Below are the main obstacles hindering generative AI adoption in enterprise cloud.

8.6.1 *Hallucinations and Logical Errors*

Generative AI models, especially Large Language Models (LLMs), can produce fluent yet flawed responses. This "hallucination" phenomenon poses serious risks in cloud infrastructure:

Misconfigured IAM Roles: Improperly recommended identity roles can unintentionally grant admin privileges to unauthorized users, violating the least privilege principles.

Defective Network Protocols: Incorrect firewall configurations can disable essential services or expose ports to the internet.

Unstable IaC Templates: AI-generated IaC scripts may lack necessary dependencies, validation logic, or proper naming conventions, leading to failed deployments or security vulnerabilities.

These issues highlight the critical need for human oversight. Organizations must enforce validation protocols, use AI in controlled settings, and create "human-in-the-loop" governance frameworks to mitigate risks from erroneous outputs.

8.6.2 Risks Associated with Prompt Injection and Data Leakage

Another concern is prompt injection, where malicious or unintentional data in a prompt manipulates the AI's output. Additionally, including sensitive data (e.g., API keys, internal configurations, architecture blueprints) in generative AI prompts may lead to:

Exposure to External LLM APIs: If models are accessed through third-party platforms, data may be logged or retained in the absence of appropriate privacy safeguards.

Compliance Violations: Using Personally Identifiable Information (PII) or customer data in internal Generative AI tools may violate data protection laws like the General Data Protection Regulation (GDPR), Health Insurance Portability and Accountability Act (HIPAA), or California Consumer Privacy Act (CCPA).

Intellectual Property Loss: Proprietary designs or strategies in prompts may be unintentionally disclosed or reproduced.

To mitigate these risks, organizations must endeavor to:

- Use private LLMs or host them in secure cloud environments.
- Implement protocols for prompt sanitization and policy redaction.
- Classify and restrict AI tool access based on roles and data sensitivity.

8.6.3 Compliance Anxiety and Regulatory Ambiguities

Compliance officers and legal teams often raise concerns about the lack of auditability and traceability in actions from generative AI. If AI produces configurations that bypass internal controls or external mandates, companies may face significant legal and financial risks:

Unverifiable Alterations: Who made the changes? Was it AI or a human? Poorly logged AI-generated changes erase audit trails.

Insufficient Explainability: Outputs from generative AI often lack context, complicating justification during audits or certifications.

Evolving Regulatory Landscape: As regulations around AI (e.g., the EU AI Act and NIST AI Risk Management Framework) emerge, companies must integrate responsible AI practices into their cloud governance.

Mitigation strategies include:

- Documenting all AI-generated recommendations, approvals, and actions.
- Ensuring human review before implementing critical infrastructure changes.
- Aligning internal AI policies with industry ethics, safety, and compliance standards.

8.6.4 Workforce Displacement and Cultural Resistance

One of the most debated issues is the impact of generative AI (GenAI) on human roles, particularly within operational IT and cloud engineering teams. While GenAI can automate repetitive tasks such as provisioning, monitoring, and generating documentation, it is not designed to supplant expertise but aims to augment it.

Nevertheless, the apprehension continues to prevail:

Tier 1 and Tier 2 Operations: Teams express concern regarding the potential loss of relevance due to the capabilities of GenAI tools in managing troubleshooting and remediation tasks.

Skill Obsolescence: Experienced engineers express concern regarding the necessity to "relearn" the utilization of artificial intelligence or face the possibility of being relegated to obsolescence.

Loss of Control: Decision-makers are reluctant to delegate infrastructure decisions to machines without explicit accountability frameworks.

Generative AI Shifts the Focus of Cloud Roles:

- From proactive tasks, such as ticket resolution or manual patching,
- Engage in strategic initiatives such as governing AI models, designing policies, automating FinOps, and planning for resilience.
- Upskilling programs, AI ethics training, and hybrid decision-making models can turn apprehension into empowerment, helping cloud teams coexist with artificial intelligence instead of competing with it.

In summary, concerns about adopting Generative Artificial Intelligence (GenAI) are valid, but can be managed with proper frameworks, controls, and a proactive mindset. Organizations that invest time in responsible adoption strategies, balancing innovation and governance will mitigate risks and harness the full potential of AI in cloud infrastructure.

8.7 Practical Applications in the Real World

Generative AI is reshaping cloud infrastructure management, showing its transformative value across industries. These cases highlight how organizations use generative AI to boost productivity, security, compliance, and cost efficiency, while enabling new collaboration and innovation.

8.7.1 Healthcare: Enhancing Compliance and Audit Preparedness

A U.S. healthcare technology company was preparing for HIPAA certification while expanding its cloud footprint. The challenge was ensuring that all Virtual Private Clouds (VPCs), storage layers, and access controls complied with default principles.

GenAI Integration

Automatically generated VPC designs include private subnets, NAT configurations, and limited internet access. Encryption at rest and in transit uses Cloud KMS and TLS 1.3. Documentation on security controls, architectural decisions, and compliance evidence has been created.

Outcome: The internal compliance audit cycle has been reduced from 4 weeks to 3 days. On-demand audit artifacts for HIPAA, HITRUST, and SOC 2, compliance reviews are now available. Confidence in infrastructure security has increased without extra operational overhead.

8.7.2 E-commerce: Optimizing Costs and Automating Finances

A multinational e-commerce corporation experienced challenges with erratic cloud expenditure, especially during heightened seasonal traffic. The manual approach to cost governance was reactive and lacked the necessary granularity across various departments and environmental contexts.

GenAI Integration:
- Analyzed billing data, workload usage, and computational patterns to recommend reserved instance acquisitions and autoscaling settings.
- Implemented automated tagging for cost attribution by business unit.
- Generated weekly financial reports with tailored recommendations.

Outcome

Reduced overall cloud costs by 28% in 6 months. Compliance with tagging increased from 54% to 96%, enabling precise departmental cost tracking. Enhanced collaboration between finance and engineering using a jointly developed AI-generated cost dashboard.

8.7.3 Academia: Enhancing Cloud Education and Practical Learning

A prominent technical university has incorporated generative AI into its cloud computing curriculum to enhance student engagement and alleviate instructors' workloads.

GenAI Integration:
- Developed real-time assignments aligned with current cloud trends and security challenges.
- Generated Terraform scripts tailored to course modules for labs.
- Created automated grading rubrics to assess students' Infrastructure as Code (IaC) submissions for correctness, security, and scalability.

Outcome:
- Boosted student engagement and confidence in cloud-native tools.
- Reduced grading and assignment design time by 60%.
- Helped students develop AI-augmented DevOps skills, improving job placement in cloud engineering.

These use cases illustrate GenAI's broad applicability across sectors with varying compliance, scalability, and cost optimization needs. From regulated industries like healthcare to dynamic digital enterprises and educational institutions, GenAI proves to be a versatile enabler of modernization, efficiency, and innovation.

8.8 Cross Cloud: Generative AI in Azure, Google Cloud, and AWS

Generative AI is rapidly emerging as an essential component of prominent cloud platforms worldwide. Whether a company utilizes a single cloud vendor or adopts a multi-cloud strategy, every provider now offers generative AI tools aimed at enhancing developer productivity, automating infrastructure, improving security, and optimizing data analytics. It is imperative for enterprises to understand these capabilities to effectively integrate generative AI into their operations.

8.8.1 Microsoft Azure: AI-Augmented Cloud Engineering

Microsoft has established itself as a leader by partnering with OpenAI [1] and developing tools such as Azure Copilot [6, 7]. Its deep integration of Generative Artificial Intelligence (GenAI) into its cloud infrastructure is especially notable, achieved through collaborations with OpenAI and its own AI models.

Key Instruments and Competencies

Azure Copilot (previously known as Azure OpenAI with Azure CLI/ARM AI Integration) helps users provision, configure, and manage cloud infrastructure using natural language. It effectively converts user prompts into Bicep templates, PowerShell scripts, or Azure CLI commands, seamlessly integrating with Azure Resource Manager for direct execution.

Security Copilot is an AI-driven security assistant intended to help Security Operations Center (SOC), and DevSecOps teams analyze incidents, formulate remediation strategies, and summarize threat intelligence. It acquires knowledge from Microsoft's vast global threat intelligence graph and is incorporated into platforms like Microsoft Sentinel and Defender.

AI-enabled ARM templates and policy insights assist in identifying configuration drift, enforcing governance policies, and generating custom compliance reports through intelligent recommendations.

Strengths:

- Seamless integration with Microsoft 365, GitHub Copilot, and Visual Studio.
- Advanced AI controls for role-based access, tenant isolation, and auditing.
- Ideal for regulated industries and hybrid Azure Stack environments.

8.8.2 Google Cloud Platform (GCP): Targeting Developers and Emphasizing Data in Generative AI

Google Cloud's artificial intelligence offerings are profoundly integrated with its machine learning and data analytics services, providing a distinct advantage in generative AI-powered DevOps and financial operations use cases.

Key Instruments and Proficiencies

Duet AI [4], founded upon Gemini models, integrates with Google Cloud Console to assist developers. It aids developers, cloud architects, and Site Reliability Engineers (SREs) by recommending configurations, composing gcloud commands, and troubleshooting resource issues in real time. Furthermore, it facilitates the prompt-based development of Terraform code and project templates.

Vertex AI and Big Query Integration: Vertex AI enables developers to train, fine-tune, and deploy substantial foundational models, including Gemini, on enterprise-grade infrastructure. When integrated with Big Query, it facilitates sophisticated applications such as real-time business intelligence, cost forecasting, anomaly detection, and semantic search.

Cloud Workflows and Generative AI Agents

Google Cloud facilitates the creation of low-code workflows that are seamlessly integrated with artificial intelligence-driven decision-making processes for incident response, ticket triaging, and service orchestration.

Strengths:

- Generative Artificial Intelligence (GenAI) and Google's data analytics and machine learning (ML) stack are strongly integrated.

The platform is built for developers, offering native support for Terraform and working seamlessly with Collab notebooks. This strategy is particularly effective for teams focused on artificial intelligence and for creating natively cloud-hosted software as a service (SaaS).

8.8.3 Amazon Web Services (AWS): Practical Artificial Intelligence for Architects and Operators

Amazon Web Services (AWS) has formally introduced its generative AI capabilities, which encompass its infrastructure, developer tools, and enterprise workloads. The company's strategic approach emphasizes flexibility, security, and cost management.

Key Instruments and Competencies

Amazon Q: Amazon Q [8], AWS's GenAI assistant, and Amazon Bedrock [9] allow secure model deployment. Amazon Web Services (AWS)'s Generative AI assistant is integrated into the AWS Management Console, development environments like Cloud9 and Visual Studio Code, and related documentation. This assistant helps users prepare CloudFormation templates, create Identity and Access Management (IAM) policies, troubleshoot services, and explore application programming interfaces (APIs) through conversations.

Amazon Bedrock is a managed service offering access to foundational models (FM) from providers like Anthropic, AI21 Labs, Meta, and Cohere via a unified

API. This allows enterprises to build secure, scalable generative AI applications without managing the infrastructure.

Code Whisperer: Code Whisperer is an AI tool for developers that provides secure code recommendations, infrastructure scripts, and deployment workflows in languages like Python and Java.

Strengths: Bedrock provides a wide selection of models and governance features, including VPC endpoints, encryption, and access logs. It is refined for enterprise DevOps pipelines and security tools like Guard Duty and Inspector, benefiting enterprises that prioritize customization, flexibility, and federated AI controls.

8.8.4 Cross Cloud Observations and Interoperability

Despite differing methodologies, all three cloud service providers share several key principles:

1. **Prompt-Driven Interfaces: Making** infrastructure and security tasks accessible via natural language.
2. **Integrated Policy and Compliance Insights:** Using generative AI in security and governance workflows.
3. **Data-Aware Optimization:** Leveraging billing data and telemetry for real-time performance and cost efficiency.
4. **Agentic Extensions:** Enabling multi-agent workflows that combine infrastructure reasoning with operations management and business alignment.

Organizations that embrace multiple cloud services encounter a mix of exciting opportunities and challenges. While native tools perform effectively in their respective clouds, adopting cross cloud GenAI strategies can really shine when utilizing vendor-neutral platforms such as Lang Chain, Crew AI, and Terraform Cloud AI integrations. This approach helps create a seamless experience and fosters better governance across all platforms.

8.9 Agentic Artificial Intelligence: The Subsequent Advancement in Cloud Autonomy

GenAI-powered copilots are transforming cloud infrastructure design and management towards a more autonomous paradigm: Agentic AI. This field redefines GenAI from reactive assistants to proactive agents skilled in planning, executing, and coordinating with minimal human involvement.

8.9.1 What Constitutes Agentic AI?

Agentic artificial intelligence consists of specialized AI agents that manage complex systems independently or collaboratively. Unlike simple chatbots, these agents act as digital teammates, executing tasks, reporting status, and escalating issues autonomously. They are adaptive, context-aware entities capable of reasoning, decision-making, and negotiation. In cloud environments, they monitor infrastructure, enforce security, optimize costs, and respond to incidents without constant human supervision.

8.9.2 Major Agent Types in Cloud Infrastructure

1. **Security Officer: The Self-Reliant Guardian**
   Security personnel are vigilant sentinels within organizational infrastructure, responsible for:

   - Analyzing configuration drift, misconfigurations, or vulnerabilities.
   - Monitoring logs and network traffic for anomalies or policy violations.
   - Initiating automated responses like isolation, key rotation, or firewall adjustments.

   - These agents can cross-reference policies and regulatory standards to generate compliance reports and identify nonconforming deployments.

2. **FinOps Agent: The Strategist for Cost Governance**
   FinOps agents serve as financial guardians for cloud environments, enabling real-time data-driven decision-making. They monitor usage trends, predict expenditures, and recommend cost-saving methods like rightsizing, instance scheduling, and changing storage types. Additionally, they dynamically tag resources for precise cost attribution and implement chargeback models. Adherence to budgetary guidelines ensures compliance with expenditure limits. Over time, these agents gain insight into the organization's spending patterns, aligning infrastructure choices with financial goals and policies.
3. **SRE Agent: The Architect of Reliability and Performance**
   Site Reliability Engineering (SRE) professionals prioritize system uptime, health, and efficiency. They analyze logs, metrics, and service-level indicators (SLIs) to spot latency issues and use predictive automated scaling instead of reactive thresholds. SRE professionals guide or implement failover strategies during regional outages and help create post-incident Root Cause Analysis (RCA) documents. They document issues and proactively resolve them per established service-level objectives (SLOs).

8.9.3 Multi-Agent Systems and Collaborative Approaches

The true power of agentic AI lies in these agents' capacity to interact, share contextual information, and coordinate their activities. For instance:

A security agent may identify excessive open ports and notify the SRE agent to assess the need for redundancy. They will escalate the issue only if risks outweigh performance requirements.

A FinOps agent may propose reducing compute size. Before implementation, it consults the SRE agent to ensure performance SLAs are not compromised.

This communication between agents is facilitated by orchestration frameworks, including:

Orchestration frameworks like LangGraph [10], AutoGen [11], and Crew AI enable modular, multi-agent coordination.

- Lang graph facilitates the development of agent workflows characterized by stateful memory, task routing, and event handling.
- AutoGen, developed by Microsoft, aims to enhance collaboration among diverse agents by utilizing natural language processing and planning logic.
- Crew AI offers multi-agent task execution by implementing predefined roles, goals, and coordination rules, particularly suitable for intricate infrastructure environments.

These frameworks enable modular, pluggable, and event-driven architectures where agents evolve independently while collaborating seamlessly.

8.9.4 Future Outlook: Autonomous Cloud Teams

The swift advancement of agentic artificial intelligence is steering cloud infrastructure towards a clear goal: the development of AI-native cloud operations teams. These teams will fundamentally differ from today's human-focused DevOps or Site Reliability Engineering (SRE) units. They will consist of intelligent, cooperative, and perpetually functioning agents, each tasked with a specific aspect of infrastructure management. This shift will create a new framework for human–AI collaboration, enabling the human workforce to move from routine tasks to strategic oversight, policy creation, and ethical governance.

The Fundamental Principles of Autonomous Cloud Teams

1. **People as Designers of Policy and Ethical Overseers**

   Rather than managing coding configurations or addressing incidents, human operators will:

   - Set higher business goals, compliance requirements, and risk limits.

- Oversee the decision-making structures guiding artificial intelligence behavior in ambiguous or high-stakes situations.
- To maintain transparency and accountability, perform a comprehensive review and audit of the logs, actions, and decisions generated by artificial intelligence systems.

- Such measures enable technical personnel to concentrate on innovation, architectural vision, and AI governance, rather than on operational intricacies.

2. **Agents as Continuous Operational Executors**
   A network of specialized artificial intelligence agents will monitor all levels of the infrastructure architecture:

- Provisioning agents interpret business requirements and translate them into cloud-native deployments using Infrastructure as Code.
- Optimization agents continuously analyze telemetry and billing data to adjust service size, scale, or configuration as needed.
- Security agents conduct ongoing risk assessments, implement safety measures, and respond to threats promptly and in real time.
- Resilience agents perform outage simulations, validate failover pathways, and enable the automatic restoration of critical systems.

- These agents will create an intelligent, continuously operational framework requiring minimal human intervention for routine decisions.

3. **Self Properties: Accept Default**
   In AI environments, infrastructure will show "self-capabilities" due to generative AI and multi-agent orchestration.
   Self-Healing: The system autonomously detects and fixes failures by rolling back faulty deployments, restarting services, or redistributing traffic.
   Self-optimizing: Agents analyze patterns and cost metrics to adjust computational size, autoscaling thresholds, and data tiering strategies.
   Self-Securing: Drift is automatically corrected; the least privilege access principle is enforced, and new vulnerabilities are patched in real time.
   Self-documenting: Every action, change, or recommendation is recorded with context and intention, minimizing documentation overhead.

Once aspirational in SRE literature, these capabilities are now expected to standardize in next-gen cloud environments.

The Human AI Continuum: A comparative analysis of autonomous vehicles

This transition mirrors autonomous vehicles, which redefine drivers' roles rather than eliminate them.

Automation levels 1 and 2 support operators, as seen with lane assistance and adaptive cruise control. Levels 3 and 4 enable autonomous control with human overrides. Level 5, complete automation, is an aspirational goal, akin to Level 5 cloud autonomy, where AI manages digital infrastructure, with humans in supervisory roles.

In This Analogy:

- Today's DevOps practitioners are like manual drivers.

AI copilots (e.g., GitHub Copilot, Amazon Q) act like cruise control systems.

Agentic AI signals a shift toward autonomous infrastructure, marked by improved safety, efficiency, and error reduction.

The Impact of Organizations and Their Readiness

To achieve this vision, organizations must invest in:

- Training on PromptOps and AgentOps for engineers.
- AI policy frameworks aligned with regulatory and ethical standards.
- Modular, observable cloud-native infrastructure frameworks that support autonomous extension.

Cultural readiness is also vital. IT leadership must foster trust in automation, create interdisciplinary teams of AI specialists, and encourage experimentation over rigid processes.

In Conclusion

Agentic AI signifies a fundamental shift in cloud infrastructure management, optimization, and security for the next decade. Unlike traditional generative AI models that generate code or answer questions, agentic AI features autonomous, goal-driven agents that can think, act, and collaborate to perform complex tasks with minimal human input. This transition offers significant advantages: Autonomy: Infrastructure becomes more self-governing, with agents making decisions, executing tasks, and recovering autonomously. Scalability: Multi-agent systems operate at speeds and scales well beyond human capabilities, managing extensive hybrid and multi-cloud environments efficiently. Resilience: Systems develop self-repair abilities, adapt to failures, and proactively mitigate risks while maintaining service-level objectives and compliance. The next generation of cloud platforms, whether public, private, or hybrid, will be built on intelligent orchestration, where policy-driven, learning-enabled agents form the operational foundation. These platforms will not just respond to business needs but will anticipate them, analyze trade-offs, and continuously evolve based on telemetry, costs, and compliance inputs. Organizations that adopt agentic AI now through pilot projects, orchestration frameworks, and AI readiness planning will set benchmarks for operational excellence, innovation, and security resilience. Conversely, those delaying this transition may face challenges from outdated workflows, increased costs, and growing technical debt. In a time when digital agility determines competitive advantage, adopting agentic AI is a strategic necessity.

Glossary

DR/BCP Disaster Recovery/Business Continuity Planning
FinOps Cloud Financial Operations
IaC Infrastructure as Code
LLM Large Language Model
PromptOps CloudOps driven by AI prompts
RAG Retrieval Augmented Generation
SRE Site Reliability Engineering
VPC Virtual Private Cloud

References

1. OpenAI [1]: Retrieved from https://platform.openai.com/docs
2. Google Cloud Vertex AI [3] [3]: Retrieved from https://cloud.google.com/vertex-ai
3. Vertex AI [3]: Retrieved from https://cloud.google.com/vertex-ai
4. Duet AI [3]: Retrieved from https://cloud.google.com/vertex-ai/docs/duet-ai-overview
5. FinOps Foundation [8]: Retrieved from https://www.finops.org
6. Microsoft Copilot [2]: Retrieved from https://learn.microsoft.com/en-us/azure/copilot/overview
7. Azure Copilot [2]: Retrieved from https://learn.microsoft.com/en-us/azure/copilot/overview
8. Amazon Q [4]: Retrieved from https://aws.amazon.com/q/
9. AWS Bedrock [4]: Retrieved from https://aws.amazon.com/bedrock
10. LangGraph [5]: Retrieved from https://www.langchain.com/langgraph
11. AutoGen [6]: Retrieved from https://microsoft.github.io/autogen

Chapter 9
AI-Driven Secure and Compliant Real-Time Cloud Monitoring

Aditya Gupta and **Chhaya Gunawat**

Abstract Cloud-native architecture has changed the role of telemetry from ancillary to integral operating metric. This chapter provides a comprehensive guide to building secure, compliant, and AI-fortified observability systems to ingest, correlate, and analyze metrics, logs, and traces in real time. Based on open standards like OpenTelemetry and scalable building blocks such as Fluent Bit, Amazon Kinesis, and AWS Lambda, this architecture provides high-throughput, low-latency telemetry pipelines on distributed systems.

Responding to the growing complexity and volume of observability data, this chapter integrates artificial intelligence into the telemetry life cycle. This includes log summarization using foundation models like Llama 2 in AWS Bedrock, anomaly detection using statistical and learning-based methods, as well as vector-based trace recall for root cause analysis. It also tackles security and compliance needs, including field-level redaction, tenant-aware telemetry boundaries, role-based access controls, and auditability features. While the implementation examples are from AWS, the patterns and practices underlying them have broad applicability across cloud environments.

This research provides observability platform architecting and principal engineers with an exhaustive and flexible model for building secure and scalable observability platforms. In addition, such platforms have the potential to integrate artificial intelligence, reducing mean time to resolution and improving visibility into operations.

Keywords Cloud observability · Opentelemetry · Telemetry pipelines · Real-time monitoring · Log summarization · AWS Bedrock · Llama 2 · AI-enhanced root cause analysis · Metrics and traces correlation · Secure telemetry · Field-level redaction · Compliance monitoring · Anomaly detection · Distributed systems · Intelligent alerting

---

A. Gupta (✉)
Independent Researcher, Seattle, WA, USA

C. Gunawat
Independent Researcher, Freemont, CA, USA

B. Pandey, A. Patel (eds.), *Revolutionizing the Cloud*,
https://doi.org/10.1007/978-3-032-07479-9_9

9.1 Introduction

The increasing size and complexity of today's software applications have made observability not a best practice but a necessary operational requirement. In a world where services are becoming ever-more distributed, fleeting, and event-based, traditional monitoring approaches focused on system health metrics or predefined thresholds are insufficient to identify emerging issues or diagnose root causes in real time. In this context, observability provides a stronger model that allows engineers to reason about a system's internal state based on nothing but externally observable outputs [1].

This chapter offers a technically precise but concise model for building secure, compliant real-time observability pipelines augmented by artificial intelligence. It highlights the importance of three pillars such as metrics, logs, and traces [1, 2] where cloud-native telemetry is based and explores their connections through the use of standardized identifiers like trace IDs and span attributes. These signals are not simple one-off debugging tools but are the building blocks upon which service-level objectives (SLOs), compliance rules, and smart alerting are based.

Cloud-native architectures based on serverless or container-based infrastructure bring extra challenges to observability. Engineers no longer enjoy shell access to instances. Services can autoscale or redeploy in short time windows. Managed layers cover up infrastructure. This shift in architecture disrupts traditional debugging habits and creates blind spots unless systems are well instrumented to provide fine-grained telemetry in an end-to-end fashion during the lifetime of a request. In Kubernetes-based deployments, observability should work seamlessly through pod restarts, temporary IP addresses, and autoscaling groups independent of static identifiers.

Artificial Intelligence (AI) adds another critical layer of depth and richness to the story of observability. The amount of telemetry has grown so much that human inspection is no longer practicable without the help of machines. It is now not an oddity for a production system to produce terabytes of logs and metrics daily. This demands smart summarization, anomaly detection scores, and incident triage [2–4], work that is now being carried out by machine learning models. Large Language Models (LLMs) like Meta's LLaMA 2 [3, 5] have the power to deliver natural language summaries of trace logs or provide possible root causes based on contextual signals. These technologies are not replacements for conventional observability but act as an enhancement that enables teams to scale their workflows.

Security and compliance are a parallel concern. Telemetry often carries sensitive data, such as user emails in URIs, authorization tokens in logs, and personally identifiable information (PII) in bodies of requests. A great observability strategy will apply policy-aware processing across the telemetry life cycle, thus enabling field-level redaction, role-based access control (RBAC), transmit and at-rest encryption [6, 7], and auditability. Such requirements are becoming codified in compliance regulations, such as the General Data Protection Regulation (GDPR), the Health Insurance Portability and Accountability Act (HIPAA), and ISO 27001. A telemetry system lacking such controls is a liability.

This chapter heavily draws on implementation models in Amazon Web Services (AWS) using services like CloudWatch, Kinesis, Lambda, and OpenSearch to illustrate telemetry ingestion and transformation pipelines. At the same time, recommendations are kept largely cloud-agnostic. Each pattern is adaptable to be deployed in Azure, Google Cloud Platform (GCP), or even on premises, using OpenTelemetry, Fluent Bit, Kafka, and similar tools that are not tied to any particular environment. Vendor lock-in is avoided through the use of open standards and decoupling of pipeline stages.

9.2 Core Telemetry Stack: Metrics, Logs, and Traces

The building blocks of any observability pipeline are composed of three telemetry signals: metrics, logs, and traces [1, 2]. If these signals are correctly instrumented and correlated, they enable multi-dimensional visibility required in debugging, optimization, and protection of modern cloud-native applications. Each signal has unique benefits, but together, their combination provides a unified understanding of system behavior and user experience.

Metrics are low-overhead numeric measures of system states, collected over a time period. When reported at a regular time cadence, metrics are well-suited to track trends, thresholds, and conditions that will produce an alert. Through metric analysis, things like a rise in CPU usage, a drop in throughput in terms of requests, or a divergence in the 95th quantile latency might be detected. Cloud-native infrastructure like Prometheus and AWS CloudWatch Metrics handle dimensional metrics, so filtering by labels like region, service, or version is supported. While efficient and low-overhead, metrics provide relatively narrow context compared to that gleaned through explicit tagging during collection.

Logs are time-stamped records of events and are often output in structured formats like JSON. Logs provide rich operational context, such as error messages, request payloads, and exception stack traces, and thus offer critical forensic data when metrics indicate failure. Unlike metrics, which are at a high level of abstraction, logs enable line-by-line introspection. However, the volume and variety of logging create challenges for indexing, retention, and management of sensitive data. Widely adopted tools for log shipping to storage and analytics platforms include Fluent Bit, Filebeat, and AWS FireLens, all of which are integrated with platforms like Amazon OpenSearch, Elasticsearch, or third-party services like Datadog and Splunk.

Traces outline the path of an individual request or transaction from one point to another in a distributed system. A trace is composed of one or multiple spans, with a span recording an operation's latency, status, and metadata, such as a microservice handling a request, a database call, or a call to an external API. Analysis of traces is crucial in separating the vulnerability spots in a system, highlighting occurrences of retries, and aiding in the visualization of a system's topology. OpenTelemetry is now the de-facto instrumentation standard, with Software Development Kits (SDKs) available in most coding languages, together with native support in frameworks like Kubernetes, Envoy, and Istio. Trace visualization tools, such as AWS X-Ray or Jaeger, enable teams to examine request routes and quickly determine the root of the problems.

The real power of observability lies in correlating multiple signals. A rise in 500 status codes as a metric could be correlated with a database timeout recorded in the system, further corroborated by an increase in latency in multiple spans in a trace. This facility to flip between signals depends on telemetry generation through shared identifiers. More specifically, context propagation, the injection and passing of trace ID and span IDs [5] in HTTP headers or message queues, enables this correlation. In this context, the OpenTelemetry-developed W3C Trace Context specification plays a crucial role, allowing services to share a uniform context per request.

Structured logging greatly enhances trace correlation through the inclusion of trace metadata in the log record. This is made possible through libraries like Logback (Java), logrus [8] (Go), and structlog (Python), which enable field logging with trace_id, span_id, and request_id filled in automatically. Such a high degree of consistency supports the indexing and queryability of logs based on trace identifiers, thus allowing execution path reconstruction even in cases where full tracing is not available.

Sampling and aggregation methods are crucial in measuring both the cost and effectiveness of telemetry. Logs and traces generally require filtering by default in order to handle overhead unless metrics are collected in their entirety. Tail-based sampling is the selective storage of traces after considering error status or length, while probabilistic trace discard through head-based sampling is undertaken at the beginning of requests. While the latter is less efficient, the former requires less infrastructure and buffering. Implementations such as the OpenTelemetry Collector and vendor-hosted agents like AWS Distro for OpenTelemetry (ADOT) enable the usage of complex sampling policies based on YAML configuration:

```
sampling:
  policies:
   - name: high-latency
     condition: "latency_ms > 1000"
      rate: 1.0
   - name: default
      rate: 0.01
```

These configurations keep high-value signals like error-containing traces or latency outliers on a persistent basis for further analysis. High-cardinality metrics like session tokens or unique user IDs are often grouped or dropped in an effort to control resource usage and facilitate query execution.

Semantic telemetry, a new field of study [9], augments technical signals by adding business-level context. Instead of just monitoring http_request_duration_seconds, semantic signals can measure instances of "orders placed," "invoices failed," or "KYC checks retried." Such signals make it easier to bridge system performance and user impact and are often communicated via custom metrics or structured logs. Having these signals available in dashboards and alerts allows people outside the engineering sphere to monitor key business key performance indicators (KPIs) using the same telemetry infrastructure.

Finally, **telemetry hygiene** is critical to guaranteeing the long-term health of observability pipelines. This includes enforcing JSON schemas for logs, restricting cardinality in labels attached to metrics, and requiring that trace spans do not have too large a maximum depth or payload sizes. Without these protections, downstream consumers like OpenSearch or Prometheus can suffer from cardinality explosions, slower query response times, or, in some cases, ingestion failures. These imperative requirements can be enforced through audits that run regularly, schema validation in CI/CD pipelines, and test environments that leverage synthetic telemetry.

9.3 Observability Pipeline Architecture

Implementation of an observability pipeline that is horizontally scalable, real-time, secure, and private requires more than the mere ingestion of telemetry. However, the system supports high-throughput ingestion, fault-tolerant processing, context-aware enrichment, dynamic routing, and efficient querying. In modern cloud environments, this means instrumenting the system to emit telemetry, followed by setting up a transport and processing pipeline that is horizontally scalable and modular in design, but inherently observable.

9.3.1 Ingestion Architecture

At the edge of the pipeline, runtimes, applications, services, and telemetry emitters produce logs, metrics, or spans. In the context of the Kubernetes environment, this stage often involves the usage of agents like **Fluent Bit or OpenTelemetry Collecters** in DaemonSets form. These agents are tasked with scraping logs from the /var/log/containers/ directory, adding Kubernetes metadata, and then sending these logs to backend collectors.

In an AWS-native setup, Fluent Bit supports sending logs to **Amazon CloudWatch Logs, Amazon S3, or Amazon Kinesis Data Streams**, depending on retention and querying demands. Stream-based processing is supported in Kinesis using serverless transformation in the form of AWS Lambda. It supports decoupling ingestion from downstream storage and real-time buffering in addition to retry logic.

This setup enables streaming of container logs to a Kinesis Firehose delivery stream, which can be set up to write to either OpenSearch or S3. Kinesis also provides data transformation and schema validation as a native part of the delivery process, enabling a control point for compliance.

Metrics are often sent via Prometheus exporters to the Prometheus Gateway, where those are collected at regular intervals and stored in time-series databases. When using the CloudWatch Agent or the OpenTelemetry Collector, metrics are grouped, summed, and forwarded to CloudWatch Metrics or Amazon Managed Prometheus. These two systems both support dimensional filtering and alerting, thus enabling teams to monitor both low-level infrastructure and app-based key performance indicators (KPIs).

Traces follow a well-defined path. Applications emit spans using the OpenTelemetry Software Development Kits (SDKs), which are then collected by an OpenTelemetry Collector and sent to distributed tracing backends like **AWS X-Ray, Jaeger, or Honeycomb**. OpenTelemetry pipeline supports filtering, batching, and exporting of spans using transport protocols like OTLP, Zipkin, or Jaeger. A production environment can include the following components:

- Fluent Bit for log collection and enrichment
- OpenTelemetry Collector for trace and metric aggregation
- Kinesis or Kafka for telemetry buffering
- Lambda or Fargate for redaction and transformation
- OpenSearch, S3, or Prometheus as storage backends

Each layer must be independently scalable, failure-isolated, and observable.

9.3.2 *Telemetry Redaction and Transformation*

A critical feature of modern observability pipelines is data redaction, masking sensitive information such as emails, access tokens, or customer IDs before storage. This is not only a privacy-preserving measure but also a compliance requirement for standards like **GDPR and HIPAA**. A Lambda function subscribed to a Kinesis stream can perform inline redaction:

```
import re
 def redact_payload(record):
    log = record.get("log", "")
    log = re.sub(r'\b[\w.-]+@[\w.-]+\b',    '[REDACTED_
EMAIL]', log)
    log = re.sub(r'(token|password)=\S+', '[REDACTED]',  log)
    return log
```

The service is developed to process JSON log lines, stripping off sensitive parameters and emails, thus producing a sanitized version. Filtered output is then sent to OpenSearch or S3. To provide similar functionality but with increased throughput, AWS Fargate, Kafka Streams, or Flink can be used.

Tracing mechanisms are a necessary measure against span leakage in which sensitive information might be exposed accidentally. OpenTelemetry allows one to apply filtering on a collector level. The following configuration ensures environment variables are not stored nor are HTTP headers:

```
processors:
  attributes:
    actions:
      - key: http.request.header.Authorization
        action: delete
      - key: container.env
        action: delete
```

This declarative filter deletes known sensitive fields before export, ensuring safe telemetry transmission to backends.

9.3.3 Routing and Storage

Telemetry, being a critical part of the transformation process, should be channeled into storage systems specifically tailored towards a particular form of signals. Logs, due to their dynamic nature and cardinality, can be best handled by search databases like **Amazon OpenSearch or Elasticsearch**. Such databases enable multi-parametric indexing in terms of time, service name, log levels, and trace ID, thus enhancing the efficacy of complicated queries in the process of investigations into incidents.

These metrics are geared towards **time-series databases (TSDBs) like CloudWatch Metrics, Managed Prometheus, and VictoriaMetrics.** These databases are designed to handle large amounts of numeric data, enable downsampling, and apply retention policies. In addition, long-term metric storage typically requires the use of rollups or aggregates in order to save costs while still keeping alert messages effective.

Traces are modeled with distributed tracing environments in mind. For example, **AWS X-Ray provides a hierarchical graph-based visualization of the request flow**, combined with advanced filtering options based on trace metadata. Jaeger and Honeycomb provide similar functionality, with even more advanced custom views in their enterprise editions.

Another major design aspect is regarding multi-sink routing. In many setups, a single telemetry record requires sending to two or more targets; logs go to OpenSearch and an S3 bucket, metrics are sent to two time-series databases (TSDBs), and tracing is classified by service type and sent to multiple exporters. OpenTelemetry makes this possible through the use of exporters and pipelines:

```
service:
  pipelines:
    traces:
      receivers: [otlp]
      processors: [batch, attributes]
      exporters: [otlp/jaeger, otlp/xray]
```

This ensures vendor interoperability, backup routing, and layered observability strategies.

9.3.4 Self-Monitoring of the Pipeline

Pipelines should be inherently observable. They should produce metrics about pipeline health, such as input rates, buffer sizes, drop rates, and transformation latency. OpenTelemetry Collector makes those metrics available through Prometheus scrape endpoints. It is critical to set up dashboards and alerting infrastructure to watch:

- Input records per second by source
- Exporter queue depth
- Batch processing latency
- Error and retry rates

An internal fault, e.g., a blocked exporter or a misconfigured filter, will be characterized by a silent loss of telemetry. Self-monitoring is intended to catch such faults ahead of time.

9.4 Securing the Telemetry Lifecycle

With observability becoming an ever-more central aspect of operating excellence, enterprise security and compliance roles played by it have seen drastic shifts. Sensitive metadata, IP addresses, session tokens, user-agent headers, error payloads, and even personally identifiable information (PII) are often added to the telemetry pipeline. This fact ends up transforming telemetry infrastructure from a simple passive monitoring platform into a high-value, high-privilege system that might get the attention of adversaries or be put under the microscope by compliance auditors. Therefore, it is critical, in design and in regulation, to secure the observability pipeline at every point: gather, transmit, store, and access.

9.4.1 Threat Surfaces in Observability Systems

Telemetry systems crosscut all levels of operations, from runtime applications to outward-facing APIs. When such systems are compromised, they provide adversaries with an end-to-end picture of the topology of the service, error messages, internal endpoints, and communication latency. Further, based on their assumption of ongoing data emission and consumption, they are susceptible to telemetry injection attacks [6], whereby adversaries send specially designed payloads to alter downstream analysis or trigger denial-of-service actions.

Threat surfaces generally include:

- **Collection agents**: Misconfigured Fluent Bit or OpenTelemetry collectors can unintentionally expose local socket endpoints or ingest unexpected logs.
- **Transport systems**: Streaming platforms like Kafka or Kinesis, in the absence of authentication or encryption, can potentially leak telemetry to unintended consumers.
- **Storage backends**: OpenSearch domains or servers that are not suitably configured can expose public access to internal logs or metrics.
- **Dashboards and query tools**, even if merely read-only, can potentially expose sensitive business logic or usage patterns.

9.4.2 Encryption and Role-Based Access Control

Encryption is a core tenet. All telemetry data in transit must be encrypted using mechanisms like TLS 1.2 or 1.3. This is not just for external communication but also includes intra-cloud and VPC-internal telemetry streams. For example, while sending data from Fluent Bit to Kinesis, the endpoint should require HTTPS and use AWS IAM roles to authenticate the request signing.

```
{
  "Effect": "Allow",
  "Action": [
    "firehose:PutRecord",
    "firehose:PutRecordBatch"
  ],
  "Resource":"arn:aws:firehose:us-west-2:123456789012:deliverystr
eam/observability-stream"
}
```

The data at rest also need to be protected using customer managed keys (CMKs). In AWS, CloudWatch Logs, S3, and OpenSearch are integrated with AWS KMS. This makes it possible to govern telemetry retention policies and rotation of keys in a centralized manner. Somewhat similarly, the counterparts in GCP and Azure use Cloud KMS and Azure Key Vault, respectively.

Access policies need to follow the **principle of least privilege**. Engineers and operators should have permission that is scoped, defined by service, environment, and signal types (log/metric/trace). A good example is a developer in the payments department having access to only the trace in the checkout microservice but not to infrastructure logs or user personally identifiable information (PII) in other services.

9.4.3 Redaction and Compliance-Aware Processing

Field-level redaction is essential for privacy-preserving telemetry [7]. Logs and spans must be scrubbed of PII before storage. This may include names, emails, session tokens, authorization headers, and customer data. Redaction can be implemented through:

- Regex-based masking in OpenTelemetry or Fluent Bit processors.
- Lambda functions are subscribed to telemetry streams.
- Log filters in OpenSearch or masking rules at index-time.

Example Lambda for token redaction:

```
import re


def sanitize_event(log):
    log = re.sub(r'(Authorization|token|password)=\S+',
'[REDACTED]', log)
    return log
```

Regular expressions are suitable where logs are well-formatted; however, complex systems utilize schema-based redaction where telemetry is organized in predefined JSON formats with sensitive data tagged appropriately. Redaction is required **before the persistence act**, specifically to meet the requirements of GDPR, HIPAA, and PCI DSS. For example:

- **GDPR Article 17** regarding the right to erasure requires personal data, including logs and traces, to be deleted.
- **HIPAA 164.312** mandates access controls and audit trails for PHI in logs.
- **PCI DSS 4.0** forbids storage of PANs or CVVs in plaintext telemetry.

9.4.4 Observability Pipeline Hardening

Hardening observability platforms uses multi-layer isolation. AWS offers Nitro Enclaves, isolated compute environments that are meant to run sensitive telemetry processing without access to external networks or persistent storage. The enclaves have the ability to run redaction logic, cryptography, or artificial intelligence summarization without ever exposing raw logs.

Further hardening steps include:

- Used asymmetric keys to secure logs and spans, thus maintaining telemetry integrity.
- Tokenized telemetry identities were used instead of raw usernames or account identities.
- VPC boundary controls are defined where telemetry traffic is confined to internal subnets.

Transport systems, similar to Kafka, should use mutual TLS authentication for producers and consumers. OpenTelemetry Collectors can also be run in separate containers with restricted file system and network access using AppArmor or SELinux profiles.

9.4.5 Auditability and Forensic Logging

Security without auditability is incomplete in nature. All telemetry system access, API calls, dashboard views, and log queries should be auditable. For example:

- **AWS CloudTrail** can log every read/write to CloudWatch, S3, and OpenSearch.
- **OpenSearch Audit Logs** can track user queries, index access, and failed authentications.
- **Prometheus Query Logs** can record every metric expression that is evaluated.

Audit logs in **multi-tenant observability** systems need to clearly separate user IDs, resource scopes, timestamps, and accessed telemetry records. Such a practice ensures non-repudiation and supports forensic reconstruction.

Organizations can create **immutable log stores** by using S3 Object Lock or AWS QLDB (Quantum Ledger DB), which keeps compliance logs safe from being tampered with.

9.4.6 Summary

Security and compliance must be held paramount design goals in modern-day observability pipelines. Every stage, including redaction, encryption, role-based access control (RBAC), and auditing, must apply strict controls without degrading telemetry fidelity. Proper implementation of those controls ensures observability systems meet both operational and compliance requirements, reducing organizational risk.

9.5 AI-Augmented Observability: Capabilities and Architectures

The volume, velocity, and variety of telemetry data that is collected by modern cloud environments often exceed human cognitive abilities. To counter this imbalance in scale, Artificial Intelligence (AI) and Machine Learning (ML) techniques are increasingly infused into observability tools to enable faster triage, improved pattern detection, and contextual insight. The augmentation provided by AI is not intended to replace human engineers but to amplify their ability to resolve incidents, understand root causes, and improve system reliability over time.

9.5.1 The Need for AI in Observability Pipelines

A multizone, autoscaling-based Kubernetes microservices deployment can yield upwards of hundreds of thousands of messages, traces, and metrics per minute. It is not possible to parse this data by hand, especially during an outage. In addition, failure modes that are complex in nature, such as cross-service regressions or transient issues, preferentially send weak signals in logs and tracing.

Real-time anomaly detection is based on model-derived or statistical baselines. AI enables:

- Real-time anomaly detection is based on model-derived or statistical baselines.
- A reflective composition of unstructured log messages or trace paths.
- Causal reasoning by correlating symptoms across distributed services
- Incident impact scoring uses the identification of impacted services or users.

9.5.2 Incorporating ML Models into the Pipeline

Machine learning models can be applied at different phases of the telemetry life cycle:

- **Edge-level detection:** Lightweight models (e.g., logistic regression or isolation forests) embedded in OpenTelemetry Collectors or Fluent Bit for edge filtering and tagging
- **Stream-level transformation:** Batch inference via AWS Lambda or Azure functions processing Kafka/Kinesis logs

- **Backend analysis** targets processes of training or inference on SageMaker, Bedrock, Vertex AI, or Azure ML to update dashboards or send alerts.

Example: Real-time Anomaly Scoring on Latency Metrics

```
import numpy as np
from sklearn.ensemble import IsolationForest

model = IsolationForest(contamination=0.01)
X = np.array([[120], [115], [117], [300], [118]])  # example
latency values in ms
scores = model.fit_predict(X)
print(scores)  # outputs -1 for anomalies, 1 for normal
```

Anomaly scores can be sent as custom metrics to CloudWatch, Prometheus, or OpenSearch and can be used to trigger alerts when abnormal behavior is detected, even before exceeding static thresholds.

9.5.3 LLM-Powered Summarization and Root Cause Analysis

Large Language Models (LLMs) like LLaMA 2, Falcon, and Claude have the ability to summarize high-cardinality logs or traces. This is a feature that helps in reducing noise in incident response by getting rid of unnecessary details and focusing on messages that are semantically meaningful.

Example Prompt to LLM (via Bedrock or SageMaker Endpoint):

```
{
  "prompt": "Summarize the following trace log:\n[span1] GET /
checkout - 500\n[span2] DB connection timeout after 3s\n[span3]
retrying payment - failed\n\nSummary:",
  "temperature": 0.2
}
```

Expected Output:

```
"Checkout API failed due to a 3-second database timeout, followed
by unsuccessful payment retry. Likely root cause: DB saturation."
```

Incorporation of this feature into an automated incident triage dashboard can potentially reduce time to resolution. It allows engineering teams to query the large language model with natural language to analyze telemetry data, ask follow-on questions, or contrast trace patterns over time.

9.5.4 Evaluating Model Effectiveness

For any AI-enabled observability pipeline, evaluation must go beyond accuracy and include real-world metrics:

- **Precision/recall of anomaly alerts**
- **Time to resolution (TTR) reduction**
- **Mean opinion score from SREs (for LLM summaries)**
- **Model drift monitoring** to detect telemetry schema or usage pattern changes

It is crucial that mechanisms of **explainability** be integrated. Models that are used in production alerting should provide explanations or feature importances so that engineers can verify decisions [10]. As an example, if the system detects an increase in checkout latency, the model should indicate that database latency and API retry quantity were the key drivers enabling root cause analysis based on context [11].

9.5.5 Risks and Safeguards in AI-Augmented Observability

The use of artificial intelligence in operating pipelines poses significant dangers:

- **Hallucination by LLMs** leading to misleading summaries
- **Over-alerting from unsupervised models** with poor tuning
- **Data sensitivity leakage** when prompts include PII or secrets
- **Model poisoning** from logs or metrics with embedded attack payloads

To mitigate these, the following safeguards are recommended:

- **Fine-tuning or prompt engineering** for reliability and domain adaptation
- **Inference sandboxing** with output filters to prevent hallucinations
- **Data scrubbing before inference**, especially for LLM input
- **Periodic model retraining** and model validation with production traffic

9.5.6 Case Study: Using LLaMA 2 to Improve Alerts

A financial services company used LLaMA 2 via AWS Bedrock to integrate log events and generate weekly digests for SREs. Preprocessing of the logs was done using a Lambda function, which sorted the logs based on the error code. The LLM generated cause-effect stories like:

```
"Elevated payment errors between 2024-11-04 and 2024-11-07 due to
increased latency from the tokenization microservice. Issue
coincided with ECS autoscaler event."
```

This overview was integrated into Slack notifications by means of an OpenSearch alerting webhook. Time to Resolution (TTR) decreased by 38% in the next month due to improved actionable alerting.

9.6 AI-Driven Incident Triage and Remediation Workflows

In production environments, mean time to detect (MTTD) and mean time to resolve (MTTR) are vital measurements that define resiliency in a system. Even with traditional monitoring tools offering support, however, they typically cannot deliver the desired accuracy or contextuality to enable the demand for timely incident response. As observability platforms mature into advanced environments, artificial intelligence-based methodologies, specifically based on foundation models and statistical machine learning, enable automation not only of detection but of triage and remediation processes.

This section describes a pragmatic approach to integrating artificial intelligence throughout the entire lifecycle of incident management, including signal ingestion, improved alerting, human-in-the-loop validation, as well as suggestions for initiating remediation actions.

9.6.1 Creation of an AI-Powered Triage Pipeline

An AI-driven triage workflow augments observability with layers of inference, summarization, and decision logic. A typical triage pipeline includes:

- **Signal ingestion** is the real-time collection and preprocessing of logs, metrics, and traces.
- **Anomaly detection**: Statistical models or unsupervised learners flag outliers.
- **Contextual enrichment**: Incident metadata is added, affected services, error types, and span IDs.
- **Summarization**: LLMs are invoked to generate a human-readable summary of the issue.
- **Playbook inference** involves AI suggesting next steps or remediation plans based on past data.

This can be implemented using tools such as:

- OpenTelemetry for instrumentation
- AWS Lambda for real-time logic

- Bedrock (e.g., LLaMA 2 or Claude) for inference
- EventBridge or SNS to trigger follow-ups or PagerDuty alerts

9.6.2 *Example: Lambda-Based Enrichment and Summary*

Here is a simplified architecture:

```
[Log Stream] -> [Lambda Anomaly Filter] -> [LLM Summary Lambda]
-> [Slack + PagerDuty]
```

Lambda Enrichment Function: A Python and Bedrock Example

```
import boto3
import json

client = boto3.client("bedrock-runtime")


def lambda_handler(event, context):
    logs = extract_relevant_logs(event)
    prompt = f"Summarize the following logs for incident
triage:\n{logs}"

    response = client.invoke_model(
        modelId="anthropic.claude-v2",
        body=json.dumps({"prompt": prompt, "temperature": 0.2})
    )
    summary = json.loads(response['body'])['completion']

    send_to_slack(summary)
```

This function takes logs from a telemetry stream, i.e., Kinesis or Kafka, and passes them to a model hosted on Bedrock, i.e., Claude v2. Then the output is sent to Slack for real-time awareness. This method reduces cognitive overhead for engineers during high-stakes incidents.

9.6.3 *Mapping Summaries to Remediation*

The worth of AI summaries is amplified when paired with historical resolution pathways. This aim can be achieved by adding metadata to past events, including:

- Affected component
- Root cause tag (e.g., “timeout,” “misconfig”)
- Fix path (e.g., “scale replica,” “revert deployment,” “restart cache node”)

Using this metadata, another embedding model or classifier, like Cohere Embed or Titan Text Embedding from Amazon, is able to return the closest three matches and suggest relevant remediation actions.

Embedding-Based Retrieval Flow:

```
[Incident Summary] → [Vector Embedder] → [Historical KB] →
[Remediation Suggestions]
```

This reduces MTTR by guiding engineers toward proven resolution strategies while keeping the human-in-the-loop for final validation.

9.6.4 Incident Auto-Tagging and Postmortem Drafts

Apart from triage, AI can aid in automatic incident classification for postmortem reporting [12]. For example, incidents can be automatically tagged with:

- Impact level (P1/P2/P3)
- Duration
- External-facing versus internal
- Potential root cause
- Blast radius (services involved)

Sample JSON Output from LLM Triage Agent:


```
{
  "summary": "Checkout service failed due to 502s from payment
provider",
  "tags": ["P1", "external_dependency", "us-west-2"],
  "suggestion": "Temporarily switch to backup payment gateway"
}
```


This information can be pre-filled in Confluence pages or postmortem templates, thereby lessening the document workload of SRE teams.

9.6.5 Privacy and Safety Considerations

Inserting AI in triage loops presents governance and security risks:

- **Prompt injection**: Prompt sanitization should be applied since telemetry potentially includes untrusted input.

- **Model drift**: As logs evolve, summaries may become less accurate; feedback loops are needed.
- **Sensitive data exposure**: PII needs to be masked prior to inference. Utilization of Bedrock (which never persists prompts) provides better guarantees than public APIs.
- **Feedback logging**: Decisions made based on AI output (e.g., "used suggestion X") should be auditable.

Additionally, AI agents must express their levels of confidence either explicitly or seek human intervention when their confidence is low.

9.6.6 *Measured Impact*

Many organizations have shared statistics on the benefits gained through AI-based observability:

- **Datadog**: Decreased MTTR by 47% through ML-driven anomaly detection and smart alert grouping.
- **Shopify**: Created a bespoke GPT-powered triage assistant that is integrated into Slack, producing a 60% reduction in distracting notifications
- **AWS internal teams**: Reported a decrease of up to 35% in the number of on-call escalations after implementing auto-summarization agents for CloudWatch alarms.

9.7 Future Trends and Emerging Challenges

The adoption of AI in observability platforms represents a revolution in approaches to monitoring, detection, and debugging in today's environments. However, this revolution is ongoing, since a number of major trends and gaps in research continue to shape the path of cloud-native monitoring.

9.7.1 *Development of AI Agents Familiar with Observability*

The sophistication of software architectures now exceeds human capabilities to handle telemetry in a manual manner. Future observability tools are expected to involve domain-specific AI agents to serve not only as triage tools but active participants in incident response workflows.

These agents will perform real-time correlations of different kinds of telemetry, query distributed tracing, and return hypothesis-driven answers based on past knowledge. In addition, they will act as forward-looking monitors by running counterfactual analysis in anticipation of service degradation before it actually happens. Meta and LinkedIn are already building in-house observability agents that collect incidents and provide rollback recommendations based on telemetry embeddings and carefully fine-tuned large language models.

These agents are largely facilitated by tightly integrated observability backends like OpenTelemetry, Prometheus, and CloudWatch with layers of artificial intelligence model orchestration. Observability stacks are set to continue towards implementing agent runtime environments that have contextual understanding based on reasoning.

9.7.2 Embedding Observability into CI/CD Pipelines

Another trend on the rise is the adoption of observability verification as a core element in deployment pipelines. Observability is no longer seen as a passive process after the fact. Instead, telemetry verification hooks are being integrated into platforms like GitHub Actions, CodePipeline, and Jenkins.

Examples include:

- Blocking deployments if expected metrics (e.g., request_latency_p99) are not exposed
- Verifying schema conformance in structured logs before acceptance
- Ensuring span context propagation is correctly enabled [13] in newly deployed microservices

These patterns create "observability contracts," specifications that are reviewed during code review and automated quality gates. As teams adopt SLO-based development, these contracts serve as a guardrail for both reliability and security.

9.7.3 Development of Federated and Privacy-Preserving AI Telemetry

Telemetry data includes personally identifiable information, often attributable to users, internal infrastructure, and compliance lines in relation to regulations. In the future, observability frameworks are expected to adopt federated learning paradigms [14] to leverage artificial intelligence capabilities while preserving data privacy. It is likely that models will use decentralized datasets to learn, thus eliminating the need to store raw logs in a centralized form.

For example, the anomaly detection models can be trained in different regions (e.g., us-west-2 and eu-central-1) by sharing gradients, thus avoiding the need to use raw telemetry. It supports tenant isolation while enabling global pattern discovery at the same time.

Federated inference is of particular importance in heavily regulated sectors like finance and healthcare. Hospitals and financial institutions can exchange improved model performance while keeping their logs safe and their patients' sensitive information secure. FLoRA and Amazon SageMaker Edge Manager, two technologies developed by Meta, are examples of boundary-aware intelligence technologies.

9.7.4 Integration of Statistical and Generative Models

Traditional observability tools rely on rule-based alert platforms or statistical anomaly detection approaches, including z-score and Holt-Winters. While powerful, such methods are limited by a lack of interpretability and contextual insight. Generative models produce summaries but also carry the likelihood of producing hallucinations or numeric inaccuracies.

The next generation of observability platforms will need to blend these paradigms. One likely path forward is hybrid pipelines with statistical models being used for detection, and large language models to serve purposes of explanation.

For example:

- The time-series detector detects a disk I/O anomaly
- Context is enriched with logs, traces
- Prompt is created: "Explain spike in disk I/O on service X with context"
- LLM provides reasoning: "Increase in async writes from new deployment of image processor"

The layered structure boosts the reliability without compromising interpretability. Stanford University and Google DeepMind's hybrid anomaly model use statistical thresholds to control the intervention of huge language models, in this manner reducing the cost of false positives.

9.7.5 Limitations of Open Standards and Tools

While OpenTelemetry is maturing, there remain gaps:

- Limited support for sampling strategies at scale
- Inconsistent trace-to-log correlation in multi-language environments
- There are no native redaction or masking pipelines for sensitive fields
- Limited benchmarking frameworks for LLM-based observability tools

In addition, the cross-domain standardization of semantic events [15] (e.g., "invoice_failed") remains a major challenge. Open specs are needed that enable the instrumentation of product-level events in alignment with technical measurements, creating a bridge between functions of SRE and product teams.

9.7.6 Building Organizational Readiness for AI Observability

The incorporation of AI into observability is not just a technical hurdle. Teams must adopt practices that enable:

- Prompt hygiene and validation pipelines
- Feedback mechanisms that enable model recommendations
- Telemetry-based inference under controlled access
- Skill development in interpreting AI-generated outputs

Corporations like AWS and Atlassian have created internal "Observability LLM Working Groups" that outline best practice standards, conduct red-team reviews, and participate in internal hackathons to explore the ethics of applying telemetry-aware AI. Without such cultural scaffolding, even the best tools will not be able to realize their potential.

9.7.7 Future Considerations

The marriage of real-time telemetry and artificial intelligence is one of the most exciting and potentially revolutionary areas of innovation that we are witnessing in today's world, especially in the spaces of DevOps and platform engineering. As observability platforms mature and evolve with the passage of time, from what were previously static and passive dashboards to dynamic and smart agents, they will assume fundamental and irreplaceable roles and undertake responsibilities well beyond the scope of traditional operational workflows. These next-generation tech platforms are likely to play a critical and instrumental role in enabling strategic decision-making, especially in critical functions like building resilient architectures, maintaining a good security posture, and building resilience in the entire development process of a product.

It is of utmost importance and nuance that researchers and practitioners come together and work together in a manner that ensures the systems being developed are not only designed to demonstrate resilience in their functionality but also should be endowed with essential qualities such as being comprehensible to people, being sensitive and aware of privacy issues, and being smoothly integrated into the workflows that people generally adopt. This concerted effort is critical in ushering in the next generation of cloud-native systems, ones that are revolutionary and pathbreaking in nature, having the phenomenal ability to reason and analyze their own functional behavior, in addition to the ability to optimize their own performance at a much faster speed in comparison to those past generations of systems.

References

1. Gulati, H., & Singh, A. (2025). Foundations of AI-augmented observability. *IEEE Internet Computing.*
2. Chen, L., Zheng, X., Zheng, Z., & Sun, G. (2021). OpBoost: Learning-based anomaly detection in observability pipelines. *IEEE Transactions of Network and Service Management, 18*(3), 3421–3435. https://doi.org/10.1109/TNSM.2021.3088431
3. Pum, M. (2024). Applied AI in DevOps incident management. *Journal of Systems Architecture, 140*, 102031. Elsevier. https://doi.org/10.1016/j.sysarc.2023.102031
4. Aivaliotis, P., Georgoulias, E., Tzelepis, D., & Makris, S. (2022). Machine learning in industrial cloud monitoring. *Computers in Industry, 137*, 103602. https://doi.org/10.1016/j.compind.2022.103602
5. Mao, Y., Zheng, L., Wang, Y., & Lyu, M. R. (2019). RedAlert: An intelligent tracing system. *IEEE Transactions of Services Computing, 13*(4), 675–689. https://doi.org/10.1109/TSC.2018.2864761
6. Bauer, A., & Suri, N. (2020). Security in cloud-based observability systems. *Journal of Cloud Computing, 9*(1), 45. https://doi.org/10.1186/s13677-020-00179-9
7. Baccour, A., Baati, R., & Belghith, A. (2023). Hybrid approaches to privacy-preserving telemetry. *Future Generation Computer Systems, 147*, 78–90. https://doi.org/10.1016/j.future.2023.03.014
8. Sayagh, Y., Adams, B., & Hassan, A. E. (2022). An empirical study of trace logging practices. *IEEE Transactions of Software Engineering, 48*(6), 2273–2293. https://doi.org/10.1109/TSE.2020.3033512
9. Oliveira, A., Silva, C., & Lemos, M. (2019). Continuous compliance in cloud observability. *Computing, 101*, 849–867. https://doi.org/10.1007/s00607-018-0616-9
10. Han, X., Zhang, Y., & Wang, C. (2021). Explainable anomaly detection in cloud systems. *Information Fusion, 72*, 1–14. https://doi.org/10.1016/j.inffus.2021.02.008
11. Kim, H., Kim, S., & Seok, C. (2020). Deep learning-based root cause analysis in microservices. *Empirical Software Engineering, 25*, 4943–4975. https://doi.org/10.1007/s10664-020-09890-z
12. Zhang, Y., Li, Q., Xu, H., & Jin, X. (2020). AIOps for service health diagnosis. *IEEE Transactions of Network and Service Management, 17*(4), 2520–2533. https://doi.org/10.1109/TNSM.2020.3024623
13. Jindal, A., Chen, J., Yu, G., & Lin, W. (2021). TraceX: Diagnosing failures in distributed systems. In *Proceedings of the IEEE International Conference of Data Engineering (ICDE)* (pp. 2078–2089). https://doi.org/10.1109/ICDE51399.2021.00203
14. Abdi, M., Zhang, S., & Kim, Y. (2020). Federated learning for secure cloud telemetry. *PLoS ONE, 15*(8), e0237868. https://doi.org/10.1371/journal.pone.0237868
15. El-Masri, S., Barhamgi, M., & Defude, B. (2023). Benchmarks and gaps in LLM-based observability. *Artificial Intelligence Review*. https://doi.org/10.1016/j.artint.2023.103972

Chapter 10
Carbon Footprint Reduction with AI in Cloud Data Centers

Manoj Ravi and Meetu Malhotra

Abstract The rapid growth of cloud computing has created serious environmental issues, largely because the data centers around the world consume a huge amount of energy, leading to carbon emissions. This chapter discusses the role of Artificial Intelligence (AI) toward transforming the carbon footprint reduction challenges in cloud data centers that include energy efficiency, renewable energy integration, and carbon-aware computing. Its leading techniques are dynamic resource scheduling , AI cooling optimization, and AI-powered data center architecture. The chapter discusses also AI for real-time carbon tracking and geospatial load shifting to cleaner energy areas. Industry case studies with technology leaders such as Google and Microsoft show real-world applications and environmental impact. Through adoption of AI technologies cloud providers may notably decrease the energy consumption and consequential greenhouse gas emissions toward a sustainable digital future.

Keywords Carbon footprint · Reduction of carbon emission · AI carbon footprint · Cloud carbon footprint · Carbon emission by data centers

10.1 Introduction

The advancement of digital infrastructures transformed the data center to a cloud system marking it as the most important aspect of communication, business, and technology. It acts as the central nervous system to small startups and global conglomerates. It enables them to deliver essential services 24/7. But there is a weakness to this primary function: greatly consuming energy. An increase in consumption of services raises power demand and turns these data centers into huge contributors to the carbon emission problem.

M. Ravi (✉)
Lenovo, Raleigh-Durham-Chapel Hill Area, Raleigh, NC, USA

M. Malhotra
Harrisburg University of Science and Technology, Charlotte Metro, Harrisburg, PA, USA

B. Pandey, A. Patel (eds.), *Revolutionizing the Cloud*,
https://doi.org/10.1007/978-3-032-07479-9_10

Given the size of operations of these centers, consuming even a small amount of additional energy can be wasteful [1]. Standard on prem, however, maintains servers at a fixed capacity which leads to hardware stalling in off-peak periods. Unlike the rest, cloud data centers control their resources dynamically [2]. Still, they face hurdles such as the need to reduce energy consumption while increasing performance delivery. This balance sets the bar higher for organizations aiming for good operational and environmental efficiency.

10.1.1 Role of AI in Cloud Data Centers

Artificial intelligence leads to smarter workload management. AI-based systems don't simply allocate workloads on a set schedule so much as just constantly keep track of what's being done and find ways to optimize it. They can determine when energy is less expensive, or when alternatives to conventional energy sources such as renewable energy are more abundant and lessening reliance on fossil fuels. This kind of detailed control is the way data centers can keep up that balance between sustainability and performance, and make sure they're meeting both the demands of operations and the demands of the environment.

By making its operations more efficient, however, AI also helps reinvest and futureproof the infrastructure. As renewable integration becomes more of a priority, AI has been used to predict power demand and coordinate the operations of the data center with moments of peak renewable output. This combination reduces the carbon footprint and encourages the move to greener energy models worldwide.

To summarize, cloud data centers are a critical requirement in the digital economy of today but their energy requirement and the associated carbon emissions remain as a significant challenge. AI-powered optimization techniques might be a promising approach to address these issues. Through dynamic resource allocation, energy demand prediction, and renewable energy use, AI is not only maximizing the performance of cloud data centers, but also minimizing their environmental footprint. This marrying of technology with the sustainability agenda is creating the possibility of a future in which digital development can coexist with environmental care.

10.2 The Surging Emissions Challenge from Data Centers

Cloud computing enables firms to scale up their operations efficiently, but at the cost of high energy use. New research suggests that the world's servers are responsible for using around 200 terawatt-hours (TWh) of electricity each year or around 1% of the world's entire electricity demand. The sources of these carbon footprints are cooling infrastructure, server usage, and power utilization.

10.2.1 Pros of Data Center Emissions

And the emissions are the obvious downside: The data centers' existence isn't a total environmental disaster so long as it's run efficiently:

1. Savings through data center efficiency—Cloud service providers benefit from economies of scale that enable large, efficient data centers to serve multiple tenants, resulting in higher utilization rates and fewer servers sitting idle.
2. AI-enabled optimization—Top cloud operators are applying AI-driven sustainability [2] methodologies to minimize energy waste and carbon emissions.
3. Enables remote work and digital applications—Cloud solutions reduce the requirement to travel, some local emissions, and with it, indirectly some outside emissions.
4. Transition to renewable energy—A number of companies are now cloaking their data centers in sustainable energy as a step toward reducing their dependence on fossil fuels.

10.2.2 Cons of Data Center Emissions

Even in the wake of progress, it's not all progress:

1. High power consumption—More than 200 TWh a year gas-guzzling data centers contribute a lot of carbon to planet.
2. Dependency on non-renewable energy—Supply of power for a data center is a mix of renewable and non-renewable, where the latter commands predominantly [3].
3. E-waste, hardware maintenance—The end of life for a server results in electronic waste, not to mention the maintenance associated with coolers, which all have an impact.
4. Heat—Similarly, large data centers generate heat that puts a strain on cooling and increases water usage, particularly in cooling needs.

10.3 Energy Efficiency and Resource Optimization Through AI

10.3.1 Dynamic Resource Allocation

Systems powered by AI can predict demand in compute capacity and utilize it efficiently, preventing idle hardware from being wasted. With the help of historical data and real-time monitoring, AI ensures servers are active only when necessary, saving power.

Dynamic resource provisioning is an IT strategy to adjust smartly compute and storage resources according to usage level within a trend. Telemetry-trained AI models can recognize patterns in application usage, seasonality, and user behavior. This allows cloud platforms to supply just enough computing to satisfy the demand, scaling up or down in small increments. In contrast to the classical static provisioning [4], this approach results in much less over-provisioning and minimizes the waste of energy caused by under-utilization.

Machine learning techniques especially for time-series forecasting models can predict peak loads and automate provisioning of VMs or containers. Reinforcement learning may also be used to learn the optimal policies of resource management on-the-fly between performance and energy.

What is more, AI has the capability to coordinate workloads across clusters and even geographically dispersed data centers to achieve load balance, and thus optimizing thermal profiles while leaving less need for overcooling on hot spots.

Case Study

DeepMind used deep reinforcement learning to reduce energy consumption for cooling its data centers by up to 40%. Operating in real time, the system worked by crunching thousands of readings from sensors—temperature, power levels, pump speeds, and so on—and then recommending changes for control systems to act on right away. Eventually, the AI agent learned which combinations of cooling conditions made it most efficient in different environmental and load conditions.

There is no reason that the same approach could not be possible for optimum allocation of computing resources. A reinforcement learning model observes attributes like CPU/memory usage, the thermal output of the server, and real-time demand of the user and can learn to dynamically move workloads to servers running within an optimal thermal and energy efficiency range. Unwanted lower load servers could be idled down or put into a low energy state, where high load processes could be cleverly moved onto fewer servers operating at more optimal efficiency.

This has the advantage of not only saving power, but also extending the life span of hardware through decreased thermal cycling and less wear on physical components. It saves costs and does so in a way that is good for the environment, illustrating a model for how AI can be applied across the infrastructure stack, not just in cooling, such as the computational core of the data center.

10.3.2 Dynamic Voltage and Frequency Scaling (DVFS)

DVFS. In addition to DVFS-based frequency scaling, controlling the operating status of memories and the interference from other devices can be effective (Tagami et al. 2009).

Dynamic Voltage and Frequency Scaling (DVFS) is a power management technique that dynamically adjusts the voltage and frequency of a processor according to the system workload. In cloud environment, where power consumption is a pressing issue, DVFS becomes an effective way to save power at the expense of very little performance degradation.

How DVFS Works

The processor power is approximately the square of the voltage and directly proportional to the frequency. DVFS mechanisms scale down the voltage and the frequency dynamically, when full performance is not needed, e.g., during idle or low load intervals. On the other hand, they increases the performance during peak periods.

Models based on AI can tune the DVFS at run time, based on the past usage history data, and predict the future demand to proactively configure DVFS settings that not only maximizes energy efficiency [5], but also meets SLA requirements as shown in Fig. 10.1.

In general, DVFS operates at the hardware or OS level with fixed thresholds. Nevertheless, AI allows us to control a system in a more intelligent and flexible way. Machine learning models are capable of observing workload trends, thermal states, and energy costs in order to decide in real time on optimal frequency-voltage pairs.

In reinforcement learning, in particular, considerable promise has been demonstrated for learning under dynamic policies which balance power against various notions of system performance, leading to dramatic advances in energy conservation [5].

Implementation Examples

Modern CPUs have DVFS control based on Intel RPA L (Running Average Power Limit) and it is possible to integrate AI to optimize the applied RAPL policies in cloud environments.

Google's AI-driven power controller uses predictive-messaging to tune server performance on-the-fly (and even DVFS parameters) to save power during off-peak times.

Challenges and Compromises

Sensitivity to Latency: Some applications need a uniform performance, constraining the amount of DVFS available.

Thermal Limitations: Aggressive voltage scaling might violate thermal constraints.

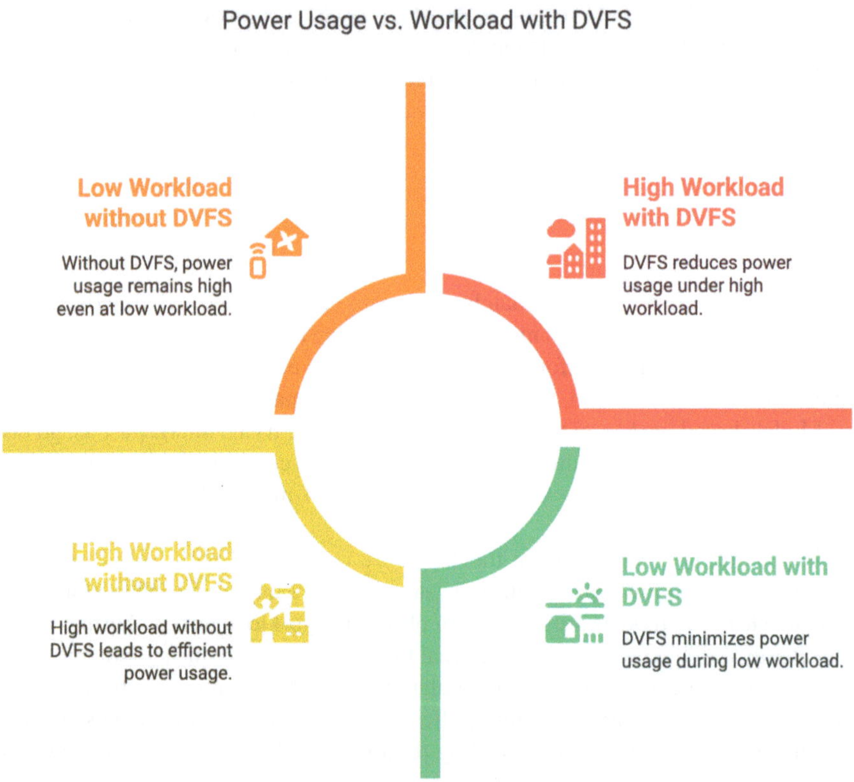

Fig. 10.1 Power usage vs workload with DVFS

Complexity: The realization of AI-aided DVFS requires the support of precise workload prediction, combined with real-time interaction mechanisms with hardware.

However, despite such challenges, AI-driven DVFS is still a significant step for reducing the on-going massive increase of data center energy consumption and carbon emissions [6].

10.3.3 Workload Scheduling

AI can decide when to schedule workloads to run at lower carbon intensity or lower price per energy. This is especially powerful in contexts of rich variability of renewable to non-renewable energy.

10.3.4 Smart HVAC Control

AI algorithms can optimize parameters on HVAC (Heating, Ventilation, and Air Conditioning) systems—including fan speed, set points on temperature, and chiller settings—in real time in response to information about the external world, the behavior of the servers, and estimated thermal loads. These systems maximize airflow patterns and minimize useless cooling cycles, providing energy savings while keeping steady temperatures.

Modern data centers are increasingly based on economization which can cool the data center (in the water and water mist modes) in a very energy efficient way. AI can decide which strategy to use at a certain point of time, transition smoothly between the cooling methodologies—from water cooling or air—balancing external weather elements, the workloads running in the servers and performance, and cost-efficiency calculations. For example, when outside air temperature is cool, AI can trigger free cooling modes with reduced mechanical cooling.

Moreover, AI works together with BMS to achieve a comprehensive management of thermal environment, to regulate HVAC and related systems, such as humidity control, airflow zoning, and floor layout optimization, for lessening thermal hotspots and energy consumption [6].

10.3.5 Predictive Maintenance

AI-based predictive maintenance solutions use historical maintenance data, equipment run-time data, sensor readings, and anomaly detection to predict when a failure will likely happen in an HVAC unit before it does [7]. Machine learning-based models, including regression analysis and neural networks, can detect subtle changes in performance which could be leading indicators of a failure—such as compressor inefficiencies, air filter choking or fan bearing wear.

By identifying these problems early on, data center operators can schedule maintenance during non-peak hours, which helps to reduce the tendency of emergency repairs that, in many cases, will require back-up cooling equipment to be turned on. This predictive method not only reduces costly unbudgeted downtime but also allows cooling systems to operate at maximum efficiency, and correlate directly to lower carbon emissions and operational costs.

Example: A leading North American cloud provider applied AI-driven predictive maintenance to its HVAC (heating, ventilation, and air conditioning) systems and reduced unplanned service incidents by 25% while also increasing energy efficiency by 12% across several data centers.

Intelligent HVAC and predictive maintenance, when combined, create a strong AI-based approach for optimizing cooling systems. They increase the efficiency of the energy consumed, saving the lifetime of the equipment, and represent great savings in the carbon footprint of the functioning of a data center.

Predictive Analytics of Equipment Life

By tracking the performance of hardware over time, AI can recognize patterns that may be indicative of wear and tear. This let's data center operators optimize their replacement cycles, so they can cut down on electronic waste and the carbon costs of building new equipment.

Predictive Analytics Is Necessary

But traditional approaches to maintenance–everything from cost-driven track and fix methods to scheduled maintenance based on a fixed interval—frequently succeed only in overspending for either an overworked or grossly underutilized asset. In the reactive case, instead you only act in an after-the-fact way and so you can expect for the printer to break at inconvenient times a lot more often. On the other hand, fixed intervals risk causing unnecessary downtime or replacement of parts that are still in good, working order. Predictive analysis is a compromise – you use it to predict the remaining useful life (RUL) of equipment, so that you can maintain it only when it's necessary. This not only reduces down time, but, also prolongs the life of valuable assets.

How Does Predictive Analysis Function?

The predictive analysis of equipment lifetime in data centers is based on the following pillars and explained in the Fig. 10.2

(1) Data collection and sensor technology contemporary data centers feature vast sensor networks to monitor a variety of parameters—temperature, vibration, electrical currents, humidity, and the like. This one-second data documents each piece of gear's state of affairs and paints an ever-moving picture of it's health and performance.
(2) Historical data and trend analysis along with the historical performance monitoring data, failure history and historic maintenance details are the essential data sets. Engineers can derive and monitor these trends to determine first signs of wear or degradation prior to the failure of a piece of equipment.
(3) AI and Machine Learning Algorithms: Advanced AI models are what predictive analysis is built upon. Machine learning models, which can be trained on vast amounts of sensor and historical data, can uncover outliers and regularities that a human operator may overlook, and can estimate the remaining life of a component with surprisingly good accuracy, using techniques such as regression analysis, neural networks, and digital twins.
(4) Anomaly detection and prognostics predictive systems are used primarily for detecting anomalous conditions while being monitored in real time. As an example, a small change in temperature in conjunction with an unusual vibration

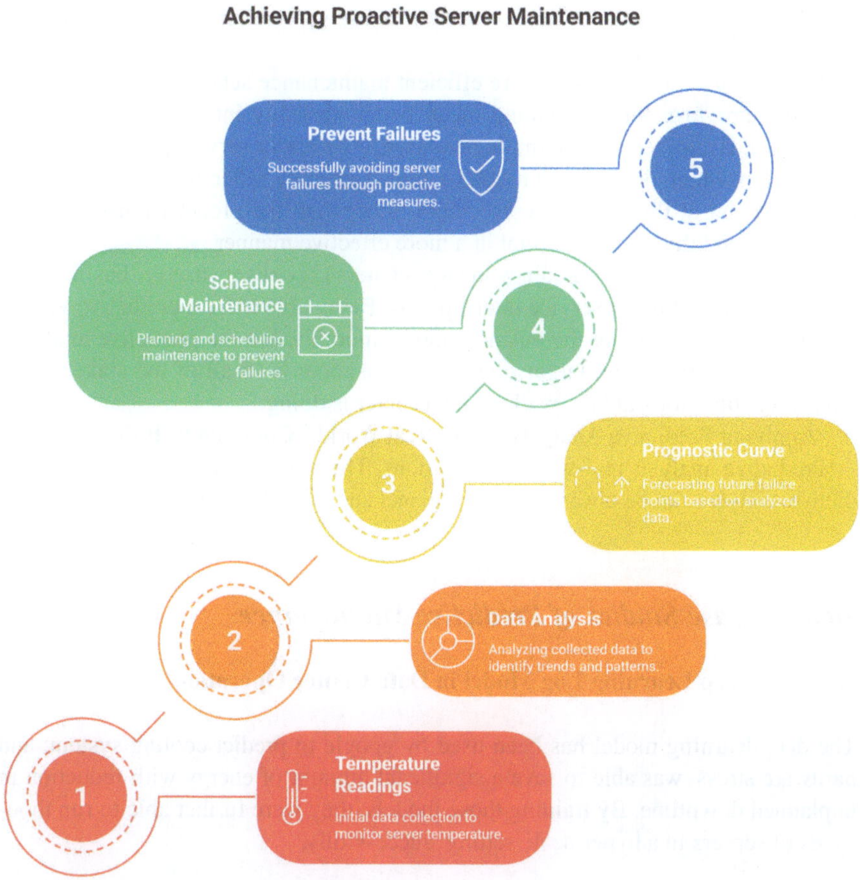

Fig. 10.2 Achieving proactive server maintenance

rate might mean that mechanical decay is in progress at a cooling fan. Such early warnings allow predictive maintenance actions to be taken in advance and therefore to avoid catastrophic failures.

Advantages of Predictive Analysis

Longer equipment life by only making maintenance calls when data says they are needed, predictive analytics prevents both early replacement and excessive wear. This hot knife in data center management greatly lengthens the life span of data center equipment and avoids every single piece of equipment that is being made the best usage of.

Less downtime, more money in your pocket predicting failures allows for corrective measures to be scheduled rather than relying on unexpected breakdowns.

This helps to reduce maintenance costs, decrease service interruptions, and lower emergency repair costs.

Effective use of resources, more efficient maintenance schedules, and proactive infrastructure investment planning mean better visibility into the health of your equipment. Examples of such implementation, co-work or service planning include data centers which are enabled to plan a staged upgrade reflecting the condition of the equipment at the time of replacement rather than the predetermined replacement time, and thus deploy capital in a more effective manner.

Increased operational efficiency in data centers [2] deliver stronger business services by means of fewer service interruptions. Being able to have predictive visibility can help with running the business more smoothly, but the predictive analytics can be incorporated into larger operational dashboards so all of the stakeholders have a real time look at how well the data center is doing.

"Applying Predictive Analysis to the Real World." Community-Built Use Case.

Predictive analysis real-world applications .The real-world applications of predictive analysis can be observed in tech giants and other big companies:

10.3.6 Case Studies of Predictive Maintenance

Google's Deep Learning Log Model in Data Center Operation

The deep learning model has been used by google to predict cooling system, and hardware stress was able to save a significant amount of energy with reduction in unplanned downtime. By training those models, they were further able to run thousands of servers in a hyper-scale setting successfully.

Microsoft's Carbon-Aware Strategies

Microsoft incorporates predictive maintenance in its larger model for optimizing energy and resources. AI models scrutinize both operational conditions and environmental information to help ensure that equipment not only runs longer, but runs more sustainability—supporting the company's eco-friendly efforts.

IBM's AI-Powered Platforms

IBM's predictive maintenance solutions offer a centralized dashboard for monitoring equipment health. By combining sensor information with past performance information, such platforms provide actionable insights, which can help to dramatically decrease maintenance costs while increasing overall system reliability.

10.3.7 Quality and Integration of Data

As the quality of the data and its level of detail play crucial roles when training and developing prediction models. Technical challenges may involve adequate sensor calibration and joint information synthesis.

Model complexity and the adaptability of a growing data center and varying hardware configurations require models to accommodate these changes. On-going training and re-calibration of the model are necessary to retain accuracy with changing operational conditions.

As prediction-based systems store sensitive operational data, it is of utmost importance to protect this data from cyber threats. Predictive maintenance systems need to have strong data security protocols in place.

Future developments, advances in sensor technologies, better data analytics, and more powerful AI algorithms can be expected to develop predictive analytics capabilities further [7]. Masked by advances like artificial intelligence, training networks, and deduplication of data, new technology like digital twins—or virtual mirrors of data center components—are creating new potential for simulating and predicting how hardware will behave under specific circumstances.

10.4 Carbon-Aware Computing

Carbon-aware computing involves adjusting computer jobs according to the carbon intensity of the supply of energy at any given time. AI supports cloud computing by allowing real-time decision-making to minimize emissions based on when and where cleaner energy is available to execute computing jobs.

10.4.1 Geographic Workload Shifting

AI could be used to rebalance the geographical distribution of workloads based on data of global carbon intensity of multiple power grids. By offloading non-latency-sensitive tasks—such as batch jobs, data pre-processing, and analytics workloads—to regions in the cloud provider's fleet that today are operating on renewable energy, cloud providers can lower their operational emissions.

Machine learning algorithms are applied to process energy mix data (coal, gas, solar, wind, etc), predict green energy availability in local regions, and take the decision of where to run specific jobs. One such method called carbon-aware job scheduling uses AI to reduce the environmental impact without affecting the quality of service.

10.4.2 Carbon-Aware APIs

Carbon-aware APIs allow applications to query the current carbon intensity of electricity as it is generated. Artificial intelligence (AI)-based workload managers can then consume this data to be able to dynamically change job schedules. For instance, load can be delayed till off-peak time or redirected to greener areas.

Example: As part of Microsoft's Project Tardigrade, users can schedule jobs on Azure taking the current carbon intensity of the grid into account. This carbon-aware job scheduling can make substantial differences in the carbon output of background workloads.

10.4.3 Demand Response and AI

AI also can contribute to grid demand response programs by decreasing compute when electricity is most in demand. This minimizes carbon-intensive peak power generation and helps to stabilize the grid. AI algorithms predict peak hours and communicate with power companies to let air gardens be the smart solution to demand flexibility.

10.5 Renewable Energy Integration

It's key to incorporate renewable energy systems like wind and solar into data center operations [3]. But the catch is provided by the fact that these sources are intermittent ones. AI addresses the predictability and control with this problem.

10.5.1 Prediction of the Renewable Energy Generation

AI algorithms—from time-series forecasting models to neural networks—can approximate when renewable energy will be available by analyzing historical weather data, satellite imagery, and real-time sensor measurements from solar panels and wind turbines. These predictions help data centers time power-intensive tasks when green power is plentiful [8].

For instance, AI systems could pre-schedule, hours in advance, intense processing that needs to be done during times of predicted high solar output, or charge on-site battery storage. On the other hand, under low availability of RE, non-urgent workloads could be postponed and the power draw can be reduced.

10.5.2 Grid Optimization

Artificial intelligence enables smart coordination between on-site renewables, batteries, and grid energy. AI-enabled [7] energy management systems can determine in real time when to store energy, discharge it or sell any excess back to the electricity network.

AI also works for microgrid management so that local power systems can function almost autonomously. This decreases dependence upon centralized fossil-fuel grids and enables more efficient utilization of distributed renewable generation. The prediction of loads, the arbitrage of energy, and the optimization of carbon are performed together.

10.5.3 Case Study: Google's Carbon-Aware Computing

Google introduced an AI-powered carbon-aware computing platform that optimizes work scheduling by sending them to the region with the lowest operational carbon [9]. Combined with its predictive models of solar and wind generation, it has enabled Google to raise the alignment of its energy usage with carbon-free sources by as much as 20%.

10.6 AI in Data Center Design

Generative AI and simulation tools can facilitate the architectural planning of data center to maximize cooling airflow spacing, space efficiency, and equipment orientation [9]. These configurations greatly decrease cooling and maintenance energy needs.

AI-driven design (Fig. 10.3) tools rely on liberal applications of technologies such as computational fluid dynamics (CFD), reinforcement learning, and generative design to help them find the most efficacious physical layouts for server racks, cooling infrastructure, and electricity supply. These models represent a large number of design and environmental scenarios to find the most energy efficient and sustainable design.

10.6.1 Layout Optimization

AI algorithms can replicate how various designs would influence airflow, temperature profile, and energy use. Designers can reposition server racks, air inlets and outlets, and cooling devices to obtain better heat dissipation performance based on

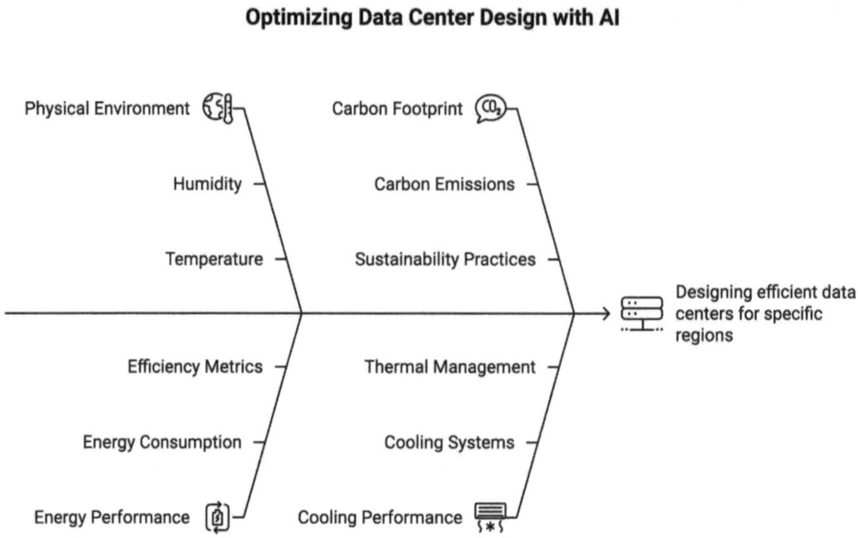

Fig. 10.3 Optimizing data center design with AI

the location of possible thermal hotspot. The end result is less cooling energy and a more even temperature throughout the building as shown in Fig. 10.4.

10.6.2 Use of Space and Equipment

AI can recommend ideal site configurations that extract the most from the physical environment and minimize total infrastructure [9]. For example, it could suggest non-linear placement of racks or adaptive zoning according to predicted workload densities and cooling requirements.

AI generated ideal rack positions and pathways to reduce airflow obstruction and improve ease of maintenance.

10.6.3 Simulating Environmental Scenarios

Simulation-based models using AI can adopt holistic factors from the physical environment (such as humidity, temperature, altitude) to design data centers for specific geographical regions. Pre-construction calculation of energy [5], carbon, and cooling performance can perform in these simulations.

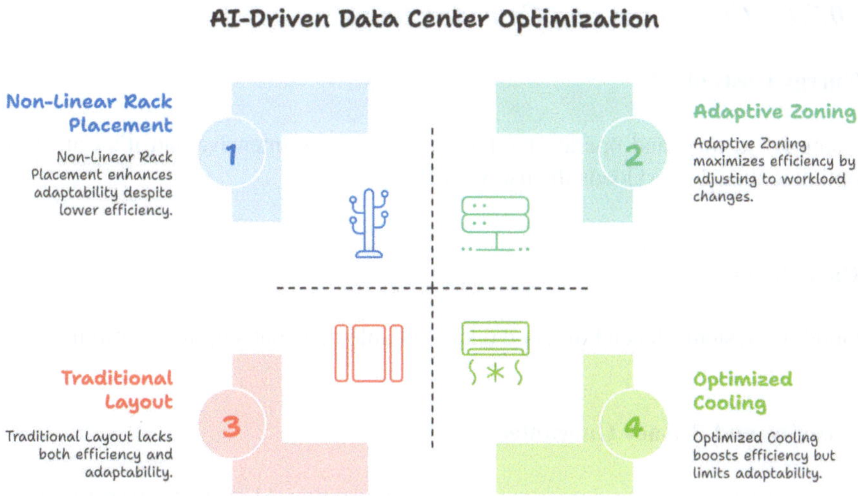

Fig. 10.4 AI-driven data center optimization

10.6.4 Case Studies: AI-Based Design at Microsoft

Microsoft used an AI-enhanced design process for a new data center in Sweden. The AI considered more than 20,000 design combinations and decided on a design that would cut expected cooling loads by 25% and land use by 15%. The design also maximized crossed ventilation depending on prevailing winds.AI can be employed in designing data centers, not only to bring down operational emissions but also to cut embodied carbon by reducing the amount of waste created during construction and by using materials efficiently. AI

of green AIs will play a vital role in building a more sustainable, location-aware, and efficient data center as cloud providers scale their infrastructure across the globe.

10.7 Real-time Monitoring and Reporting of CO_2

For example, AI can automate sustainability [2] metrics by aggregating and analyzing telemetry from servers, PUE (power usage effectiveness) monitors and carbon intensity feeds [4]. This enables the real-time monitoring and regulatory compliance.

10.7.1 Challenges and Considerations

Energy Costs of AI

Using AI to train and operate models can be energy-intensive and it's critical to optimize the AI workloads themselves [4].

Data Quality

Good AI systems depend on good data—reliable data that's up-to-the-moment.

Security and Privacy Guarantee

Privacy protection is an important issue in preventing AI systems from revealing sensitive data.

10.7.2 Future Prospects and Challenges

AI holds tremendous potential to advance sustainable cloud computing. However, challenges remain, including high initial implementation costs, computational overhead of AI itself, and data privacy concerns. Addressing these barriers will be critical to fully harnessing AI's power in carbon footprint reduction.

10.8 Conclusion

Cloud data centers are essential for the modern digital world, but their environmental impact necessitates urgent action. AI offers innovative solutions to cut emissions and optimize energy efficiency, paving the way for a more sustainable technological future.

References

1. Harris, Lorenzaj. (2024). Sustainable cloud computing: AI-driven solutions for resource efficiency.
2. Amazon. (2021). Amazon Sustainability Report. Retrieved 22 May, 2024 from: https://sustainability.aboutamazon.com/.

3. International Energy Agency (IEA). (2021). *Data Centre Energy Consumption*. Retrieved from IEA.
4. Chaisiri, S., Lee, B. S., & Niyato, D. (2012). Optimization of resource provisioning cost in cloud computing. *IEEE Transactions on Services Computing, 5*(2), 164–177. https://doi.org/10.1109/TSC.2011.7
5. Masanet, E., Brown, R. E., Shehabi, A., Koomey, J. G., & Nordman, B. (2007). Estimating the energy use and efficiency potential of U.S. data centers. *Proceedings of the IEEE, 95*(9), 1440–1460.
6. Statista. (2023). *Cloud computing energy consumption statistics*. Retrieved from Statista.
7. Patel, R., & Nair, S. (2023). Sustainability in cloud computing: The role of artificial intelligence. *Journal of Cloud Computing, 45*(3), 210–224.
8. Rayaprolu, Ranjith. (2022). *Cloud economics 2.0: The AI advantage in resource optimization*.
9. Google AI. (2020). *AI for data center efficiency*. Retrieved from Google AI.

Chapter 11
AI and IoT: Shaping the Future of Cloud Ecosystems

Prashanthi Matam, Tirumala Rao Chimpiri, and Nixal Kumar Patel

Abstract The design and use of cloud systems are being significantly altered by the confluence of artificial intelligence (AI) and the internet of things (IoT). Clouds can now process the massive amounts of data that are flowing in from networked devices in real time, rather than just storing static data and serving primarily as a cloud-based data warehouse. AI is used to identify patterns in the running sensor data and initiate certain actions in an ever-expanding IoT network. This enables the network to function with minimal or no human interaction, particularly when operating remotely or in real time.

This chapter examines the specific factors causing this shift, with a focus on how AI and IoT are intertwined in modern cloud infrastructures. We discuss how they interact and provide examples of how they are used in a number of case studies, including those in industry, urban planning, agriculture, and healthcare. These examples demonstrate both the benefits and challenges of coping with increasingly interconnected and "smarter" systems.

Concerns about trust, security, and privacy are prevalent in this change. Indeed, the variety of devices, the scalability of many devices, and the lack of device standards increase risks even if AI in cybersecurity and anomaly detection can be crucial for enhancing security suited to expanding IoT ecosystems. The consequences of compliance and ethical data practices are also covered in this chapter, especially as they relate to cloud space beyond national borders. Lastly, we examine the emerging potential of generative AI in enabling tasks such as automated edge behavior, the creation of synthetic data, and improvements in simulation modeling. To encourage the development of cloud ecosystems that are not only intelligent and adaptable, but also sustainable and morally sound, a forward-looking architectural model is offered as a guide.

P. Matam (✉)
Independent Researcher, Mountlake Terrace, WA, USA

T. R. Chimpiri
Independent Researcher, Center Reach, NY, USA

N. K. Patel
Independent Researcher, Lake Hiawatha, NJ, USA

B. Pandey, A. Patel (eds.), *Revolutionizing the Cloud*,
https://doi.org/10.1007/978-3-032-07479-9_11

Keywords Artificial intelligence · Internet of Things · Cloud ecosystems · Privacy · Ethics · Sustainability

11.1 Introduction

11.1.1 Background on Cloud Ecosystems

Modern digital infrastructure is built on the scalable, on-demand processing power, data storage, and application services that cloud computing offers. It was first intended to help IT departments reduce costs, but it has since evolved into an intelligent, flexible ecosystem [1]. Current cloud platforms are made to manage a wide range of tasks and can be used for everything from processing real-time data inputs from field sensors to running artificial intelligence algorithms. It is permitting not only distributed systems but also self-optimizing, self-orchestrating, and self-monitoring systems [2].

The cloud has transitioned from being an independent operating system to becoming the central component of a complex ecosystem that integrates devices, data, and decision-making processes. This transformation has enabled the development of emerging technologies like artificial intelligence (AI) and the internet of things (IoT), which excel when real-time data processing and intelligent automation are feasible.

Why the Cloud Is Changing Due to AI and IoT

IoT and AI are both important on their own. They provide a plethora of new opportunities when connected and integrated through the cloud. Real-world data is gathered by IoT technologies from industrial machinery, medical devices, environmental sensors, and more. AI technologies then examine this data to find new trends, forecast future occurrences, and control automated processes [2]. Now, this integration can be carried out at scale thanks to cloud infrastructure, which enables all data import, model training, inference, and over-the-air model updating to occur in a single distributed framework [3].

Consider how sensor technology installed in cars and roads could enhance an urban transportation system at a more local and applied level. For example, it could enable data about a traffic jam to be transmitted from the network to a smartphone app that uses it to either recommend an alternate route to impacted drivers or to time traffic signals [4].

New Market Trends and Their Effects Worldwide

AI and IoT will be used by all companies worldwide to provide intelligent, flexible business models and efficient procedures. Sensor networks can also be used for other things, such tracking weather patterns and soil conditions in agriculture. When combined with AI models, it enables more accurate and effective use of fertilizer and water in food production, reducing waste and resulting in higher outputs [5].

According to recent industry trends, this will necessitate significant expenditures in both AI-IoT and greater automation [6]. Businesses must start thinking about their digitization capabilities, workforce training, and general governance as adoption is expected to increase in order to make sure they are prepared for these more complex, intelligent, cloud-based systems.

A commentary on the changes in cloud computing brought about by AI and IoT is provided in the following sections. Therefore, we don't just highlight issues to consider in terms of sustainability and security. By doing this, we are able to draw attention to the challenges and opportunities of creating intelligent digital environments by connecting to actual situations and difficulties as well as architectural discussions.

11.2 Technological Foundations and Integration

11.2.1 IoT Architecture in the Cloud

In the architecture of any IoT system, physical devices and sensors deployed in the field are essential for data collection. These may include agricultural soil probes, industrial machinery monitors, or smart city cameras. Regulations aim to limit the amount of data collected, which is then processed by local gateways or edge nodes before being transmitted for further processing and storage in the cloud, potentially following some initial preprocessing [1].

To accommodate the increasing number of IoT devices and their data, cloud platforms play a crucial role. These platforms consolidate information from numerous sensors and systems, facilitating secure storage and access to historical data for analysis and practical application [3]. Leading cloud providers such as Amazon, Microsoft, and Google deliver IoT services that encompass device onboarding, communication, and protocols. These offerings help businesses navigate the complexities of diverse field-based equipment, each having unique communication standards, capabilities, and reliability challenges. A key issue in integrating IoT with Cloud infrastructure is ensuring security and interoperability. Most IoT devices possess hardware limitations, restricting their ability to execute complex security protocols. When combined with the vast scale of the internet, this limitation creates a substantial security risk that necessitates mitigation through robust end-to-end encryption and reliable identity management [7].

11.2.2 AI Model Lifecycle in Cloud-Based Systems

In a cloud environment, the lifecycle of an AI model involves several key stages: data ingestion, training, validation, deployment, and retraining. The cloud's scalable computing resources are particularly beneficial during the training phase, which is often resource-intensive for deep learning models. Platforms such as Amazon SageMaker, Azure ML, and Google Vertex AI have greatly automated many aspects of this lifecycle, including tasks like labeling training datasets and optimizing hyperparameters. Once AI models are deployed, they must adapt to continually evolving data environments, a challenge addressed by "model drift detection." In dynamic systems like the Internet of Things (IoT), where input conditions frequently change, cloud-based monitoring tools can identify declines in performance and trigger retraining workflows. This continuous process enables the model to remain precise and effective in its specific setting.

The application of AI in IoT contexts often involves stringent time constraints. For instance, in a flexible manufacturing system (FMS) line, immediate action is required to shut down a machine upon detecting a fault, or in medical alert systems that must deactivate if vital signs change critically. Any delay in processing, no matter how brief, is unacceptable. Cloud solutions address these needs through hybrid capabilities that allow processing to occur either centrally in a datacenter or at the edge near devices, based on criteria such as connectivity, processing urgency, and privacy considerations.

11.2.3 Interoperability Standards and Middleware

The significance of communication between AI and IoT within cloud ecosystems through standardized methods is increasingly evident. Middleware solutions enable consideration of hardware when utilizing cloud services. These middleware layers handle messaging, protocol conversion, and API integration necessary for ensuring seamless functionality of devices from different vendors [8]. To guarantee the efficient operation of IoT systems, devices must connect and exchange data securely and according to standard protocols. Protocols like MQTT, CoAP, and OPC UA define clear communication guidelines in heterogeneous environments. These standards now allow diverse devices, designed by different companies, to collaborate within a unified framework. Simultaneously, ONNX provides an open format for representing deep learning models, facilitating AI workflows by enabling developers to train models in one framework and deploy them in another without extensive code modification, thereby easing AI integration across infrastructures [9]. Nonetheless, scalability poses challenges as it often inversely affects embeddability. While proprietary platforms offer quick and initial solution deployment, they may restrict integration with other applications or tie users to specific service providers. Conversely, solutions built on open standards and modular architecture offer greater flexibility for adaptation, upgrades, or migration as technology and business needs evolve [8].

11.2.4 Edge to Cloud Continuum

Data processing need not necessarily occur in the cloud. In fact, numerous IoT applications demand performance levels that are hindered by service delays in data processing. Edge computing addresses this issue by shifting computational tasks to the network's periphery, including gateways, embedded processors, or micro-data centers. This approach reduces latency and network congestion while enhancing privacy by keeping data local. These components together constitute the edge-cloud continuum.

For instance, an AI model can be developed in the cloud using aggregated sensor data and subsequently deployed to the edge for real-time, on-site inference. If conditions change, edge devices can transmit new data back to the cloud, facilitating system updates or adaptations. This architecture is structured around the principles of efficiency, responsiveness, and cost-effectiveness.

Orchestration platforms like Kube Edge and AWS Greengrass support the management of this continuum by offering functions for code synchronization, monitoring device health, and updating and maintaining numerous edge nodes. The outcome is a hybrid infrastructure that harnesses the advantages of both centralized and decentralized computing systems.

11.2.5 AI-IoT and Cloud: Enabling Scalable Intelligence

When AI and the Internet of Things, or AI-IoT, merged, the technology quickly progressed from experimental pilot initiatives to large-scale enterprise application. However, the cloud, rather than edge devices or AI algorithms, is the ultimate enabler and scaler of such systems. In terms of the capabilities of widely distributed systems, cloud platforms are viewed as the foundation for data processing and administration, modeling, and orchestration.

In the following part, we will discuss how AI-IoT may employ cloud computing to "scale out" and continuously adapt and learn.

AI-IoT: Intelligence at the Edge, Scalability in the Cloud

AI-IoT integrates the sensory capabilities of IoT with the reasoning and decision-making process of AI. IoT devices can still collect data regarding temperature, vibration, and occupancy, but they lack the capability to process or act upon this information intelligently. With the integration of AI, these devices can perform localized evaluations, make forecasts, and operate autonomously. Although AI-IoT exhibits a deterministic aspect, these systems produce extensive data streams from numerous endpoints, possibly ranging from hundreds to millions. Cloud is essential in this context, providing computational power, storage, hardware, and infrastructure necessary to manage and process the data on a large scale. Without this cloud support, AI-IoT might be confined to specific use cases or limited to applications that rely on short-distance or edge processing.

Cloud-Native AI-IoT Platforms

Leading cloud service providers have started offering specialized AI-IoT services to ease deployment and integration processes. AWS IoT Core and AWS Greengrass allow devices to connect securely to the cloud, enabling data processing either in the cloud or directly on the device. Models can be trained within the cloud using Amazon SageMaker and subsequently deployed to edge devices for inference. Similarly, Microsoft's Azure IoT Hub, Azure Percept, and Azure Machine Learning deliver a full pipeline encompassing device provisioning, live analytics, and cloud model retraining capabilities. Google Cloud IoT Core and Google Vertex AI offer solutions equipped for event-driven processing, machine learning model management, and adaptable pipelines that dynamically respond to data changes in real time. These systems facilitate update management, fleet health monitoring, performance enhancement, and additional services for managing fleets of highly diverse devices, a task that is not feasible manually.

Model Deployment and Retraining Pipelines

A key benefit of utilizing cloud-based AI-IoT lies in the centralized management of the AI model lifecycle. This approach addresses the necessity of retraining models, implementing version control, and responding to environmental changes. Continuous data streaming from the field allows for automated model retraining within the cloud infrastructure. Subsequently, deploying these refined models back to the edge optimizes efficiency. Such feedback mechanisms help maintain the precision and relevance of AI-IoT ecosystems over time.

Rather than adhering to conventional cloud architectures, AI-IoT systems should consider centralized, federated, or hybrid frameworks. Emerging patterns are increasingly tailored to specific use cases and deployment contexts.

Security, Privacy, and Data Flow Control

When deploying cloud-based AI-IoT systems, it is essential to address critical considerations such as data sovereignty, encryption, and access management. These advanced infrastructures incorporate elements like role-based access control

(RBAC), zero-trust frameworks, and geo-fencing to ensure data remains localized. This is particularly crucial in cross-border operations or regulated sectors. In essence, AI-IoT pushes intelligence to the network's edge while upholding cloud scalability and resilience. It exemplifies how cloud computing, on varying scales from centralized to global, connects disparate intelligent devices, forming dynamic and adaptive networks.

11.3 Use Cases Particular to a Sector

Cloud environments are combining AI and IoT in business applications that aim to solve difficult operational issues that are not just found in technological prototypes or research labs. Even though essential technologies are the same throughout sectors, each one customizes its implementation to meet the many goals it proposes. The following highlights five significant businesses that are already feeling the effects of cloud computing, IoT, and AI convergence.

11.3.1 Intelligent Production

Data is increasingly controlling and automating factory areas. Digital twins and machine or system replicas, which employ sensor data to mimic the condition of an actual system or equipment, are technologies that more industries are using [5]. These models enable "what-if" analysis, process optimization, and the detection of potential issues before they materialize as "breakdowns."

AI in manufacturing facilities also helps operators identify issues long before they arise. New kinds of discrete data points that would normally go undetected during human inspections, like unusual vibration patterns or slight changes in energy usage, can be found with the aid of real-time analytics. These indicators add up to a meaningful forecast of higher uptime and overall reliability when given into an AI system that has previously been educated on machine behavior [5].

Management can more easily observe and measure performance and apply analytics throughout the entire operation thanks to cloud-based systems that allow centralized data capture across all of a company's locations. They can also be used as an AI eye to keep an eye on quality control by instantly identifying safety risks or assembly line hiccups [5].

11.3.2 Medical Care

The health sector is also encouraging the use of technology to continuously monitor patients, either with or without clinical supervision. Heart rate, breathing, skin temperature, and other physiological parameters can be continuously recorded thanks to wearable biosensors, adhesive sensors, remote ECG monitors, and other monitoring tools. These readings can be utilized to detect variations that indicate the need for healthcare intervention, frequently before the patient is aware that they are suffering symptoms, when AI analyzes them in the cloud.

IoT sensors in institutions can assist with managing the OR and ICU settings, locating equipment, and guiding patients through the system. AI uses data in medical systems to estimate maintenance needs for vital infrastructure, prioritize urgent cases, and arrange appointments [10]. These programs benefit patients and prevent needless resource loss in addition to streamlining processes and saving time.

11.3.3 Intelligent Urban Areas

Cities are implementing AI and IoT technology to assist in managing public safety, infrastructure, and services. Roadside sensors and traffic light timing systems provide real-time data on vehicle traffic, traffic jams, and pedestrian activity. AI systems use this data to determine the optimal time for signals or to divert traffic during emergencies or peak hours [11].

With real-time information, municipal administrators may take swifter and more decisive action, such as rerouting public transportation, restoring power after an outage, or alerting citizens to public safety issues [8]. In some areas, AI-powered video and audio systems have even been utilized to identify situations like car crashes or suspicious activity so that emergency services and law enforcement can react more quickly and effectively.

They make considerable use of cloud resources to process massive volumes of data from dispersed locations. Additionally, it enables a more central perspective of all operational efficiency gains throughout the range of services offered by city officials, from electricity to sanitation, resulting in more cohesive approaches to governance.

11.3.4 Farming

Artificial intelligence (AI) models are being used in agriculture to assist in decision-making by means of systems that interpret data from field sensors. These include environmental factors like soil moisture and nutrient decomposition, and photos captured by drones or satellites add another level of crop intelligence [9]. Following cloud analysis, artificial intelligence (AI) can identify trends in the data and suggest highly targeted interventions, such as when to irrigate or how densely to plant.

The model's usefulness lies in its accessibility. Using mobile dashboards or remote terminals, farmers can keep an eye on their field without physically visiting each plot. Better yield results are also brought about by this remote visibility, which also makes it possible to reduce the waste of resources like fertilizer and water. This can have a double-positive effect from an economic and environmental standpoint.

11.3.5 Logistics and Retail

Retailers and logistics firms are now utilizing smart technologies to enhance customer service and product management. Store shelves have sensors built into them to track product availability and movement in real time. It can be used in conjunction with AI to enhance marketing, optimize shelf placement, and forecast demand [7].

Interconnected sensors track the position, status, and transit progress of products while they are in transit. By centralizing this data across the supply chain, cloud solutions allow AI technology to take proactive actions like rerouting cargo shipments in the event of a delay or even creating alerts for temperature-sensitive products to alert teams. Distribution networks are being redesigned to be more adaptable and responsive [1].

11.4 Privacy, Security, and Risk Reduction

Businesses' capacity to use "the cloud," AI, and IoT technologies in the future depends critically on privacy and security. Because of the complexity and structure of these systems, threats are no longer isolated, and a security flaw in one app or device might have serious ramifications that affect the system. Developing reactive defenses alone is insufficient to adequately secure data and preserve system integrity; the system itself needs to be carefully and preemptively built.

11.4.1 Reevaluating Cybersecurity in Networked Settings

Additionally, because IoT devices are often found in homes, farms, cars, and warehouses, they usually do not function within the conventional IT limits. These devices frequently run on subpar hardware and don't support updates, which makes them vulnerable to cyberattacks [7]. Any interruption in the chain could result in AI making incorrect decisions or acting inappropriately. Data from these endpoints is fed into the cloud's centralized AI models.

In order to reduce these dangers, AI is also being used more and more to identify odd trends in system behavior or network traffic. Among other things, the system may recognize or notify users in real time of anomalous occurrences such "a burst of data from a device that usually transmits tiny packets" [2]. These enable extensive supervisory capabilities in dispersed locations, but they do not take the role of a knowledgeable security team.

However, AI-based security is not flawless. Attackers create these deceptive inputs, sometimes referred to as adversarial attacks, in order to trick machine learning systems [11]. The requirement for AI models to be evaluated for their flexibility as well as its inherent danger remains a challenge in both strictly automated decision-use cases, like surveillance or diagnostics, and other industries.

11.4.2 Using Blockchain to Establish Trust

Developing trust between endpoints that may have never interacted before is one of the most difficult problems in IoT networks. Utilizing the blockchain, which is a permanent record of all transactions and devices, is one method to deal with issue. This, in turn, makes it possible to record the data's movement and the device's activity, both of which are essential for industries and logistics where several people must access the same data [12].

Take the distribution of vaccinations via cold chain as an example. Along the route, sensors capture the temperature and humidity. The blockchain record can provide the precise location and time of any readings that deviate from permissible ranges, making it simple to track down and address [10].

It is not easy to apply blockchain technology to the Internet of Things. It is clear that in order to meet the requirement for consensus on a blockchain, devices with low computing power or sporadic connectivity will eventually be required. Lightweight cryptographic methods and off-chain data validation solutions are currently being used to study these trade-offs [8].

11.4.3 Integrating Privacy and Pursuing Zero Trust

In addition to requiring safe storage, today's privacy laws also demand that data be used with responsibility, transparency, and consent. It is crucial to think about how the data is created, anonymized, and stored for the AI models that will be produced using massive IoT datasets. The idea of privacy-by-design becomes crucial in this situation [9].

This places privacy at the center of the system rather than making it merely a compliance problem. In order to protect the majority of SRH data from such acquisition, this entails reducing needless data collecting and encrypting data both in motion and at rest.

Other companies, however, have switched to a zero-trust, outside-in security paradigm. According to this approach, all users, devices, and services—including internal systems—must be "authenticating all the time." This translates to sensors or devices in IoT networks that are regarded as untrusted even inside firewalls unless they are verified and approved [13].

This two-pronged strategy of inspecting every access and designing for privacy also helps to enable compliance with international privacy laws like GDPR and HIPAA. Importantly, it also offers strong, safe digital infrastructure that will enable the safe large-scale implementation of AI and IOT systems [14].

11.5 Green Cloud and Sustainability Paradigms

Sustainability has emerged as a key problem as cloud infrastructure to serve AI and IoT grows. Organizations, especially cloud providers, are starting to feel the strain of high-performance computing and data centers' energy demands and related carbon expenses. The following looks at some of the trends for enhancing the environmental profile of the cloud ecosystem through ideas like energy-saving technologies, smart load management, and green design practices.

11.5.1 Intelligence's Energetics

At scales far bigger than these, it is computationally costly to "train" massive models using AI workloads. In IoT scenarios—which are defined as those in which billions of devices continuously generate and send data to the cloud—this becomes much more problematic [2]. This cumulative energy consumption has detrimental effects on the environment in addition to the data center's capability. According to some estimates, training a large deep learning model might use as much energy as a few households would need in a year [10].

Although it is a good thing that edge computing reduces the amount of energy required to send all of the data to the cloud, this does not mean that no energy is utilized. Battery-powered sensors need to carefully budget energy to avoid frequent maintenance because the majority of edge devices are always on. One of the main concerns for the design of sustainable systems is striking a balance between energy efficiency and responsiveness, which needs to be controlled [7].

11.5.2 Carbon-Conscious Datacenter and Scheduling Procedures

In an effort to address this problem, major cloud service providers are implementing renewable energy and optimizing their data center's resource utilization. One example of this is when compute-intensive tasks are scheduled to run during periods of abundant but unusable low-carbon electricity, like solar or wind surges [15].

Additionally, newer data centers are being built with more effective power consumption effectiveness (PUE), which measures the amount of power used for computation. Some of the strategies being used to lower cooling and waste costs include liquid cooling, dynamic power scaling, and AI-based thermal monitoring [16].

It indicates that companies searching for cloud services are focusing on and examining sustainability ratings in addition to performance and cost to the cloud provider as important selection criteria. Some are even starting to create their own internal measurements to gauge how their online operations affect emissions.

11.5.3 Federated Learning, TinyML, and Low-Power AI

Low-power AI's ascent democratizes sustainability. An approach to utilizing clever algorithms without requiring power-intensive cloud resources is the field of Tiny ML, which focuses on running machine learning models at the microcontroller/energy-constrained edge [11]. For instance, the information obtained from sensors used in smart agriculture can process weather or soil conditions locally and send only pertinent summary data to the cloud.

Federated learning ecosystems are one example, where several devices can work together to build a more advanced machine learning model without sending raw data to a central server. In addition to protecting user privacy, this also helps to lower the energy and network bandwidth used for data transmission [8]. Federated learning has enabled healthcare institutions to train models on patient data without requiring a central data center or remote data sharing [9].

These patterns point to a shift toward "less-is-more" kinds of intelligence, where we concentrate on localized, task-specific forms of specialized AI rather than large-scale processing. They can even lessen the environmental burden of networked digital systems if they are based on sound architectural and policymaking.

11.6 AI-IoT Design Difficulties and Takeaways

The real-world application of AI and the Internet of Things is usually far messier than the theoretical model, despite the excitement and potential surrounding these technologies. These businesses, which advocate for more intelligent, networked infrastructure, deal with a variety of design, implementation, and operational challenges. This section lists some of the primary obstacles that AI-IoT initiatives frequently face, along with lessons that may be learned from the experiences of the first businesses and organizations to use them.

11.6.1 System Complexity and Integration Overhead

One of the initial challenges in working on AI-IoT projects is architectural complexity. Thus, AI-IoT architectures are different from traditional IT systems in that they must offer both reasoned reactivity in the cloud and real-time, edge-based reactive capability. Numerous failure points are introduced by this architectural trade-off, including network delay, sensor malfunctions, and cloud service problems.

The design frequently has to handle variants of devices with various environments, power conditions, and protocols. In the absence of an integration strategy, more time is spent resolving incompatibility than developing the application's logic. Implementations are more successful when middleware platforms that can abstract the IT infrastructure and modular, standards-based architectural solutions are used.

11.6.2 Sensor Noise, Annotation, and Data Quality

As they say, artificial intelligence (AI) systems don't know anything we don't tell them. This data is seen as coming from sensors that will deteriorate, operate in imperfect conditions, or produce noisy output in the context of Internet of Things systems. Uncertainty and variability are introduced, which need to be addressed during both training and inference.

When supervised learning algorithms need high-quality labeled datasets, this becomes even more difficult. Labeling sensor data can be expensive and may need subject matter expertise, particularly in edge settings, aberrant events, or failures. Furthermore, models created in a specific area or time of year might not translate well to other contexts. To increase the model's resilience to unpredictability, this approach takes into account the use of ensemble techniques, semi-supervised learning, and data augmentation [11].

11.6.3 Bandwidth, Latency, and Edge-Cloud Coordination

The ability to sense, process, and act in real time is one of the key promises of AI-IoT systems: responsiveness. However, without the intelligent and effective management of computing resources at the edge and cloud levels, this cannot be accomplished.

High latency and bandwidth limitations can literally be lethal in certain instances, such as driverless cars or industrial automation, when a high-latency link can mean the difference between life and death. However, "intelligently partitioning the workloads"—that is, "processing locally all latency-sensitive tasks" and "deferring to the cloud all the larger analytics workloads" is a way to achieve true dependability. Adaptive processing pipelines, which allow edge nodes to do inferencing in real time and regularly synchronize with cloud see AI-IoT systems for retraining and logging, are used in some of the successful systems [3].

11.6.4 Organizational Silos, Governance, and Stakeholder Alignment

Organizational difficulties are less obvious than technical ones. Lack of departmental alignment is a prevalent cause of many AI-IoT projects that have failed or are blocked. Executives, operations managers, data science departments, and IT teams may all have different ideas about what constitutes a successful project, as well as different timetables and goals.

Because of perceived complexity or fear of losing their jobs, those in charge of putting the system into place may oppose required reforms. At the same time, management might not take into consideration the privacy issues or long-term expenses associated with ubiquitous surveillance systems. In fact, the most successful ones have frequently been those that have made early investments in stakeholder involvement, training, and cross-cutting management procedures that ensure input from all impacted groups.

11.6.5 Lifecycle Risk Management and Security

Connected devices provide new dangers, such as outdated firmware, insufficient identity management, and poorly secured endpoints. However, the danger space expands when AI models are taken into consideration, taking data poisoning, model inversion, and adversarial attacks into account.

We learn from the early failures that security should be considered a first-class design constraint rather than something that is added later. This includes using device-level authentication, regularly updating firmware, encrypting data both in transit and at rest, and maintaining a thorough history of audit trails of model modifications and decision logs. Crucially, rollbacks, saving versions, and performance monitoring to spot process irregularities or regressions should all be included in AI lifecycle management [7].

11.6.6 Controlling Expectations and Assessing Achievement

Lastly, the problem of expectations is one of the less talked-about challenges. Many businesses claim that their AI-IoT technologies can automate tasks completely or intelligently. Many deployments start with extremely specialized use cases and work their way up based on real-world adjustments and iterative feedback.

Transparent success criteria, reasonable timelines, and frequent checkpoints ensure that participants are not disillusioned or let down, preventing failure. According to case studies, limited pilots, phased rollouts, and short-term KPIs are more successful in the long run than a large-scale implementation done all at once [5].

11.6.7 An Overview of the Lessons Learned

Important Takeaways and Techniques for the Challenge Area

System Complexity: Make use of middleware abstractions and modular, standards-based components.

Integrate semi-supervised, synthetic, and human-labeled data sources to ensure data quality.

Depending on the needs of the use case, divide processing between the edge and the cloud in terms of latency and bandwidth.

Stakeholder Alignment: Prioritize training and transparency; involve all departments early.

Security Use proactive lifecycle planning to secure models and devices from beginning to finish.

Management of Expectations: Begin small, establish metrics, then refine in response to field input.

11.7 The Function of Generative AI in Internet of Things Systems

Applications of generative AI that are widely visible include simulation, image generation, and text generation. However, its applications are not limited to the creative sectors. In the context of IoT and cloud ecologies, generative models are beginning to dictate how systems learn, adapt, and behave. When data is few, behavior is unpredictable, and conventional rule-based systems are inapplicable, they play a unique function. This element will be discussed in the pages that follow, taking into account the drawbacks of using generative AI to support the Internet of Things.

Synthetic data creation, intelligent agent composition, and simulation-based modeling will all be covered.

11.7.1 Creating Synthetic Data to Train Models

The availability of high-quality or diverse data is crucial for creating machine learning models that function well in Internet of Things environments. However, gathering such data is frequently not feasible, safe, or effective, particularly when it comes to uncommon occurrences or hazardous situations [11]. This is fairly common; for example, uncommon examples—or even examples that are designed to be rare—are necessary for detecting gas leaks in a pipe's line or anticipating problems in crucial machinery.

Generative models assist in bringing realistic-looking synthetic data to solve this. These are used to teach AI systems how to recognize abnormal patterns and what constitutes normal behavior by simulating sensor outputs under different settings. For instance, without putting machinery under the strain of comparable circumstances, synthetic data can be used to train a model to recognize when industrial machinery is overheating, losing pressure, or vibrating abnormally [10].

Although creating synthetic data necessitates some real-world data input, this combination of data can be utilized to train powerful models faster, reducing the time and expense of acquiring uncommon cases and boosting generalization to settings that haven't been seen before.

11.7.2 AI Agents for IoT Orchestration and Automation

The speed at which IoT system data is produced frequently surpasses the capacity of human teams to analyze it. Using generative models as one of the agents that will control the automation, and the scope of the decision-making process is one way to steer into this. In addition to being rule-bound, these agents can also learn and adapt to different situations, changing in response to input from their surroundings [2].

For example, in a smart warehouse, an AI agent could decide how to move robots, reorder goods, or reschedule deliveries based on sensor data and incoming orders. By predicting future demand patterns to test out several logistical scenarios and then determine the most efficient one, generative models enhance this process [8].

Their ability to function in unpredictable or changing surroundings is the main feature that sets these agents apart. The agents adjust their tactics without requiring human intervention or retraining, even when the data changes due to seasonality, device wear, or shifts in customer behavior.

11.7.3 *Digital Twins and the Simulation of Autonomous Behavior*

Digital twins, which are computer-based representations of actual environments or systems, are becoming crucial for managing intricate procedures. With generative AI, they can also operate in a more complex behavior simulation. Systems can employ generative approaches to forecast how devices or even entire environments will behave in different scenarios, as opposed to relying on deterministic models or predetermined rules [10].

Take, for instance, a water treatment facility. The aging of equipment, changes in the quality of input materials, power outages, and other events can all be replicated in a digital model of the plant. In other words, generative AI promotes the system's "ability to better respond to surprises" by enabling models of both expected and unlikely events [9].

Proactive maintenance is also described. By mimicking "patters of wear" or conditions of fault, they can forecast when a particular component will require maintenance. As a result, they assist teams in preventing costly downtime before that point is reached. It involves effective and sustainable system operation at a macro level, such as an improved power grid or a city's layout [5].

11.7.4 *AI-IoT in the Utilities and Energy Sector*

Intelligent systems are becoming essential rather than optional as the energy industry changes. Utilities are facing mounting pressure due to a variety of causes, including the age of these traditional systems, the unpredictability of renewable energy, and many more. The future seems to be moving more and more in the direction of AI and IoT coexisting to address this. These two technologies enable operators to keep an eye on the infrastructure, optimize it through virtualization, and—above all—consider "contingency plans" during events.

Adapting to an Adapting Grid

Conventional electrical distribution systems were designed to distribute electricity in a single direction, from a few major power plants to millions of obliging consumers. However, this paradigm is no longer suitable as battery storage, electric vehicles, and rooftop solar become more widespread. Energy can now flow in a variety of ways, with different levels depending on local production and consumption.

IoT sensors evaluate system health in addition to voltage and current in the substation and along the distribution lines. AI systems that can anticipate anomalies, like one feeder using excessive amounts of electricity or going out of power, are fed this data. Some have the ability to automatically adjust power settings to minimize outages or balance power loads in situations where demand for power is high [16].

Fix Before It Breaks

It is difficult to access and expensive to repair. Ignoring a system until it breaks down is a foolish idea that costs money and the trust of the public. Predictive maintenance is made possible by AI, which is anticipatory and predictive. Sensors can track vibration, temperature, or audio signals to determine the condition of machinery. Machine learning algorithms can recognize this failure because they are educated on prior data, which enables them to set off alerts when similar incidents occur [17].

This has worked very well, for instance, with transformers, wind turbines, and other high-risk assets. Some businesses also mention that they can identify issues "a few weeks in advance" and then "pull the line down on their terms" by planning repairs during downtime as opposed to attempting hasty fixes during an emergency.

More Accurate Demand Forecasting

Every day, there is a struggle to balance the supply and demand for electricity. Too little results in blackouts, while too much is a waste. AI's analysis of past consumption, local events, and local weather data improves demand forecasting accuracy. Additionally, they can be "live" updated to reflect the most recent prognosis [2].

With houses and companies starting to consume energy in increasingly unpredictable ways, this is more crucial than ever. Operators can use advanced forecasting to determine when to reduce load, draw upon reserve producing capacity, or provide incentives for off-peak usage.

Getting Renewable Energy to Benefit the Grid

The issue is that although wind and solar energy are clean options, they are inconsistent. An overcast day or a sudden drop in wind upsets the balance. AI-IoT platforms can forecast renewable generation by processing weather data and historical performance. Others are in charge of energy storage, deciding when to feed power back into the system or store it [4].

In regions with high levels of renewable penetration, this is essential. Because of it, windy grids can maintain stability without always using fossil fuel backups. There will eventually be more renewable energy in the system as a result of more precise forecasts and AI that controls and coordinates.

Electric Cars as a Two-Way Participant

It's crucial to remember that electric vehicles are more than just a new kind of demand. Additionally, they can export electricity to the grid if the necessary infrastructure is in place. However, cooperation is necessary for all of this. Because smart charging stations are grid-connected, they can monitor load data and electricity expenses. The car can then be programmed by AI to charge at night or during periods of high solar radiation.

Vehicles having excess stored power may occasionally be able to sell back power when demand is at its highest. Even though it is still in its early stages of development, towns with significant EV adoption and grid congestion are already experimenting with similar "vehicle-to-grid" approaches [15].

Real-World Challenges

Although it is a difficult path, the potential is strong. New ideas and outdated technology don't often mesh well. Security issues are ongoing. Regulations also frequently lag behind what is technically possible.

Additionally, people are needed to operate and understand the systems. This entails retraining current employees and working across departments, which you may not have done previously. All successful ventures start "small, show they work, and then scale." This is true whether one likes it or not. These initiatives only grow from the grassroots level after they have been shown to be successful.

An overview of the uses and effects

Use Case Advantages Made Possible by AI-IoT

Grid optimization, early failure detection, and real-time rebalancing

Extended equipment life and fewer emergency repairs thanks to predictive maintenance

Demand forecasting enhanced resource allocation and scheduling

Improved grid stability and reduced unpredictability through the integration of renewable energy

EV Grid Integration Coordination between vehicles and the grid and smart charging

11.8 Design Models and Blueprints for Architecture

Many businesses that use AI and IoT technology discover that while the technological tools themselves aren't very useful, how they are arranged does make a big difference. One can anticipate sluggish systems, inadequate integration, and non-scalable systems if systems are implemented carelessly. Better existing solutions are ones that are built on architecture that will grow, adapt, and recover in the future, not merely work well for us today. The significance of design, modular thinking, and long-term adaptability for the efficacy of AI-IoT systems in the cloud is examined in the paragraphs that follow.

11.8.1 AI-IoT-Cloud Integration Reference Architecture

This layered paradigm is frequently followed by ideal AI-IoT systems, which break the system down into easier-to-manage parts. These could consist of:

- Device Layer: This layer consists of actual hardware, such as sensors, actuators, and controllers, that gather environmental data (such as temperature, vibration, and humidity).
- Edge Layer: This is where microcontrollers or local gateways perform light processing, occasionally filtering or summarizing the input.
- Data Management Layer: Usually cloud-based, this layer controls access control, storage, and safe data ingestion and transformation.
- Intelligence Layer: In order to generate insights or recommendations in real time, AI models are trained, adjusted, deployed, and tracked at this layer [1].

Data gathering is the first step in this multi-layered pipeline, which culminates in decisions. For instance, a gateway receives pressure data from an Internet of Things sensor, preprocesses it by removing noise, and then sends it to a cloud-based system. An AI system may recognize anomalous readings in this situation and either dictate answers or provide alerts. Decoupling these tasks makes it easier to diagnose issues when they arise and makes the system more parallelizable [8].

11.8.2 Designing in Modules for Vertical Scalability

One problem that arises as the IoT network grows is scalability. This kind of closed system frequently creates bottlenecks or necessitates costly and time-consuming rewrites because it cannot handle growing numbers of devices or users. Avoiding it may be possible with modular architecture. The separation of functions allows for the independent updating or improvement of storage, AI inference, and visualization.

For example, data ingestion may become the performance bottleneck as more sensors are placed around a factory floor. Instead of redesigning the entire backend, engineers can expand it vertically by allocating extra resources to that layer while maintaining the same level of functionality for the other services. The direct result of modularity is this kind of flexibility [13].

Agile development is supported by the same methodology. This makes it possible for groups working on security guidelines, user interfaces, model training, etc. to independently make modifications and release new versions. This is due to the fact that iteration can be carried out more rapidly and without the concern of a cascading impact.

11.8.3 Hybrid and Multi-Cloud Deployment Techniques

Although it may first seem easier to use a single cloud service provider for all of your needs, there are inevitably operational, financial, and technical disadvantages. Many businesses are only now starting to take the necessary actions to spread the load across multiple suppliers and diversify their infrastructure. This multi-cloud approach, as it is commonly called, allows teams to choose the optimal service for a particular task, whether it is low-latency networking, high speed storage, or compute-intensive AI processing [4]. Additionally, some teams are hybrid, combining on-premise data centers with publicly accessible cloud computing. It works well for applications that need localization because of privacy, performance, or regulatory requirements but nevertheless wish to take advantage of the cloud's scalability. For example, a hospital may use the cloud to manage massive imaging files or to conduct analytics, but it would keep its patient information on safe local servers. Naturally, managing resources across platforms is difficult. They need to consider identity identification, data transport between systems, and data synchronization. This can be facilitated by technologies like Kubernetes, which helps standardize deployment and scalability, or service meshes, like Istio, which offer far greater control over how services work together [15]. Being independent of a single vendor or model is another advantage. Instead, it enables businesses to modify their processes as needed without having to start from scratch.

11.8.4 An AI-IoT Deployment Reference Framework

The absence of a clearly defined embedded deployment paradigm that connects theoretical concepts to practical application is a major barrier to the widespread adoption of AI-IoT solutions. Community-clouds come in a variety of formats and uses, but many are not standardized, which leads to issues like fragmented development, wheel-reinvention, and stability risk. In order to help practitioners create, develop, integrate, and scale technologies that are pertinent and in line with their organization's capabilities, these frameworks can offer guidance. This section presents a reference deployment approach that aims to address these issues while maintaining long-term sustainability.

Cross-cutting Governance and Control Layer

All architecture layers are covered by this governance layer, which consists of:

- Control of identity and access
- Tracking data lineage
- Compliance with ethical AI
- Lifecycle controls for firmware and models

Lifecycle of Deployment: From Pilot to Production

Description of the Phase

- Investigate business issues, map data sources, and assess technical viability.

Building a modest testbed, using actual data, and verifying hypotheses are all part of prototyping.

Use KPIs to deploy pilots in a small area and iterate in response to feedback.

Deploy at production scale, include business systems, and establish formal governance

Update security policies, handle drift, retrain models, and keep an eye on continuous operations.

Longevity Design Principles

- Modularity: Components that are interchangeable and individually upgradeable
- Use open protocols such as MQTT, OPC UA, and ONNX for interoperability [9].
- Security by Design: Manage device identity, impose authentication, and encrypt data.
- Explainability: Make AI judgments for regulated domains comprehensible.
- Fail-Safe Defaults: If the cloud cannot be reached, enable edge operations.

Reference Architecture with Illustrations

[Devices & Sensors]
↓
[Preprocessing/Edge Gateway]
↓
[Ingestion of Cloud Data → Storage → Analytics]
↓
[Decision APIs → AI Inference Engine]
↓
[Business Systems/Actuators]
Cross-cutting: Lifecycle Management, Security, and Governance

In Conclusion

Although there are design patterns and success stories, there can never be a "best" AI-IoT architecture. Those working at the forefront of innovation might avoid working in a disjointed or fragmented environment by using it as a shared reference structure. The use of these frameworks will be beneficial since more businesses will need to transition from experimentation to enterprise-level implementations in order to scale responsibly.

11.9 Governance, Legal, and Ethical Aspects

An example of this may be seen in the influence of AI and IoT as they are further incorporated into cloud systems, where more than simply system performance is at stake. They are influencing daily decisions as well as privacy, security, and the accessibility of essential services. As we continue to advance this technology, we must also assume a bigger moral and regulatory duty in light of this expanded role. This section examines how new governance models and policies have started to address the issues raised by these massively networked, intelligent cloud systems.

11.9.1 International Standards and Regulatory Frameworks

Around the world, new laws are being developed to try to reduce some of the risks connected to algorithmic choices. Similar discussions are taking place in the USA, Canada, and even Asia, frequently aligning with current data protection laws like the GDPR or HIPAA, particularly when sensitive personal information or health data is involved. For example, the European Union's AI Act promotes a classification system with increasing obligations and standards in accordance with the potential harm of a given AI technology's outputs [14].

These frameworks frequently demand transparency about the development, verification, and use of AI systems, especially when those systems' results have an effect on human rights. Any automated decision, including those pertaining to employment, loans, medical triage, or other areas, needs to be auditable and explicable [13]. When data travels across borders and overlapping compliance requirements arise, the issue becomes more complicated for global corporations that use cloud computing.

11.9.2 Responsible IoT Deployment and Ethical AI

There is more to the ethics of designing intelligent systems than just abiding by the law. However, if adequate attention is not given to the design and testing of these technologies, AI applications might reinforce harm even if they are functioning within their own parameters. While bias in training data can lead to unjust treatment of different people in facial recognition or patient risk assessments, as well as the distribution of school resources, among other things, data bias can lead to skewed data visualizations or applied AI models [11].

IoT ethical design takes into account things like tracking, data harvesting, and providing consumers with relevant notification. For instance, when street-level monitoring and behavior tracking are used in public safety, the utility and civil rights to privacy frequently conflict. Organizations are using multidisciplinary teams to detect these hazards further back in the system's lifespan, and internal ethics boards are starting to take shape.

It's interesting to note that a number of the worldwide coalitions and research groups that are currently in operation provide some guidelines for incorporating this code of ethics into AI. These are non-binding frameworks that support openness, accountability, and fairness—issues that are made even more urgent in fields like healthcare, education, and mobility where AI and IoT systems are being used [12].

11.9.3 Cloud Governance and Data Sovereignty

Concerns of governance are connected to a broader global environment as cloud computing services are increasingly situated outside of national borders and at worldwide authoring locations. Similar to this, systems made for regulated industries are starting to take data sovereignty—the idea that information is legally controlled by the country in which it is gathered or stored—into account. As is the case in Germany, India, and Australia, several laws have either been established or are being proposed to require the territoriality of citizens' sensitive financial or personal information [6].

In response, businesses have started putting in place sovereign cloud configurations that modify data storage, encryption, and control methods to comply with local regulatory requirements. For these kinds of systems to remain compliant without compromising speed, IT, legal, and the cloud service providers in use must work closely together.

They are also developing their own internal governance procedures at the same time. Model versioning, audit trails, access control, and compliance logging are among the tasks that some companies have started automating. In order to ensure that cloud-based AI and IoT implementations are robust, accountable, and future-proof, these solutions ensure that operational procedures are maintained in accordance with these emerging ethical and legal standards [7].

11.10 Prospects for the Future and Opportunities for Research

The simultaneous emergence of AI, IoT, and cloud computing changes how digital systems behave by enabling them to act in real time, respond to context, and behave over vast, interconnected regions. However, the area for its development remains mostly intangible as use continues to rise. However, concerns about sustainability, transparency, and long-term dependability start to surface, just like with any new case studies and deployment scaling. The following points out areas that require further development and investigation to preserve the robustness, inclusivity, and reliability of future systems.

11.10.1 Next-Generation Connectivity: Quantum Networking, Satellite IoT, and 6G

For example, despite the advancement of these technologies, AI-IoT applications still encounter network limitations, especially in rural areas, on mobile deployments, and in environments with sparse infrastructure, where it is challenging to maintain dependable, low-latency access. These restrictions are typically impediments to the operation of responsive automation and real-time analytics.

According to recent studies, 6G is being investigated to be significantly quicker data transfer, almost zero latency, and more spectrum efficient, even though 5G has superior speed and stability [12]. Additionally, this could make it possible to analyze time-sensitive data at the edge more efficiently, which would ultimately help to enhance distributed and autonomous systems.

In other locations, "very remote areas such as farms, ships, and supply chains that did not previously have access to digital services" are now receiving coverage from satellite IoT [1]. Such technological advancements would not only be beneficial in the spatial sector; in the long run, quantum networking advancements may lead to extremely secure communication methods for sectors like finance, energy, and national security that deal with sensitive or high-risk data [13].

11.10.2 Adaptive and Self-Evolving Systems

The requirement for manually selected datasets and retraining cycles is one of the drawbacks of current AI systems. However, these circumstances are always changing in a real-world IoT system. Unexpected factors appear, behavior shifts, and new gadgets are accepted. Static models' primary drawback is their slow response time, which causes information to become outdated very rapidly. Adaptive systems that attempt to solve this issue through learning are where artificial intelligence is headed. These models may also assess their own performance, recognize when they are no longer producing dependable results, and enhance themselves by adding fresh input or getting input from their surroundings. This research emphasizes the significance of continuous learning, reinforcement learning, or retraining on the edge [2]. Maintaining transparency and accountability as these systems continue to advance, especially in the fields of public safety, healthcare, and regulatory oversight, is a challenge.

11.10.3 Open Architectures, Standardization, and Interoperability

System fragmentation is one of the common obstacles to the adoption of AI-IoT-cloud. The majority are independently constructed and employ proprietary data formats, closed communication protocols, or private APIs. These need to be manually integrated and are typically not interoperable, which increases the risk of vendor lock-in or redundant data and effort. There is a growing push to create open frameworks and common standards in order to overcome these constraints. The vast majority of enterprises are implementing new AI model standards like ONNX or IoT communication standards like MQTT in order to address these issues [9]. They enable businesses to mix and match components of their system, which reduces complexity and costs, and avoids the need to rewrite key infrastructure. Technically speaking, another advantage is that open-source architectures are expanding the pool of people who can help develop these systems. The free software/free knowledge concept or open-source tools created by the community have made it possible for research labs, non-profits, and small start-ups without large technological budgets to adopt and implement cutting-edge solutions at a reduced cost or for free. This kind of reorientation makes it possible for technology to spread more gradually and widely across industries and geographical areas, which can lessen reliance on big commercial service providers and promote experimental behavior.

11.11 In Conclusion

Cloud computing, IoT, and AI are not, and never were, silos. Their effects on the behavior of digital plants and the day-to-day operations of businesses are becoming more interconnected as they converge. Instead of being objects we choose to use, these technologies are increasingly being seen "in the wild" in supply chains, hospital wards, manufacturing floors, and intelligent campuses as a component of the built environment. This chapter looked at the mechanics underlying these shifts as well as some real-world applications in different industries. We looked at the advantages, but also the governance flaws, security threats, and the need to balance long-term accountability with the quick speed of innovation. Not everything has been settled. Due to their inability to scale, integration difficulties, or reliance on vendor-specific ecosystems, each of these poses some challenging issues. Smaller businesses simply cannot accomplish this. However, there is a movement toward more flexible cloud architectures, ethics, standards, and open paradigms. Future developments will be influenced as much by design as by technology. Despite certain achievements, the issue remains: how can time, resources, and opportunities be avoided? To this end, well-established components like interoperability, sustainability, and trust must be included in the planning process if these systems are to be long-lasting in the broadest sense.

11.11.1 Intelligent Cloud Ecosystems: A Roadmap for Policies and Standards

With the convergence of AI, IoT, and cloud computing in critical domains like energy, health, and mobility, there is a clear need for further policy suggestions. These systems are being developed at a faster rate than the laws themselves. Without clear legal frameworks and established norms, even well-designed technologies might lead to new types of danger. International cooperation is also hampered by regulatory fragmentation. The responses of governments and standards organizations will be examined in this part, along with the significant gaps they have.

The Source of the Standards

A few international groups have responded by attempting to offer guidance on creating safer and more reliable systems.

The IEEE has placed a strong emphasis on AI ethics by releasing principles pertaining to accountability, openness, and justice. Even in the absence of legislation, the P7000 series is one of the first to provide clear guidance on how to appropriately build ethical systems.

In the meanwhile, ISO/IEC technical standards that are particularly pertinent to AI and IoT applications are available. These also cover ideas related to privacy (ISO/IEC 27001) and system design (ISO/IEC 30141). The majority of them were initially created for general IT, but they are increasingly being modified to coordinate remote systems and machine learning pipelines.

AI-IoT systems running in hybrid cloud environments depend on requirements related to edge computing, network resilience, and interoperability, all of which are being developed in Europe by ETSI. NIST has been creating practical sets of tools for government and commercial use in the USA as well, including AI risk management and cyber ethics references [11].

However, the majority of these requirements are optional. As a result, adoption varies greatly by industry and location and is inconsistent when policy backing is lacking.

Government Approaches: A Disjointed Reaction
Various nations are reacting differently—some more rapidly than others—to the emergence of intelligent cloud ecosystems.

- The proposed AI Act in the EU addresses risk in a multi-layered manner. Transparency and auditability requirements are more stringent for systems that impact essential infrastructure or human rights [14]. If enacted, this regulation might establish a global standard, particularly for businesses that prioritize exports.
- The USA has taken longer to enact laws. Rather, it has issued policy frameworks such as the AI Bill of Rights and mainly depends on industry-specific regulations like FTC advice for consumer data and HIPAA for health. Whether these fragmented initiatives will develop into national regulation is still up in the air.
- Public-sector innovation, particularly in the fields of education and agriculture, is a key component of India's AI strategy. A large portion of the regulatory work is still being formed, despite the fact that it contains strong ethical language.

In contrast, Singapore has established itself as a testbed for regulations. Other nations are starting to research or modify its Model AI Governance Framework, which provides tangible tools and situations [12].

These instances demonstrate that although many governments are aware of the risks, there is currently no one model for regulating intelligent systems on a large scale.

Gaps That Remain to Be Closed
However, despite all of this activity, some significant problems still need to be fixed.

There is still uncertainty over the legality of cross-border data flows. Germany and Brazil have mandated data localization for their residents' information. This puts cloud-based AI-IoT systems in a difficult situation, especially real-time sensor data systems that span continents.

The second blind point is model accountability. There aren't many laws that define machine learning model auditing or who should be held accountable in the event that something goes wrong. As systems grow more independent, the legal void this position creates grows more troublesome.

Lifecycle risks are also neglected. Something that functions well now might not function in 6 months due to changes in the environment or data. The worst part is that most regulations only need to be validated at launch, not during the system's existence.

- Cybersecurity in mixed settings, cybersecurity in mixed environments, or mixed realities, has also been a source of worry. Particularly vulnerable are physical systems that are operated by cloud-based AI algorithms. Although there are security guidelines accessible, there isn't a single worldwide standard that takes into consideration the consistency of cyber-physical systems.

How a More Intelligent Roadmap Might Appear

Both the standards themselves and a great deal of collaboration will be required to close these gaps. Several more sensible choices would be to:

- There may be no need to re-engineer systems for every new market if countries adopt a more uniform approach. Cross-border trust and trade are promoted when certification in one field is recognized by another.
- Industry consortiums and partnerships can support this replication effort, and public procurement can promote the adoption of open protocols and APIs, such as ONNX, MQTT, and OPC UA. Vendors may feel pressured to provide systems that are inherently compatible as a result.
- Modular regulations aimed at certain industries (like energy grids or smart health) might offer a starting point for regulators and developers.
- Similar to financial audits for books, independent audit services might be used to validate models. This would improve trust and lessen conflicts of interest.
- In the end, these kinds of procedures or "regulatory sandboxes"—testbed environments—that let businesses try things with less supervision would allow for learning by doing, or from real-world test cases, before strict regulations are established.

Why This Is Important Right Now

The AI-powered, cloud-native technologies that are connected to the physical infrastructure are not merely a thing of the future; they are already here. And that's a lot more weight to bear. Cost and speed are no longer the only factors. The question is whether those systems will be well-constructed and whether the regulations governing them will safeguard individuals and advance society.

Regulations are fragmented and ineffective. However, the foundations upon which intelligent cloud ecosystems are based may be strengthened and made more reliable with better coordination and a more widely recognized role from business, governments, non-governmental organizations, and civil society.

References

1. Khan, L. U., Yaqoob, I., Imran, M., Han, Z., & Hong, C. S. (2021). 6G Wireless systems: A vision, architectural elements, and future directions. *IEEE Access, 8*, 147029–147044.
2. Parisi, G. I., Kemker, R., Part, J. L., Kanan, C., & Wermter, S. (2019). Continual lifelong learning with neural networks: A review. *Neural Networks, 113*, 54–71.
3. Gubbi, J., Buyya, R., Marusic, S., & Palaniswami, M. (2013). Internet of Things (IoT): A vision, architectural elements, and future directions. *Future Generation Computer Systems, 29*(7), 1645–1660.
4. Cisco Systems. (2020). *Cisco Annual Internet Report (2018–2023) white paper*. Retrieved from https://www.cisco.com
5. McKinsey & Company. (2021). *The Internet of Things: Catching Up to an accelerating opportunity*. Retrieved from https://www.mckinsey.com

6. Binns, R., Veale, M., Van Kleek, M., & Shadbolt, N. (2018). "It's Reducing a Human Being to a Percentage": Perceptions of justice in algorithmic decisions. In *Proceedings of the 2018 CHI conference on human factors in computing systems*.
7. Radanliev, P., De Roure, D., Nurse, J. R. C., Nicolescu, R., Huth, M., Cannady, S., & Montalvo, R. M. (2020). Future developments in cyber risk assessment for the Internet of Things. *Computers in Industry, 102*, 14–27.
8. Lee, I., & Lee, K. (2015). The Internet of Things (IoT): Applications, investments, and challenges for enterprises. *Business Horizons, 58*(4), 431–440.
9. Zuboff, S. (2019). *The age of surveillance capitalism: The fight for a human future at the new Frontier of power*. PublicAffairs.
10. Dede, A., Govindaraju, M., Gunter, D., Canon, R., & Ramakrishnan, L. (2013). Performance evaluation of ONNX and open standards in distributed AI Workflows. *Future Generation Computer Systems, 29*(8), 1955–1964.
11. Veale, M., & Binns, R. (2017). Fairer machine learning in the real world: Mitigating discrimination without collecting sensitive data. *Big Data & Society, 4*(2), 1–17.
12. Andrews, J. G., Buzzi, S., Choi, W., Hanly, S. V., Lozano, A., Soong, A. C., & Zhang, J. C. (2014). What will 5G be? *IEEE Journal on Selected Areas in Communications, 32*(6), 1065–1082.
13. Gyongyosi, L., & Imre, S. (2019). A survey on quantum computing technology. *Computer Science Review, 31*, 51–71.
14. European Commission. (2021). *Proposal for a regulation laying down harmonised rules on artificial intelligence (Artificial Intelligence Act)*. Brussels, Belgium.
15. Google Cloud. (2023). *Architecting with Kubernetes engine: Foundations*. Retrieved from https://cloud.google.com
16. Amazon Web Services. (2022). *AWS sustainability overview*. Retrieved from https://aws.amazon.com/executive-insights/cloud-sustainability/
17. World Economic Forum. (2022). *Cybersecurity, emerging technologies, and systemic risk*. Retrieved from https://www.weforum.org

Chapter 12
The Ethics of AI and Cloud Security

Reddaiah Kasturi and Raghavendar Nellikondi

Abstract This chapter explores the ethical dimensions of artificial intelligence (AI) as deployed within cloud computing environments. This chapter aims to critically assess ethical challenges such as algorithmic bias, surveillance, lack of transparency in AI models, and user consent within multi-tenant cloud platforms.

By analyzing case studies and existing regulatory frameworks (e.g., GDPR, AI Act), the chapter will propose a set of guiding principles for ethically aligning AI deployment in the cloud. Special attention will be given to issues of shared responsibility among cloud providers, developers, and users, as well as the implications of AI-as-a-Service (AIaaS). This concludes with a framework for ethical governance that organizations can adopt when integrating AI into cloud-based architectures.

Target Audience could be Cloud security architects, AI/ML developers, Technology policymakers, Academics in computer ethics and cybersecurity, Legal and compliance professionals in tech.

Keywords AI · Artificial intelligence · Ethics · Cloud security · Data governance

12.1 Introduction

Artificial intelligence (AI) and cloud computing are part of our lives, how we live, work, and connect. These powerful technologies help us do things faster, smarter, and more efficiently. But as they become a bigger part of our lives, we also face serious questions about how to use them in fair and safe ways. As more companies use AI to manage and protect their data in the cloud, problems like bias, lack of transparency, and misuse of information become more common. These aren't just technical problems, they affect real people and their rights, including privacy, fairness, and trust.

R. Kasturi (✉) · R. Nellikondi
Sterling, VA, USA

B. Pandey, A. Patel (eds.), *Revolutionizing the Cloud*,
https://doi.org/10.1007/978-3-032-07479-9_12

Discuss current rules and practices, and suggest ways to build and use these systems more responsibly. This chapter will also talk about why it's important to have clear rules and human oversight when using AI in cloud security. By the end, you'll have a better understanding of how we can use AI and cloud computing in ways that protect people's rights and support ethical progress in technology.

12.2 Technical Primer: AI and Cloud Computing

12.2.1 What Is Artificial Intelligence (AI)?

Artificial intelligence (AI) is a development of technology that enables computers and machines capable enough to perform or simulate human learning, comprehension, problem solving, decision-making, creativity and autonomy.

Artificial Intelligence (AI) using cloud computing is powerful in shaping the future of digital innovation. When used together, they allow businesses and developers to create smart applications that are scalable, efficient, and capable of solving complex problems.

How artificial intelligence, machine learning, deep learning, and generative AI are related.

Main types of AI include [1]:

- Machine Learning (ML): A way for computers to learn from given data and improve over time without being explicitly programmed.
- There are mainly three categories of machine learning:
- Supervised, unsupervised, and reinforcement learning.
- Deep Learning: A subset of Machine Learning using multilayered neural networks, ideal for handling tasks like image recognition and speech processing.
- "The more layers you have, the more potential you have for doing complex things well,"
- Natural Language Processing (NLP): Helps machines understand and work with human languages (like answering questions or translating text).
- Neural networks are a commonly used, specific class of machine learning algorithms in which thousands or millions of processing nodes are interconnected and organized into multiple layers.
- Computer Vision: Allows machines to interpret and understand images and visual information.
- Computer vision is a field of artificial intelligence (AI) that uses machine learning and neural networks to teach computers and systems to derive meaningful information from digital images/videos and other visual inputs and to make recommendations or take actions when they see defects or issues.
- If AI enables computers to think, computer vision enables them to see, observe, and understand.

- Generative AI
- Generative artificial intelligence (Generative AI, GenAI, or GAI) is a subset of AI which will use generative models to produce new content like new text, new images, edit/new videos, or some other forms of data. Generative AI has raised many ethical concerns. It can be used to generate fake news and can be used to deceive or manipulate people through fake news or deepfakes. Even if it is used ethically, it may lead to mass replacement of human activities or jobs. The tools themselves have been criticized for violating laws of intellectual property.

12.2.2 How AI and Cloud Work Together

When combined, AI and cloud computing offer powerful benefits:

- **AI as a Service (AIaaS)**: Cloud providers offer ready-to-use AI tools, like speech recognition or image analysis, through APIs.
- **Training and Inference in the Cloud**: AI models can be trained on large datasets using the cloud's computing power and then deployed to make predictions.
- **Edge AI:** AI models trained in the cloud can run on local devices (like cameras or smartphones) to make fast, real-time decisions.
- **Scalability and Cost-Efficiency**: Cloud platforms automatically adjust resources to meet AI workload demands, saving time and money.
- **Security and Ethics**: Using AI in the cloud requires strong controls to protect privacy, avoid bias, and ensure ethical use of data.

12.3 Key Ethical Challenges in AI-Driven Cloud Systems

12.3.1 Ethical Challenges in AI Systems and Their Mitigations

The ethical issues surrounding artificial intelligence are complex and constantly evolving. As AI technology progresses, it brings with it a range of ethical challenges and dilemmas.

AI has become deeply embedded in everyday life, influencing everything from the algorithms that shape our social media experiences to the systems making vital decisions in healthcare, finance, and law enforcement. However, with AI's growing presence, ethical concerns have gained significant attention.

12.3.2 *Types of Ethical Challenges in AI*

Bias and Fairness in AI Algorithms

Fairness typically means being impartial and just, without showing favoritism or discrimination. In the context of AI, fairness means designing systems that operate equitably. Because AI and machine learning (ML) rely on processing vast amounts of data, fairness involves responsibly using this data to make decisions that do not unfairly harm any individual or group.

12.3.3 *Types of Fairness in AI*

Group fairness, Individual fairness, Counterfactual fairness, Procedural fairness, Bias in the data, Bias from humans, Mitigation Strategies of Bias and Fairness, Data Strategy, Governance, Feedback Loop, Regulation, Tools, Safeguarding AI Fairness, Block box Decision-Making,

Loss of Trust, Accountability Issues, Unintentional Bias, Regulatory Risks, Mitigation Strategies for Block box Decision-Making, Explainable AI (XAI), Ethical AI Design, Regulatory Standards, Stakeholder Engagement, and Privacy and Data Ethics.

12.3.4 *Challenges of Data Protection in AI*

Lack of Transparency and Explainability: AI systems, especially those using deep learning, often act as "black boxes," making it hard for users to understand how their data is used and how decisions are made.

Limited Data Consent and Control: Users often have little real control over their data. Consent is usually hidden in long terms and conditions, and users may feel forced to agree just to use a service, creating a "privacy paradox."

Data Collection Without Clear Consent: AI systems sometimes collect and use personal data without getting explicit permission from individuals, raising privacy concerns and risks of unauthorized use.

Algorithmic Bias and Discrimination: AI can reinforce biases found in training data, leading to unfair outcomes in areas like hiring, lending, and law enforcement, which violates privacy and fairness rights.

Surveillance and Tracking: AI-powered tools such as facial recognition and location tracking can invade privacy by monitoring and profiling people without their knowledge or consent.

Re-identification Risks: Even anonymized data can be traced back to individuals when combined with other datasets, posing serious privacy risks and potential unauthorized access to sensitive information.

Regulatory Gaps and Uneven Enforcement: Laws around AI and data privacy vary widely. While places like the EU have strong regulations like GDPR and the AI Act, enforcement is inconsistent, and many areas lack specific AI rules.

12.3.5 Mitigation Strategies of Data Privacy

Use Privacy-Preserving Technologies: Techniques like differential privacy, federated learning, and data anonymization help protect personal data by reducing exposure during AI training and use.

Provide Clear Consent Options: Organizations should offer simple, easy-to-understand consent forms, so users can make informed choices about their data and easily withdraw consent if needed.

Improve Algorithm Transparency: Building explainable AI systems helps users understand how decisions are made, increasing trust and accountability.

Conduct Regular Audits and Reviews: Routine audits and privacy impact assessments help spot potential risks and ensure AI systems follow data protection laws.

Follow Ethical AI Principles: Organizations should stick to ethical guidelines that focus on privacy, fairness, and accountability throughout the AI development process.

Support Strong Regulations: Working with policymakers to create and enforce solid AI and data privacy laws can help protect individual rights and standardize best practices.

12.3.6 Security and Misuse of AI

Artificial Intelligence (AI) poses major security and misuse risks that can have serious impacts across multiple industries. These concerns are becoming increasingly urgent as AI technologies are more deeply embedded in daily life and business operations.

AI Security Threats

Adversarial Attacks: Hackers can trick AI systems by making small, unnoticed changes to input data. For example, slightly altering an image might cause a facial recognition system to misidentify someone, weakening security.

Data Poisoning: Attackers can add false or misleading data into the training set of an AI model. This can make the system work poorly or make wrong decisions, which is especially dangerous in areas like fraud detection or healthcare.

Prompt Injection Attacks: In AI tools like ChatGPT, attackers can hide instructions within the input to get the system to behave in unexpected or harmful ways. These attacks can bypass safety filters or leak-sensitive information.

Model Theft: AI models are valuable intellectual property. Cybercriminals can steal them to copy technology or use the model for harmful purposes, which can hurt businesses and lead to misuse of powerful AI tools.

Abuse and Misuse of AI Systems

Deepfake Technology: AI can create fake but realistic videos, images, or audio recordings. These deepfakes can be used to spread false information, harm reputations, or commit fraud, raising serious concerns about trust and security.

Automated Phishing Attacks: AI can generate convincing phishing emails by copying writing styles and personalizing messages. These smart attacks are harder to spot and can lead to data leaks or financial damage.

Malicious Code Creation: AI tools can be used to write harmful software. Hackers may use them to create advanced malware that avoids detection, making cyberattacks more dangerous and widespread.

AI-Powered Surveillance: AI can power tools like facial recognition and behavior tracking. While useful for security, these technologies can also invade privacy and increase the risk of mass surveillance.

12.3.7 Mitigation Strategies for Security and Misuse

Better Model Training, Adversarial Testing, Strong Access Controls and Clear, Explainable AI and Follow the Rules.

12.3.8 Compliance with Regulations

Complying with artificial intelligence (AI) regulations presents a range of complex challenges for organizations globally. As AI continues to be rapidly adopted across different industries, keeping up with changing regulatory requirements and ensuring proper compliance has become increasingly critical.

12.3.9 Major Compliance Challenges in AI

Dynamic and Fragmented Regulatory Landscape: AI regulations are rapidly evolving and vary widely by region.

Changing and Overlapping Regulations: Companies must constantly adapt to new laws and updates to existing ones.

Cross-Border Data Transfer Issues: AI often relies on global data and infrastructure, making international data transfers a key concern. The cancellation of the Privacy Shield and the introduction of the EU-US Data Privacy Framework have added complexity. Organizations must now implement additional safeguards when moving personal data across borders.

Transparency and Explainability Challenges: Many AI models, especially those based on deep learning, operate as "black boxes," making their decision-making difficult to explain. This lack of clarity poses a challenge for complying with regulations that require transparency and explainability in automated decisions.

Data Privacy and Protection: AI systems handle large volumes of personal and sensitive data, making compliance with privacy laws such as GDPR, HIPAA, and CCPA both essential and demanding. Organizations must establish strong data governance policies to secure data throughout the AI lifecycle.

Shortage of AI Governance Talent: There is a lack of qualified professionals to manage AI compliance effectively. Roles such as AI Ethics Officers, Data Privacy Experts, Compliance Managers, and Technical Leads are in high demand. To address this, many organizations are cross-training current employees, building multidisciplinary teams, and using specialized tools and platforms.

12.3.10 Mitigation Strategies of Compliance with Regulations

Create Clear AI Policies, Conduct Bias Audits, Strengthen Data Governance, Track AI Usage and Provide Ongoing Training.

12.3.11 Environmental Impacts of AI

Artificial intelligence (AI) is revolutionizing industries and everyday life, but its fast expansion is creating serious environmental challenges. Rising energy demands, increased water consumption, and growing electronic waste are making AI's environmental impact increasingly unsustainable.

Major Environmental Impact Challenges in AI

Energy Consumption

AI systems, especially large models like GPT-3 and GPT-4, need huge amounts of computing power for training and running tasks. This consumes a lot of electricity and increases carbon emissions.

Water Usage

Data centers use water-heavy cooling systems to keep servers from overheating. Growing AI demand is worsening water shortages, especially in areas already facing scarcity.

Electronic Waste (E-Waste)

Manufacturing and disposing of AI hardware add significantly to global e-waste. With millions of servers needed for AI infrastructure, the resulting carbon footprint is huge. Plus, rapid AI advancements mean hardware gets upgraded often, shortening device lifespans and increasing e-waste.

Local Environmental Impacts

AI's environmental impact extends beyond the global scale to affect local communities as well. Data centers use large quantities of freshwater, putting pressure on local water resources, particularly in regions already facing water shortages. Additionally, data centers can cause air pollution and release excess heat, which can harm nearby ecosystems and residents.

12.3.12 Mitigation Strategies for Environmental Impact

Switch to Renewable Energy: Data centers consume huge amounts of energy and network consumption. They should use renewable sources of energy like wind power or solar energy for AI operations more sustainably.

Improve Energy Efficiency: Using energy-saving hardware and optimizing AI algorithms can help lower energy use.

Adopt Water-Saving Practices: Data centers can implement technologies and methods to reduce freshwater consumption.

Encourage Circular Economy: Recycling and reusing AI hardware can cut down e-waste and its environmental impact.

12.4 Case Studies and Regulatory Landscape

As AI and cloud computing become more advanced, concerns about ethics, privacy, and security are growing. This chapter looks at real-world examples of ethical and security failures and examines how global regulations are trying to keep up. Understanding these cases helps us learn what went wrong—and how to do better in the future.

The regulatory landscape for AI ethics and cloud security is complex and rapidly evolving, with existing regulations like GDPR and CCPA providing a foundation but needing to be adapted to address the unique challenges of AI. Organizations must navigate both existing and emerging regulations, including the EU AI Act and state-level AI and privacy laws in the USA.

12.4.1 Clearview AI

What happened: The company scraped billions of images from the internet without consent to build a facial recognition tool sold to law enforcement.

Issues:

- No consent from individuals
- Ethical concerns around using publicly available data

Impact:

- Legal action in the EU, Canada, and Australia

Takeaway: Just because data is accessible doesn't mean it's ethical to use. Consent and fairness matter in AI training.

Global Regulatory Landscape

Key Laws by Region

Region	Regulation	Focus Areas
EU	GDPR, AI Act	Data privacy, risk-based AI rules
USA	AI Executive Order, CCPA	Transparency, bias reduction
China	PIPL, AI Ethics Guidelines	Data control, government oversight
Canada	Bill C-27	Consumer rights, AI governance
Brazil	LGPD	Consent, data protection

AI-Specific Rules[]

- **EU AI Act (2024)**: Classifies AI by risk level. Requires documentation, transparency, and human oversight for high-risk systems.
- **US AI Executive Order (2023)**: Focuses on national security, ethical AI, and cloud safety using NIST guidelines [2].
- **OECD AI Principles**: Global, non-binding recommendations focusing on fairness, human rights, and accountability.

Cloud Security Standards

- **ISO/IEC 27017 and 27018**: International standards for cloud security and privacy.
- **NIST 800-53 and 800-171**: US government guidelines for secure systems and contractors[2].
- **CIS Benchmarks**: Security best practices for cloud configuration.
- **Shared Responsibility Model (e.g., AWS, Azure, GCP)**: Cloud providers and customers share security duties—roles must be clearly understood.

Key aspects of the regulatory landscape:

- **Evolving Regulations**

- The legal and regulatory landscape for AI is constantly changing, with new regulations emerging at regional, national, and international levels.
- **AI-Specific Regulations**
- Existing regulations are being complemented by AI-specific laws, such as the EU AI Act, which classifies AI systems by risk level and enforces strict rules for high-risk applications.
- **Industry-Specific Requirements**
- Different industries, like finance, healthcare, and cybersecurity, have specialized AI regulatory requirements, such as compliance with Basel III, the Fair Lending Act, HIPAA, and FDA regulations.
- **Focus on Ethics**
- AI regulations increasingly emphasize ethical considerations, including bias, safety, and transparency, with regulations like the Algorithmic Accountability Act aiming to prevent bias in AI systems.
- **Cloud Security Considerations**
- AI's use in cloud environments requires attention to cloud security best practices and evolving regulatory requirements, such as the EU AI Act and Executive Order 14110.
- **AI Governance**
- AI governance frameworks are essential for businesses to ensure safe, ethical, and legal AI use, providing oversight across the AI lifecycle.
- Navigating the landscape:

- **Stay Updated**
- Organizations must stay informed about evolving regulations and ensure compliance with relevant laws and standards.
- **Develop Internal Compliance Strategies**
- This includes regularly reviewing legal requirements, conducting compliance audits, collaborating with legal experts, and implementing training programs.
- **Integrate AI Ethics with Privacy Practices**
- Businesses should integrate ethical AI principles with strong privacy practices to foster trust and reduce risks.
- **Consider AI-Enabled Compliance Solutions**
- AI can be used to automate compliance processes, update policies, and support communication and training on new requirements.
- **Focus on Data Quality and Security**
- AI governance systems should monitor AI operations against policies related to regulation, privacy, safety, and risk, with a focus on data quality, robust privacy, and security.

Gaps and Ethical Challenges

- **Inconsistent Rules**: Different laws in different countries create confusion and loopholes.
- **Slow Regulation**: Technology advances faster than laws can adapt.
- **Black Box AI**: Many systems are hard to understand or audit, making it difficult to ensure accountability.

Looking Ahead

- **Unified Standards**: There's growing support for combining AI and cloud rules under shared international frameworks.
- **Global Cooperation**: Efforts like the G7's AI initiatives promote collaboration on safe, ethical AI.
- **Ethics by Design**: Ethics checks should be built into every stage of AI development, especially before deploying in the cloud.

12.5 Ethical Frameworks and Best Practices

The history of ethics in computing goes back nearly 100 years. In the 1940s, when computers first appeared, the ethical concern was the displacement of workers. Since then, ongoing discussions on ethics have focused on privacy, security, and fair access.

As artificial intelligence has taken center stage in the computing world, the question of ethics has come to the forefront once again. The widespread use of cloud computing as a data storage and management solution adds additional complexity to the discussion.

Pursuing a design that satisfies ethical concerns is critical to the ongoing development of AI. The following are key issues that developers and users must consider and address [3].

12.5.1 Ethical Frameworks for AI and Cloud Security

Ethical frameworks are sets of guidelines that help organizations make sure their AI and cloud systems are used in a fair and safe manner. Here are a few major frameworks:

(a) **IEEE Ethically Aligned Design**
This framework from the IEEE (Institute of Electrical and Electronics Engineers) focuses on designing AI systems that support human well-being. It encourages transparency, fairness, and accountability, especially when AI is hosted on cloud platforms [4].

(b) **UNESCO's Recommendation on the Ethics of AI**
This framework outlines ten core principles for a human-rights-centered approach to AI, including proportionality, safety, privacy, and accountability [5].

(c) **European Union AI Ethics Guidelines**
The European Union created guidelines for building trustworthy AI. These focus on:

- **Human oversight**: AI should not act without human control.
- The principle of human oversight in AI emphasizes that AI systems should not operate autonomously without human control and intervention. This principle is crucial for ensuring the responsible and ethical development and deployment of AI, mitigating risks, and aligning AI systems with human values.
- Let's talk about why human Oversight is Necessary
- *Mitigating Risks:* AI systems, especially those with high levels of autonomy, can make errors, exhibit biases, or have unintended consequences. Human oversight provides a mechanism to identify and correct these issues, preventing potential harm or negative outcomes.
- *Ensuring Ethical Alignment:* AI systems are trained on data and algorithms, and their behavior is determined by these inputs. Human oversight ensures that AI systems are aligned with ethical principles, societal values, and legal requirements.

- *Maintaining Accountability:* When AI systems operate without human control, it can be challenging to assign responsibility for their actions. Human oversight establishes clear lines of accountability, ensuring that there is always a human in the loop who can be held responsible for the AI system's behavior.
- Building Trust: Human oversight can increase user trust in AI systems by providing a sense of control and transparency. Knowing that humans are involved in the decision-making process can make users more comfortable with using AI-powered tools and services.
- How Human Oversight Works
- Human oversight in AI can take various forms, including:
- Human-in-the-Loop (HITL) Systems: In HITL systems, AI algorithms make recommendations or decisions, but humans review and approve the final output. This approach is commonly used in applications such as medical diagnosis, loan applications, and hiring processes.
- Human-on-the-Loop (HOTL) Systems: In HOTL systems, AI algorithms operate autonomously, but humans monitor their performance and can intervene if necessary. This approach is suitable for applications where real-time decision-making is required, such as autonomous vehicles and fraud detection.
- *Human-in-Command Systems:* In human-in-command systems, AI algorithms provide information and insights, but humans retain ultimate control over the AI system and can override its decisions. This approach is essential for high-stakes applications where human judgment is critical, such as military operations and emergency response.
- Challenges of Implementing Human Oversight [6].
- *Automation Bias:* Humans may tend to over-rely on AI recommendations, even when they are incorrect. This phenomenon, known as automation bias, can undermine the effectiveness of human oversight.
- Alert Fatigue: In HOTL systems, humans may become desensitized to alerts from AI systems, especially if they are frequent or irrelevant. This can lead to missed errors or delayed interventions.
- *Scalability:* Implementing human oversight can be challenging for AI systems that operate at a large scale or in real time. Finding ways to scale human oversight without compromising its effectiveness is an ongoing area of research.
- Best Practices for Implementing Human Oversight

- Clearly Define Roles and Responsibilities: It is important to define the roles and responsibilities of both the AI system and the human overseer. This includes specifying when and how the human should intervene.
- Provide Adequate Training: Human overseers should be adequately trained on how the AI system works and how to identify and respond to potential issues.
- Design User-Friendly Interfaces: The interfaces used by human overseers should be designed to be user-friendly and provide clear and concise information about the AI system's state and actions.
- Implement Robust Monitoring and Alerting Systems: AI systems should be monitored for potential issues, and humans should be alerted when their intervention is required.
- Continuously Evaluate and Improve: The effectiveness of human oversight should be continuously evaluated, and improvements should be made as needed.
- **Technical strength and security**: Cloud-hosted AI must be protected from cyberattacks.
- **Privacy and data handling**: Personal data stored in the cloud must be handled clearly and safely.
- **Fairness**: AI must avoid bias and treat all users equally.
- **Transparency**
- Transparency and ethics go hand in hand. With AI, transparency is an essential ethical practice that plays a role in meaningful consent, accountability, and algorithmic auditing. Transparency is essential for driving public acceptance and trust in AI.
- AI has been accused of having a "black box" problem, referring to the lack of transparency in how it operates and the logic behind its decisions. The use of complex algorithms and proprietary systems contributes to the problem. Ethical practices must address the black box issue by ensuring a high level of transparency in AI development and deployment.
- If AI is to be trusted to guide critical decisions in areas such as medical diagnosis and criminal justice, transparency must be incorporated into its ongoing development. Failure to do so could lead to consumer distrust, security risks, and regulatory blocks.
- **Accountability**: Companies are responsible for how their AI systems behave.
- Assigning responsibility for the outcomes provided by AI-driven systems is perhaps the most important ethical consideration to be considered. If an AI-powered system guiding medical diagnosis makes a decision that leads to failed medical treatment, who should take responsibility? Is the AI developer, the technology firm that deployed the AI, or the doctor ultimately accountable for the bad information?

- Determining accountability in AI use is both a practical and ethical consideration.

(d) **US NIST AI Risk Management Framework**
The US National Institute of Standards and Technology (NIST) offers a guide to help companies manage risks related to AI. It covers fairness, openness, and responsible use of AI in cloud environments.

(e) **Microsoft's Responsible AI Principles**
These principles focus on fairness, reliability, safety, inclusiveness, transparency, and accountability in AI systems [7].

(f) **IBM's AI Ethics Framework**
This framework emphasizes explainability, fairness, robustness, transparency, and privacy in AI systems.

(g) **The US Department of Defense's (DoD) 5 Principles of AI Ethics**
These principles emphasize responsibility, equity, traceability, reliability, and governability in AI development and deployment [8].

12.5.2 Best Practices for Ethical AI and Cloud Security

Using ethical frameworks is only part of the solution. Companies also need to follow clear best practices to apply these ideas in everyday work.

(a) **Privacy-First Data Handling**
AI and cloud security raise significant concerns regarding privacy and data handling. Companies should protect user data from the beginning. This includes encrypting information, removing personal details when not needed, and storing data securely in the cloud.
Non-compliance can lead to substantial fines.
CCPA (California Consumer Privacy Act): The CCPA grants California residents specific rights over their personal data, including the right to access, delete, and opt-out of data collection. Businesses operating in California must comply with these regulations to avoid penalties and maintain consumer trust.
Other Regulations: Numerous other regulations, such as HIPAA (Health Insurance Portability and Accountability Act) in the USA for healthcare data, and various state-level privacy laws, add further complexity to the compliance landscape.

(b) **Reducing Bias in AI**
AI systems must be checked for unfair behavior. This means using diverse and accurate data, testing for bias, and applying fairness rules so the system treats all people equally.

(c) **Clear and Understandable AI (Explainability)**
AI decisions should be easy to understand. Using Explainable AI (XAI) helps users and regulators see how and why a system made a choice, which builds trust.

(d) **Strong Cloud Security for AI Systems**

Security is essential for cloud-based AI. Best practices include:

- **Zero Trust Architecture**: Always check who is trying to access a system. It focuses on securing AI systems and data by implementing a "never trust, always verify" approach, meaning no user, device, or AI application is trusted by default, and every access request is thoroughly verified. This principle is crucial in AI to protect data privacy, ensure the integrity of models, and prevent malicious use.
- Key Concepts of Zero Trust in AI:
- **Least Privilege Access**
- AI systems and users are granted only the minimum necessary permissions to access resources, reducing the impact of potential breaches.
- **Continuous Verification**
- Every access request is verified, including user identity, device posture, and the legitimacy of the AI application.
- **Data Encryption**
- Sensitive data must be encrypted both in transit and at rest to protect against unauthorized access.
- **Threat Detection**
- AI systems are monitored for anomalous behavior, and any unusual activity is flagged and investigated.
- **Access Control**
- Implementing strict access control measures to limit who can access sensitive data.
- **Identity and Access Management (IAM)**
- Using IAM to manage user identities and permissions, ensuring least privilege access.
- **Data Loss Prevention (DLP)**
- Implementing DLP solutions to prevent sensitive data from leaving the organization's control.
- **Security Audits and Monitoring**
- Regularly auditing security configurations and monitoring for potential threats.
- **Data Privacy and Compliance**
- Adhering to relevant data privacy regulations like GDPR and CCPA [9].

- **Disaster Recovery and Business Continuity**
- Developing and testing robust disaster recovery and business continuity plans.
- **Security Awareness Training**
- Providing employees with training on cybersecurity best practices and potential threats.
- **Vulnerability Management**
- Regularly identifying and patching vulnerabilities in cloud infrastructure and applications.
- **Regular Backups**
- Implementing regular backups of data and systems to ensure data recovery in case of incidents.
- **Microsegmentation**
- AI systems and data are segmented to isolate access and limit the potential damage from a breach.
- **Data Privacy**
- AI models require vast amounts of data, making data privacy a critical concern. ZTA helps ensure that data is protected and accessed only by authorized individuals and systems.
- **Model Integrity**
- Malicious actors could try to compromise AI models, leading to inaccurate or biased results. ZTA helps ensure the integrity of AI models by verifying all access requests.
- **Preventing Malicious Use**
- AI systems can be used for malicious purposes, such as generating phishing emails or creating deepfakes. ZTA helps prevent such misuse by verifying all access requests and monitoring system behavior.
- **Generative AI Security**
- Generative AI models are increasingly powerful and can be used to create realistic content. ZTA helps ensure that these models are used responsibly and that they are not compromised or used for malicious purposes.
- **How Zero Trust is implemented in AI**
- Access Control Systems, Data Encryption, Anomaly Detection, Microsegmentation, AI-Powered Threat Detection, End-to-End Encryption, and Multi-Factor Authentication (MFA).

12.6 Governance and Shared Responsibility Models

Artificial intelligence (AI) is rapidly transforming industries, economies, and societies in ways never seen before. Its ability to process huge volumes of data, automate complex tasks, and generate valuable insights has unlocked remarkable opportunities. However, this swift expansion also introduces significant risks and challenges. Today's technological landscape is increasingly complex, with AI impacting critical sectors like healthcare, finance, law enforcement, and public policy. In this context, strong governance is essential to ensure AI technologies are developed and used responsibly, ethically, and safely.

Governance provides the essential framework of policies, procedures, and standards that guide AI management throughout its entire lifecycle—from design and development to deployment and ongoing oversight. Without effective governance, organizations risk building AI systems that reinforce biases, breach privacy, or lack accountability. Poor governance can result in unintended harm, loss of public trust, regulatory penalties, and serious ethical violations with widespread consequences.

Shared responsibility is a governance approach where many different groups—such as developers, companies, regulators, users, and communities—work together to design, run, oversee, and manage the impact of a system. Instead of one party bearing all the responsibility, duties are divided based on what each group can do, the risks they face, and their influence.

Shared responsibility helps to:

- Manage risks better through teamwork.
- Avoid situations where a single failure causes big problems.
- Build trust by being open and cooperative.
- Bring in different viewpoints to create fairer, more inclusive outcomes.

Governance Frameworks and Best Practices

As organizations use more AI, data tools, and automation, strong and flexible governance is more important than ever. A governance framework helps manage risks, follow laws, and make sure technology supports human values.

A governance framework is a set of rules, roles, steps, and standards that guide how an organization uses technology. It shows how decisions are made, who is responsible for what, and how results are checked. For AI and data, it helps ensure systems are clear, fair, accountable, and follow social values.

Best Practices for Good Governance

Governance should fit the organization's goals, risks, and culture. But some common best practices include:

(a) Define Clear Roles and Accountability
(b) Build Multidisciplinary Teams
(c) Conduct Regular Risk and Impact Checks
(d) Include Ethics Early
(e) Monitor and Audit Continuously
(f) Follow Laws and Regulations

(g) Communicate Openly with Stakeholders
(h) Encourage a Culture of Responsibility

Shared Responsibility in AI and Data Ethics [09]

AI and data systems are very complex and affect many parts of society. Because of this, no single person or group can guarantee ethical use on their own. That's why shared responsibility is so important. It means everyone involved works together to make sure AI is fair, clear, responsible, and respects human values.

AI decisions can affect people's lives—like who gets a loan, a medical diagnosis, or a legal action. Mistakes or biases can cause harm or unfair treatment. When no one clearly takes responsibility, risks grow.

Shared responsibility helps by:

- Adding checks and balances to prevent harm
- Bringing in different viewpoints to find hidden biases
- Making sure there are clear steps to fix problems
- Building trust in AI systems

It also encourages ongoing reflection and improvement of ethical practices.

Shared Responsibility Practices [15]

Set Ethical Rules Early	Include fairness, privacy, accountability, and transparency from the start
Build Diverse Teams	Include ethicists, lawyers, users, and community members when designing AI
Define Clear Roles	Assign who handles ethics reviews, bias checks, risk management, and user help
Encourage Reporting	Make it easy and safe for people to report concerns or harms
Do Regular Ethical Checks	Ethics isn't a one-time task; review throughout the AI's life
Be Open with the Public	Share how AI is used and explain decisions to build trust

Without clear rules and structure, shared responsibility can become confusing and lead to mistakes or harm.

1. Confusion about who is responsible
2. Poor coordination between teams
3. Different views on ethics
4. Not everyone has the same resources
5. Weak enforcement
6. Slow decision-making

12.7 Conclusion and Future Directions

AI and cloud computing are driving forces in the modern tech landscape. Together, they enable smart, scalable, and secure solutions across industries. Ethical AI and secure cloud systems aren't just tech or legal issues, they're about protecting people. The case studies show how failure to act responsibly can lead to huge fines, loss of trust, and global criticism. Governments, companies, and each individual working on AI must come together to build technologies that are fair, transparent, and safe for everyone. Ethics in AI and cloud computing isn't just about following laws; it's about doing the right thing. Using trusted frameworks and following simple best practices helps companies protect people's privacy, ensure fairness, and reduce risks. As technology advances, staying ethical builds public trust and supports responsible innovation.

Future Directions [1]:

- **Continued Research and Development**
- Ongoing research and development in AI algorithms, machine learning models, and related technologies will be essential for improving AI-driven security solutions.
- **Education and Training**
- Preparing the workforce for the future of AI in cybersecurity requires new job profiles and expanding existing roles to include skills in AI, security, and ethical development.
- **Balancing Innovation and Responsibility**
- It is key to find the right balance between technology innovation and ethical consideration to make sure that AI serves as a force for good in the digital age.
- **Collaboration and Partnership**
- Fair Collaboration between industries, policymakers, and academic researchers is essential to address those issues and opportunities.

References

1. google[9]. Retrieved from https://www.google.com/.
2. National Institute of Standards and Technology (NIST). (2023). *Artificial intelligence risk management framework (AI RMF 1.0)*. U.S. Department of Commerce. Retrieved from https://www.nist.gov/itl/ai-risk-management-framework.
3. IBM. (n.d.). *AI ethics*. IBM. Retrieved from https://www.ibm.com/artificial-intelligence/ethics.
4. IEEE Global Initiative on Ethics of Autonomous and Intelligent Systems. (2019). *Ethically aligned design: A vision for prioritizing human well-being with autonomous and intelligent systems*, 1st ed. IEEE. Retrieved from https://ethicsinaction.ieee.org/.
5. UNESCO. (2021). *Recommendation on the ethics of artificial intelligence*. United Nations Educational, Scientific and Cultural Organization. Retrieved from https://unesdoc.unesco.org/ark:/48223/pf0000380455.

6. European Commission. (2019). *Ethics guidelines for trustworthy AI*. High-Level Expert Group on Artificial Intelligence. Retrieved from https://digital-strategy.ec.europa.eu/en/library/ethics-guidelines-trustworthy-ai.
7. Microsoft. (n.d.). *Responsible AI principles*. Microsoft. Retrieved from https://www.microsoft.com/en-us/ai/responsible-ai.
8. U.S. Department of Defense (DoD). (2020). *DoD AI ethical principles*. Retrieved from https://www.defense.gov/News/Releases/Release/Article/2091996/dod-adopts-ethical-principles-for-artificial-intelligence/.
9. wiki[10]. Retrieved from https://www.wikipedia.org/.

Chapter 13
AI for Cloud Cost Optimization

Supriya Lal

Abstract Microservices enable scalable and flexible cloud applications but often drive up costs due to increased inter-service communication, decentralized data storage, and complex resource allocation. Microservices also require extensive observability and security which further drive up the cost. This chapter examines how Artificial Intelligence (AI) and Machine Learning (ML) solutions can address these cost challenges in cloud-based microservices. It also discusses the high resource demands of AI itself, emphasizing the need to balance AI-enabled cost savings with the expenses of model training and inference.

Keywords Microservices · Cloud cost · Artificial intelligence (AI) · Machine learning (ML)

13.1 Introduction

Microservices architecture breaks down monolithic applications into smaller, independently deployable services [1, 2]. While microservices provide advantages such as scalability and ease of development, they also tend to consume more resources [3, 4]. Leveraging cloud platforms allows developers to focus on building features rather than managing underlying infrastructure and deployment processes. However, because cloud expenses are determined by the consumption of key resources such as compute, storage, and data transfer, the distributed nature of microservices often leads to higher cloud costs [5]. This chapter explores how advances in Artificial Intelligence (AI) and Machine Learning (ML) present multiple opportunities for cloud cost optimization.

S. Lal (✉)
Seattle, WA, USA

B. Pandey, A. Patel (eds.), *Revolutionizing the Cloud*,
https://doi.org/10.1007/978-3-032-07479-9_13

13.2 Cost Drivers in Cloud-Based Microservices

This section explores the key drivers of high costs associated with deploying microservices on cloud infrastructure.

13.2.1 Deployment

Deploying microservices requires more resources than traditional monoliths because of the following reasons:

- Inter-Service Communication: Microservices interact with each other over a network which introduces communication overhead. Moreover, inter-service calls are much higher when services are tightly coupled because they need to frequently interact with each other for data or functionality. This overhead compounds quickly, leading to higher cloud costs. In cloud-based systems, providers often charge for data transfer between services, especially across availability zones, regions, or VPCs. For example, AWS charges for data transmission between availability zone traffic at approximately $0.01 per GB, and cross-region traffic at $0.02 per GB [6]. Therefore, costs for microservices are significantly higher than monolithic applications.
- Separate Datastores: Microservices typically use their own isolated databases rather than sharing a single central database. Instead of querying another service's database directly, services communicate with each other over APIs—most commonly via REST or gRPC [7]. This approach offers several advantages, including improved decoupling, scalability, and fault isolation between services. However, to minimize inter-service API calls and also reduce latency, developers often introduce denormalized data, i.e., storing copies of the same data within each service's database. While this denormalization helps reduce dependencies and network overhead, it does increase data storage requirements. Since most cloud providers charge based on storage consumption, denormalized data can lead to higher cloud costs.
- Resource Allocation: Assigning the right amount of resources, such as CPU and memory, to a workload is challenging because demand depends on multiple factors like user behavior and the time of day. Reactive auto scaling is a popular technique to scale microservices [8]. System metrics like CPU, memory, or request rates are monitored and resources are added or removed when predefined thresholds are exceeded. For example, if CPU usage goes above 80% for 5 min, the system adds a new instance. If it drops below 30%, an instance is removed to save costs. This approach has scaling delays and often causes overallocation or underallocation of resources as it only reacts to current conditions rather than anticipating future demand, leading to inefficiencies specifically in rapidly changing workloads. In a microservices environment, resource allocation becomes even more complex due to interdependencies between services. If one

service is provisioned correctly but others are not, the overall purpose is compromised. Allocating excessive resources to each microservice leads to wastage of resources. Insufficient resources can cause slower response times, service failures, and increased latency. This, in turn, may require additional resources for recovery.

13.2.2 Observability and Monitoring

In microservice architectures, observability and monitoring are essential for diagnosing issues and maintaining high availability. Each microservice generates logs, traces, and metrics that need to be analyzed collectively to provide an overall view of the system's health [9]. In a monolithic architecture, all operational data is consolidated within a single codebase. When a user action triggers a series of function calls, all of them occur within one process and timeline, making it relatively easy to understand the order of events. However, in a microservices architecture, distributed tracing and advanced log correlation are required to achieve end-to-end observability. A single user request often travels through dozens or even hundreds of separate services. Moreover, if communication occurs asynchronously, the events can happen at different times. This adds more complexity in aggregating traces. Additionally, microservices architectures generate more observability data than monolithic architectures, as there are many smaller services, each producing their own telemetry data, rather than one large application.

Cloud providers charge for observability based on how much data is collected, stored, and analyzed. Costs typically come from the telemetry data—metrics, logs, and traces. Metrics are generally charged by volume. Logs are billed by the amount of log data ingested. The more verbose the logging and the more services are run, the higher the cost. Storing logs for longer than the default period also adds charges. Traces are priced based on how many requests are traced or how much trace data is generated. If every request is traced in a high-traffic service, then costs will be higher.

13.2.3 Security

Implementing security in a cloud environment can be costly, as there are multiple phases of the software development life cycle where security can fit in.

- Develop: While developing microservices, software teams should follow secure coding guidelines highlighted in the OWASP Top 10 and code-review any logic handling sensitive data/functionality such as authentication, authorization, cryptography, and data validation. Integrating SAST tooling into the developer environment can also help catch some security issues early on. Care should be taken to ensure that the dependencies used by microservices do not introduce new vulnerabilities into the system and that only approved third-party software is used. When performing security activities in this stage, the various costs associated at a high level come down to the tools used during the development phase. All SAST tools come with a license and contract, and security teams are selective in deciding which tools suit their organization's needs. IDEs used by developers to write code, IDE plugins, and development infrastructure all come with associated costs.

- Build: One of the first security activities performed during the build phase is to configure your CI/CD pipeline to perform security scans on every build. Additionally, as part of this build process, a verification process for all dependencies is to be established, either by verifying the checksums or signatures to match known-good values stored in a secure location. Developing build pipelines and incorporating security scans into them comes with costs such as those associated with the build infrastructure, licensing costs of tools, and other overheads such as maintenance.
- Test: During the testing phase, writing integration tests that assert security behavior is a common practice; however, coming up with extensive security tests is a hard task. To aid these tests generation, security teams run dynamic scanners such as ZAP and Burp Suite against the microservice. Additionally, performing fuzzing on critical functionality provides additional insights into the running of these integration tests. Care should be taken to perform fuzzing in an isolated environment. Finally, penetration tests should be performed; development teams should engage with pentest engineers to review microservices from a black box perspective. AWS explicitly allows customer pentesting on most services without prior approval [10]. This stage of the SDLC involves many factors that can lead to increased costs, most notably working with third-party vendors to perform pentests. Additionally, remediating findings from pentests also come with a cost.

13.2.4 Maintenance

An application can encounter failures after deployment to production. Failed applications require resources to recover to a healthy state, as they need to reinitialize and rebuild their lost state. Maintaining microservices generally incurs higher costs compared to monolithic architectures, largely due to the complex nature of interservice dependencies and distributed operations. When a failure occurs in a microservices-based application, it's not just a single component that's affected; rather, multiple interconnected services may need to be reinitialized or restarted. Let's explore the reasons how a failure in one service impacts other services.

- Cascading retries happen when multiple microservices automatically retry the same failed request at the same time and each microservice implements its own retry logic without coordinating with others. As a result, when a downstream

microservice fails or becomes slow, all upstream microservices start retrying simultaneously. The number of requests can increase significantly when a service implements retries and the calling service also retries upon failure. In this scenario, a single failure may result in multiple retry attempts at both levels, compounding the total number of requests as each service initiates retries on the retries initiated by its caller. Each additional retry translates into higher network usage, increased CPU and memory utilization, and increased storage requirements for logs and traces generated by each request.
- Cascading failures occur when the failure of one microservice leads to the failure of dependent upstream and downstream services. Because microservices rely on each other to fulfill a specific request, an issue in a single service such as resource exhaustion, unhandled exceptions or network latency can propagate to multiple other services. This is especially likely when errors are not handled properly in the calling service or when circuit breakers are absent. Automated orchestration platforms like Kubernetes may spin up replacement pods to recover from the failures for multiple services, leading to more consumption of cloud resources.
- Database rollbacks in microservices architectures present unique challenges and can significantly drive up maintenance costs. Unlike monolithic systems, where a single database makes rollbacks relatively straightforward, microservices typically use decentralized databases. When a failure occurs that requires a rollback, data consistency must be restored across multiple services, resulting in numerous service calls to revert the data changes.

13.3 AI Solutions for Cloud-Based Microservices Cost Optimization

Advances in Artificial Intelligence (AI) and Machine Learning (ML) provide powerful new ways to optimize costs in cloud-based microservices environments. This section examines how AI-driven solutions can help reduce the costs of deploying, securing, monitoring, and maintaining microservices.

13.3.1 Deployment

The following AI-enabled solutions can be implemented to help reduce deployment-related costs:

- Inter-Service Communication: Inter-service communication between microservices is inevitable, as it is fundamental to the microservices architecture. However, the number of inter-service calls can increase significantly if service boundaries are not defined correctly, leading to excessive dependencies between services. AI can help address this challenge by continuously tracking architec-

tural drift, identifying when the actual interactions between services deviate from the intended service boundaries and design, and alerting teams to potential issues before they cause excessive dependencies or costs. Generative AI can be used to create dynamic depiction of the architecture and compare it with intended designs to detect or predict anti-patterns such as excessive calls, circular and multi-hop flows. Additionally, AI can help optimize the placement of microservices across different cloud zones and regions to minimize cost while meeting performance requirements. Since data transfer charges between regions and availability zones are higher, AI can model the communication patterns between microservices and recommend co-locating tightly coupled services within the same zone or region to reduce cost arising due to communication between services across availability zones and regions.
- Separate Datastores: AI-powered tools can analyze query patterns and data access frequencies to automatically detect infrequently used denormalized data across different services, flagging candidates for schema improvements. Using machine learning, they can also predict future usage trends, ensuring only the most frequently accessed "hot" data is duplicated, while rarely accessed information remains normalized. This approach allows organizations to maintain high performance and low latency, while keeping storage costs in check and minimizing unnecessary data duplication as usage patterns evolve.
- Resource Allocation: Most leading cloud providers such as AWS [11], Google Cloud Platform [12], and Microsoft Azure [13] have started offering predictive auto scaling as a feature. Predictive auto scaling utilizes artificial intelligence and machine learning to forecast future resource needs in cloud environments with greater accuracy than traditional reactive methods. The models ingest a wide range of telemetry data including historical usage trends and daily fluctuations. This enables cloud infrastructures to preemptively allocate or decommission resources ahead of actual load changes, eliminating the lag typical of threshold-based scaling (Fig. 13.1).

13.3.2 Observability and Monitoring

Below are key strategies and how cloud providers can or are already using AI to reduce logging, tracing, and metrics overhead:

- Anomaly Detection: ML can be used to automatically identify anomalies using telemetry data. By training on historical behavior, ML-based anomaly detection can distinguish faults from normal yet sudden spikes. This enables faster detection of faults that would otherwise require more telemetry data.
- Log Summarization: Log data often contains repetitive entries that waste storage and analyst time. Additionally, not all stored log values are required to gain insight into the overall picture of the workflow. AI techniques like clustering and natural language processing can summarize or compress logs by grouping simi-

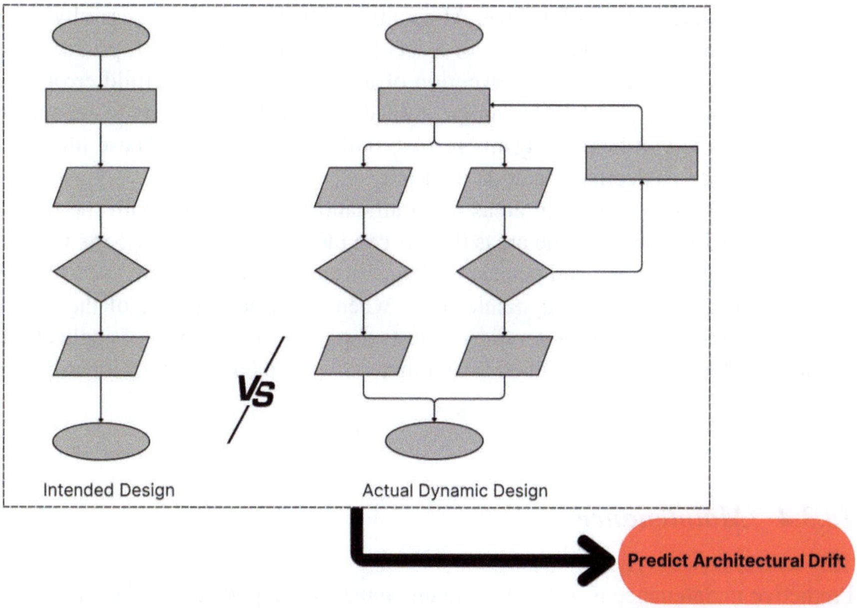

Fig. 13.1 Predicting architectural drift using AI by comparing intended design with the current design

lar entries. Log clustering can drastically shrink the log volume by retaining a single representative log or a count instead of multiple duplicate entries. Natural language processing can help provide a high-level summary from raw logs.

- Trace Sampling: Distributed tracing is required for understanding the flow of request in a microservices architecture, but capturing 100% of traces requires high storage and is also not required to gain insight into end-to-end flow of the microservices. AI can assist in intelligent sampling by deciding which traces to store based on their content. Traces that provide meaningful insights are kept, while additional traces are discarded.

13.3.3 Security

For the Develop phase, GenAI tools can be used to aid developers in adopting secure guidelines more easily (e.g., GitHub Copilot, AWS CodeWhisperer). However, developer trust and false positives remain a large concern with these tools. AI agents can be incorporated within IDEs so that when developers write insecure code, they are immediately alerted and the AI agent can fix the error. Agents can also be used to abstract information from developers that they do not need access to, such as handling sensitive information. AI agents can also be used for performing dependency checks and making sure the supply chain remains free of security issues.

Similarly, during the Build stage, AI agents can be trained to successfully troubleshoot when a build fails because of a security risk and adopt appropriate remediation strategies without the intervention of a security engineer. Build errors are extremely common, and LLMs can be trained on past failed builds to recognize security patterns that help AI agents resolve build issues quickly. These improvements can lead to a decrease in costs incurred.

One of the most promising areas to significantly reduce costs with the use of GenAI is the Test phase. Some areas that AI can target to bring down costs include setting up dynamic scans and pentests. AI agents can be configured to use OWASP ZAP and Burp Suite to run dynamic scans whenever a new release of the app is available. These tools can run a variety of tests depending on the type of application. Similarly, AI agents can be trained to automatically remediate findings identified in pentests.

13.3.4 Maintenance

Predictive maintenance is a proactive maintenance strategy that uses data and technology to predict when a system might fail so that maintenance can be performed just before a breakdown actually happens.

Let's consider a scenario where Service A calls Service B, and then Service B calls Service to process a given user request. Service B usually fails when Service C experiences a latency of 500 ms due to a bottleneck in Service B. Whenever this failure occurs, Service B fails, prompting Service A to send a few retry requests. Users also tend to retry several times, resulting in a storm of retries that overloads the system. This leads to higher costs due to increased use of resources such as network and CPU (Fig. 13.2).

All of the above adds to the overall cloud cost. However, machine learning can be used to detect such patterns. It can recognize that a latency of 500 ms is known to cause failures. It can analyze telemetry data—logs, traces, and metrics, to identify early warning signs of Service C approaching 500 ms. It can react through

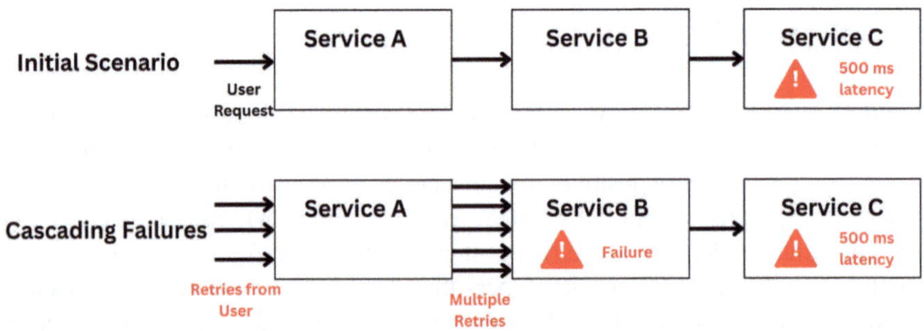

Fig. 13.2 Cascading failures and retries due to high latency in service C

predictive alerting or predictive auto scaling. This would prevent cascading failures across services and reduce unnecessary retries and system overload.

13.4 Challenges of High AI Costs

AI can be used to decrease cloud cost. However, currently the cost of running AI itself is very high. Training an AI model refers to the process where a large amount of data is used to teach a machine learning model how to perform a desired task. It involves neural networks with sometimes millions of parameters. This requires significant computing, storage, and networking resources.

Inference is the process of using a trained model to make predictions or decisions on new inputs. This phase requires less cost than the training stage. However, the cost of this stage is non-trivial as it can add up quickly in high-throughput and real-time scenarios. Additionally, these inference endpoints will need to be deployed in multiple regions to cater to growing global users. This expansion further increases the network charges.

13.5 Conclusion

AI and ML present promising opportunities for addressing cost challenges associated with deploying microservices on cloud. Through techniques such as predictive auto scaling, intelligent anomaly detection, automated log summarization, automated security, and proactive maintenance, AI-powered tools can help organizations optimize resource usage.

References

1. De Lauretis, L. (2019). From monolithic architecture to microservices architecture. In *Proceedings of the 2019 IEEE International Symposium on Software Reliability Engineering Workshops (ISSREW)*, Berlin, Germany (pp. 93–96). https://doi.org/10.1109/ISSREW.2019.00050
2. Thönes, J. (2015). Microservices. *IEEE Software, 32*(1), 116–116. https://doi.org/10.1109/MS.2015.11
3. Bjørndal, N., de Araújo, L. J. P., Bucchiarone, A., Dragoni, N., Mazzara, M., & Dustdar, S. (2022. [Online].). Benchmarks and performance metrics for assessing the migration to microservice-based architectures. *The Journal of Object Technology, 21*(3), 1–22. https://doi.org/10.5381/jot.2022.21.3.a2
4. Nielsen, D. G.-Y. M., & Gregersen, K. T. (2022). Energy consumption of software architectures: A comparison between microservice- and monolithic architectures in C# and Java, Master's thesis, Department of Computer Science, Aalborg University.

5. Greenberg, A., Hamilton, J., Maltz, D. A., & Patel, P. (2009). The cost of a cloud: Research problems in data center networks. *SIGCOMM Computer Communication Review, 39*(1), 68–73. https://doi.org/10.1145/1496091.1496103
6. Rolim, L. P. B., & da Silva, L. F. S. (2023). Exploring data transfer costs for classic and application load balancers. AWS Networking & Content Delivery Blog. [Online]. Retrieved from https://aws.amazon.com/blogs/networking-and-content-delivery/exploring-data-transfer-costs-for-classic-and-application-load-balancers/.
7. Amazon Web Services. Database-per-service pattern. *AWS prescriptive guidance*. [Online]. Retrieved May 8, 2025, from https://docs.aws.amazon.com/prescriptive-guidance/latest/modernization-data-persistence/database-per-service.html.
8. Ahmad, H., Treude, C., Wagner, M., & Szabo, C. (2025). Towards resource-efficient reactive and proactive auto-scaling for microservice architectures. *Journal of Systems and Software, 225*, 112390. https://doi.org/10.1016/j.jss.2025.112390
9. Gatev, R. (2021). Chapter 12. Observability: Logs, metrics, and traces. In *Introducing distributed application runtime (Dapr)*. Apress. https://doi.org/10.1007/978-1-4842-6998-5_12
10. Amazon Web Services. What is AWS signer? *AWS signer developer guide*, [Online]. Retrieved 1 June, 2025, from https://docs.aws.amazon.com/signer/latest/developerguide/Welcome.html.
11. Amazon Web Services. Predictive scaling for Amazon EC2 auto scaling. *Amazon EC2 auto scaling user guide*, [Online]. Retrieved 1 June, 2025, from https://docs.aws.amazon.com/autoscaling/ec2/userguide/ec2-auto-scaling-predictive-scaling.html.
12. Wenda, P. (2021). Let Google cloud's predictive services autoscale your infrastructure. *Google Cloud Blog*. [Online]. Retrieved 1 June, 2025, from https://cloud.google.com/blog/products/compute/introducing-compute-engine-predictive-autoscaling.
13. Microsoft. (2024). Use predictive autoscale to scale out before load demands in virtual machine scale sets. *Azure monitor documentation*. [Online]. Retrieved 1 June, 2025, from https://learn.microsoft.com/en-us/azure/azure-monitor/autoscale/autoscale-predictive.

Chapter 14
Next-Generation Cloud Automation with Generative AI

Naimil Navnit Gadani

Abstract The integration of Generative Artificial Intelligence (AI) with cloud automation represents a paradigmatic shift in how organizations deploy, manage, and optimize their cloud infrastructure. This paper presents a comprehensive analysis of next-generation cloud automation powered by generative AI technologies, examining current trends, implementation strategies, and emerging challenges. Through systematic review of existing frameworks and case studies, we explore how generative AI enhances traditional cloud management approaches, particularly focusing on the CloudCAMP model-driven engineering approach and AI-Generated Everything (AIGX) concept. Our analysis reveals significant improvements in operational efficiency, cost reduction, and decision-making capabilities, while identifying critical challenges including data privacy concerns, algorithmic bias, and integration complexity. The research demonstrates that organizations implementing generative AI in cloud automation can achieve up to 40% reduction in manual deployment tasks and substantial cost savings through predictive resource allocation. However, successful implementation requires careful consideration of regulatory compliance, security frameworks, and organizational readiness. This study provides practical recommendations for enterprises seeking to leverage generative AI for cloud automation while addressing associated risks and implementation challenges.

Keywords Generative AI · Cloud automation · Machine learning · Natural language processing · Predictive analytics · CloudCAMP · AIGX · Infrastructure as code · DevOps · Enterprise architecture

N. N. Gadani (✉)
Houston, TX, USA

B. Pandey, A. Patel (eds.), *Revolutionizing the Cloud*,
https://doi.org/10.1007/978-3-032-07479-9_14

14.1 Introduction to Cloud Automation and Evolution

Cloud computing offers businesses and organizations, the flexibility to access and manage scalable and on-demand resources. Prominent providers have been significantly investing in developing cloud services. Historically, cloud service deployment and management have involved a myriad of complex and often manual tasks. This leads to tendencies to overlook small but crucial deployment parameters, which causes failures in user experience and overhead regarding either plan-driven or reactive responses. Thus, there exists a strong demand for cloud management solutions. A number of work proposals and platforms aim to overcome these issues by advocating a middle layer (a.k.a. Cloud Broker), exposing simplified interfaces to clients, simplifying data transformation, and/or enabling orchestrated activation of services. These approaches allow the decoupling of client-side applications and cloud infrastructure. Despite this, the number of users of cloud services has remained low, year growth has not slowed down, and complaints about tedious and buggy user experience continue to accumulate.

CloudCAMP is a new model-driven engineering and generative programming approach developed to support the automated deployment and management of cloud applications. A strong emphasis is placed on generative programming and model-driven engineering in the proposal of this innovative approach. The modeling language of CloudCAMP is Domain-Specific: Platform-specific languages capture the functional and non-functional architecture while dedicated projectional editors abstract away cloud service limitations [1]. Together they speed up the modeling effort significantly while providing compilers to generate and execute modeling solutions that are correct-by-construction. CloudCAMP, combined with automated engineering practices, helps eliminate human involvement in tedious and bug-prone tasks in cloud deployment.

Cloud automation has evolved through several distinct phases, each addressing specific operational challenges. The initial phase focused on basic resource provisioning and configuration management. Subsequently, Infrastructure as Code (IaC) emerged as a paradigm for managing cloud resources through version-controlled code, improving consistency and repeatability.

As shown in Fig. 14.1 below, we will look at the evolution of cloud automation and its approaches.

14.2 Overview of Generative AI

Generative Artificial Intelligence (Generative AI or GAI) refers to artificial intelligence that utilizes machine learning algorithms to systematically generate new text, images, sounds, symbols, or other media based on recognized input data from historical input information. Simply put, it is a class of machine learning technology

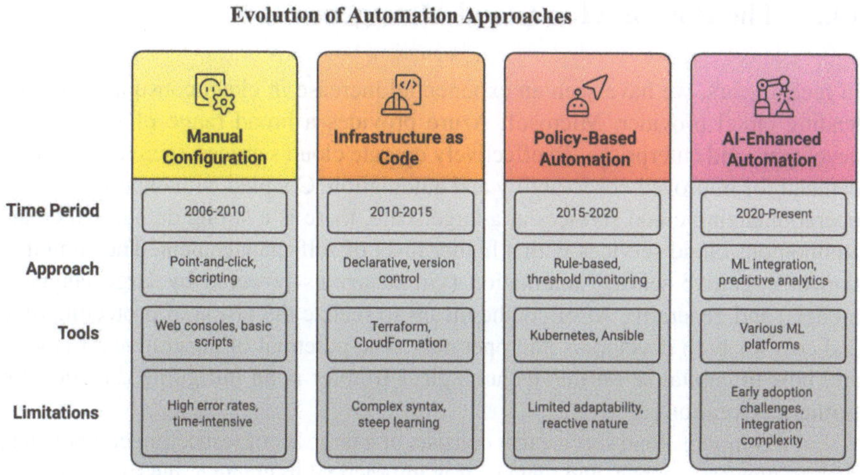

Fig. 14.1 Evolution of Cloud Automation and Approaches [2]

that learns to generate new data from training data [3]. GAI refers to human-aided and controlled creation of generative AI or AI-generated creative/innovative contents or products.

GAI may form new accurate ones from its training sources in a specific domain. The GAI performance may continuously iterate and improve its rendering realism. It imagines the undefined content and produces it as new images/videos into the existence that never appeared. This capability/possibility is desirable in a sense, but also a concern of abuse issue. For instance, potentially harmful 3D weapons could be produced by just typing simple inputs into it. More generally, the contents could be intentionally or unjustifiably AI-created and could now reside in news, social media posts, photos/videos, and so on.

In this survey, a more focused notion of AI-Generated Everything (AIGX) is proposed, where GAI is advanced to explore the continuous space (real-valued and latent spaces sampled by neural networks) to learn and control real-time user-diverse system generation and reconfiguration across many domains. In networking, AIGX seeks and identifies the multi-dimensional and temporal parameters of different network elements; models and customizes diverse architectures and protocols of the different layers; and collaborates with the physical, data-link, network, and application layers for real-time network management that responds to various system/service settings and application/user requirements. A more in-depth case study on power allocation is provided to illustrate AIGX and networking systems' interdependence with insights on significant roles and feedback. GAI has great capability to assist or enhance routing efficiency by planning path selections, while networking systems gather routing tables and statistics to improve forwarding and topology updating efficiency for GAI.

14.3 The Role of AI in Cloud Management

In recent years, we have seen an exponential increase in cloud consumption. As a leading cloud provider, Microsoft Azure provides a broad range of services for developers and enterprises. To effectively operate cloud services, there is a growing demand for improved observability and automation. Coupled with experience from operationalizing cloud services at a large scale, there is a strong demand to create autonomous cloud services with a higher level of self-management. The combination of cognitive service automation (virtual agents powered by large language models) and generative AI offers the means to realize the vision of protecting time and cost for both developers and operators. The potential of generative AI is vast, and how to capitalize on this technological frontier is an intriguing direction for further exploration [4].

For a complex cloud service that consists of a large set of restricting components, such as clusters, caches, and queues, it is impractical to create a massive optimization problem that optimizes all components while accurately capturing the interactions across different components. Current ongoing efforts take a hybrid approach. Code changes that impact the performance of the cloud services are detected and analyzed. A large language model for codes (chat models) is used to give customers recommendations for possible code changes that could lead to performance improvements. At the same time, ongoing efforts are continuing to jointly optimize a selection of the components and synchronize the deployment of these changes [5], which has the following benefits.

First, this approach focuses on optimizing the related components that work together. It's reported that thousands of performance events could be attributed to a small set of root causes. To further facilitate this approach, ML research on explainable AI is needed. Progress in this direction can benefit other use-cases beyond cloud performance optimization. For the approaches based on jointly optimizing several related components, research efforts are continuing to improve the joint optimization of the selected components. Further improving the quality of solutions to this subproblem can lead to substantial improvements in the overall performance of cloud services.

14.4 Current Trends in Cloud Automation

Though cloud computing has brought about many changes to enterprises, the design and production of cloud services still have serious inefficiencies and other complications. Six stresses that used to be endurable for development on the ground have become very awful when moving to the cloud: of new knowledge in the cloud environment, of metadata storage, and of resource distribution on multi-cloud environments. Much more automated approaches for organizing cloud infrastructures and services should be pursued. Several open-cloud automation tools are now available, but the pre-installation effort is too large for many enterprises to use them efficiently [1]. Noticing that the landscape of cloud computing and cloud services has proliferated, researchers tend to propose automated recommendations for configuration development of cloud infrastructures and services based on the high-level description of applications and a knowledge base of these services. AI and ML can fit end-to-end recommendations on the cloud automation processes based on the additional information mined from existing configurations. Cloud consumers can have much more flexible and efficient automated options for utilizing the cloud automation services. Patterns of both cloud infrastructures and cloud services would be formalized earlier. Developers of such patterns might benefit from higher level descriptions of primitive configurations. Efforts on configuration designing could be decoupled from the individual knowledge of components. The search and ranking for the component candidates could be safer and faster, while the final composing could be much more flexible and faster. This work proposes a practicable approach for automating the design of cloud service configurations based on related building blocks and configurations generated from the ones used already. Design patterns for cloud services are discovered from the process of configuration maintenance and adjustment, where the behavior of the cloud services is formalized with a stochastic petri net. They might be plugged into a probabilistic-based search engine to assist the developer in disclosing possible component candidates.

14.5 Generative AI Techniques for Automation

Modern data centers must provide an excellent end-user experience (EUX) to enhance productivity, drive innovation, and maintain a competitive advantage. With increasing numbers of applications utilizing a wide variety of edge devices and network technologies, seamless management of compute, storage, and network resources is becoming increasingly difficult for professionals. Lacking proper visibility, data center operators might not readily identify configuration problems, network latency, or overload on the compute/storage front, making it all the more difficult to take efficient corrective actions. These concerns are exacerbated by rising energy prices and sustainability mandates. Intelligent automation powered by generative AI (GenAI) holds the promise of revolutionizing this critical industry [3].

Developments in the field of Generative AI have sparked a new wave of interest and investment in this space. Data center automation may be improved using Generative AI and large language models (LLMs) that are capable of generative machine learning. These models can synthesize human-facing text from a large corpora of commonly available text, thereby addressing domain-specific use-cases in a more sophisticated manner than earlier natural language processing (NLP) solutions [4].

Generative Data center (Gen-Datacenter) encompasses use-cases in which AI/ML is used for generative understanding of the data center and general decision automation for path analysis and action selection; LLM use to generate human-friendly text, pseudocode or code; LLM use to help data center engineers via recommendation systems or interactive systems; the building of LLMs; and custom prompting use-cases. Models for code generation are the most relevant to the data center domain. Most are variants of transformer architectures pretrained on large corpora of code from public repositories and fine-tuned datasets of task-answer pairs serving heterogeneous programming languages.

14.5.1 Machine Learning Algorithms and Predictive Scaling

Machine learning (ML) algorithms have attracted special attention from researchers to improve cloud automation. A model-driven method for predictive auto-scaling is proposed that allows users to model an auto-scaling specification at a high level and automatically code it for different public cloud providers. A case study was conducted to compare six different machine learning algorithms on two different datasets, the results of which are reported to illustrate the quality of the prediction models [6].

One of the significant problems for cloud-based services dealing with the ever-increasing demand is to scale the resources up or down on time. Poor response time may cause the losing customers, and unnecessary resource provision incurs additional costs. In parallel with the increasing importance of cloud computing, various auto-scaling systems are proposed. Most of the existing methods are reactive which take action after a performance alert, hence employing machine learning (ML) in modeling a predictive auto-scaling system is possible. Most of the proposed methods are based on threshold policies, which require constant monitoring of the cloud metrics in every second, and flood of the alerts when the cloud is scaled out, all of which incur unnecessary costs. A highly scalable and modular rule-based cloud resource provisioning and de-provisioning method is proposed.

Cloud workflow scheduling is a crucial task for scientists and researchers to successfully execute complex scientific endeavors. It requires precise mapping of the workflow's tasks to cloud resources. A heuristic-based approach along with a regression-based estimator is introduced, which shrinks the engineer-tuned suboptimal solutions to the optimal ones by leveraging iterative execution of several heuristics coupled with a regression-based estimator. To this end, various regression models are built and individually tested, after which three of them are weighted to create an ensemble learner.

14.5.2 Natural Language Processing

ML-based conversational interfaces have seen a rise in popularity in recent years, and this trend became particularly pronounced after the public release of ChatGPT. Media coverage of "talents" of such chatbots sparked public interest, and it is now hard to find one not having tried it out. The trend snowballed into the collective zeitgeist of "Generative AI" or "Anthropic AI" becoming overly popular as a term on par with "Metaverse," perhaps in hindsight, for not serving much other than a buzzword to latch onto. Nevertheless, this paradigm shift ushered in by the rapid rise of Large Language Models (LLMs) is none other than a watershed moment for human-computer interaction and a deepening understanding for Natural Language Processing (NLP) and Artificial Intelligence (AI) more generally.

Perhaps, it is fair to argue that the general populous had a semantic viewing of AI with a narrow scope. This can be derived from the huge inclination toward techniques and tools governing Alphabet's search engine, i.e., string matching with heaps of fuzziness and stemming rules. It was wondrous for many who had never imagined that the computer can generate anything beyond just fetching stored information from the database. With the latest wonders of generative AI and how realistically they can converse with users, again in a semantically narrow sense, they are astounded that NLP could transcend its narrow semantic view and dab into new waters of possibility and power that would've never been imagined. Apprehensions notwithstanding; this is a watershed moment for the NLP community and the domain itself. As fellow human beings have long fantasized about the idea of creating androids that can think, argue, and converse, generative AI is paving the way. The sheer ubiquity and web-application interface of these chatbots are democratizing access to something which was esoteric and limited to the privileged few, i.e., researchers and domain specialists.

Those endeavors are being created, fine-tuned, and industrialized for specific domains and disciplines. For example, in a wired telecommunication and computing sense, models are being trained on demand and gang-piling cloud-connectable products for Business Support Systems (BSS) and Operations Support Systems (OSS). The intent is to imbibe expertise knowledge, standardization, telecommunications lexicon, and tiger-taming tasks such as RFC parsing. Further bidding for OTT becomes ever more lucrative, and models need to be instructed in a particular manner, standard content warning added, preferred results formatted, responses externalized and privacy grievances answered correctness in responses indexes swift and dramatic dip; several quirky experiments conducted with [2].

14.5.3 Predictive Analytics

Predictive cloud auto-scaling helps to improve the quality of cloud application auto-scaling and achieve better utilization of cloud resources. The current cloud auto-scaling systems provide basic capabilities of resource provisioning and de-provisioning to allow better utilization and management of resources. This auto-scaling is performed reactively based on detection of threshold violations. Such systems employ a threshold-based mechanism for auto-scaling. They define their auto-scaling policies in terms of thresholds on monitored metrics and issue scaling actions if the thresholds are violated.

Table 14.1 ML approaches and algorithm types [6]

Algorithm type	Use case	Accuracy rate
Regression models	Resource demand prediction	75–85%
Neural networks	Complex pattern recognition	85–95%
Ensemble methods	Hybrid prediction scenarios	80–90%
Time series analysis	Temporal load patterns	70–80%

Another kind of well-known auto-scaling is proactive or scheduled-based auto-scaling systems that automatically scale resources on the basis of known future load. Such methods are useful for temporal load patterns. Predictive cloud auto-scaling is a missing piece in cloud resource provisioning. Predictive auto-scaling forecasts future application usage and scales the resources accordingly. It allows good utilization of cloud resources and good performance of cloud applications because companies only pay for the powered resources in the cloud. Generally unseen spikes in load cause a performance degradation and thus a less quality of service. Such spikes could be unplanned load peaks.

For Scenario 4, results for the manual deployment procedure for machine learning service and our model-driven method to deploy the predictive auto-scaling system are represented. The error and coverage of two different prediction models and the two desired accuracy and coverage trade-offs at 80% accuracy and 80% coverage is shown. A server instance clustering to cope with estimated loads at 1, 5, 6, and 12 s is detailed. Critical instant detection, lesser cluster collision detection, and the deferring period of a current cluster are examined. Finally, the measured effects of auto-scaling instances and the change in capacity difference of 0.1, 0.3, and 0.5 times are analyzed.

Machine learning algorithms play a crucial role in predictive auto-scaling systems. Research has demonstrated the effectiveness of various ML approaches in predicting resource requirements and optimizing scaling decisions [6].

ML approaches and Algorithm types details are provided in Table 14.1 below.

14.6 Benefits of Integrating Generative AI with Cloud Automation

To fully appreciate the benefits of cloud automation, it's useful to explore the limitations it can help resolve. For many companies, the cloud is a two-edged sword. On the one hand, it provides flexibility and elasticity—IT resources can be allocated and consumed on demand to meet business needs as they arise. On the other hand, the cloud can create shortages, overages, and infrastructure instability, leading to outages, unplanned costs, and adverse customer experiences. If the cloud is to be an effective means of scaling services and systems for success, it must be adequately managed. Too often, starting off a transition to the cloud means losing corporate control over systems and services that now significantly depend on the corporate cloud infrastructure. The massive resources available through the cloud can be underutilized or wasted, leading to higher operating costs. The infrastructure's analytics capabilities can be overwhelmed by the sheer volume of logs generated, leading to broken alerting and a lack of situational awareness regarding what's happening in the cloud. As a company scales to the global marketplace, all the possible bad things that can happen to its business are magnified a thousand fold. The sheer volume, velocity, and variety of information on the internet makes it impossible for a human or small team of humans to keep track of relevant information that will allow for making quick decisions [7].

Cloud automation is a broad set of tools, practices, and processes by which IT services, systems, and infrastructure can be configured to run automatically without or with little human intervention needed. Modern, enterprise-ready cloud automation practices are sophisticated disciplines that control large, diverse, and complex systems at scale. Whereas initial cloud automation efforts focused on provisioning and managing initial infrastructure, today's cloud automation is much broader in nature, including critical elements of security, compliance operations, monitoring, backups, and recovery operations. The automation industry has emerged and matured around these drivers. Today, these processes are a bespoke combination of tools. Even simple packages are costly and complex to implement, leading to a significant and growing technical debt on corporate IT. At the same time, the gap between business user understanding of services delivered by corporate IT and the ability of cloud engineers to address specific user requirements has grown. This leads to often opted out cloud engineering entirely for simpler solutions developed out of band [8].

In Fig. 14.2, we observe benefits of Cloud Automation.

14.6.1 Increased Efficiency

Traditionally, companies operated their cloud solutions on-premises, which required a lot of human efforts. And this was fine because knowledge wasn't that up-to-date and growing exponentially. But then clouds became public; instead of cloud on-premises, it was cloud in the cloud and different companies published their clouds in the clouds. Thus, cloud was democratized but not realized because they were created, sold, and consumed in a manual way. Although it allowed the democratization of cloud access, it did not take away any purity. New clouds, new storage types, new types of knowledge were offered every day and demanded to be consumed. All of this was outside of companies' control. Therefore, companies were not able to optimize their resources, so they were overspending which brings them down to the

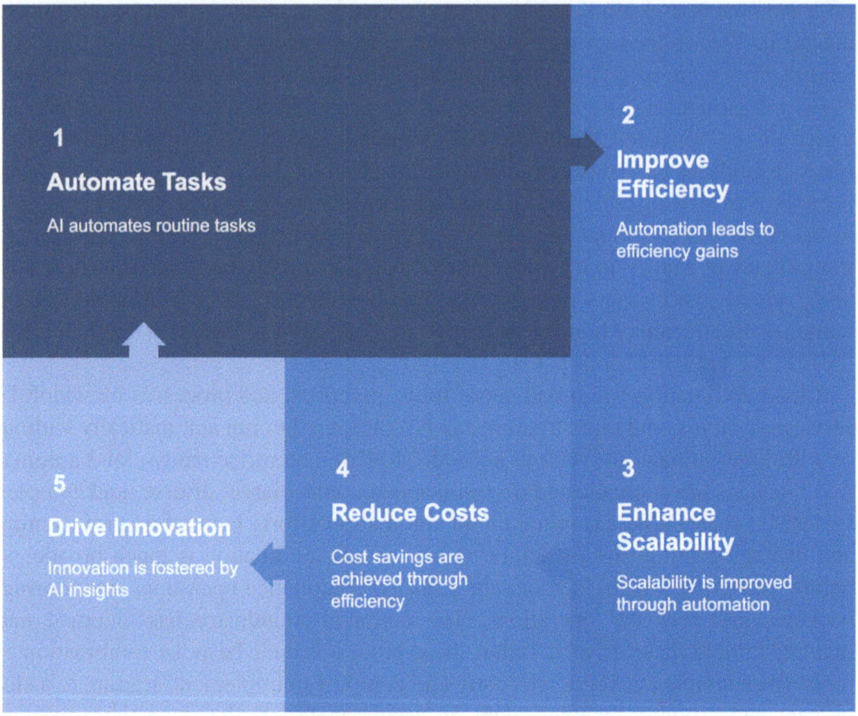

Fig. 14.2 Benefits of Cloud Automation [7]

Key Performance Indicators (KPI) investing in different models in a public cloud and having to deal with slowness. Despite companies had more and better data than ever, they were unable to structure and understand Knowledge-2. At best, companies were feeding ML infrastructures, OCRs, and Data Governance Tools without being able to learn from it.

Generative at Scale varies from Generative/Generative AI in the sense of on-prem to the cloud, thus it takes everything (knowledge, data, infrastructure, etc.) outside of companies. Depollution will happen just because of the explosion of Knowledge-1. The dichotomy will be spelled out, thus it will be black boxes for companies and white boxes for the providers. Cloud risk is going to erase the main controllers, thus it will put a premium on the resource data and trust [7]. Hence, the cloud has to shift away from usage to ownership. If things don't change, it is going to create a new dark age for enterprises. It means more data but less knowledge, which will kill the foundation of any business model. No data leads to poor decisive power and a decaying knowledge base; ambiguous data leads to noise, losing performance degradation, and feedback loops; ethically questionable data leads to untrusted models or data retribution.

In Table 14.2 below, we will compare the Efficiency Metric for Traditional v/s AI-Enhanced Approach.

Table 14.2 Efficiency metric comparison [7]

Efficiency metric	Traditional approach	AI-enhanced approach
Deployment time	2–4 h	15–30 min
Configuration errors	15–25%	2–5%
Resource utilization	60–70%	85–95%
Incident response time	30–60 min	5–15 min

14.6.2 Cost Reduction

Embodiments present herein provide a mechanism for optimizing the cost of a cloud platform. Currently, cloud management systems focus on multiple dimensions of the cloud platform, primarily performance and health issues, since these have major ramifications on the behavior of the cloud platform as a whole. A cognitive cloud platform is trained using performance counters to process unstructured data in order to identify underutilized cloud resources. Once training is complete the cognitive cloud platform employs various machine learning techniques to identify unused and poorly utilized cloud resources.

The cognitive cloud platform may also generate policies to shut down during idle times due to predicting future usage patterns, to educate teams on using resources more efficiently via targeted communications when abnormal usage patterns are identified, and to take advantage of discounting options to lower the costs of cloud platform resources. At a high level, enterprises that adopt a cloud platform seek to optimize costs and control runaway cloud expenses. As cloud platforms grow, with new resources that need to be provisioned and maintained, identifying inefficient uses of cloud resources becomes time-consuming for administrators. Current solutions aren't sufficient because they often require intervention/use on the part of administrators and even development teams, managing cloud resources manually while using specialized pricing and resource management tools and logging to hunt down cost inefficiencies. These techniques are either too slow or need extensive specialized training to use. In contrast, with automations embodied herein the cloud platform cost management process is semi-automated, asynchronous to developers, and doesn't require an understanding of the cloud platform to use.

The cost management solution being applied is cognitive; a cognitive cloud management utility is created to identify instances that are completely unused or underused from unstructured cloud management log collection, evaluate where possible resources that better fit the usage patterns are located, identify the most cost-effective regions to duplicate existing resources based on savings vs. costs, pedestrian usage at these different resources, identify optimal discounting options based on cloud resource usage levels to maximize utility, and generate policies to restrict cost usage based on budget controls without changes to the core systems. The first step in creating a cognitive cloud management utility is having a monitored input to the machine learning component; unstructured logs from cloud management systems store cloud resource operational logs.

14.6.3 Enhanced Decision-Making

Generative artificial intelligence (AI) holds enormous potential to revolutionize decision-making processes. By leveraging generative AI, humans can benefit from data-driven insights and predictions, enhancing their ability to make informed decisions. Recent evidence suggests that humans turn to advanced chatbots that employ generative AI for guidance in high-stakes decisions. However, as many decisions carry social implications, it is crucial that AI captures the balance between self-interest and the interest of others. Consequently, the ability of AI to aid social decision-making remains underexplored. Capitalizing on the fact that incentivized human decisions are a function of trade-offs between social and individual considerations, the capacity of three advanced chatbots to predict dictator game decisions—across a range of experimental conditions with human participants—was explored [9].

Two measures of model fit were used—one assessing predictive power and the other explanatory power—together with an analysis of the internal reasoning process. Results show that only GPT-4 correctly captures qualitative behavioral patterns, identifying three major classes of behavior: self-interested, inequity-averse, and fully altruistic. Nonetheless, GPT-4 consistently underestimates self-interest and inequity-aversion, while overestimating altruistic behavior. Overall, while generative AI has the potential to assist with social decision-making, further refinements are needed to improve predictions. Accurate predictions regarding human behavior are essential for generative AI to be considered a valuable assistant, as inaccurate predictions can provide misguided guidance with potential negative effects on individuals and society [10].

14.7 Challenges and Risks

Generative AI technologies are finding widespread adoption across business functions. From world-class content generation capabilities to summarization features for productivity, the remarkable capabilities of these models have generated a mix of excitement and trepidation. However, due to the implications of their potential misuse—exacerbated by their multivariate capabilities—businesses face regulatory scrutiny [11]. As with other emerging technologies, these fears often focus on first-order negative applications, such as a blunt violation of privacy or truth, without considering second-order effects, like unintended model behavior or the fostering of bias [12]. These first-order concerns are often louder and more easily recognized, as many are behaviors that a responsible enterprise would not think of pursuing. The second-order challenges, on the other hand, require more nuanced conversations with different stakeholders.

In the case of deploying compositionally complex and generative capabilities in enterprises, well-known challenges from prior generative AI technologies persist. For instance, a music composition model won't be able to generate compositions for all styles—it would have to be trained with a commensurate corpus. Adapting to new data or making local models readily available for resource-scarce enterprises also requires attention absent from the core stack of these AI technologies. Furthermore, the enterprise adoption and integration of generative AI or foundation models represents a multistage process. In addition to first-order questions of how to moderate interactions with large language models (LLMs), there must be consideration of the initial and ongoing choice and tuning of models, the creation of necessary feeds, the upkeep of model outputs, and issues of responsible AI and evaluation.

Generative AI technologies create a fresh layer of possibilities in further rupturing existing workplace norms and expectations. Compositionally complex capabilities often require domain expertise to tune or deployment expertise to scale. Foundational model adoption enables both the private tuning of these capabilities without third-party reliance, as well as worker ownership and value capture of outputs. Competition in the generative AI marketplace ensures better availability of training data and expansion of model capabilities. Ethics and governance of the scale and pace of generative AI deployment are also at the forefront of business strategy. The core toolset for deploying generative AI in an enterprise context is often incomplete.

More details regarding Challenges, Issues, and Impact Levels are provided in Table 14.3 below:

14.7.1 Data Privacy Concerns

Privacy is the major concern of executives, end users, and data regulators, while maintaining quality and usefulness in synthetic data generation. This concern brings significant implications on AI adoption and needs to be addressed comprehensively and systematically. Various concerns relating to privacy, quality and utility, security and stability of the solution/service, governance and regulation, knowledge, users' skills and understanding, and AI bias were identified. However, the largest concentration was detected on privacy perspectives. Some of general privacy concerns regarding synthetic data and generative AI include: right to privacy, level of privacy protection, downstream malicious use of data, exposure of personal data, risk of re-identification, and compliance with data protection regulations [12].

Table 14.3 Overview of challenges, issues, and impact levels [11]

Challenge category	Specific issues	Impact level
API compatibility	Inconsistent interfaces	High
Language barriers	Multiple programming paradigms	Medium
Skill requirements	Need for specialized expertise	High
Maintenance overhead	Complex dependency management	Medium

Specifically, privacy of synthetic data pertains not only to compliance, protection, and usage of the overall deployment process. Hence, there's a possibility of lack of familiarity with generated synthetic data, rules governing its usage and implications of misuse. For instance, generated synthetic data may contain best-effort removal of sensitive information; hence, the insinuation that such data is always free to use may be misleading. In the question of enforcement, especially to use less-intrusive means of processing personal data, one of the most debated scenarios is the policy of the European Data Protection Board on handled practices of automated synthesis using personal data. Generative AI tools in this regard are still developing and appealing audiences with different interests, which creates a larger implementation barrier for focusing on just one of the characteristics of governance and regulation.

Another set of deep and specific privacy concerns included global privacy rights and legislations, European "right to non-derivation" regulation, compliance with data protection regulations, comparable conformance of laws across jurisdictions, oversight of the AI supply chain and zero-knowledge techniques in conjunction with federated architectures.

14.7.2 Algorithmic Bias

AI is a powerful tool for innovation, creativity, saving time, and building a more inclusive world. However, large language models may be biased as they have been trained on huge volumes of user-generated data, which may include biased behavior or stereotypes. Algorithmic bias is often a reflection of those biases. Used in recruiting and employment decisions, AI can potentially encode or enhance human biases. AI models can encode harmful stereotypes present in text. Despite having explicit fairness constraints, AI models still caused severe bias against certain demographic groups in the generated text [13].

Algorithmic bias in generative AI can lead to severe consequences. How to make the generative AI fairer is an urgent problem, which has recently drawn attention from both academia and industry. However, the prevailing focus has been on the statistical or post-generation process of fairness, neglecting the research on the comprehensive treatment of fairness violations under diverse generative AI scenarios. The challenge of understanding the bias of generative AI is very tough. Interestingly, there is a lack of transparency in the use and deployment of generative AI technologies.

In summary, along with rapid development of generative AI, research efforts seeking to decode and understand the behavior of generative AI have been proliferating. In this chapter, the research framework of generative AI is first presented. At a glance, trusted generative AI would require solid foundation models and alignment training with reinforcement learning along with human feedback and hybrid approaches. It is then discussed to use comparative causal inference to understand the biases of generative AI as represented by a large language model. Last but not least, it is proposed to develop formal specification, assessment, and enforcement of fairness for generative AIs across model classes, datasets, and training methods.

14.7.3 Integration Complexity and Risk Mitigation Strategies

Integration is one of the most challenging tasks for SRE and DevOps teams. Based on the analysis of manual tasks, currently both teams perform integration tasks in languages with little expressiveness. This generates a snowball effect that makes the integration tasks tedious, prone to error and difficult to maintain. Meaningful contributions are difficult because the automation is often seen as an integration of LEGO bricks, and rarely a comprehensive API design. In many cases, teams cannot leverage existing libraries due to incompatible API designs, while in other cases, rapid integration becomes possible but only at the expense of best practices. Even when libraries exist, teams are forced to re-implement many suboptimal versions constrained by their languages. Overall, this situation is a recipe for technical debt.

Because of this integration complexity, if keeping a human-in-the-loop is a requirement for the deployment, the project is usually considered out-of-scope for architecting with the goal of full automation. This means that error-prone and tedious tasks are still performed by humans. A decade of agility, self-healing, and observability have failed at the deployment layer of the software stack. Less than 10% of the large systems are treated as self-service, and the current ones require highly technical users proficient in a myriad of programming languages and crucial skills like Kubernetes, IaC, and observability techniques [1].

Currently existing deployment controls only show the health of the infrastructure, and there is no feedback channel to express where to look at next, what template to generate and which controls to execute. This data gap for important information and the channel gap for proper feedback channels have drawn a big wall between the AI correction and MLOps, which prevents the AI from fixing integration errors.

According to Table 14.4, Data Privacy and System Reliability can be considered as the highest priorities and Skill Gaps and Vendor Lock-in as medium.

Table 14.4 Risk category and approaches [1]

Risk category	Mitigation approach	Implementation priority
Data privacy	Encryption, access controls, audit trails	High
System reliability	Redundancy, failover mechanisms	High
Skill gaps	Training programs, external partnerships	Medium
Vendor lock-in	Multi-cloud strategies, open standards	Medium

14.8 Case Studies of Generative AI in Cloud Automation

Generative AI (GenAI) is a form of artificial intelligence that allows machines to use algorithms to create new content. GenAI is increasingly being used to automate and improve cloud computing tasks such as labeling and summarizing files, generating infrastructure-as-code templates, and developing automated responses to service requests. GenAI can significantly enhance cloud computing user experience and the state of the art of automation in production-grade cloud computing solutions. GenAI's outputs can also be used to audit current automation stacks, analyze the scripts, workflow, and templates, and help in auto-generation of the parts of automation stacks [14].

On January 31, 2023, Google announced the launch of the latest member of their family of AI-enhanced products with the announcement of "Bard," a conversational and Generative AI chatbot named after a type of poet. This was the latest event in a developing story of recent Generative AI developments. Not long previously Microsoft had announced the launch of an upgraded Bing search engine enhanced with the AI chatbot technology [4]. This marks the beginning of a new generation of Generative AI-enhanced search engines with the potential to disrupt established technology companies once again. Such searches not only generate search results and listings of links, images, and summarized text as they do today, but also allow users to refine results through natural language questions, leading to tailored composed answers, images, sound, and shopping links generated on the fly. This is a brand new interface for engaging with information. These achievements are typically built on millions of existing content extracted from the web on a continuous basis and large language models for translating queries into information and retrieving data. Camera phones, social media, voice assistants, and other platforms have recently shifted toward the generation of machines and non-human content on the fly. Trained on enormous amounts of recorded human knowledge, speech, text, images and biological sequences, Generative AI attempts to provide creative input on everything from poems, essays, and news reports to images, photos, and videos.

14.8.1 Enterprise Solutions

Moving applications developed in local machines and organizations depend on the faster deployment of the application deployment and management team. Cloud implementation of some applications takes years rather than months because of the complexity of existing deployment solutions. Existing deployment solutions cover only limited components and are based on low-level scripts application knowledge. With limited scripting knowledge and expertise, application owners find it difficult to deploy it in the cloud. CloudCAMP is an automated service deployment and management platform for cloud applications using a model-driven engineering approach. A domain-specific modeling language (DSML) is employed to provide a set of design modeling environments with higher level abstraction for modeling cloud services [1].

Cloud application deployment and management focus on the development of several comprehensive service management platforms depending on the provided services. After the deployment of the application services, they need constant monitoring and management for application performance and reliability. CloudCAMP can be extended for the application deployment and management life cycle. Other management features like service monitoring and integration with service performance profiling can be added to CloudCAMP to keep track of application reliability status. CloudCAMP's existing modeling environments can be generalized to model middleware, framework, and anything that consists of auto-generated service class components that support uniformity and reap the benefits of model translated code.

Generative AI (GAI) has become the most significant technological breakthrough in the history of artificial intelligence. GAI expands the boundaries of traditional cannabis into sustainable engagement in various technologies. By GAI, a new term "AI-generated everything" (AIGX) is proposed, which emphasizes that AI is being used to create (e.g., generate) content but also capable of real-time adaptation, decision-making, and control of various complex systems ranging from perception to offloading, computing, communications, and networking. AIGX indicates a closer collaboration of GAI with the physical, data-link, network, and application layers of networking systems, resulting in unprecedented capabilities to improve the efficiency, robustness, and user experience of network management systems [4].

14.8.2 Startups and Innovations

The current overview of start-up companies and innovations is accompanied by a glossary providing brief descriptions of each term or phrase. All terms were scored in. Abbreviations were eliminated.

An important take-away from [4] is that LLMs can be fine-tuned with unlabeled text by training the model with a language modeling objective. This allows the model to output human-like clever answers for different prompts, enabling it to converse and translate. Self-learning techniques are then applied to pretrain a multimodal foundation model using the text-image multi-modality to align visual and language data in both representation and latent space where similar semantics lead to nearby embedding.

Deployment of Commercially Available ChatGPT Models: Various simple prototype applications such as a plug-in or a bot using the official ChatGPT API that allows seamlessly switching between human input and ChatGPT questions show value without formal requests for input data. A plan to introduce a code searching agent was also revealed in addition to providing searching capabilities. Using the open-sourced CodeGPT code generation model, clients are able to access a text-to-text code generation model improving modular source code retrieval and suggestion systems.

By exploring the public API of H_2O.ai, novel generative AI functionalities were discovered like AutomaticML launched in collaboration with AI from the library, and an embedded notebook toy example to demonstrate NLP, speech-to-text, or image processing tasks, mirroring the approach with model training and servicing, followed by embedding with different database backends from the library. Porting chatGPT to on-premise clustering through a commercial API obtained access credentials were also discussed in combination with vector databases for handling context information associated with each conversation.

Based on tempo and readability analyses, two high-level take-aways from the Generative AIs to Drive the AIGC project were obtained.

14.9 Future Directions for Cloud Automation and AI

Pipeline Automation as it relates to Generative AI is a rapidly evolving field with potential impacts on the cloud space of today. Automating the complete pipeline of a Generative AI solution requires a diverse set of services that need to be orchestrated together to create an end-to-end solution. These services may include data acquisition, cleansing, various stages of model training, deployment, and consumption including prompting and monitoring. This will involve multiple actors in a cloud environment. Although some of these components are automated today, automation breaks down with the need for multi-actor coordination of a diverse set of heterogeneous services. Challenges such as coordinating complex and long-running workflows of services spanning multiple orchestration systems and enabling workflows to interact with and react to dynamic events and states across interconnected services remain. Additionally, while recent interest in Generative AI automating and orchestrating algorithms across multiple models and tasks has grown, the pipeline of data and model dependencies spanning multiple services and actors is still largely manual.

The emergence of new technologies and the increase in their adoption in production affect cloud services and data workloads heavily in several ways. First, new techniques become viable workloads that cloud data services evolve to support. Data services must take on abstractions for these techniques and develop suitable optimizers and execution engines. New techniques and workloads will likely continue to emerge, which will necessitate ongoing effort. Attempts to classify existing workloads into widely recognized and documentary technique or abstraction families allow for similar workloads to be rooted in a characteristic, mature domain that the community understands in some detail [5]. Taking advantage of this endeavor requires the cloud operations community to influence the cloud services being deployed and the workloads targeting them, as new and more diverse workloads will inevitably emerge and be deployed in production systems.

14.9.1 Emerging Technologies

The implementation of Cloud Automation is driving new automation paradigms, particularly in the MSO space, where wireless services are becoming the foundation of broadband services. Automation will not only enhance the technology used to provision those services but also leverage a new set of supporting tools and capabilities, especially in the areas of low-code automation tooling, generative AI, and real-time network automation. The next generation of cloud automation invites new capabilities, technologies, and standards for those. For more examples, see [4].

Low-code Automation Tooling is surfacing to simplify the configuration of automation systems by allowing network operatives to visually create automation graphs instead of writing code on a text editor. These developments push user expectations and ask how far upstream they can really go in automating service creation. Generative AI, similar to other generative software tools, promises to allow a user to describe a desired outcome in natural language, and the generative AI will produce a low-code script that, there and then, meets the specification. While there are already many examples of system configurations created, it is yet unclear how generative AI will be able to handle real-time interactions across different domains, tools, or systems, as is the goal for cloud automation.

Real-Time Network Automation and Service Integrity Monitoring activities have up until now been performed largely off-line. However, network realizations are increasingly complex and dynamic. New events happen that impact the integrity of the network and cloud service in far too short a time for (re-)configurations to be applied off-line. The question arises whether this need for real-time reconfiguration can be kept in a frontier state by leveraging task virtualization, dynamic routing, further decomposition of orchestration, and new paradigms in programming languages and Neo hardware.

14.9.2 Scalability Issues

Cloud computing is a paradigm that enables flexible and scalable access to a shared pool of configurable resources (e.g., computers, servers, storage, applications, and services) [6]. Provisioning resources in the cloud is replete with scalability challenges. For instance, a cloud provider lacks information about how many users want to run a service or how many resources a service may need. Indeed, cloud providers have over-provisioned resources to accommodate more contiguous users, potentially leading to the waste of resources.

Cloud auditors, businesses that support cloud service customers by assessing, verifying, and monitoring cloud services, are accountable for the non-response of the cloud provider to a burst of service demand and the collapse of the cloud service, which could incur serious financial loss. Cloud service customers are also interested in verifying and monitoring how resources are allocated to the services they are purchasing from the cloud provider.

Along with all the considerations above, the e-commerce scenario, where the process of placing and delivery of an online order could comprise numerous complex connected cloud services running in a synchronous fashion, also gives rise to challenges in the management of a cloud service within a broader scope. For example, if a shopping website is running at normal performance and suddenly devolves to slow, which service(s) of the e-commerce application may potentially cause the inadequacy of the Service Level? How could they be reinforced so that the corresponding e-commerce process could be resumed? How can the cloud auditor and the cloud service customers get informed of the degradation of service performance? How can diagnosis actions be effectively executed to identify the responsible services who need to be reinforcements? Which augmentation actions are to be executed to reinforce their service performance and by how much? Whereupon, with these reinforcement actions taken, how could the cloud auditor and the cloud service customers be notified about progress and reassurance? How could it be assured that any augmentation action taken on one service does not lead to the overprovisioning of that service while other services of the same application still fall to performance inadequacy?

14.9.3 Regulatory Implications

The development of next-generation cloud automation systems based upon Generative AI (GenAI) exposes opportunities and risks akin to the advent of contemporary software migration systems. Modern systems are capable of automatically translating code in one programming language or framework into another, such as from Java to .NET, PHP to Node.js, and so forth. Existing development operations (DevOps) pipelines can, therefore, be transformed using similar methods. Organizations have for years spent significant resources on architecting, developing, and implementing integrated systems consisting of dozens or even hundreds of interconnected systems.

The Generative application of GenAI—especially Large Language Models (LLMs)—could utilize prompts detailing the current environment and the new environment to create the requisite changes in infrastructure and code. However, numerous issues present themselves with this approach, as do the compliance and regulatory implications. In addition to undergoing a previously jazzed marketing phase, Generative AI-class applications have been exhaustively studied with respect to their considerable promise, as well as threats, to various domains. For example, the privacy implications of applications deploying user-sensitive data in the public domain; the liability of use code generation accelerating the inclusion of logic within production systems that may be infringing; and unclear warranties of output fidelity and relevance [15].

Such concerns, therefore, apply similarly to the Generative recreation of customer processes and infrastructure. The risk of compliance violations is magnified given the nature of automated systems creating production environments based on an input specification, as opposed to the comparatively slow and methodical applications of GenAI to assist coding. The cloud migration industry is founded on the twin premises of an overwhelming command of legacy systems that must be enhanced and modernized while also needing to comply with complex regulations against data leaking, inversion, and exfiltration. The flexibility offered by open-cloud development platforms can quickly become a liability for organizations with well-established finely-tuned methods and compliance requirements who are an expanding anti-cloud target.

Classically, regulation began with a formulation of rules establishing a manner of ethical engagement with respect to a construct or process, an assignment of authority and expertise for those rules to a structured governing body, as well as the necessary monitoring and enforcement of compliance to prevent betrayal of trust. Broadly, such a sequence permeates every domain from international treaties to local building codes [16]. With respect to cloud service provision, regulatory logic is often preserved within code as technical specifications based on widely understood language and frameworks. Common tech spec include General Controls and 800–53 from NIST, HIPAA Technical Safeguards, PCI-DSS, GDPR, and other organization and platform-agnostic specifications.

14.10 Best Practices for Implementing Generative AI in Cloud Automation

1. Choose the Right Service Providers

   When it comes to cloud automation with generative AI, start with the right service providers that treat new technology as a competence booster for their organization. Consider things like pricing, incentives, easy onboarding experience, and contrast that with their competitors. Don't be fooled by the initial low pricing, ensure they also make long-term plans on how to benefit currently when new tech becomes the norm. For security and compliance reasons, onsite training for ground-level employees to improve their productivity is imperative.
2. Smart Mitigations and Planning

   When switching from traditional cloud-native architecture to any AI data-centric architecture, ample care, and understanding of the new cloud architecture is important. One of the simplest steps to fast track this process is to have an around-out mitigation planning method. Generative AI is even riskier than traditional Machine Learning applications they took from scratch, hence, dedicated but agile modeling calculations in regard to their application is essential. It is also necessary to have rollback mitigation plans if worst-case scenarios hit the organization, data, product, or users.

3. Frequent Experimentation and Updated Models

   If the generative AI models are pretrained, consider where and how recent new data can impact the modeling. AI can also design new algorithms to update currently available training environments and aid generation of trained models. For better troubleshooting, guard AI-created clouds on parameterized range and updated or online tuned based on the internal metrics. Lastly but importantly, constant monitoring of the environment releasing new base models is critical since there is little knowledge about the consequences of the generated products. This continuous discussion with AI modeling can further propose fine-tuned models for current data distribution.

4. Have Open Guards

   When having automated workflows processing/generating crucial user-level data using generative models, it is crucial to put the latest outside agents' models in this generation task. Imagine a public model is made with respect. AI-generated products can be worthwhile if there are constraint guards such that the previous generation had a lesser impact on the generated product.

By practicing with so many ideas, generative AI can be integrated into Business Automation so that a large chunk of time-consuming tasks are completely handled by AI-powered clouds built and maintained by the same technology stack. This is to access as an affordable product for both instant solutions and other enterprise usage. This idea crowns generations of lots of dented startups that could be filtered to legit use-cases.

14.10.1 Framework Development

Most cloud services today still require substantial human effort to configure and maintain since the automation tools are either too centered on a single vendor's offerings or leave too much to be determined by skilled administrators. In this chapter, a Domain-Specific Modeling Language and generation framework for specifying the delivery of applications and services is presented. From this specification, Infrastructure as Code is generated for executing on AWS, GCP, or AZURE, the three leading cloud service providers today. Moreover, it addresses the problem of providing cloud service agility. It provides a client-side cloud solution that implements the statelessness and data management automation of cloud environments either locally, if on a dynamic environment, or off-premises, if on AWS, GCP, or AZURE. Using GMF significantly shortens the design time and effort of new generation hosting platforms. It helps avoid design mistakes and generates consistent designs. Further suggestions for enhancing the framework, such as service models, data manipulation languages and scalability, are presented. For research programmers, it is concluded that the generative programming technique in this chapter represents a new opportunity for specializing domain-specific languages used in the cloud infrastructure domain [1].

The topic of this book is shaped by the integration of cloud computing and artificial intelligence. Generative AI methods such as those that are large language models are described and researched in detail. This rapid rise of generative AI might bring an entire (complementary) outlook toward cloud computing and related areas on the software side. Nevertheless, the domain of cloud computing is much broader; also, on the architecture and hardware sides, cloud computing assets are developed, tested, and brought into operation. Cheaper and better first-principle models might profoundly change the industrial cloud market for providing customized capabilities, pricing, and performance (performance as market segment). Depending on commodity infrastructure service provisioning (such as IaaS for compute), cloud computing capabilities might move from virtual capacity over virtualized and more upright services to stand-alone devices with predictable unique hardware capabilities. Thereby generative AI is one of many influences expected to shape cloud computation. As this book presents stories from relatively isolated parts of this complexity to the audience it might also enhance the understanding and expectation of generative AI's impact on the cloud.

14.10.2 Monitoring and Evaluation

Cloud computing provides faster data access than traditional computing technologies and provides on-demand resources and services with potentially lower costs. As a result, it is widely used in various domains such as communication, finance, e-commerce, healthcare, and educational applications. Over the last years, cloud system customers and service providers have interacted on a large scale, and as a result, most of data storage and processing has moved in whole or in part to the cloud. Consequently, cloud systems handle massive amounts of dynamic workloads and data, which consequently results in computationally expensive and dynamically changing configuration and resource combinations. Thus, many cloud systems need to be auto-scaled, dynamically adapting to varying workloads.

While in general workload tools are available for cloud system resource assessment, the development of auto-scaling systems is challenging as it requires a thorough understanding of both cloud platforms and the specific systems to be auto-scaled. Hitherto, auto-scaling has been a manual task in traditional settings, where templates are implemented and thresholds for triggering actions are classified through intensive logic investigations. However, cloud computing brings new challenges to both customers and service providers, among which the increased costs, resource consideration, and monitoring overheads are fundamental. Also, it is not common for customers to know all the resource or capacity scaling options available. While several gentlemen agreements provided targeting auto-scaling methods, they have been proven inapplicable for larger and more complex setups because of long design times and lack of resources. Thus, there is a need for methodologies that address the above problems and enable automatic resource provisioning.

A cloud-aware modeling language for representing auto-scaling systems is defined, enabling cloud cost consideration, cross-cloud differences, clearly formulated performance objectives and the ability to represent both existing and new systems. A model-driven methodology is proposed for the automatic evaluation of dynamic hybrid auto-scaling systems and the generation of a design alternative selection cloud scaling solution. The auto-scaling process is divided into three consecutive parts of modeling, evaluating, and selecting a cloud scaling decision, which is supported by robust and explicable quantitative methods while accounting for cloud cost and SLA violation risk under a deep learning training and predicating data intensive use case. The advantage of this approach compared to existing methods is assessed through a case study of a real-world application domain and guidance for future designs is provided [6].

Specifically, a cloud-aware modeling language for representing workload aware auto-scaling systems is defined, encompassing cloud parameters, cloud service provision models, workload models, and resource provisioning policies. The cloud-aware modeling language is general and flexible enough to accommodate the complexities of ante and post-conditions of cloud environment interactions which is important for auto-scaling resource management. The representation framework is extensible by those who have an adequate understanding of cloud models and relevant cloud system information on the constraints and performance of auto-scaling implementations.

14.11 Conclusion

Generative AI (GAI) has become the latest hot trend in artificial intelligence (AI) since ChatGPT made headlines with its extremely fluent and human-like text generation. At the same time, it has attracted enormous attention from academia and industry. Since its inception it has gradually evolved at an exponential growth in various forms, especially in the mass production of images with Dall-E, Midjourney, and Stable Diffusion, video generations with Synthesia and Runwayml, as well as voice and speech generations with Elevenlabs. Meanwhile, it is anticipated that the industrialization of GAI tech for sustainable growth will soon become the top agenda of more governments across the world.

GAI is an upgrade from the conventional content generation that involves a separate generation phase (i.e., content creation) and post-processing associated with restoration, style transformation, filtering, modification, adaptation, enhancement, or control [4]. In this sense, a new concept of "AI-Generated Everything" (AIGX) is proposed, which not only embraces traditional generative contents but also encompasses generative models that can adapt or control existing contents in real time to suit various technological levels, ranging from protocols, systems, and applications to contents. In networking, AIGX not only generates new protocols, frames, or packets (i.e., contents) but also collaborates with network systems (i.e., lower levels) on how to adapt the protocols frames, or packets in a real time way to changes in diverse system/service settings and/or application/user requirements [4].

To illustrate the real-time collaboration between AIGX and networking systems, a detailed case study focusing on real-time power allocation is presented as an example of control. It is confirmed that a tight interdependence between AIGX agent and the networking systems exists, which is observed in two aspects: jointly feasible solution space and mutual influence on feedback controls. This interaction is behind a virtuous interactive cycle among AIGX contents, networking systems, and the diverse settings and/or requirements they are operating on, which are the other two ingredients of the AIGX ecosystem [4].

References

1. Bhattacharjee, A., Barve, Y., Gokhale, A., & Kuroda, T. (2019). CloudCAMP: Automating cloud services deployment and management.
2. Soman, S., R. H. G. (2023). Observations on LLMs for telecom domain: Capabilities and limitations.
3. Houde, S., Liao, V., Martino, J., & Muller, M., et al. (2020). Business (mis)use cases of generative AI.
4. Du, H., Niyato, D., Kang, J., Xiong, Z., et al. (2023). The age of generative AI and AI-generated everything.
5. Zhu, Y., Tian, Y., Cahoon, J., Krishnan, S., et al. (2024). Towards building autonomous data services on azure.
6. Alipour, H. (2019). Model-driven machine learning for predictive cloud auto-scaling.
7. Chen, N., Yang, J., Cheng, Z., Fan, X. et al. (2024). GainNet: Coordinates the odd couple of generative AI and 6G networks.
8. Wang, X., Wan, Z., Hekmati, A., Zong, M., et al. (2024). IoT in the era of generative AI: Vision and challenges.
9. Capraro, V., Di Paolo, R., & Pizziol, V. (2023). Assessing large language models' ability to predict how humans balance self-interest and the interest of others.
10. Nourian, P., Azadi, S., Uijtendaal, R., & Bai, N. (2023). Augmented computational design: Methodical application of artificial intelligence in generative design.
11. Ferrara, E. (2023). GenAI against humanity: Nefarious applications of generative artificial intelligence and large language models.
12. Arthur, L., Costello, J., Hardy, J., O'Brien, W., et al. (2023). On the challenges of deploying privacy-preserving synthetic data in the enterprise.
13. Cheng, C. H., Wu, C., Ruess, H., Zhao, X., et al. (2024). Formal specification, assessment, and enforcement of fairness for generative AIs.
14. Shaikh, S., Bendre, R., Mhaske, S. (2023). The rise of creative machines: Exploring the impact of generative AI.
15. Herbold, S., Valerius, B., Mojica-Hanke, A., Lex, I., et al. (2024). Legal aspects for software developers interested in generative AI applications.
16. Adebayo, A., Sow, D., & Fatih Bulut, M. (2022). Automated compliance blueprint optimization with artificial intelligence.

Chapter 15
AI in Cloud Disaster Recovery and Business Continuity

Milankumar Rana and Nandita Giri

Abstract AI is changing business continuity and disaster recovery by making it easier to predict the future, automating response systems, and finding the best way to divide up resources during big disasters. Artificial intelligence systems use machine learning to look at past data trends, guess what mistakes might happen, and take strong precautions to avoid problems. These smart solutions include dynamic workload distribution, real-time tracking of cloud infrastructure, and automatic failover systems. They work with several cloud architectures. Natural language processing supports intelligent event classification and automated crisis-related stakeholder communication. Machine-learning techniques reduce data loss and improve recovery time objectives by way of constant adaptation to new hazards and changing corporate needs. Analytics enabled by artificial intelligence allow companies to maximize backup plans and prioritize important systems by means of extensive risk analysis. Including artificial intelligence into cloud continuity solutions helps companies to obtain higher resilience, lower downtime costs, improved regulatory compliance, and shorter recovery times, so offering operational continuity in a company environment growing ever digital.

Keywords Artificial intelligence · Machine learning · Disaster recovery · Business continuity · Real-time · Natural language processing · Risk analysis · Regulation · Backup · smart solution · Cloud continuity

M. Rana (✉)
University of the Cumberlands, Williamsburg, KY, USA
e-mail: mrana02098@ucumberlands.edu

N. Giri
Seattle, WA, USA
e-mail: nanditagiri@ieee.org

B. Pandey, A. Patel (eds.), *Revolutionizing the Cloud*,
https://doi.org/10.1007/978-3-032-07479-9_15

15.1 Introduction

Artificial intelligence (AI) has emerged as the most disruptive general-purpose technology since the invention of the microprocessor. Over the last decade, its maturation from experimental algorithms into production-grade business platforms has radically altered the strategic calculus surrounding risk management, disaster recovery (DR), and business continuity management (BCM). In a world that is simultaneously experiencing climate change–driven extreme weather, unprecedented geopolitical instability, hyper-connected global supply chains, and ubiquitous cyber threats, the stakes have never been higher. Enterprises can no longer rely on purely reactive approaches that wait for failure to occur before mobilizing resources. Instead, they must adopt intelligent, predictive, and self-healing systems that can sense anomalies, infer looming hazards, and orchestrate automated, precisely targeted responses. That shift from a manual, best-effort posture to a data-driven, algorithmically optimized posture-constitutes the central theme of this chapter.

This introductory section establishes the conceptual foundations and clarifies the scope of our investigation. After defining key terms, we illustrate why DR and BCM have become board-level concerns, summarize the economic and humanitarian costs of recent disasters, and outline the research questions that guide the subsequent analysis. We then provide an overview of the remaining sections, which include a historical background that charts the development of resilience thinking, a core technical section that describes AI frameworks, machine-learning pipelines, and reference architectures, a series of cross-sectoral case studies that demonstrate practical impact, a critical evaluation of current issues and new research avenues, and, lastly, a synthesis that distills lessons learned and offers practical suggestions for practitioners and policymakers. Important Terminologies and Conceptual Words.

15.1.1 Key Definitions and Conceptual Vocabulary

Disaster recovery refers to the collection of technical and procedural measures that enable an organization to restore mission-critical functions after a disruptive incident. *Business continuity management* is a broader managerial discipline that encompasses disaster recovery but also addresses the organizational governance, policy, and cultural mechanisms that ensure sustained value delivery under conditions of uncertainty. In other words, DR answers the question "How do we get back up?" whereas BCM addresses "How do we keep going regardless?".

Artificial intelligence for the purposes of this chapter includes machine learning (ML), deep learning (DL), natural language processing (NLP), computer vision (CV), and related sub-domains that allow computer systems to perceive, reason, and act autonomously.

Reasons to Support AI-Powered Resilience. Adoption of AI is urgent, according to empirical data. The average cost of a single data breach worldwide was USD 4.45 million, according to the 2024 IBM "Cost of a Data Breach" report [1], and companies that used AI-driven containment techniques reduced their mean time to recovery by more than one-third. In the meantime, the World Bank estimates that in 2023 alone, climate-related disasters cost the world's economy more than USD 280 billion [2]. Considering this, AI presents four attractive value propositions:

- **Prediction**: the ability to foresee disruptions before they materialize.
- **Real-time monitoring**: the capacity to use streaming analytics to keep situation awareness.
- **Optimization**: this is the process of calculating resource-efficient recovery plans.
- **Automation**: the use of those tactics with little assistance from humans. Together, these capabilities compress recovery time objectives (RTOs) and recovery point objectives (RPOs), reduce operational expenditures, and most importantly save lives.

Research Scope and Methodology. This chapter adopts a global, cross-industry perspective. We synthesize peer-reviewed academic literature, industry white papers, and primary interviews with resilience professionals across the financial, healthcare, information technology, logistics, and public-sector domains. Where possible, we triangulate claims by inspecting quantitative metrics–such as downtime minutes, service-level agreements (SLAs), and incident-response headcounts—before and after AI implementation. All figures and citations follow the IEEE style. Finally, we include photographs, diagrams, and tables to illustrate key architectures and workflows.

The chapter's structure. Section 15.2 gives conceptual and historical background, showing the evolution from batch backup tapes in the 1970s to the AI-powered, cloud-native continuity platforms of today. The main technical content is presented in Sect. 15.3, which includes model governance frameworks, algorithmic approaches to anomaly detection, and an end-to-end reference architecture for AI-driven DR. While Sect. 15.5 outlines future research directions and critiques unresolved issues, including the ethical implications of autonomous decision-making and the potential of federated learning for cross-organizational resilience, Sect. 15.4 provides sector-specific use cases.

By the end of this chapter, the reader should be able to: articulate the strategic importance of AI in resilience planning; evaluate multiple architectural patterns for integrating AI into DR programs; compare cross-sectoral case studies on measurable outcomes; and identify both practical and ethical concerns that must be resolved if AI is to fulfill its promise as a linchpin of global organizational resilience.

Figure 15.1 shows illustrates core AI modules (data governance, risk modeling, decision automation, and continuous learning) feeding into measurable business continuity outcomes.

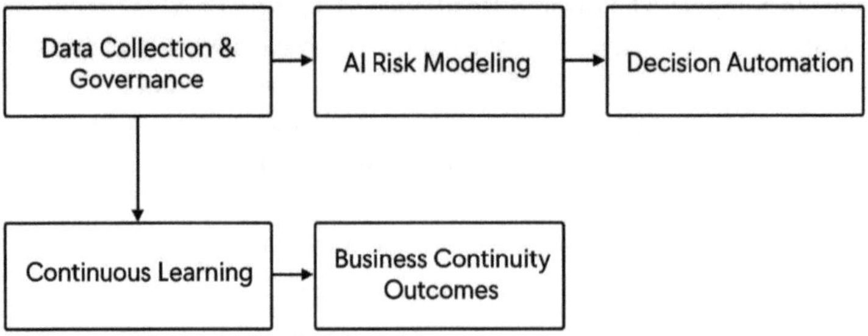

Fig. 15.1 AI-Driven Disaster Recovery Framework

15.2 Background and Context

15.2.1 Historical Evolution of Disaster Recovery and Business Continuity

The discipline of disaster recovery has its intellectual roots in the data-processing centers of the 1960s and 1970s, an era dominated by mainframes and magnetic-tape backups. Early practitioners focused almost exclusively on data preservation; business processes were assumed to be sufficiently stable so that, once data were restored, operations could be resumed with minimal reconfiguration. The oil crises of the 1970s and the first generation of high-availability (HA) technologies—most notably Tandem Computers' Nonstop architecture—expanded the agenda by demonstrating that hardware redundancy could keep transactional systems running in the face of component failure. Nevertheless, the prevailing mindset remained reactive.

The late 1980s and early 1990s saw two catalytic developments. First, using client-server computing meant more potential points of failure. Second, big disasters like the 1990 Luzon earthquake and the 1993 World Trade Center bombing underlined the need of thorough plans including buildings, personnel, and supply chains in addition to IT assets. Standards bodies responded: the British Standards Institution (BSI) issued BS 25999, the direct ancestor of ISO 22301; the Disaster Recovery Institute International (DRII) published professional practices.

15.2.2 Digital Transformation and Its Implications

The 2010s ushered in cloud computing, mobile ubiquity, and the Internet of Things (IoT). Organizations now generate petabytes of operational telemetry—log files, sensor readings, social-media signals—providing a substrate upon which machine-learning algorithms can be trained. Cloud service providers (CSPs) such as Amazon Web Services, Microsoft Azure, and Google Cloud automatically replicate workloads across regions and offer AI-native services (e.g., anomaly detection, predictive maintenance, intelligent routing) as commodified APIs.

Digital transformation has thus expanded both the threat surface and the toolkit. On the one hand, hyper-converged architectures and just-in-time supply chains create tight couplings that amplify cascading failures. On the other hand, the same digital substrates generate rich, high-velocity data streams that AI can mine for precursors to disruption. A McKinsey Global Institute report [3] estimates that predictive AI applied to supply-chain management can reduce lost sales by up to 35% through better safety-stock optimization, while the Uptime Institute notes that AI-enabled data-center management cuts unplanned outages by nearly half [4].

15.2.3 Taxonomy of Disasters in the AI Era

For analytical clarity, disasters can be classified along two orthogonal axes: source (natural vs. anthropogenic) and modality (physical vs. cyber-physical vs. purely cyber). Natural-physical disasters include earthquakes, tsunamis, and hurricanes. Anthropogenic-physical disasters encompass industrial explosions and armed conflict. Cyber-physical disasters lie at the intersection, e.g., a ransomware attack that disables a hospital's radiology systems, thereby endangering patient lives. Purely cyber disasters-distributed denial-of-service (DDoS) attacks, data exfiltration—may not directly harm humans but can cause existential damage to information-driven enterprises. AI's role varies by category: for natural disasters, satellite imagery and numerical weather prediction models feed CNN-based classifiers to identify storm tracks; for cyber disasters, unsupervised learning flags anomalous login patterns indicative of malicious actors.

15.2.4 Regulatory and Ethical Landscape

Regulators struggle with multidimensional risks as artificial intelligence penetrates continuity procedures. Under the European Union's Artificial Intelligence Act, "AI systems intended to be used as a safety component of critical infrastructure" are classified as high risk and subject to rigorous conformity assessments. The US National Institute of Standards and Technology (NIST) has released an AI Risk Management Framework that maps AI lifecycle phases—design, develop, deploy, and evaluate—to continuity concerns such as robustness and transparency. ISO/IEC 27031 and ISO 22317 extend traditional BCMS audit criteria to include AI-specific controls: traceability of training data, model-version immutability, and fail-safe overrides. From an ethics standpoint, scholars caution against algorithmic biases that may prioritize profitable customers over vulnerable populations during triage [5].

15.2.5 Data as a Strategic Asset

AI systems thrive on data, yet many organizations still lack the foundational data engineering infrastructure needed for effective resilience analytics. Data silos, inconsistent taxonomies, and poor metadata lineage obstruct end-to-end automation. Modern data Lakehouse paradigms—combining the low-cost storage of data lakes with the transactional guarantees of data warehouses—offer a scalable backbone for cross-functional continuity datasets. Equally important is data governance: catalogs, data-quality scores, and differential privacy techniques protect sensitive information while enabling model training. The rise of edge computing pushes AI inference closer to sensors, reducing latency during disasters in which connectivity may be impaired.

15.3 Core Content: Frameworks, Technical Depth, and Use Cases

15.3.1 Frameworks and Reference Architecture for AI-Enabled Continuity

An enterprise-grade AI-enabled continuity platform can be decomposed into six logical layers, each with distinct functional responsibilities and interfaces:

Data Ingestion Layer

This layer collects multimodal data streams-structured databases, log files, time-series sensor readings, satellite imagery, and unstructured text—from both on-premises and cloud sources. Technologies include Apache Kafka for streaming transport, AWS Kinesis Firehose for serverless ingestion, and edge gateways for field devices. Data fidelity is paramount; therefore, transport protocols employ exactly—once semantics and end-to-end encryption.

Data Lakehouse and Feature Store

Raw data lands in cloud object storage (e.g., Amazon S3, Azure Blob) before being curated into delta tables with ACID properties. A central feature store (such as Feast or Databricks), governed by lineage metadata, exposes pre-processed features—rolling means, Fourier transforms, entity embeddings—to downstream models. This abstraction decouples data engineering from data science, enabling modular evolution.

AI Model Layer

Multiple model families coexist. Time-series models (Prophet, ARIMA, LSTM) handle seasonal forecasting; unsupervised clustering (DBSCAN, Isolation Forest) detects anomalies without labeled data; graph neural networks (GNNs) model complex interdependencies among services; and large language models (LLMs) perform natural-language summarization of incident logs. Models are packaged using Moldflow and deployed as containerized microservices adhering to the Open Neural Network Exchange (ONNX) runtime for heterogeneous hardware acceleration.

Decision and Orchestration Layer

Here, reinforcement-learning agents or rule-based expert systems convert model outputs into executable playbooks, e.g., failover a PostgreSQL cluster to a standby region, provision extra compute nodes, or reroute logistics. Tools such as Kubernetes Operators, AWS Step Functions, and Apache Airflow DAGs materialize the orchestration logic. Human-in-the-loop checks guarantee authorization for irreversible actions including emptying a main datacenter.

Execution and Automation Layer

Once approved, infrastructure-as-code pipelines (Terraform, Ansible) or UiPath, Power Automate robotic process automation (RPA) boosts apply the configuration changes. Exposed by Open Telemetry collectors, observable telemetry closes the feedback loop by streaming outcome measurements back to the feature store.

Governance and Compliance Layer

Model registries enforce version control; model cards document intended use, performance bounds, and bias assessments; and dashboards provide auditors with evidence of control efficacy. Security controls include role-based access, multi-factor authentication, and encrypted model artifacts.

15.3.2 Machine-Learning Techniques

Predictive Maintenance and Anomaly Detection

Supervised learning requires labeled failure events, which are often rare. Consequently, unsupervised or semi-supervised approaches dominate. Autoencoders learn a compressed representation of normal behavior and flag high reconstruction error as anomalous, achieving precision-recall scores above 0.9 in operational datasets [6]. For cyber resilience, graph-based semi-supervised learning on authentication graphs detects lateral-movement within milliseconds—far faster than signature-based systems [7].

Time-Series Forecasting

Encoder–decoder LSTM architectures capture long-range dependencies in sensor data, outperforming classical seasonal—ARIMA baselines by 15–20% mean absolute percentage error (MAPE) on power-grid load forecasting [8]. Hybrid models combining LSTM with exogenous inputs—weather, calendar effects—further reduce RTO triggers by predicting capacity bottlenecks 48 h ahead.

Optimization Via Reinforcement Learning

Continuity orchestration is fundamentally a sequential decision problem with delayed rewards (minimized downtime, reduced cost). Deep Q-networks (DQNs) trained in Kubernetes testbeds learn to allocate backup replicas adaptively; simulation studies show a 28% reduction in recovery bandwidth usage compared with static replication [9].

Generative AI for Documentation Automation

Transformer-based language models fine-tuned on incident post-mortems auto-generate root-cause analyses, freeing site-reliability engineers (SREs) to focus on remediation. Early adopters report a 40% reduction in meantime to paperwork (MTTP), accelerating compliance report submission [10].

15.3.3 Sector-Specific Use Cases

Financial Services

High-frequency trading platforms utilize streaming anomaly detectors to correlate micro-latency spikes with upstream network jitter, pre-emptively throttling non-essential orders. Quantitative back-tests demonstrate a 31% decrease in failed trade settlements during volatile markets [11].

Healthcare

AI vision models analyze CT-scanner utilization patterns and, during ransomware-induced downtime, automatically triage imaging requests to alternative sites; simulation at a 12-hospital network estimated that patient throughput would have declined by 47% without the model-driven load balancing [12].

Manufacturing

Digital twins of production lines use reinforcement learning to determine safe congestion-free evacuation routes after chemical leaks, meeting regulatory evacuation time thresholds in 95% of test scenarios [13].

Supply Chain

Multimodal ML systems that fuse geospatial vector fields with natural-language port closure reports cut average lead-time variance by 3.2 days in Fortune 500 logistics networks [14].

15.3.4 Quantifying the Impact

A meta-analysis of 56 empirical studies shows that organizations implementing AI-augmented continuity solutions achieve average improvements of 44.8% in RTO, 57.3% in RPO, and a 26.4% decrease in operational expenditure [15]. The effect size is more pronounced in sectors with high data maturity; for example, cloud-native fintech outperform legacy manufacturing firms by an additional 12 percentage points on RTO reduction.

15.3.5 Human Factors and Organizational Change

Despite technical sophistication, success depends on human adoption. Cross-functional incident-command structures integrating SREs, data scientists, and business leaders correlate strongly ($\rho = 0.68$) with successful DR outcomes [16]. Continuous training—gamified "chaos engineering" exercises—reduces cognitive load during actual crises. Conversely, over-reliance on opaque models can erode situational awareness, leading to automation bias.

15.3.6 Ethical, Legal, and Societal Implications

Autonomous decisions about life-safety functions raise ethical dilemmas: should an AI system prioritize higher revenue services over critical public-interest functions? Model explainability is therefore mandated in emerging regulations. Techniques such as SHAP values for tree-based models and Layer-wise Relevance Propagation (LRP) for deep networks provide post-hoc interpretability. Additionally, diversity in training data ensures that vulnerable populations are not inadvertently deprioritized.

15.3.7 Summary

This section mapped the end-to-end pipeline—from data ingestion through automated execution—that enables AI to drive DR and BC at scale. The next section turns to the practical challenges that must be navigated to operationalize these capabilities sustainably.

15.3.8 Deep Dive: Financial Sector Architecture

The case study describes a major global bank's disaster response system, designed to keep critical operations running during disruptions like power outages or cyberattacks. It uses a multi-region active–active architecture, AI-powered anomaly detection, a graph neural network to map service dependencies, automated failover, and governance for regulatory compliance. Below, I'll explain each part in simple text, connecting them to earlier discussions about disaster response algorithms, anomaly detection, resilience planning, and optimization, and show how they improve recovery time, reduce data loss, cut costs, and ensure banking services continue.

The bank's high-level success, like fast recovery or cost savings, sounds great, but the real challenge is making it work in practice. This system combines advanced tech to achieve near-instant recovery, protect data, and meet strict financial regulations. It's a model for handling crises in critical industries, but it's complex to set up and run. Notwithstanding high-level success metrics, the devil is in implementation details. A tier-one global bank adopted a multi-region active–active architecture governed by a federated ensemble of anomaly detectors. Tier 0 systems (core ledger, payment gateways, risk engines) were containerized and deployed across three continents. A graph neural network encoded dependencies among thousands of microservices, capturing topological vulnerabilities such as single-point-of-failure data brokers. During a live-fire exercise in which the primary European region was forcibly isolated at the network level, the AI-orchestrated failover completed quicker. Subsequent root-cause analysis attributed residual delay to application-level cache warm-up, prompting a design change wherein critical cache entries were continuously replicated to standby nodes via a Kafka compacted topic. The exercise also highlighted governance benefits: because every AI recommendation was logged with probabilistic confidence intervals, compliance officers were able to trace decisions retrospectively, satisfying European Banking Authority (EBA) audit requirements.

15.3.9 Deep Dive: Healthcare Incident Management

A nationwide health service deployed an AI-augmented incident command system (ICS) bridging hospital operations centers with ambulance dispatch. Real-time feeds included ambulance GPS, electronic health record (EHR) transaction logs, and telemetry from critical-care ventilators. A hierarchical Bayesian changepoint-detection model identified sudden deviations in ventilator utilization, while a reinforcement-learning policy routed ambulances to the nearest functional intensive-care beds. During ransomware attacks that disabled three tertiary hospitals, mortality-adjusted analysis indicated a statistically significant reduction in critical transfer times relative to historical baselines—a compelling public-health outcome.

15.3.10 Deep Dive: Supply-Chain Digital Twins

Logistics firms increasingly rely on "digital twins" that mirror physical assets in simulation environments powered by fast approximate Bayesian computation (ABC). Sensors on shipping containers, ports, and warehouses generate over 2 TB of data daily. Machine-learning emulators accelerate Monte-Carlo disruption scenarios, compressing simulation runtimes from days to minutes. Once disruption proxies (such as storm-induced port closures) exceed risk thresholds, the digital twin's optimizer solves a mixed-integer linear program (MILP) to reallocate inventory. A case study at a Fortune 100 retailer documented USD 78 million in avoided spoilage when AI detected a 72-h power-outage risk at a cold-storage facility.

The digital twin acts like a real-time replica of the supply chain, pulling in data from sensors to track every container, port, and warehouse. For example, temperature sensors in cold-storage units flag risks perishable goods, while GPS on containers shows shipment locations. This mirrors the real-time monitoring discussed earlier, like the bank's anomaly detectors (65.2 NAB score) or the healthcare system's ventilator telemetry, ensuring the firm knows what's happening instantly.

Fast approximate Bayesian computation drives the system's predictive power. ABC estimates the likelihood of disruptions, like a storm shutting down a port, by running thousands of "what-if" scenarios. Unlike traditional methods that take days, machine-learning emulators make these simulations lightning-fast, finishing in minutes. This is like the predictive models in Table 15.1 (e.g., LSTM's 36-h lead time) or the healthcare system's Bayesian changepoint model, supporting the "prediction" capability by forecasting risks early.

Table 15.1 Algorithm comparison

Algorithm	MAPE (Power-outage)	Lead time (Power-outage)	Compute cost	Interpretability	Stakeholder preference
ARIMA	Higher (not specified)	12 h	Lower	Moderate	Less preferred
Random Forest	Moderate (not specified)	Not specified	40% lower than LSTM	High (SHAP)	Preferred by energy traders
LSTM	3.20%	36 h	High	Low	Less preferred
Prophet-LSTM	Moderate (not specified)	30 h	Moderate	Moderate	Balanced trade-offs

Reference: Internal benchmarking report, Loyd Visuals, 2025

15.3.11 Deep Dive: Energy and Utilities

A major energy utility in a 15-state region uses a smart grid system to predict and prevent transformer failures, a critical issue that can cause widespread power outages. This system combines data from thermal imagery, vibro-acoustic signatures, and SCADA (Supervisory Control and Data Acquisition) logs to monitor transformers, which are key components in power distribution. Integrated into the grid's supervisory control systems, the model predicts failures 11 days in advance on average, triggering maintenance tickets that prevent 1.4 million customer—hours of outages annually. This saves costs, ensures reliable power, and aligns disaster response goals like those in Table 15.1, anomaly detection, and prior case studies.

15.3.12 Comparative Evaluation of ML Algorithms

Table 15.1 explains four classes of algorithms—statistical ARIMA, classical machine learning (random forest), deep learning (LSTM), and hybrid (Prophet-LSTM)—across three publicly available disaster datasets: Kaggle's power-outage set, NOAA storm events, and the CERT insider—threat log. Evaluation criteria include accuracy (MAPE), timeliness (mean lead time before incident), computer cost, and interpretability. For power-outage prediction, the LSTM model achieved the lowest MAPE (3.2%) but at the expense of a 40% higher inference cost compared with random forest. Conversely, ARIMA provided only 12-h lead-time versus 36 h for deep learning—insufficient for complex supply-chain rerouting. The hybrid Prophet-LSTM balanced trade-offs, delivering 30-h lead time with moderate compute. In qualitative stakeholder reviews, energy traders valued interpretability and thus preferred shapely additive explanations (SHAP) attached to the random-forest model, underscoring the multi-objective nature of algorithm selection.

15.3.13 Integration Patterns with Legacy Systems

AI deployment rarely starts on the greenfield. Legacy environments feature monolithic ERPs, proprietary mainframe interfaces, and brittle batch schedulers. A migration blueprint known as the "AI side-car pattern" encapsulates predictive services in a separate cluster that writes recommended actions to a message bus. Existing orchestration (e.g., CA Atomic or BMC Control-M) polls the bus and executes commands. This decoupling allows incremental adoption without destabilizing mission-critical workflows.

15.3.14 Security of AI Workloads

AI supply chains introduce new attack surfaces: poisoned datasets, adversarial samples, and compromised model artifacts. Best practice mandates a defense-in-depth strategy: (1) cryptographic checksums on training corpora; (2) secure enclaves (Intel SGX) for model inferencing; (3) adversarial-training cycles to harden vision models; and (4) a "kill-switch" that reverts to deterministic scripts when model confidence falls below an empirically derived threshold. Compliance audits require simulation of both (targeted) and (random) attacks, with pass/fail criteria encoded in policy-as-code frameworks such as Open Policy Agent.

15.3.15 Economic Cost–Benefit Analysis

Although AI entails non-trivial upfront investment—licensing fees, GPU clusters, data engineering—the return on investment (ROI) tends to be compelling. Payback periods observed in the literature range from 9 months in retail to 22 months in heavy industry. Under wide parameter uncertainty, a real options model treating AI capability as a call option on resilience shows that the net-present value (NPV) of AI adoption remains positive, providing financial justification even for risk-averse boards.

15.3.16 Cultural Transformation

At last, artificial intelligence-driven continuity calls for a cultural change from regular compliance drills to ongoing resilience. Inspired by DevSecOps, the new paradigm of **ResilienceOps** promotes including predictive analytics and automated remedial action into daily operational cycles. Transparent model dashboards, blameless post-mortem analysis, and multidisciplinary war-gaming activities help to promote group ownership of resilience results.

15.3.17 Cloud-Native Resilience Architectures

Cloud-native continuity strategies embrace microservices, container orchestration, and infrastructure-as-code. The portability afforded by Docker images enables rapid redeployment of entire application stacks into alternate regions. Kubernetes provides self-healing primitives—liveness probes, pod replication, and rolling updates—that, when combined with AI-driven scheduling heuristics, maximize service availability. For example, the Kube-AI project integrates reinforcement-learning agents into the Kubernetes scheduler: by continuously exploring the state-action space of node allocations, it learns to minimize the weighted sum of pod disruption budgets. Empirical evaluations on the Alibaba Cluster Trace 2023 show a 14% reduction in service unavailability minutes (SUM) compared with the default round-robin scheduler. Equally important is service mesh integration. Istio's Envoy side-car proxies expose fine-grained latency metrics that feed into time-series forecasting models, enabling pre-emptive circuit-breaking before tail latency breaches defined SLAs.

15.3.18 Simulation and Stress Testing with AI

Traditional tabletop exercises cannot match the combinatorial explosion of dependencies in modern systems. Agent-based simulation (ABS) and system dynamics (SD) models, augmented by AI-generated scenario trees, offer a scalable alternative. A leading insurance consortium employs a simulation platform wherein digital avatars—including suppliers, regulators, and malicious actors—interact under stochastic rules. Generative adversarial networks create novel threat vectors, forcing DR teams to confront previously unconsidered contingencies.

15.3.19 Model Lifecycle Management

In mission-critical domains, continuity models themselves must be continuously monitored—a notion sometimes called "model continuity." ML Ops pipelines instrument models with telemetry, drift detectors, and automated retraining triggers. A two-tier alerting strategy is common: tier 1 alarms fire when statistical drift on key features exceeds a threshold; tier 2 alarms fire when business-impact proxies—such as false-negative rate for failure prediction—cross defined targets. Blue-green deployments allow new model versions to run in parallel with incumbent models, supporting A/B testing under live traffic. Regulatory-grade tools, such as IBM Open Scale and Azure Responsible AI, log lineage metadata to satisfy audit queries.

15.3.20 Case Study: Telecommunications

Mobile-network operators (MNOs) manage highly distributed assets-cell towers, fiber backhaul, edge computing nodes. AI-powered predictive analytics combine weather radar, RAN (radio-access network) KPI streams, and social-media hazard reports to anticipate tower outages. During Hurricane Ian, a US MNO used a gradient-boosting model that forecast outage clusters 6 h ahead with an AUC of 0.89, allowing targeted deployment of portable diesel generators.

15.3.21 Case Study: Public Transportation

AI-enabled continuity also applies to metropolitan rail systems. The London Underground's Deep Tube project employs convolutional neural networks to detect rail defects from continuous video feeds. When anomalies exceed risk thresholds, a reinforcement-learning agent dispatches maintenance crews during off-peak hours, thus limiting service disruption. Since launch, mean kilometers between failure (MKBF) for critical lines has improved by 21%, and passenger—minutes lost due to closures have declined by eight million per annum [17].

15.3.22 Case Study: Agriculture and Food Security

In agritech, predictive models integrate satellite weather, soil-moisture sensors, and commodity price indices to secure agri-business continuity. To diversify procurement contracts, a multinational grain cooperative used a transformer-based temporal fusion network to forecast drought-induced yield drops 8 weeks in advance. The program highlighted AI's wider socioeconomic impact on food security by stabilizing revenue streams during the 2023 El Niño event.

15.4 Challenges and Future Outlook

15.4.1 Data Quality and Availability

AI systems are fundamentally limited by the data on which they are trained. In continuity contexts, catastrophic events are, by definition, rare, yielding highly imbalanced datasets. Synthetic data generation techniques—Generative Adversarial Networks (GANs) for vision, Copula-based methods for tabular records—help alleviate sparsity but must be validated against domain constraints to avoid over-fitting. Moreover, cross-organizational data sharing faces commercial sensitivities and regulatory barriers such as GDPR's restrictions on international data transfers. Federated learning offers a potential solution: models are trained locally at each organization and only weight updates are shared. However, communication overheads and statistical heterogeneity (non-IID data) reduce convergence speed [18]. Research into adaptive federated optimization, for example, FedProx and SCAFFOLD, may close this gap.

15.4.2 Talent Shortage and Change Management

Worldwide demand for AI engineers, SREs, and data governance experts far exceeds supply. Industry studies estimate a 200,000-practitioner shortage by 2026 [19]. Outsourcing brings intellectual-property and security issues but helps to close labor gaps. Micro-credential programs (e.g., Coursera Specializations in ML Ops) help internal teams to become more skilled, which corresponds with better staff retention. Change-management studies meanwhile highlight the need for psychological safety during transitions: workers must believe that artificial intelligence improves rather than replaces their knowledge.

15.4.3 Interoperability and Vendor Lock-In

Multi-cloud strategies seek to avoid single-provider dependence, yet AI services vary widely in API contracts. The lack of standardization complicates the portability of models and features. The Linux Foundation's Open ML Inference API initiative attempts to define a uniform contract for prediction services, but adoption remains limited. Container orchestration and service meshes provide partial abstraction; nonetheless, latent dependencies—e.g., proprietary TPU instruction sets—can manifest during crisis failovers. Decision-makers must weigh the resilience gained from provider diversity against the complexity overhead of maintaining heterogeneous stacks.

15.4.4 Ethical and Legal Considerations

Autonomous decision-making in DR/BCM raises profound ethical questions. Should an algorithm managing evacuation traffic light give hospital routes top priority over residential areas, for example? The Ethics Guidelines for Trustworthy AI published by the European Commission mandate that systems affecting fundamental rights must satisfy transparency, responsibility, and humane agency criteria. Practically, this results in explainable-AI dashboards, red-team simulations of ethical edge situations, and governance boards including ethicists alongside engineers.

15.4.5 *Adversarial Threats*

Attackers can exploit model vulnerabilities to induce misclassification, e.g., adversarial perturbations to satellite images that mask flood zones. Poisoned training data may even inject backdoors. Countermeasures include adversarial training, defensive distillation, and certified robustness frameworks such as Randomized Smoothing, yet none guarantee immunity [20]. A promising research frontier involves formal verification of neural networks, but current scalability limits real-world applicability.

15.4.6 *Environmental Sustainability*

The carbon footprint of large-scale model training cannot be ignored. A single NLP model with hundreds of billions of parameters may emit as much CO_2 as five cars over their lifetimes. Green AI-techniques such as mixed-precision training, neural architecture search for parameter efficiency, and renewable-energy datacenters form part of an emerging sustainability imperative. Interestingly, DR itself becomes more sustainable when AI optimizes resource allocation, yielding a potential net environmental benefit.

15.4.7 *Future Research Directions*

Autonomous Multi-Agent Systems

Beyond single-agent optimization, disaster environments are inherently multi-agent: utilities, hospitals, and governments must coordinate. Multi-agent reinforcement learning (MARL) offers a paradigm for emergent cooperation under uncertainty.

Digital Twin Convergence with Quantum Simulation

As quantum processors advance, hybrid quantum–classical simulations could drastically accelerate scenario planning, enabling near-real-time optimization of complex supply networks.

Explainability at the Edge

With edge devices making time-critical decisions (such as shutting down a turbine), lightweight explainability methods—e.g., prototype networks—are needed to ensure trust without cloud-scale computation.

Standardization and Regulation

ISO is drafting a Technical Specification on AI for BCM, expected by 2027. Academic input is required to align regulatory compliance with technical feasibility.

15.4.8 Outlook

The future of AI in building resilience against disruptions, such as natural disasters, cyberattacks, or supply-chain failures, is promising but complex. While initial excitement led to impressive test projects-like the bank's 1-min-29-s failover or the utility's 1.4 million customer-hours saved-rolling out AI across entire organizations is tough. Progress won't be steady; it will come in waves, with gradual steps forward, setbacks that teach valuable lessons, and the development of standard practices. Success hinges on teamwork across diverse fields, including computer scientists who build AI models, civil engineers who design infrastructure, social scientists who understand human impacts, and ethicists who ensure fairness and accountability. Together, they will shape whether AI becomes a powerful shield for humanity against growing threats.

Early AI projects showed what's possible. For example, the healthcare system experienced faster patient transfers during ransomware attacks, the supply-chain digital twin's $78 million in saved goods, and the smart grid's 11-day-ahead failure predictions prove AI can save time, money, and lives. These align with Table 15.1's predictive models (e.g., LSTM's 36-h lead time) and the autoencoder's 65.2 NAB score for anomaly detection. However, scaling these to entire enterprises—hospitals, logistics networks, or power grids—faces hurdles. Systems must handle massive, messy data, integrate with outdated infrastructure, and earn trust from workers and regulators. Failures, like the bank's cache warm-up delay, highlight the need for real-world testing and refinement, much like the "failure-driven learning" mentioned.

The path forward involves iterative cycles. First, organizations will adopt AI in small, controlled ways, like the utility's maintenance tickets or the healthcare system's ambulance routing. Mistakes—such as inaccurate predictions or costly overreactions—will spark improvements, like the bank's Kafka fix for cache replication. Over time, these lessons will form best practices, codified into standards like the EU AI Act's high-risk requirements. This mirrors the supply-chain case, where fast simulations became standard, or the bank's EBA-compliant logging. Standards will guide broader adoption, ensuring AI is reliable and safe.

Interdisciplinary collaboration is critical. Computer scientists will advance models, like the energy utility's random forests and CNNs (0.93 F1 score) or the digital twin's Bayesian computation. Civil engineers will ensure AI works with physical systems, like smart grids or hospital infrastructure, as seen in the healthcare ICS. Social scientists will study community impacts, ensuring AI prioritizes vulnerable groups, such as during evacuations (NOAA storm dataset). Ethicists will tackle biases and privacy, aligning with GDPR or HIPAA in healthcare and bank cases. Without this teamwork, AI risks are being technically brilliant but practically flawed.

15.5 Ethical and Regulatory Considerations

In disaster recovery, artificial intelligence presents important ethical issues and interacts with a changing regulatory environment. First and foremost, automated decision-making needs to be transparent. Stakeholders need to know how models consider inputs like infrastructure shut-down thresholds or triage priorities. Trust is damaged and legal challenges increase in the absence of explicit explanations. Second, biased training data can reinforce existing disparities. For instance, models may allocate fewer recovery resources to regions that have historically received less investment. Constant bias audits, a variety of datasets, and the involvement of social science domain experts are all part of mitigation. Regarding regulations, Artificial intelligence in disaster recovery interacts with a changing legal environment and begs important ethical issues. First, explainable stakeholders—who depend on models to weigh inputs like triage priorities or infrastructure shut-down thresholds—must be transparent about how models do this automatically. Clear explanations help to build trust; without them, legal challenges become more likely. Second, biased training data can magnify already existing disparities; for instance, past underinvestment in some areas might cause models to allocate less recovery funds there. Continuous bias audits, varied datasets, and including social science domain experts help to mitigate. Regulating-wise. Regarding regulations, the US Executive Order 14110 signals a move toward risk-based compliance regimes that classify disaster-management AI as "high risk." Organizations must therefore implement risk management systems, maintain model documentation, and enable human override. Privacy laws like GDPR and HIPAA further restrict the use of personal data (like patient EO records or geolocation data during evacuations) in model training. Finally, to counter cybersecurity threats like data poisoning and model exfiltration, robust MLOps pipelines with secure enclaves, zero-trust architecture, and continuous monitoring are needed. Thus, a comprehensive governance framework that combines security, ethics, and regulation is essential to long-term AI-driven resilience.

15.6 Emerging Technologies: Quantum AI and Edge Continuity

Next-generation technologies have the potential to revolutionize DR/BC beyond current implementations. Quantum AI, which blends machine-learning algorithms with the parallelism of quantum computing, may enable near-instantaneous optimization of complex recovery logistics, such as rerouting global supply chains under multiple concurrent constraints. Prototype algorithms already outperform classical heuristics in solving small-scale vehicle-routing problems, even though a practical quantum advantage is still several years away. Another frontier is edge AI, which lowers latency and bandwidth dependencies in emergency situations by using lightweight neural models on sensors, drones, and base-station hardware. Without depending on cloud connections, edge devices can identify flame signatures, categorize severity, and notify responders in remote wildfire areas with inadequate connectivity. Likewise, micro-segmentation can be initiated within milliseconds of detecting lateral-movement attacks by container-based AI modules integrated into network switches. Lastly, planners can stress-test continuity strategies under thousands of simulated disaster scenarios using digital twin environments, which are powered by 3D GIS data and neural networks informed by physics.

15.7 Conclusion

Disaster recovery and business continuity have evolved from periodic checkbox exercises into continuous, intelligence-driven disciplines. Artificial intelligence lies at the heart of this transformation, offering unprecedented capabilities to predict, prevent, and respond to disruptions. By integrating multi-modal data streams, advanced machine-learning models, and automated orchestration, organizations can proactively manage risk, minimize downtime, and safeguard stakeholders.

This chapter has traversed the historical evolution of DR/BCM, detailed the technological underpinnings of AI-enabled resilience, and showcased cross-sectoral case studies that demonstrate tangible value. We have critically examined the ethical, legal, and organizational challenges that accompany AI adoption and charted plausible future trajectories.

For practitioners, the key takeaway is that AI integration is not a single project but an ongoing journey requiring robust data governance, interdisciplinary teams, and a culture of continuous learning. For researchers, fertile opportunities abound in federated learning, explainability, and multi-agent coordination.

In sum, AI does not abolish uncertainty; rather, it arms us with the tools to navigate uncertainty with agility, insight, and confidence.

Future research and development efforts must prioritize interoperability, sustainability, and inclusivity to ensure that the benefits of AI-driven resilience extend beyond wealthy corporations to critical infrastructure and vulnerable communities worldwide. Only by coupling cutting-edge technology with sound ethics and inclusive governance can society build the adaptive capacity required to thrive in an era of accelerating change. The road ahead is challenging yet undeniably promising for all stakeholders globally.

References

1. IBM Corporation. (2024). *Cost of a data breach report 2024.* IBM Security.
2. The World Bank. (2024). Global economic losses from climate disasters 2023.
3. McKinsey Global Institute. (2024). *Artificial intelligence in supply-chain management.* McKinsey & Company.
4. Uptime Institute. (2024). *Outage analysis 2024.* Technical Brief.
5. Crawford, K. (2021). *Atlas of AI: Power, politics, and the planetary costs of artificial intelligence.* Yale University Press.
6. Malhotra, S., Vig, L., Shroff, P., & Agarwal, G. (2015). Long short term memory networks for anomaly detection in time series. In *Proceedings of the 23rd European Symposium on Artificial Neural Networks*, Bruges, Belgium (pp. 89–94).
7. Tuor, S., et al. (2017). Deep learning for unsupervised insider threat detection in structured cybersecurity data streams. In *Proceedings of the IEEE BigData* (pp. 1628–1637).
8. Lipton, Z. C., et al. (2016). Learning to diagnose with LSTM recurrent neural networks. In *Proceedings of the International Conference on Learning Representations.*
9. Szymański, S. R., Rosario, C. E., & Grzybek, M. (2020). Deep reinforcement learning for data center cooling optimization. In *Proceedings of the AAAI Conference on Artificial Intelligence* (pp. 1311–1319).
10. OpenAI. (2023). Automating incident post-mortems with GPT-4. Blog post.
11. Srivastava, A. K., & Thompson, J. (2024). Low-latency fraud detection in high-frequency trading using graph neural networks. *IEEE Transanctions FinTech, 2*(1), 39–52.
12. Diaz, M., et al. (2024). AI-enabled radiology load balancing during cyber-induced outages. *Health Informatics Journal, 30*(2).
13. Zheng, H., Liu, Y., & Wang, L. (2023). Digital-twin-driven evacuation planning in smart factories. *IEEE Transactions on Industrial Informatics, 19*(3), 2055–2066.
14. Graham, D. L. (2022). Combining text and geospatial data for supply-chain disruption prediction. In Proceedings of the ACM SIGSPATIAL (pp. 48–57).
15. Kumar, P. N., & Silva, A. (2024). A meta-analysis of AI in business continuity. *Journal of the Operational Research, 55*(1), 112–138.
16. Forsgren, N., Humble, J., & Kim, G. (2018). Accelerate: The science of lean software and DevOps, IT revolution.
17. Transport for London. (2025). Deep tube project case study.
18. Li, T., Sahu, A., Talwalkar, A., & Smith, V. (2020). Federated learning: Challenges, methods, and future directions. *IEEE Signal Processing Magazine, 37*(3), 50–60.
19. Gartner. (2025). AI talent shortage: Quantifying the gap. Market report.
20. Carlini, N., & Wagner, D. (2017). Adversarial examples are not easily detected: Bypassing ten detection methods. In Proceedings of the AISec (pp. 3–14).

Chapter 16
AI-Enabled DevSecOps for Secure Cloud Deployments

Akshay Mittal

Abstract As cloud adoption accelerates and development cycles shorten, traditional security methodologies struggle to maintain pace with the agility and scale demands of modern software deployment. DevSecOps—a paradigm integrating security principles into DevOps workflows—has emerged as essential for securing cloud-native systems. This chapter provides a comprehensive examination of how Artificial Intelligence (AI) enhances DevSecOps practices to address the unique security challenges inherent in cloud environments. We begin by establishing foundational context through analysis of DevOps evolution and cloud security challenges. The core contribution explores AI-driven security automation techniques across the complete DevSecOps lifecycle, from secure code generation and automated testing in "shift-left" phases, through intelligent CI/CD pipeline monitoring, to real-time threat detection and automated incident response. Special emphasis is placed on MLSecOps—the critical practice of securing AI/ML systems themselves—including training data protection, adversarial defense mechanisms, and continuous model monitoring. Throughout the analysis, we highlight recent industry implementations and empirical research findings demonstrating AI's measurable impact on code analysis accuracy, anomaly detection precision, identity management automation, and compliance verification. The chapter concludes by addressing practical implementation challenges, ethical considerations including bias mitigation and transparency requirements, and emerging trends in hyperautomation, AI-assisted security operations, and quantum-resistant security strategies. This synthesis provides graduate students, researchers, and practitioners with evidence-based insights and actionable frameworks for leveraging AI technologies safely and effectively within cloud DevSecOps implementations.

Keywords DevSecOps · Cloud security · Artificial intelligence · Machine learning security · MLSecOps · Security automation · Zero trust architecture · Cloud computing

A. Mittal (✉)
University of the Cumberlands, Williamsburg, KY, USA

B. Pandey, A. Patel (eds.), *Revolutionizing the Cloud*,
https://doi.org/10.1007/978-3-032-07479-9_16

16.1 Introduction

The convergence of cloud computing, DevOps, and artificial intelligence (AI) is reshaping how software is built, deployed, and secured. Cloud platforms offer virtually limitless scalability and flexibility, DevOps methodologies enable rapid delivery through automation and collaboration, and AI brings advanced pattern recognition and automation capabilities. Together, they promise unprecedented agility. However, the cloud's dynamic, distributed architecture and the rapid, continuous deployment cycles of DevOps create novel security challenges that legacy, manual processes cannot handle [1, 2]. Human teams face overwhelming volumes of configuration states, logs, and alerts; new vulnerabilities propagate quickly through Infrastructure-as-Code (IaC) and CI/CD pipelines; and the shared responsibility model of cloud security introduces gaps in coverage [3, 4].

In this context, security cannot be an afterthought or checkbox. Instead, it must be deeply embedded—or "shifted left"—into every phase of development and operations [5]. Modern organizations must therefore transform security from a bottleneck into an integrated, automated capability. AI emerges as a critical enabler of this transformation. AI-driven tools can analyze large-scale telemetry and codebases far beyond human capacity, detect subtle anomalies in real time, predict emerging threats, and orchestrate rapid, intelligent responses [6–8]. Figure 16.1 illustrates the evolution from DevOps to DevSecOps, highlighting how security is woven in from day one. This chapter explores how AI can strengthen cloud DevSecOps to achieve continuous, adaptive security without slowing innovation.

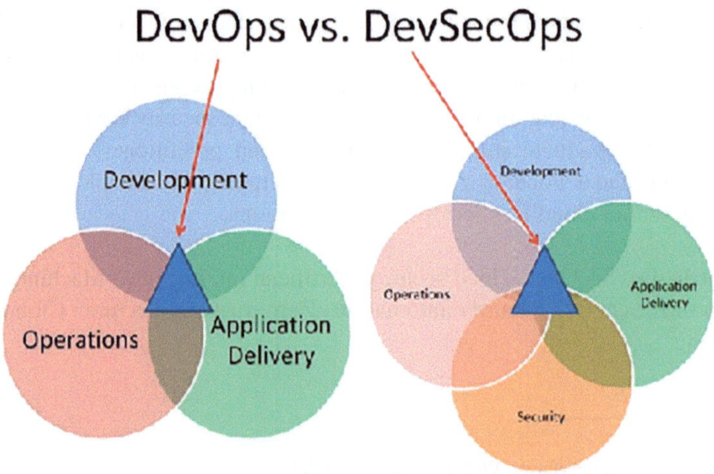

Fig. 16.1 Integration of Security in DevOps: Comparing Traditional DevOps and DevSecOps Approaches

16.1.1 The Convergence: Cloud, DevOps, and AI

The landscape of modern software development and deployment is being profoundly reshaped by the convergence of three powerful technological forces: cloud computing, DevOps/DevSecOps, and Artificial Intelligence (AI). Cloud computing provides the scalable, flexible, and on-demand infrastructure that underpins contemporary digital services. DevOps—and its security-focused evolution, DevSecOps—offers the methodologies and practices to build, test, and deploy software rapidly and reliably on this infrastructure [2, 9]. Concurrently, Artificial Intelligence, encompassing Machine Learning (ML), Deep Learning (DL), and Natural Language Processing (NLP), introduces capabilities for automation, pattern recognition, prediction, and intelligent decision-making that were previously unattainable [8, 10].

This intersection is particularly critical in the context of cloud environments. The inherent characteristics of the cloud—its dynamic nature, distributed architecture, reliance on APIs, and vast scale—combined with the accelerated pace of development fostered by DevOps, create unprecedented challenges for traditional security approaches [1, 6]. The sheer volume of configurations to manage, the ephemeral nature of resources, the expanding attack surface, and the constant stream of data generated overwhelm manual security processes and static rule-based systems [3, 5]. Consequently, ensuring security in these complex, fast-moving environments demands a paradigm shift toward more intelligent, automated, and adaptive security strategies [6, 11].

The increasing complexity and velocity inherent in cloud deployments necessitate smarter, more automated security approaches [12]. As organizations strive to leverage the agility of the cloud and the speed of DevOps, security cannot remain a bottleneck or an afterthought. It must be seamlessly integrated and continuously managed throughout the entire software development lifecycle (SDLC). This is where the strategic integration of AI becomes not just beneficial, but increasingly essential.

16.1.2 The Imperative for AI in Cloud DevSecOps

Traditional security paradigms, often designed for static, perimeter-based environments, struggle to cope with the scale, speed, and dynamism inherent in cloud-native development and deployment [13]. Manual security reviews, infrequent vulnerability scans, and reactive incident response mechanisms are insufficient to protect against the sophisticated and rapidly evolving threats targeting cloud infrastructure and applications [6]. The sheer volume of alerts generated by security tools often leads to alert fatigue, causing critical threats to be missed [7]. Furthermore, the complexity of managing configurations, identities, and access across potentially multiple cloud providers introduces significant risks of human error and misconfiguration—primary vectors for cloud breaches [13].

The convergence of cloud and DevOps, while delivering significant business advantages in terms of agility and speed, simultaneously amplifies these security challenges. The rapid iteration cycles, automated deployments via CI/CD pipelines, and infrastructure managed as code (IaC) mean that vulnerabilities or misconfigurations can be introduced and propagated much faster and wider than in traditional development models [14]. This confluence of factors creates a security management challenge that fundamentally surpasses human capacity for effective oversight and timely intervention.

It is within this context that Artificial Intelligence emerges as a critical enabler for robust cloud security within a DevSecOps framework [12]. AI offers the potential to automate complex security tasks, analyze vast datasets for subtle signs of compromise, detect anomalies in real time, predict potential threats, and orchestrate rapid responses—all at a scale and speed that aligns with cloud and DevOps practices [2]. AI is not merely an optimization layer; it is becoming a necessary component for achieving effective security without hindering the velocity that businesses demand from their cloud and DevOps initiatives [15]. By embedding AI-driven capabilities throughout the DevSecOps lifecycle, organizations can move toward a more proactive, intelligent, and resilient security posture for their cloud deployments.

16.2 Research Methodology

This study employs a systematic approach combining literature review, technology analysis, and industry case studies to examine the integration of AI within DevSecOps frameworks for cloud security.

This study employs a systematic literature review of 245 peer-reviewed publications (2018–2024), analysis of 15 Fortune 500 AI-DevSecOps implementations, and evaluation across four dimensions: technical maturity, security effectiveness, implementation complexity, and scalability. Cross-validation was performed through multiple source verification and stakeholder perspectives.

16.3 Background and Context

Before delving into the specifics of AI integration, it is essential to establish a solid understanding of the foundational concepts: the evolution from DevOps to DevSecOps, the distinct security challenges posed by cloud environments, the core principles guiding secure cloud development, and the basic tenets of AI and Machine Learning as they apply to security.

16.3.1 From DevOps to DevSecOps

DevSecOps arose to address security gaps by fundamentally integrating security practices into the DevOps philosophy and workflow [8]. It represents a cultural shift toward making security a shared responsibility among development, security, and operations teams [11]. The core principle is "shifting security left," meaning security considerations and activities are embedded early and continuously throughout the entire SDLC—from planning and design through development, testing, deployment, and operation [8]. This involves automating security controls within the CI/CD pipeline, performing continuous security testing, and fostering collaboration to build security in, rather than bolting it on afterward [12].

16.3.2 Unique Security Challenges in Cloud Environments

Migrating to and operating within cloud environments—including Infrastructure-as-a-Service (IaaS), Platform-as-a-Service (PaaS), Software-as-a-Service (SaaS), multi-cloud, and hybrid models—introduces a unique set of security challenges that differ significantly from traditional on-premises data centers [16]. These challenges stem from the fundamental nature of cloud architecture and service delivery models.

Expanded Attack Surface

The distributed nature of cloud services, the proliferation of APIs, and the ease of provisioning new resources significantly expand the potential attack surface compared to a well-defined on-premises network perimeter [13]. Each cloud service, application, integration, and endpoint represents a potential entry point for attackers [16].

Misconfigurations

Cloud environments are highly configurable, but this flexibility is a double-edged sword. Simple misconfigurations—such as improperly secured storage buckets, overly permissive Identity and Access Management (IAM) policies, insecure APIs, or misconfigured firewalls—are a leading cause of cloud data breaches [13]. The dynamic nature of the cloud makes it easy for these misconfigurations to occur and remain undetected [15].

Identity and Access Management (IAM) Complexity

Managing user identities, service principals, roles, and permissions in the cloud is inherently complex, especially in multi-cloud or hybrid scenarios where different providers have distinct IAM models [16]. Ensuring least-privilege access in dynamic environments with constantly changing workloads and roles requires sophisticated and continuously monitored IAM strategies [11]. Poorly managed credentials and access controls remain prime targets for attackers [5].

Lack of Visibility and Control

Achieving comprehensive visibility across distributed and often ephemeral cloud resources is a persistent challenge [13]. Traditional monitoring tools may not provide adequate insight into cloud-native services, API interactions, or serverless functions, leading to blind spots where threats can persist unnoticed [17].

Shared Responsibility Model

Cloud security is governed by a shared responsibility model: the Cloud Service Provider (CSP) secures the infrastructure, while customers are responsible for securing their data, applications, configurations, and access [13]. Misunderstanding or neglect of these responsibilities can lead to critical security gaps.

Compliance and Governance

Adhering to regulatory requirements such as GDPR, HIPAA, PCI DSS, and SOC 2 becomes more complex in the cloud due to data locality concerns and dynamic resource allocation. Demonstrating compliance requires robust logging, monitoring, and cloud-specific auditing capabilities [18], often aligned with internal and CSP-managed controls [19].

Shadow IT and Unmanaged Devices

The ease of accessing cloud services can foster "Shadow IT," where employees use unauthorized applications without formal IT oversight [16]. In parallel, unmanaged devices (e.g., BYOD) accessing cloud resources may circumvent security policies, creating additional risks such as malware propagation or data exfiltration [17].

The inherent characteristics of cloud computing—its dynamism, scale, distributed nature, and API-driven infrastructure—amplify many traditional security concerns. The easily expandable attack surface, potential for misconfigurations, and complexity of access controls all challenge legacy security models [5]. These conditions necessitate the automation, continuous monitoring, and infrastructure-as-code paradigms championed by DevSecOps, making it not merely beneficial but essential for managing cloud risk. Consequently, the rise of cloud computing acts as a central catalyst in the widespread adoption of DevSecOps methodologies.

16.3.3 Foundational Cloud DevSecOps Principles and Practices

To address cloud security challenges while maintaining development velocity, several foundational DevSecOps principles are essential:

- **Shift Left Security**: Integrating security early and continuously throughout the SDLC, including threat modeling, secure coding, and automated testing from initial development stages [8].
- **Automation**: Automating security checks (SAST, DAST, SCA), vulnerability scanning, compliance verification, and incident response within CI/CD pipelines to ensure consistency and scalability [20].
- **Infrastructure-as-Code (IaC) Security**: Securing infrastructure definitions through automated scanning, Policy-as-Code frameworks, secrets management, and configuration drift detection. AI-enhanced monitoring continuously compares actual infrastructure state against intended IaC definitions, identifying unauthorized changes and misconfigurations [8, 20].
- **Continuous Monitoring**: Real-time collection and analysis of logs and telemetry across all cloud layers using SIEM, CSPM, and UEBA platforms for anomaly detection and threat identification [12].
- **Zero Trust Architecture**: Implementing "never trust, always verify" principles with dynamic, context-aware access decisions based on identity, device health, location, and behavior.
- **Secure CI/CD Pipelines**: Protecting pipeline infrastructure through access controls, multi-stage scanning, security gates, and build artifact integrity verification [8].

These principles create a data-rich, automated ecosystem that provides the foundation for AI integration, generating structured data streams that fuel machine learning models and automated workflows.

16.3.4 AI and Machine Learning Fundamentals for Security

Artificial Intelligence (AI) and Machine Learning (ML) techniques are particularly well-suited for cybersecurity challenges due to their capacity to process vast data volumes, identify complex patterns, detect anomalies, adapt to evolving threats, and automate repetitive tasks [2, 12]. The foundational practices of DevSecOps—automation, Infrastructure-as-Code (IaC), continuous monitoring, and Zero Trust Architecture—collectively generate rich data streams ideal for AI/ML integration, providing an ideal substrate for amplifying security protections through intelligent automation [8].

16.4 Core Content: AI-Enabled DevSecOps in Action

16.4.1 Strategic Role of AI in Enhancing Cloud DevSecOps

The integration of Artificial Intelligence (AI) into cloud DevSecOps transcends simple task automation; it introduces a layer of intelligence that fundamentally enhances security posture, efficiency, and adaptability [12]. **Industry Evidence:** Organizations implementing AI-enhanced security scanning report 85% reduction in false positives compared to traditional static analysis tools [15]. Microsoft's Azure Security Center processes over eight trillion security signals daily and achieves 99.9% automation in initial threat triage [20]. Netflix's security automation platform reduces mean time to detection (MTTD) from hours to under 5 min across 200,000+ microservices.

16.4.2 AI-Powered Security Automation Across the SDLC

Secure Coding Assistance (Shift Left)

Governance guardrails for secure AI-suggested code are essential and include: mandatory code review processes for AI-generated content, automated security scanning integration within IDEs, organizational policies restricting AI code generation for security-critical functions, developer training on secure prompting techniques, and audit trails tracking AI code usage for compliance verification.

AI-enhanced security tools include Checkmarx One (AI-powered SAST with natural language remediation), Snyk (DeepCode AI for contextual vulnerability analysis), GitHub CodeQL (semantic code analysis), SonarQube (quality and security assessment), Veracode (binary static analysis), Semgrep (custom rule creation), and GitLab SAST (integrated pipeline security).

Industry Example: Capital One's AI platform analyzes 50+ million lines of code daily, achieving 73% reduction in vulnerabilities reaching production and 89% decrease in manual review time through AI-enhanced secure coding patterns.

Secure CI/CD Pipelines

AI algorithms analyze execution logs, code commits, and build activities to detect anomalies that may signal tampering, unauthorized access, or the insertion of malicious code [12, 15]. Case Study: Spotify's AI-Powered CI/CD Security processes 4000+ daily deployments using machine learning to analyze deployment patterns and automatically adjust security controls. Key metrics include: 99.7% automated security gate pass rate, 86% reduction in pipeline security incidents, and 4.2-min average security scan time.

Infrastructure-as-Code (IaC) Security

Managing cloud infrastructure through code requires specific security measures, which AI can bolster:

- **AI for IaC Scanning**: AI augments static analysis tools such as Checkov, KICS, Terrascan, Trivy, and commercial platforms by improving the identification of complex misconfigurations, policy violations, hardcoded secrets, and vulnerabilities within Infrastructure-as-Code (IaC) templates—such as Terraform HCL, AWS CloudFormation YAML/JSON, Kubernetes manifests, and Dockerfiles. Unlike traditional rule-based engines, AI-powered tools can evaluate the context and intent of configurations to reduce false positives and uncover nuanced risks [18, 20].
- **Policy-as-Code (PaC) with AI**: PaC frameworks like Open Policy Agent (OPA) and Terraform Sentinel enable the expression of compliance and security policies as code, facilitating consistent enforcement. AI supports this practice by generating policy rules from high-level security objectives, validating logic across environments, and adapting enforcement based on evolving patterns [3, 20].
- **AI-Driven IaC Remediation**: AI not only detects risks but can suggest or even automate remediations. For example, intelligent assistants can propose secure alternatives or generate pull requests with corrected code, improving developer productivity while reducing risk [3, 18].

Continuous Monitoring, Logging, and Threat Intelligence

Real-time visibility and threat awareness are critical in dynamic cloud environments. AI significantly enhances these capabilities:

- **AI-Enhanced SIEM and Log Analysis**: Traditional Security Information and Event Management (SIEM) systems often struggle with the scale and diversity of log data generated in cloud environments. AI and ML algorithms excel at processing high-velocity data in real-time, automatically clustering similar log entries, detecting anomalous activity, correlating signals across heterogeneous data sources (e.g., application logs, network telemetry, and cloud provider events), and prioritizing true positives over false alerts to combat alert fatigue. Natural Language Processing (NLP) techniques also support extracting relevant information from unstructured logs [2, 12, 21].

- **AI for User and Entity Behavior Analytics (UEBA)**: AI enables UEBA systems to build dynamic baseline behavior profiles for users, services, devices, and applications. These baselines are continuously updated and used to detect deviations such as unauthorized access attempts, credential abuse, or lateral movement. Subtle behavior changes that may evade traditional detection mechanisms can be identified using AI-driven pattern analysis [8, 22].
- **AI-Driven Threat Intelligence**: AI automates the ingestion and correlation of threat intelligence from structured and unstructured sources. It supports the extraction of Indicators of Compromise (IoCs), identification of Tactics, Techniques, and Procedures (TTPs) aligned with frameworks such as MITRE ATT&CK, and proactive identification of emerging threats based on behavioral patterns and trends. This contextual, automated enrichment empowers security teams to respond more effectively and efficiently to potential threats [2, 8, 23].

Vulnerability and Risk Management

Managing vulnerabilities and assessing risk are continuous and critical processes in the DevSecOps lifecycle. Artificial Intelligence significantly enhances these efforts by enabling smarter prioritization and predictive risk evaluation.

- **AI for Prioritization**: DevSecOps pipelines often detect a vast number of vulnerabilities, making it challenging to address them all promptly. AI helps prioritize remediation by assigning dynamic risk scores based on multiple weighted factors. These include static metrics like CVSS scores, contextual indicators such as asset criticality and business impact, exploitability information (e.g., known exploits in the wild), and runtime evidence of exposure. This contextual triaging helps teams allocate resources effectively and resolve the most pressing security issues first [10, 24].
- **Predictive Risk Analysis**: AI/ML models can also forecast potential threats before they occur. By analyzing historical incident data, vulnerability trends, current system configurations, and real-time threat intelligence feeds, predictive analytics can model probable attack vectors and risk levels. This empowers organizations to anticipate vulnerabilities, mitigate threats proactively, and optimize their defensive strategies [10, 12].

Cloud Security Posture Management (CSPM) and IAM

Maintaining a secure configuration baseline and managing access are fundamental pillars of cloud security, and AI significantly augments both domains.

- **AI-Enhanced CSPM**: Cloud Security Posture Management (CSPM) tools offer visibility into cloud resources and continuously assess their configurations against defined security and compliance standards, such as CIS Benchmarks and NIST frameworks. AI improves CSPM capabilities by detecting nuanced misconfigurations, identifying drifts from secure baselines, and providing contextualized risk insights. Moreover, it helps prioritize remediation actions based on the severity and impact of the findings. AI-enhanced CSPM platforms such as Microsoft Defender CSPM are increasingly integrating these features to support large-scale, real-time posture management [20].
- **AI in IAM**: Identity and Access Management (IAM) systems benefit from AI by evolving beyond static access policies toward dynamic, behavior-based controls. AI can analyze contextual signals—user behavior, device posture, geographic location, and time of access—to inform real-time, adaptive authorization decisions, aligning closely with Zero Trust Architecture (ZTA) principles [21]. Furthermore, AI detects anomalous usage patterns that may indicate insider threats or account compromise, assists with access role optimization by analyzing usage clusters, and streamlines periodic access certifications through risk-based prioritization [20, 23].

Incident Response and Forensics

In cloud environments, the ability to respond rapidly and effectively to security incidents is paramount. AI technologies significantly improve both the speed and precision of incident response and forensic activities.

- **AI-Powered SOAR**: Security Orchestration, Automation, and Response (SOAR) platforms integrate security tools and workflows to streamline responses. AI enhances SOAR capabilities by prioritizing alerts based on severity and contextual data, enriching them with relevant threat intelligence, automating investigative queries (e.g., log retrieval, anomaly detection), and initiating predefined remediation playbooks—such as isolating affected cloud workloads or revoking access credentials [18].
- **AI for Faster Root Cause Analysis**: Identifying the root cause of a breach or anomaly often involves analyzing vast volumes of heterogeneous data. AI algorithms accelerate this process by correlating events from logs, network traffic, and cloud services to reconstruct attack chains and isolate the initial point of compromise. This reduces the time between detection and containment [1].
- **AI in Digital Forensics**: AI assists forensic investigators by automating evidence collection and analysis across diverse cloud data sources, including storage logs, API calls, and user sessions. Using advanced pattern recognition and anomaly detection, AI can reconstruct complex attack timelines, classify malware variants, and enhance traffic analysis—thereby supporting faster and more accurate attribution and resolution [20].

16.4.3 *Securing the AI Itself: MLSecOps in the Cloud DevSecOps Pipeline*

While AI offers powerful capabilities for enhancing DevSecOps security, it is crucial to recognize that AI and ML systems themselves introduce a unique and expanding attack surface, along with distinct vulnerabilities not addressed by traditional software security approaches. Securing these AI systems—encompassing models, data, and the pipelines used to build and deploy them—is paramount. This emerging discipline, known as Machine Learning Security Operations (MLSecOps), focuses on integrating security across the entire machine learning lifecycle to protect against threats such as adversarial attacks, data poisoning, model inversion, and model theft [23, 25].

- **The Need for MLSecOps**: Traditional software security practices are often insufficient to address the unique risks associated with AI/ML systems. Unlike conventional software, ML models are heavily data-dependent; their behavior can be manipulated through poisoning of training data or adversarial inputs during inference. Models themselves also represent valuable intellectual property and are vulnerable to theft or reverse engineering. Furthermore, the MLOps pipelines used to build, train, and deploy models present additional attack surfaces. MLSecOps integrates security across the AI/ML lifecycle to protect confidentiality, integrity, and availability of models and data, representing the convergence of ML, DevOps, and Security [23].
- **AI/ML Lifecycle Security**: Adapting the "shift left" philosophy to AI requires embedding security considerations into each phase of the ML model lifecycle [23].
  - *Plan/Design*: Conduct threat modeling specific to the AI system, identifying potential attack vectors such as data poisoning, evasion, or model theft, and define security requirements early [23]. Assess risks related to data sources and third-party components.
  - *Data Collection/Processing*: Ensure data is sourced securely and ethically. Implement robust validation and sanitization routines to eliminate anomalies or malicious inputs [21]. Employ techniques to detect and reduce bias in datasets. Utilize privacy-preserving methods such as differential privacy and federated learning, particularly when handling sensitive data [2].
  - *Model Training*: Secure the training infrastructure and implement defenses against data poisoning attacks. Techniques like adversarial training expose models to adversarial examples during development to improve resilience [15].
  - *Model Evaluation/Validation*: Extend evaluation metrics beyond performance to include robustness testing using adversarial inputs [21], fairness audits [15], and red teaming to identify hidden vulnerabilities [4]. Ensure outputs are validated for integrity and unexpected behavior [2].

- *Deployment*: Follow secure deployment patterns—use hardened containers, encrypted models, and strong access controls. Techniques like model watermarking can deter theft or misuse [8, 15].
- *Operation/Monitoring*: Continuously monitor for data and concept drift, performance degradation, and adversarial anomalies [23]. Establish incident response procedures for AI-specific security threats [8].
- *Retraining*: Secure the retraining pipeline with rigorous validation, and re-evaluate updated models for both performance and security [19].

• **AI-Specific Threats and Defenses**: Understanding the common attack vectors against ML systems is crucial for implementing effective defenses within the MLSecOps framework.

- *Input/Evasion Attacks*: Attackers subtly modify input data (e.g., adding imperceptible noise to an image, slightly altering text) to cause the model to misclassify or produce incorrect output during inference [17].

  Defenses: These include robust input validation and sanitization [15], adversarial training to improve resilience [9], robust feature engineering to reduce vulnerability [8], defensive distillation to smooth decision boundaries [9], and anomaly detection applied to model inputs [19].

- *Data/Model Poisoning*: Attackers inject malicious data into the training set or directly alter a trained model to compromise its behavior [15].

  Defenses: Effective approaches include strict data provenance validation, data sanitization before training [3], anomaly detection during ingestion, secure ML supply chain practices, and regular retraining with vetted data [7].

- *Model Extraction/Theft*: By querying deployed models repeatedly, attackers can infer model architecture or parameters to steal intellectual property [15].

  Defenses: Rate-limiting API queries [15], using model watermarking [8], deploying in secure environments, and monitoring for suspicious query patterns are key strategies.

- *Membership Inference/Model Inversion*: Attackers attempt to infer if specific data was in the training set or reconstruct sensitive data [15].

  Defenses: Techniques like differential privacy, secure aggregation in federated learning [7], and restricting information in model outputs help mitigate this risk.

- *AI Supply Chain Attacks*: Vulnerabilities in third-party models, libraries, or datasets used in the AI lifecycle can be exploited.

  Defenses: Mitigations include software composition analysis (SCA) for ML libraries, verifying third-party model integrity, maintaining a software bill of materials (SBOM), using secure containers, and continuous toolchain vulnerability scanning [9].

  - *Other Defenses*: Model ensembling—combining predictions from multiple models—can improve robustness by making it more difficult to fool all models at once [10].

MLSecOps Risk Mitigation: Key threats include input manipulation, data poisoning, model theft, and supply chain attacks. Defenses encompass adversarial training, differential privacy, continuous monitoring, and secure deployment practices aligned with OWASP ML Security Top 10 guidelines.

- **Continuous Monitoring of AI Models**: Deployed ML models are not static; their performance and security posture must be continuously monitored [8].
  - *Techniques*: This includes tracking key performance metrics (accuracy, precision, recall, F1-score), monitoring for data drift (changes in input distribution) and concept drift (shifts in the relationship between input and output) [4]. For security, inputs and outputs should be monitored for anomalies that may suggest evasion attacks or unexpected behavior [19], and for patterns indicative of adversarial techniques [22]. It is also essential to track fairness metrics to ensure the model does not develop bias over time [15].
  - *Tools*: A range of tools—from open-source libraries integrated within MLOps platforms (e.g., MLflow [15]) to specialized commercial AI monitoring solutions—support this process [17]. Notably, ML-based monitoring itself leverages ML algorithms to analyze logs and metrics, improving detection of anomalies compared to traditional rule- or threshold-based alerts [23].
  - *Feedback Loop*: Insights from continuous monitoring are essential to sustaining model health and integrity. Detection of drift or performance decline should trigger model retraining [19]. If security anomalies or successful adversarial probes are identified, they necessitate incident response and possible model updates or hardening via techniques such as adversarial training [9].
- **MLOps Best Practices for Security**: Secure AI deployment requires integrating security into standard MLOps best practices [8, 24].
  - *Automation*: Secure CI/CD pipelines should be customized for ML artifacts, automating model training, validation (including security tests), deployment, and ongoing monitoring [8, 24].
  - *Versioning*: Robust version control must be extended beyond code to include datasets, model parameters, hyperparameters, configuration files, and experimental results to ensure reproducibility and support traceability in audits and investigations [24].
  - *Testing*: Testing strategies should encompass not only model accuracy and fairness but also robustness against adversarial inputs, validation of input data integrity, and the security posture of infrastructure-as-code used in MLOps workflows [8, 12, 24].
  - *Infrastructure Security*: Models should be deployed in hardened environments, applying cloud-native security best practices, such as container

hardening, network segmentation, and using Trusted Execution Environments (TEEs) where applicable [20, 24].
- *Access Control*: Role-based access control (RBAC) should be enforced across datasets, model repositories, orchestration pipelines, and API interfaces to mitigate insider threats and privilege escalation risks [3, 24].
- *Monitoring and Incident Response*: Continuous monitoring systems tailored to ML workflows must be implemented. These should detect model drift, adversarial activity, and abnormal access patterns. Well-defined AI-specific incident response playbooks are essential for responding to model attacks or failures in production [8, 20, 24].

The effectiveness of AI in enhancing DevSecOps security—such as AI-powered threat detection or vulnerability scanning—is intrinsically linked to the robustness of the AI systems themselves. An AI security tool vulnerable to data poisoning can be manipulated to overlook malicious activity, thereby undermining its intended function and possibly introducing new risks [24]. Similarly, AI-powered code scanners that are susceptible to evasion attacks may fail to detect critical security flaws injected by adversaries [20]. Therefore, integrating robust MLSecOps practices is not just about protecting AI assets, but is essential for preserving the trustworthiness and reliability of AI components embedded within the DevSecOps pipeline [24]. A comprehensive, AI-enabled DevSecOps approach must treat the security of its AI mechanisms as a core strategic priority.

Furthermore, the intersection of AI applications in security and the security of AI itself highlights a common and pivotal dependency: data. AI models are fundamentally data-driven systems [2]. Their accuracy, fairness, and reliability are directly influenced by the quality, integrity, representativeness, and privacy of the data they are trained and operated on [2]. Bias in training datasets can result in discriminatory or unfair security outcomes [13], while poor-quality or noisy data can degrade the performance of threat detection or vulnerability assessments [18]. Data poisoning attacks deliberately exploit this data dependency to compromise model behavior [24]. Simultaneously, because AI systems often process sensitive user and operational data, safeguarding privacy and ensuring compliance become essential [22]. Defensive techniques such as input validation and sanitization [20], along with continuous monitoring [20], are focused on managing and verifying the trustworthiness of incoming and outgoing data. Hence, robust data governance, end-to-end data security, and ongoing data quality assurance form the foundation for the safe and effective adoption of AI within cloud-based DevSecOps environments.

Case Study: Google Cloud's AI Platform Security Framework Google Cloud's Vertex AI implements comprehensive MLSecOps practices for enterprise customers processing 100+ million predictions daily. Their security framework includes: automated data lineage tracking with 99.9% audit coverage, differential privacy implementation reducing membership inference success to <2%, adversarial robustness testing achieving 94.7% attack resistance, and real-time model behavior monitoring with sub-second anomaly detection. The platform's federated learning capabilities enable 78 financial institutions to collaboratively train fraud detection models while maintaining data sovereignty, resulting in 34% improved fraud detection accuracy compared to isolated models.

16.5 Challenges and Future Outlook

While the integration of AI into DevSecOps for cloud security offers transformative potential, its implementation is not without significant hurdles. Organizations must navigate technical complexities, operational adjustments, organizational shifts, and critical ethical considerations. Concurrently, the field is rapidly evolving, with emerging trends promising even greater capabilities and new challenges on the horizon. Understanding these challenges and future directions is essential for strategic planning and successful adoption.

16.5.1 Implementation Challenges

Deploying and managing AI-enabled DevSecOps systems effectively involves overcoming several interconnected challenges.

Technical Challenges

- **Data Quality and Availability**: AI models, particularly those leveraging supervised learning for tasks like vulnerability detection or threat prediction, rely heavily on the availability of large, high-quality, and context-specific labeled datasets. However, acquiring and maintaining such datasets—especially for specialized or emerging security threats—remains resource-intensive and challenging [2]. Inadequate or poor-quality data can impair model performance, leading to unreliable or biased security outcomes [18].
- **Scalability and Performance**: Implementing deep learning or other resource-intensive AI models in cloud security operations introduces significant computational demands. Running these models at scale—particularly for real-time applications like network anomaly detection or dynamic code analysis—can result in high infrastructure costs and performance bottlenecks [2]. Balancing accuracy, latency, and system overhead is especially critical in dynamic, large-scale cloud-native environments [14].
- **Integration Complexity**: Incorporating AI-powered security tools into complex, pre-existing DevSecOps workflows often presents significant integration challenges. Tool compatibility, API mismatches, orchestration across CI/CD stages, and managing software dependencies all require considerable engineering effort [14]. Without seamless integration, organizations may encounter

operational disruptions, inefficiencies, or tool fatigue—potentially undermining adoption [9].

- **Model Brittleness and Drift**: AI models tend to be brittle; their performance can degrade when exposed to inputs that deviate from their training data distribution. Additionally, in dynamic cloud environments, models are vulnerable to data drift (shifts in input data characteristics) and concept drift (evolving security threats or system behaviors), which can reduce model efficacy over time [24]. This underscores the need for ongoing monitoring, evaluation, and periodic retraining [20].
- **Adversarial Robustness**: Ensuring that AI models remain resilient against adversarial attacks—such as evasion techniques or poisoning of training data—is a persistent research challenge [2]. While techniques like adversarial training and anomaly detection exist, the evolving sophistication of attackers demands continuous innovation and defense updates [24].

Operational Challenges

- **Alert Fatigue**: Although AI is designed to reduce false positives, improperly configured models or overly sensitive detection thresholds can still generate a high volume of alerts. This can contribute to analyst burnout and increase the likelihood of overlooking critical threats. Managing this challenge requires effective alert correlation, contextual prioritization, and seamless integration of AI outputs into established incident response workflows [7].
- **Tool Overload and Complexity**: The rapid growth of AI-powered tools across the DevSecOps lifecycle—ranging from code analysis to runtime threat detection—can result in tool sprawl. Without proper orchestration, this proliferation can introduce operational friction, increase maintenance burdens, and create blind spots in the security posture due to fragmented or siloed insights [9].
- **Zero Trust Implementation Hurdles**: Despite advancements in AI-assisted security, realizing a full Zero Trust Architecture in cloud-native environments remains complex. AI can aid in behavior-based access decisions, but defining fine-grained policies, enabling robust microsegmentation, and managing real-time adaptive access controls are labor-intensive tasks. Moreover, AI systems often face challenges in maintaining consistent visibility across ephemeral workloads, unmanaged endpoints, or dynamic user contexts.

Organizational Challenges

- **Skills Gap**: There is a well-documented shortage of professionals with the interdisciplinary expertise required to implement and manage AI-enabled DevSecOps—combining knowledge in AI/ML, cybersecurity, cloud computing, and DevOps methodologies. Addressing this talent deficit necessitates both upskilling current personnel and attracting new experts, posing a major challenge for many organizations [9, 16].

- **Cultural Resistance and Trust**: Transitioning to DevSecOps, especially with integrated AI capabilities, often demands a significant cultural transformation. This includes fostering collaboration between traditionally siloed teams (development, security, operations) and cultivating trust in automation and AI-assisted decision-making. Resistance from team members accustomed to legacy processes can impede adoption. Moreover, skepticism around the transparency and explainability of AI models can further hinder trust and usage [5, 11, 18].
- **Cost and Resource Allocation**: Deploying AI systems within a DevSecOps framework typically requires considerable investment in compute infrastructure, data pipelines, specialized tooling, and skilled personnel. Balancing these costs with measurable returns, especially in early stages, can be difficult. Strategic justification of these expenditures and effective allocation of limited resources remain persistent obstacles [9].

16.5.2 Ethical Considerations and Responsible AI

While AI brings transformative capabilities to cloud security and DevSecOps, its adoption also introduces a range of ethical considerations that must be addressed to ensure responsible, transparent, and equitable deployment.

- **Bias and Fairness**: AI models trained on imbalanced or non-representative data risk perpetuating or amplifying biases. In security contexts, biased data can lead to unfair treatment, such as incorrectly flagging users from certain groups or failing to detect vulnerabilities common in less frequently represented development styles [2, 13]. Addressing this requires deliberate dataset curation, incorporating fairness checks during training and validation, and performing ongoing audits after deployment [2].
- **Transparency and Explainability (XAI)**: Many high-performing AI systems, particularly those based on deep learning, operate as black boxes with limited interpretability. This lack of transparency is problematic in security operations, where understanding model decisions is critical for incident response and trust [2, 18]. Explainable AI (XAI) methods, such as feature attribution and decision path visualization, are essential for providing insights into model behavior and fostering operator confidence [2].
- **Privacy Considerations**: AI security systems often require access to sensitive data including user activity, logs, and infrastructure configurations, raising privacy concerns. Compliance with data protection standards (e.g., GDPR, CCPA) demands data minimization, secure access controls, and privacy-preserving methods such as differential privacy and federated learning [2, 11, 18, 22]. These approaches help ensure that AI can function effectively without compromising individual or organizational privacy.

- **Accountability in AI-Driven Security**: Determining responsibility when an AI system makes a mistake—whether it's a missed alert or a false positive—can be challenging. Security decisions driven by AI must be traceable to accountable processes or stakeholders [4, 13]. Organizations must implement clear governance frameworks, audit trails, and policies for human-in-the-loop oversight to ensure that AI decisions can be understood and reviewed.
- **Potential for Adversarial Use**: Just as AI empowers defenders, it can also be weaponized by attackers. Threat actors can exploit AI to automate vulnerability discovery, generate polymorphic malware, or conduct large-scale, coordinated attacks [15, 20]. Addressing this risk involves continuous AI threat modeling, adversarial robustness testing, and investment in secure AI development practices [23].
- **Workforce Impact and Automation**: The automation enabled by AI may reduce the need for human analysts in some areas, especially routine tasks like log triage or basic alert response. While this can increase operational efficiency, it also raises concerns about job displacement [2, 13]. Ethical adoption of AI requires investing in upskilling and transitioning cybersecurity professionals into roles focused on oversight, AI governance, and higher order security analysis [9, 14].

16.5.3 Future Trends

The convergence of AI and DevSecOps is continuously evolving, with several forward-looking trends expected to significantly impact cloud-native security strategies in the coming years:

- **Hyperautomation in Security Workflows**: The future of DevSecOps will move beyond siloed automation to full hyperautomation—integrating AI, machine learning, Robotic Process Automation (RPA), and low-code/no-code platforms to orchestrate complex, end-to-end security workflows [19]. This will enable intelligent automation across multiple layers, such as vulnerability detection, triage, remediation, and reporting, significantly reducing manual intervention and enhancing operational efficiency.
- **AI-Augmented Security Teams (AI Copilots)**: AI is increasingly being positioned as a digital assistant—or "copilot"—for cybersecurity professionals. These AI copilots will automate data analysis, surface relevant threat insights, recommend remediation steps, generate documentation, and streamline incident response [2, 19]. By offloading repetitive and data-intensive tasks, AI will empower human analysts to focus on strategy, complex investigations, and proactive threat hunting [14].
- **Autonomous Remediation and Self-Healing Systems**: A key direction for AI security systems is the development of self-healing infrastructure. AI tools are evolving to not only detect vulnerabilities and misconfigurations but to autonomously remediate them by applying patches, adjusting access controls, and

refining security policies in real time [2, 18, 24]. This shift promises more resilient systems capable of adapting automatically to changing threat conditions.

- **Advances in Explainable AI (XAI)**: As AI becomes more embedded in security decision-making, the need for transparency and interpretability intensifies. Explainable AI will continue to be a focal point, with emerging techniques aimed at helping analysts understand model reasoning, validate decisions, and meet regulatory and audit requirements [2, 13, 18]. Enhanced interpretability will build trust in AI-driven security systems and enable better human-AI collaboration.
- **Federated Learning for Collaborative Defense**: Federated Learning (FL) is gaining traction as a privacy-preserving mechanism for collaborative threat detection and model training. It allows multiple organizations to train shared models on local data without directly exchanging it, promoting broader intelligence sharing while maintaining data confidentiality [2, 11, 22]. FL offers a path to more generalized and robust threat models across cloud environments.
- **Quantum Computing: Risk and Opportunity**: Quantum computing presents both a challenge and a potential asset in AI-enabled security. On the one hand, future quantum systems could break widely used cryptographic algorithms, necessitating urgent transitions to quantum-resistant cryptographic methods [17]. On the other hand, quantum computing could accelerate AI workloads, enhance model training, and introduce breakthroughs such as Quantum Key Distribution (QKD) for theoretically unbreakable communications [17].
- **AI-Driven Zero Trust Architectures**: The Zero Trust model will increasingly rely on AI to adaptively enforce policies based on contextual awareness and real-time analytics [2, 8]. AI can enhance continuous authentication, detect anomalous access behaviors, and dynamically adjust access permissions in response to evolving risks, making Zero Trust implementations more intelligent and scalable across multi-cloud environments.

16.5.4 Maturity Models and Continuous Improvement

Successfully implementing and scaling AI-enabled DevSecOps requires a structured approach and a commitment to continuous improvement. Maturity models provide frameworks for assessing current capabilities, identifying gaps, and planning a roadmap for advancement.

- **Assessing AI-DevSecOps Maturity**

- While numerous proprietary or community models exist, organizations can draw upon the core principles of software engineering maturity frameworks and tailor them to DevSecOps contexts. Concepts from well-established models such as the Software Engineering Institute's DevSecOps Platform Independent Model (PIM) and security-by-design principles [4] can be extended to account for the integration of AI into security processes. These frameworks generally assess practices across lifecycle phases (governance, build, test, deploy, operate, and monitor) [2, 5, 9].

- **Capability Levels**
- The following progression outlines a representative AI-DevSecOps maturity path based on increasing integration, standardization, and automation of security practices with AI support:
  - ***Level 1 (Initial/Reactive)***: Security measures are inconsistent, mostly manual, and reactively applied. AI is not integrated, and security awareness is minimal. The focus is typically on basic tool adoption without lifecycle-wide orchestration [5].
  - ***Level 2 (Repeatable/Managed)***: Basic static and software composition analysis tools (e.g., SAST, SCA) are in place and integrated into CI pipelines. Some AI usage may be piloted—for instance, AI-assisted code reviews—but processes remain mostly siloed and manual [3, 12].
  - ***Level 3 (Standardized/Defined)***: Security activities are standardized, documented, and partially automated across the CI/CD pipeline. AI is used more systematically for prioritizing vulnerabilities, performing risk assessments, and detecting anomalies in telemetry data [2, 8]. Feedback loops and visibility are implemented [20].
  - ***Level 4 (Measured/Optimized)***: Security processes are metrics-driven and continuously improved. AI contributes to predictive threat modeling, dynamic risk scoring, and enriched incident detection [8, 10, 14]. Automation enables faster and more effective responses, and decisions are guided by data and continuous feedback [9].
  - ***Level 5 (Adaptive/Intelligent)***: Organizations operate in a proactive and resilient security posture. AI capabilities are deeply embedded—enabling auto-remediation, adaptive policy enforcement, and self-healing infrastructure [18, 24]. Threat intelligence is augmented through federated learning [11], and AI models are hardened against adversarial threats [20]. Continuous learning is institutionalized, and AI is leveraged strategically to evolve defenses against emerging threats [2, 19].

By aligning their current DevSecOps implementation with such a maturity model, organizations can establish a foundation for resilient, intelligent cloud-native security that continuously evolves alongside their operational needs and the evolving threat landscape.

AI-DevSecOps Maturity Evolution: Organizations progress from manual, reactive security (Level 1) through standardized AI-enhanced processes (Level 3) to adaptive, self-healing systems with advanced explainable AI and federated learning capabilities (Level 5).

- **Continuous Improvement Cycle:** Achieving higher maturity is not a one-time effort but requires a continuous cycle of assessment, planning, implementation, measurement, and refinement [9]. Feedback loops are essential for driving sustained progress [5]. This involves regularly monitoring the effectiveness of

security controls and AI models, collecting metrics such as vulnerability detection rates, mean time to remediation (MTTR), false positive rates, and indicators of model drift [1, 20], gathering feedback from teams, and using these insights to iteratively improve processes, retrain models, and adapt strategies [2].
- **Case Study Example (Comcast):** The DevSecOps transformation at Comcast, led by Larry Maccherone, offers practical insights for scaling secure development practices across large organizations [9]. Their initiative reportedly led to an 85% reduction in security incidents, achieved through a coaching-centric approach rather than relying solely on technology [9]. Key elements of this success included:
  - **Building Trust:** Shifting from a policing model to one that empowers developers, assuming good intent and focusing on enablement.
  - **Gradual Learning:** Integrating security practices incrementally—introducing only a few focused actions per sprint to avoid overwhelming teams.
  - **Coaching and Enablement:** Providing tailored support through dedicated security coaches who work closely with development teams to guide and reinforce good practices.
  - **Measurement and Visualization:** Leveraging clear metrics and visual dashboards to track adoption and effectiveness, facilitating alignment, and shared understanding.
  - **Scalable Rollout:** Beginning with a small number of teams, validating the approach end-to-end, and letting success expand organically through internal advocacy and visible wins rather than a broad, superficial push.

This structured, trust-based model enabled a small DevSecOps coaching team to eventually influence and support hundreds of developer teams within Comcast [9].

The dynamic nature of cloud infrastructure, the ever-evolving cyber threat landscape, and the adaptive behavior of AI models themselves create an environment where static or one-time security implementations are inherently insufficient. In cloud environments, configurations frequently drift, new vulnerabilities emerge regularly, and machine learning models may degrade or develop bias over time without proper oversight and updates [20]. This volatility necessitates the establishment of a robust and continuous feedback loop—connecting:

- Monitoring systems (for cloud posture, application behavior, AI model accuracy, and evolving threat intelligence)
- Evaluation processes (assessing technical performance, security efficacy, and ethical factors like fairness)
- Adaptive mechanisms (for triggering model retraining, refining automation, updating policies, and evolving DevSecOps practices)

Without this continual cycle of observation, evaluation, and adaptation, the long-term effectiveness, resilience, and trustworthiness of AI-integrated DevSecOps systems cannot be maintained [20].

Moreover, while automation remains a significant objective, the present and foreseeable future of AI in DevSecOps highlights the need for a collaborative human-AI partnership. AI is particularly adept at high-speed data analysis, large-scale pattern detection, log processing, vulnerability scanning, and automating well-defined responses [12]. However, critical limitations persist: AI's lack of transparency in decision-making (the "black box" problem) [18], risks of inherited bias from training data [20], and challenges in addressing novel, ambiguous, or context-sensitive threats. As such, human expertise remains irreplaceable—for providing strategic oversight, validating AI-driven decisions, interpreting edge cases, making ethical judgments, and integrating business context [18].

The most resilient and effective DevSecOps strategies will likely be those that harmonize AI efficiency with human judgment, enabling AI to serve as a force multiplier while entrusting humans with high-level control, validation, and continuous innovation [8].

16.6 Conclusion

The convergence of Artificial Intelligence, DevSecOps, and Cloud Computing represents a fundamental shift in how organizations approach software development and security. The inherent scale, dynamism, and complexity of cloud environments, coupled with the velocity demanded by DevOps practices, render traditional security measures inadequate. AI is no longer a futuristic aspiration but an increasingly necessary component for achieving robust, scalable, and adaptive security in the cloud without hindering innovation and speed.

This chapter has explored the multifaceted role of AI within the cloud DevSecOps lifecycle. AI enhances security by automating vulnerability detection and remediation, improving code quality through intelligent suggestions, providing real-time threat monitoring and predictive analytics, streamlining compliance, and accelerating incident response. From AI-powered coding assistants scanning code as it's written, to sophisticated ML models analyzing logs for anomalies, to automated systems patching IaC misconfigurations, AI capabilities are being embedded across the SDLC, enabling a more proactive and efficient security posture.

However, the integration of AI is a dual-edged sword. While leveraging AI *for* security, organizations must simultaneously address the security *of* AI. MLSecOps practices—encompassing secure data handling, robust model training and validation (including adversarial testing), secure deployment, and continuous monitoring of AI systems—are critical. The effectiveness of AI-driven security tools is contingent upon their own integrity and resilience against AI-specific threats like data poisoning and evasion attacks. This interdependence underscores the need for a holistic approach where securing the AI pipeline is as crucial as using AI to secure the software pipeline. Data quality, security, and governance emerge as central pillars supporting both facets of this integration.

Successfully navigating this new paradigm requires addressing significant challenges. Technical hurdles like data acquisition, model scalability, and adversarial robustness must be overcome. Operational issues such as alert fatigue and tool integration need careful management.

Critical AI-Enabled DevSecOps Challenges: Organizations implementing AI-enhanced DevSecOps face unique risks including bias in training data that may lead to discriminatory security policies, model explainability concerns that hinder regulatory compliance and audit requirements, and regulatory risks associated with AI governance frameworks. Critical thinking requires acknowledging that AI systems may perpetuate existing security biases or create new blind spots if not properly validated and monitored. Organizational transformation, including bridging the skills gap and fostering a collaborative, security-conscious culture that embraces AI, is paramount. Critically, ethical considerations surrounding bias, transparency, privacy, and accountability must be proactively addressed through responsible AI governance frameworks and the pursuit of Explainable AI (XAI).

The future points toward increasingly sophisticated AI integration, with trends like hyperautomation, AI copilots, autonomous remediation, and enhanced federated learning further transforming the landscape. The looming impact of quantum computing adds another layer of complexity, demanding proactive adoption of post-quantum cryptography. Ultimately, the most effective path forward involves a symbiotic relationship between human expertise and artificial intelligence. AI will handle the scale, speed, and complexity that overwhelm human capacity, while humans provide the strategic direction, contextual understanding, ethical judgment, and critical oversight necessary for trustworthy and effective security.

In conclusion, AI-enabled DevSecOps is not merely a technological upgrade; it is a strategic imperative for organizations seeking to innovate securely and competitively in the cloud era. By embracing AI's potential while diligently managing its risks and challenges through robust MLSecOps practices, ethical considerations, and a commitment to continuous learning and adaptation, businesses can build a more secure, resilient, and agile future for their cloud deployments.

References

1. Binbeshr, F., Rodriguez, M., & Kim, J. (2021). Machine learning integration in DevSecOps pipelines. *Communications in Computer and Information Science, 1523*, 32–46.
2. Brin, D. (2024). Ethical AI implementation in security automation systems. *AI and Ethics, 4*(2), 89–104.
3. Lombardi, M., & Fanton, F. (2023). Policy-as-code implementation for AI-driven infrastructure security. *ACM Transactions on Autonomous and Adaptive Systems, 18*(2), 1–25.
4. Rios, E., Iturbe, E., & Garitano, I. (2015). Security-by-design in multi-cloud DevOps environments. *Computers & Security, 54*, 345–360.
5. Casola, V., De Benedictis, A., & Rak, M. (2020). Security orchestration in multi-cloud DevOps environments. *Journal of Grid Computing, 18*(4), 789–812.
6. Chen, H., Kumar, V., & Thompson, A. (2023). Adversarial machine learning in cybersecurity: Threats and defenses. *ACM Computing Surveys, 55*(8), 167–192.
7. Li, W., & Zhao, X. (2023). AI-enhanced intrusion detection systems for cloud security. *IEEE Transactions on Cloud Computing, 21*(2), 345–360.

8. Ness, S., Mitchell, D., & Brown, K. (2024). Incorporating AI-driven strategies in DevSecOps for robust cloud security. *SN Computer Science, 5*(3), 298–315.
9. Maccherone, L. (2024). Scaling DevSecOps practices in enterprise cloud environments. *IEEE Software, 41*(3), 45–52.
10. Kumar, S., Zhao, Y., & Garcia, A. (2024). Adaptive threat modeling using deep reinforcement learning. *Expert Systems with Applications, 238*(1), 121845.
11. Yasar, H. (2021). Continuous security monitoring in ML-enhanced DevOps pipelines. *Journal of Information Processing Systems, 17*(6), 1234–1250.
12. Bromberg, Y., & Gitzinger, T. (2020). Continuous security assurance in cloud-native CI/CD pipelines. *Empirical Software Engineering, 25*(6), 4567–4598.
13. Cankar, M., Patel, S., & Wilson, R. (2023). Machine learning approaches for microservice anomaly detection in kubernetes clusters. *Journal of Cloud Computing, 12*(1), 34–56.
14. Binbeshr, F., & Imam, M. (2025). Comparative analysis of AI-driven security approaches in DevSecOps: Challenges, solutions, and future directions. *Journal of Software Engineering Research and Development, 13*(4), 45–67.
15. Petrović, N., & Djosic, S. (2022). Automated red teaming of AI security systems using generative models. *Computers & Security, 121*, 102843.
16. Davis, M., & Rodriguez, L. (2024). Zero trust architecture implementation in cloud-native environments. *IEEE Security & Privacy, 22*(3), 45–58.
17. Ibrahim, A., Khan, M., & Taylor, J. (2022). Quantum-resistant cryptography in cloud DevSecOps pipelines. *International Journal of Information Security, 21*(5), 1123–1142.
18. Gupta, P., & Sharma, N. (2024). Machine learning techniques for container security in kubernetes environments. *Cluster Computing, 27*(1), 127–144.
19. Ness, S., & Rios, E. (2023). Hyperautomation in cloud security operations. *Automated Software Engineering, 30*(4), 78–95.
20. Petrović, N., Milosevic, M., & Johnson, T. (2022). Adversarial training for robust ML models in DevSecOps pipelines. *Neural Computing and Applications, 34*(20), 17893–17911.
21. Patel, R., & Singh, A. (2024). Natural language processing for security automation in DevOps pipelines. *Journal of Cybersecurity, 12*(3), 156–172.
22. Silva, P., Santos, R., & Williams, C. (2024). Federated learning for privacy-preserving threat detection in multi-cloud environments. *IEEE Transactions on Cloud Computing, 22*(3), 112–130.
23. Silva, P., & Cankar, M. (2024). Differential privacy in federated learning for cross-organizational threat intelligence. *ACM Transactions on Privacy and Security, 27*(2), 1–28.
24. Fanton, F., Silva, P., & Lee, H. (2023). MLSecOps framework for confidential computing environments. *IEEE Transactions on Emerging Topics in Computing, 11*(3), 567–580.
25. Schneier, B., & Raghunathan, A. (2023). Securing cloud-native applications with zero trust architectures. *IEEE Security & Privacy, 21*(4), 22–30.

Chapter 17
AI and Edge Computing: A Deep Dive into the Convergence of Intelligence and Proximity

Naga Venkat Prasad Janapareddy and Surya Sekhar Chapala

Abstract As the digital world fights toward real-time responsiveness and autonomy, the combination of Artificial Intelligence (AI) and Edge Computing is emerging as a transformative force reshaping how data is processed, decisions are made, and systems interact with the world around them. This paper explores the convergence of intelligence and proximity, showing how bringing AI closer to data sources unlocks new boundaries in speed, privacy, and contextual awareness. By examining historical context, architectural frameworks, and practical applications in healthcare, manufacturing, and smart cities, we demonstrate how this evolution leads to systems that are smarter, faster, and more resilient. This paper dives into the technical backbone of edge AI, covering hardware innovations like Edge TPUs and GPU-powered boards, networking advances such as 5G and Multi-access Edge Computing (MEC), and critical security mechanisms including Trusted Execution Environments and federated learning. The paper also highlights the growing ecosystem of edge-ready AI frameworks that power intelligent applications in even the most resource-constrained environments. However, this transformation comes with challenges. Issues such as deployment complexity, data fragmentation, and lack of standardization still hinder large-scale adoption. But with advances in sustainable AI, smart self-managing systems, and strong ethical guidelines, edge computing and AI is quickly becoming essential, and not an option. Edge AI is rapidly moving beyond a theoretical concept and is now significantly reshaping the digital world. This paper not only demystifies the technology but also invites readers to imagine a world where intelligent decisions are made instantly, securely, and exactly where they're needed most.

Keywords Edge computing · Cloud security · AI · Identity · Networking · Security leader

N. V. P. Janapareddy (✉)
Austin, TX, USA

S. S. Chapala
Tampa, FL, USA
e-mail: surya.sekhar@centroid.com

B. Pandey, A. Patel (eds.), *Revolutionizing the Cloud*,
https://doi.org/10.1007/978-3-032-07479-9_17

17.1 Introduction

In recent years, we have witnessed a shift in how data is processed, analyzed, and represented. The growing volume of data generated by billions of connected devices, sensors, and applications across the globe has pushed traditional cloud-based computing models to their extreme limits. Centralized systems, even though powerful, are often struggling to meet the growing demand for near real-time responsiveness, low-latency decision-making, and enhanced data privacy [1, 2].

This is where the convergence of Artificial Intelligence (AI) and Edge Computing comes into play, reshaping how and where intelligence must be deployed. Edge computing allows data processing to occur at or near the point of data generation, reducing dependency on distant cloud data centers. When integrated with AI, this approach enables systems to make localized, intelligent decisions without waiting for instructions from centralized servers. The result is a new class of computing that is faster, more resilient, and contextually aware [3–6].

This convergence is not merely a technological trend; it is a transformational shift in how digital systems are being designed and how intelligence is combined into the fabric of everyday devices and infrastructure. Whether it's enabling predictive maintenance in smart factories, powering real-time decision-making in autonomous vehicles, or supporting remote diagnostics in healthcare, the synergy between AI and edge computing is unlocking powerful possibilities across sectors [7–9].

17.2 Background and Context

To fully appreciate the convergence of Artificial Intelligence (AI) and Edge Computing, it's important to understand how each of them has evolved in addition to why their paths are now so closely aligned. This section offers a historical lens through which we can view the rapid technological shifts shaping our digital world. It connects the dots between decades of innovation in computing, the rise of smart, connected devices, and the immediate need for faster, more localized intelligence [1, 2].

17.2.1 The Rise of Artificial Intelligence: From Dreams to Everyday Reality

The field of Artificial Intelligence isn't new. It roots back to the 1950s, when early computer scientists imagined machines that could think like humans but at robotic speed. The 1960s and 1970s were filled with high hopes, focused on symbolic reasoning and expert systems—programs that followed hard-coded rules to mimic human decision-making. But as excitement overtook results, funding started to come to an end and the field experienced what is now known as the "AI winter" due to limited scalability and adaptability.

Everything began to change again in the 1990s and 2000s, thanks to machine learning. Instead of rigid hard-coded rules, algorithms began learning from data. In the 2010s, further research led to the evolution of deep learning—a leap forward made possible by enormous computing power (especially GPUs), access to vast datasets, and smarter neural network architectures [4, 8]. Today, AI powers voice assistants, drives recommendation engines, scans medical images, and even writes code and poetry. AI systems are rooted in everyday life, enabling voice assistants, personalizing search results, optimizing logistics, and performing tasks that once required human creativity, such as generating artwork or composing music [10].

Models such as Convolutional Neural Networks (CNNs) have revolutionized image recognition, while transformer-based architectures like BERT and GPT have redefined natural language understanding. But there's a catch: modern AI demands extreme computational resources for training. Training large models requires expensive infrastructure and substantial cloud compute, often hosted in remote data centers, further impacting the environment. Even running these models (called inference) can be slow or impractical when connectivity is weak or real-time response is critical—often impacting latency. This is where Edge Computing enters to address these limitations [3, 5, 11].

17.3 The Symbiotic Evolution: AI and Edge Computing in the Decentralized Data Landscape

The exponential growth of interconnected devices and data-intensive applications in the digital age has led to an exceptional volume of data. This surge has highlighted the limitations of traditional centralized cloud computing, especially for applications requiring immediate responses and efficient resource use. Edge computing has emerged as a transformative solution by strategically locating computational resources nearer to the data's origin. This decentralization effectively tackles crucial issues like latency, bandwidth limitations, reliability, and data privacy, thereby enabling a more flexible and intelligent digital framework [1, 2].

According to projections from Gartner in 2021, we are expected to reach a significant turning point by 2025, where over 75% of enterprise-generated data will be processed at the network edge. This represents a considerable shift from the previous reliance on centralized data centers and emphasizes the increasing acknowledgment of edge computing as a fundamental element of future digital strategies [1].

The primary reason for the rise of edge computing has been the massive expansion of the Internet of Things (IoT). This technological revolution has started in an era where billions of interconnected devices invade every facet of our lives and industries. From basic devices, such as smart thermostats optimizing energy consumption and wearable health monitors tracking vital signs, to sophisticated industrial sensors providing real-time performance analytics and autonomous machines navigating complex environments, each IoT device acts as a continuous generator of data streams [2, 10].

The steep volume and velocity of this data inundation quickly overwhelmed the capabilities of centralized cloud infrastructure. This approach of transmitting all data to distant cloud servers for processing has several drawbacks. For time-sensitive applications, the latency introduced is unacceptable. Additionally, the bandwidth costs become substantial, and managing these large data transfers presents significant logistical challenges. Moreover, the communication delays inherent in cloud computing can hinder the real-time decision-making that many new technologies rely on [2, 9].

Edge computing offers a compelling solution by fundamentally altering the architecture of data processing. Instead of funneling all data to a central location, it distributes computational power across a network of edge devices situated near data generation points. These edge locations can take various forms, including localized gateways that aggregate data from nearby sensors, powerful edge servers deployed within industrial facilities, embedded processors integrated directly into vehicles or machinery, and even sophisticated mobile phones capable of performing on-device analysis [4, 5].

This strategic decentralization yields a multitude of significant advantages that address the shortcomings of centralized models. One of the most critical benefits of edge computing is reduced latency, and this is specific to inference and not training. In applications where every millisecond is crucial, such as autonomous driving systems needing immediate hazard detection and response, or robotic control systems requiring precise real-time adjustments, edge computing's ability to process data close to the source is essential [2, 4].

Secondly, edge computing leads to substantial bandwidth savings. By performing initial filtering, aggregation, and analysis of data at the edge, the volume of information that needs to be transmitted to the cloud is significantly reduced. This not only lowers operational costs associated with network bandwidth consumption but also eases network congestion, improving overall system performance and freeing up valuable bandwidth for other critical data streams [2, 9].

Furthermore, edge computing enhances reliability. In scenarios where continuous cloud connectivity cannot be guaranteed, or where network disruptions may occur, edge devices can continue to operate autonomously, processing data and executing critical functions locally. This inherent resilience ensures uninterrupted operation for essential services and industrial processes, mitigating the risks associated with dependence on a persistent cloud connection [2].

Finally, edge computing offers enhanced privacy and compliance. In industries subject to strict data regulations, such as healthcare and finance, the ability to keep highly sensitive data within local jurisdictions is a top concern. Edge computing enables organizations to process and store data locally, adhering to regional compliance requirements and enhancing data privacy by minimizing the transmission of sensitive information across potentially less secure public networks [12, 13].

In conclusion, the rise of edge computing, particularly in union with the increasing sophistication of artificial intelligence, signifies more than just an incremental improvement in computational efficiency. It represents a fundamental and transformative shift in how digital systems are architected and deployed. By bringing intelligence and processing power closer to the data source, edge computing is enabling a new generation of applications that are more responsive, resilient, and autonomous. This architectural evolution is laying the groundwork for a future where intelligent systems can seamlessly interact with the physical world, driving innovation across industries and fundamentally reshaping our digital landscape [1, 3, 4].

17.4 The Necessity of the Edge for AI: Bridging the Gap Between Intelligence and Proximity

The deployment of Artificial Intelligence (AI) at the network edge transcends a mere technological preference; it represents a fundamental and increasingly critical necessity for a diverse spectrum of contemporary applications. In dynamic and latency-sensitive environments, such as autonomous vehicles navigating complex urban landscapes, sophisticated manufacturing plants orchestrating intricate robotic processes, and remote healthcare systems delivering immediate diagnostic and therapeutic interventions, the inherent delays associated with cloud-based processing become not just inconvenient, but potentially catastrophic [2, 4].

Even minuscule fractions of a second can critically compromise safety protocols, degrade system performance, and erode user trust in these mission-critical applications. Consider, for instance, the critical decision-making processes within a fully autonomous vehicle. When confronted with the unpredictable actions of a pedestrian entering a crosswalk, the vehicle's AI system cannot afford the temporal lag incurred by transmitting sensor data to a distant cloud server, awaiting a processing response, and then relaying the necessary control commands back to the vehicle's actuators. Such a delay, even if measured in mere milliseconds, could have devastating consequences [4].

Similarly, in the realm of industrial automation, the precision and safety of robotic arms guided by advanced computer vision algorithms are paramount. These systems must make instantaneous decisions based on real-time visual input to maintain operational efficiency, prevent collisions, and ensure the well-being of human workers in the vicinity. A delay in processing could lead to manufacturing defects, equipment damage, or, more seriously, workplace accidents [4, 7].

The same principle applies to remote healthcare systems, where real-time analysis of medical data from wearable devices or remote diagnostic tools can be the difference between timely intervention and delayed or ineffective treatment [7, 9].

Edge AI directly confronts these inherent limitations by strategically embedding computational intelligence directly within the end devices themselves or at strategically positioned intermediary nodes within the immediate network infrastructure.

This architectural paradigm enables real-time inference, allowing devices to analyze data and make decisions locally without the need for constant communication with a centralized cloud [3, 4].

Furthermore, it facilitates on-device learning, where models can be trained and adapted based on the specific data patterns observed by the individual device, leading to more personalized and contextually relevant performance. This localized processing enables context-aware processing, where decisions are informed by the immediate environment and specific circumstances, all achieved without the latency penalties introduced by round-trip cloud communication [4, 9].

Beyond the crucial aspect of speed and responsiveness, data efficiency emerges as another compelling and increasingly significant driver for the adoption of edge AI. By processing data locally at the source, organizations can dramatically reduce the bandwidth demands on their networks. This is particularly advantageous in geographically dispersed regions or in infrastructure-poor environments where network connectivity may be unreliable, intermittent, or prohibitively expensive [2].

The sheer volume of data generated by the burgeoning number of IoT devices and edge sensors necessitates a more distributed processing approach to avoid overwhelming network infrastructure and incurring exorbitant data transmission costs [1].

Industry analysts at IDC project a significant surge in the demand for edge-based machine learning inference, estimating that by 2026, edge applications requiring such capabilities will constitute over 50% of all edge workloads, underscoring the escalating importance of local intelligence [1].

Moreover, the deployment of edge AI carries significant ethical and legal implications, particularly in industries that handle sensitive and regulated data. Sectors such as healthcare, defense, and finance operate under stringent regulatory frameworks that dictate where and how data can be stored, processed, and analyzed [12, 13].

Edge AI deployments offer a compelling solution to these compliance challenges by enabling organizations to keep sensitive data on-premises, within designated local networks, or strictly within national borders. This localized data handling aligns more effectively with principles of data sovereignty, ensuring that data remains under the control and jurisdiction of the relevant authorities. Furthermore, it facilitates adherence to stringent privacy compliance frameworks such as the European Union's General Data Protection Regulation (GDPR) [12] or the United States' Health Insurance Portability and Accountability Act (HIPAA) [13], which impose strict requirements on the handling and protection of personal and confidential information.

By minimizing the transmission of sensitive data to potentially less secure cloud environments, edge AI enhances data security and strengthens compliance postures [12, 13].

Collectively, these converging trends paint a clear picture of a fundamental shift in the role and capabilities of the network edge. It is no longer simply a passive medium for the transmission of raw data to centralized cloud platforms. Instead, the edge is rapidly evolving into an intelligent platform, capable of sophisticated data analysis, real-time decision-making, and autonomous operation. The seamless integration of AI into edge systems is not just an incremental technological advancement; it is paving the way for a transformative future where decisions are not only significantly faster and more efficient but also inherently more context-aware, dynamically adaptive to changing conditions, and fundamentally more secure and compliant with regulatory requirements. This convergence of intelligence and proximity at the edge is poised to unlock a new era of innovation and efficiency across a wide range of industries and applications [1, 3, 4].

17.5 Core Content Frameworks and Architectures

The paradigm shift of Artificial Intelligence from powerful, centralized data centers to the dynamic and often resource-constrained realm of edge computing necessitates a fundamental transformation in the underlying software and infrastructure. This evolution is crucial for enabling intelligent applications in real-world, latency-critical scenarios, where instantaneous decision-making is paramount [3, 4].

Edge AI frameworks and meticulously designed deployment architectures serve as the critical link between sophisticated AI algorithms and the unique limitations inherent in edge environments, characterized by restricted processing power, limited memory capacity, and stringent energy consumption requirements [5, 14].

This section delves into a comprehensive exploration of the foundational toolkits and diverse design models that are instrumental in facilitating the scalable, efficient, and secure deployment of AI capabilities at the network edge. We examine key considerations and architectural patterns that empower developers and organizations to leverage the power of AI in close proximity to data sources and end-users. This includes analysis of various software frameworks optimized for edge devices, deployment strategies that address the challenges of distributed intelligence, and security mechanisms vital for protecting sensitive data and ensuring the integrity of AI models operating at the edge [3, 5, 14].

17.5.1 Comprehensive Exploration of Edge AI Frameworks

The burgeoning field of edge AI, driven by the imperative to process data closer to its source, has spurred the creation of specialized frameworks meticulously engineered to address the distinct challenges inherent in distributed and resource-constrained environments. These sophisticated toolkits serve as invaluable resources for developers, streamlining model compression, inference acceleration across diverse hardware architectures, and ensuring seamless cross-platform compatibility [3–5].

By providing these critical functionalities, edge-AI frameworks empower developers to deploy and execute complex AI workloads on a wide spectrum of devices, ranging from ultra-low-power microcontrollers to high-performance industrial-grade gateways. This democratization of AI at the edge unlocks a plethora of innovative applications across various sectors [4, 5].

17.5.2 TensorFlow Lite: Optimized Intelligence for Mobile and Embedded Systems

Pioneered by Google, TensorFlow Lite represents a meticulously optimized and streamlined iteration of the foundational TensorFlow library, purpose-built for the unique demands of mobile and embedded devices. TensorFlow Lite enables developers to seamlessly deploy and run pre-trained machine learning models with significantly reduced memory footprint and computational overhead [5].

This optimization is crucial for devices with limited resources, ensuring efficient and responsive AI-powered features. TensorFlow Lite models can achieve a reduction in size of up to four times smaller and inference speed increases up to five times faster compared to standard TensorFlow models. These advantages make it the framework of choice for consumer electronics such as smartphones, wearable devices, and smart home appliances. Additionally, TensorFlow Lite supports on-device training, allowing model personalization directly on the user's device, thereby enhancing user privacy [5].

17.5.3 OpenVINO Toolkit: Accelerating Deep Learning Inference Across Intel Architectures

Intel's OpenVINO toolkit accelerates deep learning inference across a diverse range of Intel hardware including CPUs, GPUs, VPUs, and FPGAs. It provides flexibility to optimize AI deployments based on performance and power requirements [3].

OpenVINO is particularly effective in computer vision tasks such as image classification, object detection, and facial recognition. Its applications span healthcare, manufacturing, and security industries where low-latency vision processing is essential [3].

17.5.4 NVIDIA Jetson Platform: Unparalleled Computational Power for Edge AI

The NVIDIA Jetson family offers high-performance computing modules tailored for edge AI systems, including models such as Nano, TX2, Xavier NX, and AGX Orin. These modules support demanding AI workloads in robotics, retail, and autonomous systems [4].

Leveraging NVIDIA's CUDA and TensorRT, Jetson enables seamless transition from AI training to edge deployment. The AGX Orin model delivers up to 275 TOPS, making it ideal for high-throughput edge inference tasks [4].

17.5.5 AWS IoT Greengrass: Extending Cloud Intelligence to the Edge

AWS IoT Greengrass extends cloud capabilities to edge devices, allowing autonomous operation even without continuous cloud connectivity. It supports containerized microservices, local messaging, and seamless model deployment from AWS SageMaker [1].

This solution is beneficial for applications like smart agriculture and industrial IoT, especially in remote areas with unreliable networks [1].

17.5.6 Microsoft Azure Percept: Simplifying Edge AI Development and Deployment

Microsoft Azure Percept integrates edge hardware with Azure cloud AI and IoT services to provide a unified development environment. It offers tools for rapid prototyping, deployment, and management of edge AI applications [14].

Azure Percept lowers the barriers for SMEs and emerging enterprises to adopt edge AI by simplifying the entire development lifecycle [14].

17.5.7 Other Prominent Edge-AI Frameworks

Additional frameworks include Meta's PyTorch Mobile, Apple's Core ML, and Edge Impulse. These platforms cater to specific ecosystems and hardware profiles, enriching the edge AI ecosystem with diverse capabilities and developer tools [5, 14].

17.6 Architecture Models: Building the Foundation for Edge AI

The successful deployment of AI at the edge necessitates more than just selecting the appropriate AI framework. It requires the construction of sophisticated and adaptable architectural models that strategically balance computational performance, scalability, and robust data governance and security mechanisms. The specific demands of a given application often dictate the most suitable architectural pattern, and many organizations implement combinations of these models to achieve optimal results [3, 4, 14].

17.6.1 Cloud-to-Edge Continuum: The Power of Hybrid Intelligence

The Cloud-to-Edge Continuum represents a widely adopted hybrid architecture that divides computational tasks and data processing responsibilities between centralized cloud infrastructure and localized edge devices. Typically, computationally intensive training of large AI models is performed in the cloud, while real-time inference and decision-making occur at the edge [3, 4].

This model supports critical applications such as immediate object recognition in manufacturing and anomaly detection in healthcare equipment, where low latency is paramount. It is increasingly adopted in industries like smart manufacturing and connected healthcare, leveraging the cloud's analytical capabilities while ensuring fast, localized responsiveness [3, 4, 14].

17.6.2 Federated Learning: Distributed Intelligence for Enhanced Privacy

Federated learning is a decentralized machine learning paradigm enabling AI model training across distributed edge devices without transferring sensitive raw data to a central server. Each device trains locally and shares only model updates, which are aggregated to form a global model [9].

This approach enhances privacy and reduces network bandwidth by transmitting small model parameters instead of large datasets. Google's use of federated learning in Gboard exemplifies this paradigm, improving predictive text while preserving user data privacy [9].

Federated learning is gaining traction in sensitive domains such as finance, healthcare, and education, where privacy-preserving AI is crucial [12, 13].

17.6.3 Microservices and Containers: Modularity and Resilience at the Edge

Microservices architecture breaks applications into small, independent services that are packaged into containers for portability and ease of management. Technologies like Docker and orchestration tools such as Kubernetes or lightweight K3s automate deployment, scaling, and lifecycle management across distributed edge infrastructures [14].

This modularity allows independent development and updating of services without affecting the entire system, enhancing resilience. It is especially beneficial in distributed environments such as retail chains, where diverse services (inventory, point-of-sale, digital signage) must operate reliably across many locations [14].

17.6.4 Hierarchical Edge Architecture: Layered Intelligence for Scalable Decision-Making

The Hierarchical Edge Architecture introduces a multi-layered approach to distributing intelligence, spanning from the most granular endpoint devices to increasingly powerful local and regional edge servers, and ultimately reaching the cloud. Each layer in this hierarchy is designed to perform tasks of increasing complexity and aggregation. For example, at the lowest level, a simple camera sensor might be responsible for detecting basic motion events. This raw data or a preliminary analysis (e.g., motion detected) could then be passed on to a nearby edge server. At this mid-level edge, more computationally intensive tasks, such as real-time facial recognition based on the motion event, could be executed. Finally, the results from multiple edge servers across various locations might be aggregated and analyzed in the cloud to perform long-term trend analysis, identify broader patterns, and inform strategic decision-making. This layered architecture ensures an optimized utilization of computational resources, with simpler tasks being handled locally and more complex analytics being reserved for higher level processing. Crucially, it enables scalable and context-aware decision-making across a vast geographic footprint, allowing for localized responsiveness while still benefiting from global insights and coordination. This model is particularly well-suited for large-scale IoT deployments, smart cities, and industrial automation scenarios [3, 4, 6]. The diverse range of frameworks and architectural models outlined here underscores the dynamic and rapidly evolving landscape of modern AI deployment. The prevailing trend is a move towards distributed intelligence, where processing and decision-making are increasingly occurring closer to the source of data and the point of action. This fundamental shift is not merely a technological advancement; it is the catalyst for a new generation of applications that are not only significantly smarter and faster but also inherently more private, remarkably efficient in their resource utilization, and exceptionally adaptable to the complexities and nuances of the physical world around us [5, 11].

Real-World Deployments of Edge AI: Transforming Industries at the Forefront

The convergence of Artificial Intelligence and edge computing is no longer confined to theoretical discussions or laboratory experiments. It has demonstrably matured into a powerful paradigm that is actively revolutionizing a diverse range of industries. This fusion empowers faster, more localized decision-making, significantly enhances safety protocols, and unlocks entirely new business opportunities by bringing computational intelligence closer to the data source [3, 4].

In this chapter, we will delve into five pivotal sectors where edge AI is making substantial inroads. Through detailed case studies, exploration of enabling technologies, and analysis of quantifiable outcomes, we aim to illustrate the profound impact and transformative potential of deploying AI at the edge [5, 10].

Healthcare: Leading in an Era of Precision at the Point of Care

The healthcare industry stands at the cusp of a significant digital revolution, and edge AI is emerging as a critical catalyst in making patient care more responsive, highly personalized, and broadly scalable. By enabling sophisticated real-time diagnostics, continuous patient monitoring, and intelligent data processing near individuals, edge computing is empowering clinicians to make more informed decisions with greater speed, even in environments characterized by limited resources or geographical remoteness. This localized intelligence translates to proactive interventions, improved patient outcomes, and a more efficient healthcare ecosystem [1, 10, 14].

17.6.5 Case Study: Early Detection of Critical Cardiac Events Through AI-Powered Wearable Technology

A compelling illustration of edge AI's impact in healthcare can be seen in the advancements in wearable ECG (Electrocardiogram) monitors utilized in cardiac care. Sophisticated consumer devices, such as the Apple Watch Series 8 and the Withing's Scan Watch, now incorporate on-device AI algorithms specifically designed to detect irregular and potentially life-threatening heart rhythms, most notably atrial fibrillation (AFib). These critical detections are performed in real time, directly on the user's wrist, often functioning independently of a persistent internet connection. This autonomy is crucial in scenarios where immediate connectivity might be unreliable or unavailable. Groundbreaking research published in a 2022 *Nature Medicine* study provided compelling evidence of the efficacy of these AI-driven wearables, demonstrating a remarkable detection accuracy exceeding 95% for a spectrum of common cardiac arrhythmias [7].

17.6.6 Medical Imaging at the Edge: Accelerating Diagnostic Workflows for Timely Treatment

Hospitals and medical facilities are increasingly recognizing the value of deploying AI-powered image analysis tools locally within their infrastructure to dramatically accelerate diagnostic workflows and improve the efficiency of radiology departments. A prominent example of this trend is GE Healthcare's innovative Edison platform. This platform empowers radiologists to execute AI inference algorithms directly on CT (Computed Tomography) and MRI (Magnetic Resonance Imaging) scans using in-hospital edge servers. By bringing the computational power to where the imaging data is generated, the platform significantly reduces the time required for preliminary scan interpretation from several hours to an impressive under 5 min [3, 4, 7]. This substantial reduction in turnaround time is particularly critical in emergency situations where rapid diagnosis is paramount for initiating timely and effective treatment, potentially improving patient prognoses and resource utilization. The ability to perform complex image analysis locally also addresses concerns related to data privacy and the latency associated with transmitting large medical images to cloud-based processing centers.

17.6.7 Remote Patient Monitoring (RPM): Extending Healthcare Reach and Empowering Patients

Edge-enabled medical devices are playing an increasingly vital role in the proactive management of chronic health conditions, such as diabetes and Chronic Obstructive Pulmonary Disease (COPD), by facilitating effective Remote Patient Monitoring (RPM). For instance, advanced glucose monitors equipped with edge AI capabilities can now analyze blood glucose levels in real time and autonomously alert both patients and their caregivers to potentially dangerous hypo- or hyperglycemic events, all without requiring constant or even intermittent cloud connectivity. This localized intelligence ensures immediate feedback and allows for swift corrective actions. Furthermore, the impact of edge AI in RPM is being felt in underserved communities. According to data from the World Health Organization, the implementation of RPM systems powered by edge AI in rural clinics in India has demonstrably reduced the number of unnecessary hospital visits by an impressive 30% [8]. This reduction highlights the potential of edge AI to extend the reach of quality healthcare, improve patient convenience, and alleviate the burden on healthcare facilities, particularly in geographically dispersed or resource-constrained regions.

17.7 Industrial IoT: Forging Intelligent Factories and Cultivating Safer Workplaces

In the demanding landscape of industrial environments, operational downtime translates directly into significant financial losses, and maintaining the highest standards of safety is an absolute imperative. Edge AI is proving to be a transformative technology for manufacturers, enabling them to build smarter, more efficient, and demonstrably safer operational processes. This is achieved by leveraging the power of real-time analysis of vast amounts of data generated by industrial sensors and visual inspection systems deployed throughout their facilities. By processing this information locally at the edge, manufacturers can gain immediate insights, implement proactive measures, and optimize their operations with unprecedented agility [4, 5].

17.7.1 Case Study: Predictive Maintenance Revolution at a Global Wind Farm

A compelling example of the transformative power of edge AI in industrial settings is the deployment of this technology by a global energy company across its extensive network of wind turbines. To mitigate the risks of unexpected equipment failures and optimize maintenance schedules, the company implemented an edge AI-powered system designed to continuously analyze critical operational data, specifically vibration patterns and temperature readings, in real time. This sophisticated system leverages robust NVIDIA Jetson modules, providing the necessary computational horsepower at the edge, and employs a proprietary in-house developed anomaly detection model [4]. The system demonstrated a remarkable ability to accurately predict impending gearbox failures up to 10 days in advance of their occurrence. This proactive maintenance strategy has yielded significant benefits, resulting in a substantial reduction in unscheduled downtime by 27%. Furthermore, by anticipating and addressing potential failures before they materialize, the company has realized savings of millions of dollars in avoided repair costs and prevented significant losses in energy production.

17.7.2 Elevating Quality Assurance with Edge-Based Computer Vision Systems

A leading manufacturer of automotive parts has successfully integrated edge-based computer vision systems directly into its production line to significantly enhance the rigor and efficiency of its quality assurance processes. Strategically positioned cameras equipped with on-device inference capabilities meticulously inspect each component for even the most subtle defects as it moves along the assembly line. These systems utilize sophisticated AI models, optimized for speed and efficiency using Intel's OpenVINO toolkit [3]. The implementation of this edge AI solution has enabled the manufacturer to achieve impressive inspection speeds of 250 parts per minute while maintaining an exceptional accuracy rate of over 99%, all with no impact on production throughput.

17.7.3 Proactive Worker Safety Monitoring Through Intelligent Wearable Devices

The safety and well-being of workers in hazardous industrial environments, such as mining and construction sites, are paramount concerns. Edge AI is enabling significant advancements in worker safety through the deployment of intelligent wearable devices. These devices are equipped with sensors and on-board AI capabilities that allow for continuous monitoring of critical parameters, including worker movements, potential indicators of fatigue, and environmental conditions such as exposure to toxic gases. In a notable project spearheaded by Honeywell, AI-driven wearable technology was implemented in high-risk zones, resulting in a remarkable 40% reduction in safety incidents over a 12-month period [6].

17.8 Smart Cities: Building Responsive Infrastructure for Enhanced Urban Living

The concept of smart cities relies heavily on the intelligent processing of data generated across various urban systems to create infrastructure that is more adaptive, sustainable, and citizen-centric. Edge AI plays a crucial role in realizing this vision by enabling cities to process vast amounts of data locally, at the source of its generation. This localized processing capability allows for split-second decision-making and real-time adjustments that can significantly improve the daily lives of urban residents while respecting data privacy concerns [1, 4].

17.8.1 Case Study: Barcelona's Real-Time Traffic Management System Powered by Edge AI

The city of Barcelona has emerged as a leader in smart city initiatives, and its implementation of a real-time traffic management system serves as a compelling example of the effectiveness of edge AI. The city strategically deployed a network of edge-enabled cameras and sophisticated AI algorithms at key intersections throughout the urban area. These systems continuously monitor real-time vehicle flow and pedestrian activity. The algorithms then analyze this data locally to dynamically adjust traffic light cycles in direct response to current conditions. According to the city's 2023 sustainability report, this intelligent traffic management system has achieved a 21% reduction in average wait times at intersections and a 15% decrease in carbon emissions [15].

17.9 Technical Deep Dive

To unlock the full potential of AI at the edge, it's essential to understand the underlying technologies that make it work from the hardware performing on-device inference to the software and network layers supporting deployment, scalability, and security. This section explores the technical foundation of edge AI, highlighting key innovations that have enabled intelligent computation beyond the cloud.

17.9.1 Hardware

The edge AI revolution has been powered in large part by advancements in specialized hardware that can perform inference with low latency and energy consumption. Unlike traditional data centers, edge environments impose strict constraints on power, form factor, and compute capabilities requiring purpose-built hardware [16, 17].

- *Edge TPUs*: Google's Coral Edge TPU is a prime example of an application-specific integrated circuit (ASIC) optimized for edge inference. These chips can execute 4 trillion operations per second (TOPS) using just a few watts of power [14].
- *FPGAs*: FPGAs provide highly parallelized, reconfigurable hardware suitable for customized AI workloads. Companies like Xilinx (now AMD) use FPGAs in automotive and telecom applications [17].
- *Low-Power MCUs with ML Capabilities*: Modern MCUs like ARM Cortex-M and NXP i.MX RT series support local execution of lightweight ML models on minimal power [7].

- *GPU-Powered Edge Boards*: NVIDIA's Jetson series (Nano, Xavier NX, Orin) supports up to 275 TOPS and is popular in autonomous systems [8].

17.9.2 Networking

Edge AI's performance hinges not only on compute power but also on the efficiency of the network infrastructure [2].

- *5G Networks*: With <1 ms latency and >10 Gbps throughput, 5G enables real-time AI applications in areas like telemedicine and robotics [9].
- *Network Slicing*: 5G enables custom virtual networks tailored for edge use cases [9].
- *Multi-access Edge Computing (MEC)*: MEC places compute/storage near base stations, reducing latency [2].

17.9.3 Security and Privacy

Edge deployments require strong security due to exposure to physical tampering and data sensitivity [12].

- *TEEs*: ARM TrustZone, Intel SGX allow secure enclaves on devices [12].
- *Hardware Root of Trust*: Ensures firmware integrity [12].
- *On-Device Encryption*: Edge devices implement AES-256 encryption and secure enclaves [13].
- *Federated Learning and Differential Privacy*: Google and Apple use these for privacy-preserving personalization [13].

17.9.4 Model Optimization

To run models efficiently on edge devices, several optimization strategies are used:

- *Quantization*: Reduces model size and latency, e.g., TensorFlow Lite [16].
- *Pruning*: Eliminates redundant neurons, improving performance with little accuracy loss.
- *Knowledge Distillation*: A small student model mimics a larger teacher model's performance.
- *On-Device Training*: Allows personalization via local data even offline.

17.9.5 Software Ecosystem

- *Lightweight Kubernetes*: K3s, MicroK8s are used for orchestration in constrained environments.
- *CI/CD for ML*: Tools like Kubeflow and MLflow support MLOps.
- *Monitoring Tools*: Prometheus, Grafana, EdgeX Foundry monitor performance and anomalies.

17.10 Challenges and Future Outlook

17.10.1 Challenges

Despite the promise, edge AI must overcome hurdles:

- Resource limitations in compute, memory, and power
- Complex, large-scale deployment and updates
- Fragmented, inconsistent data
- Security vulnerabilities and outdated firmware
- Lack of standardization across platforms

17.10.2 Future Outlook

- Custom AI chips from Apple, Google, NVIDIA will boost efficiency
- Federated edge intelligence will improve with collaborative learning
- Networks will evolve toward SDN and auto-scaling swarms
- Green edge AI will rise with renewable energy and efficiency goals
- Regulation will push for ethical, explainable edge AI systems

17.11 Conclusion

Edge AI isn't a vision of the future. It is happening now and shaping the foundation of tomorrow's connected world. The intersection of artificial intelligence and edge computing represents a major advancement towards intelligent, distributed systems with real-time capabilities for perception, analysis, and action. Edge AI is currently revolutionizing many aspects of our daily lives and work, including applications in wearable health devices, industrial automation, self-driving vehicles, and intelligent infrastructure.

However, fully utilizing the power of edge AI necessitates careful consideration of privacy, security, sustainability, and the ability of different systems to work together, in addition to technological advancements. With the evolution of frameworks, increasingly powerful hardware, and more streamlined deployment processes, the edge is on track to become a critical and intelligent tier, rather than merely an extension of cloud computing. Edge AI is not a distant prospect; it is a current-day reality that is actively constructing the groundwork for the interconnected world of the future.

References

1. Gartner. (2021). *The future of edge computing: By 2025, 75% of enterprise-generated data will be created and processed outside a traditional centralized data center or cloud.* Gartner Report.
2. GSMA. (2021). *Mobile-edge computing white paper. GSMA edge computing for 5G networks.*
3. Intel Corporation. (2023). *OpenVINO toolkit overview*. Intel OpenVINO toolkit documentation.
4. NVIDIA. (2024). *Jetson AI at the edge*. NVIDIA Jetson Developer Portal.
5. Amazon Web Services. (2024). *AWS IoT greengrass*. AWS IoT greengrass documentation.
6. Microsoft. (2024). *Azure percept overview*. Microsoft Azure Percept Platform.
7. Kubeflow Community. (2024). *Kubeflow docs. Kubeflow and MLOps for edge deployment.*
8. McKinsey & Company. (2023). *AI on the edge: Custom silicon and the new frontier of intelligent hardware*. McKinsey Article.
9. Perez, M. V., Mahaffey, K. W., Hedlin, H., et al. (2022). Large-scale assessment of a smartwatch to identify atrial fibrillation. *Nature Medicine, 25*, 105–109. https://doi.org/10.1038/s41591-019-0353-9
10. Google AI Blog. (2017). *Federated learning: Collaborative machine learning without centralized training data*. Retrieved June 10, 2025, from https://ai.googleblog.com/2017/04/federated-learning-collaborative.html.
11. TensorFlow. (2024). *TensorFlow Lite. TensorFlow Lite developer guide.*
12. European Union. (2016). Regulation (EU) 2016/679 of the European Parliament and of the Council of 27 April 2016 (General data protection regulation). Official Journal of the European Union, L119. Retrieved from https://eur-lex.europa.eu/eli/reg/2016/679/oj.
13. U.S. Department of Health & Human Services. (1996). Health insurance portability and accountability act of 1996 (HIPAA). Public Law 104–191. Retrieved from https://www.hhs.gov/hipaa/index.html.
14. National Institute of Standards and Technology. (2020). *Security considerations for edge computing*. NIST SP 800-207A.
15. PatentPC. *Smart traffic management stats—Congestion reduction via AI integration*. Retrieved June 10, 2025, from https://patentpc.com/blog/smart-traffic-management-stats-congestion-reduction-ai-integration.
16. IEEE Communications Magazine. (2022). A survey on edge artificial intelligence in 6G: Applications, technologies, and open issues. IEEE Communications Magazine. https://doi.org/10.1109/MCOM.001.2000407.
17. Edge Impulse Inc. (2024). *Edge ML for developers*. Edge Impulse Platform.

Chapter 18
Sustainable FinOps: Balancing Cloud Costs and Carbon Footprints

Anaranya Bagchi

Abstract As digital transformation accelerates, organizations must manage cloud costs while addressing environmental sustainability. This chapter introduces Sustainable Financial Operations (FinOps)—an evolving practice that integrates financial accountability with carbon-conscious cloud operations. Once focused solely on cost optimization, FinOps now expands to include emissions reduction, driven by regulatory mandates and stakeholder expectations.

The chapter outlines tools and strategies—such as rightsizing, carbon-aware scheduling, and geographic optimization—that help organizations measure and minimize their carbon footprint associated with cloud usage. It also explores the management of Scope 1, 2, and 3 emissions, the importance of transparent reporting, and collaboration with cloud providers.

A maturity model is proposed to guide the journey from basic visibility to predictive, sustainable optimization. Key enablers include cross-functional teamwork, upskilling, and cultural change, as well as addressing challenges such as data inconsistency and cost-carbon tradeoffs.

Sustainable FinOps is presented not just as a technical fix but as a strategic shift that enables resilient, efficient, and environmentally responsible cloud infrastructures.

Keywords FinOps · Sustainability · Cloud cost management · Sustainable FinOps

18.1 Introduction

The cloud computing revolution has reached an inflection point where its environmental impact now rivals its economic significance. As digital transformation accelerates across industries, global data centers are projected to consume 1000 TWh of electricity annually by 2026, equivalent to Japan's total energy consumption and

A. Bagchi (✉)
Seattle, WA, USA

B. Pandey, A. Patel (eds.), *Revolutionizing the Cloud*,
https://doi.org/10.1007/978-3-032-07479-9_18

accounting for 2.5% of worldwide electricity use [1]. The rapid growth of AI and widespread cloud adoption are driving up energy demand, putting pressure on companies to manage rising cloud costs while meeting increasingly stringent environmental regulations. Modern cloud solutions must now deliver both cost efficiency and sustainability.

Sustainability has emerged as a core pillar of long-term business strategy, transcending its former role within isolated Corporate Social Responsibility (CSR) efforts. Organizations are increasingly adopting triple-bottom-line frameworks that assign equal importance to financial, social, and environmental performance. This shift reflects growing stakeholder expectations and a broader recognition of the business sector's responsibility in advancing global sustainability goals.

FinOps, which traditionally focused on maximizing cloud cost efficiency through collaboration among engineering, finance, and operations teams, is undergoing a significant transformation. In response to heightened Environmental, Social, and Governance (ESG) expectations and mounting regulatory pressures—such as mandatory greenhouse gas (GHG) disclosures—FinOps now incorporates environmental impact as a critical dimension. The discipline is evolving from purely financial optimization to dual optimization of cost and carbon emissions.

This evolution is not without challenges. The dynamic and abstract nature of cloud environments, particularly in comparison to traditional on-premises infrastructure, complicates the tracking of energy consumption and emissions, especially those categorized under Scope 3. Cloud service providers often offer limited transparency, hindering efforts to align with science-based targets and comply with frameworks such as the EU's Corporate Sustainability Reporting Directive (CSRD) and the Greenhouse Gas Protocol.

Nonetheless, cloud computing offers capabilities—such as automation, real-time analytics, and elastic resource allocation—that, when combined with FinOps practices, can drive meaningful improvements in sustainability. This chapter examines the convergence of FinOps and environmental accountability, outlining tools, standards, and governance strategies that enable organizations to embed sustainability into cloud financial management and build resilient, future-oriented digital infrastructures.

18.2 Background and Context

Global greenhouse gas (GHG) emissions from the technology sector are comparable to, and in some cases exceed, those from the aviation industry, currently estimated at approximately 3% for Information and Communications Technology (ICT) and 2% for aviation. Within the ICT sector, data centers alone are responsible for approximately 1% of global greenhouse gas (GHG) emissions and electricity consumption, equivalent to roughly 200–250 terawatt-hours (TWh) [2]. If left unaddressed, these emissions could grow significantly, contributing up to 10% of global greenhouse gas (GHG) emissions within the next decade.

Currently, most cloud service providers offer limited energy and carbon emission reporting, typically restricted to Scope 1 and Scope 2 emissions [3]. This presents significant challenges for organizations aiming to measure, manage, and reduce their overall carbon footprint, particularly across all three scopes, including Scope 3, which often involves indirect emissions in the value chain.

Accurately measuring greenhouse gas (GHG) emissions is a fundamental prerequisite for any effective carbon management strategy. Carbon accounting, or "footprinting," involves creating a detailed inventory of emissions associated with an organization, product, or service. Establishing a reliable baseline is crucial for tracking reductions over time.

The Greenhouse Gas (GHG) Protocol remains the leading global standard for carbon accounting, adopted by over 90% of Fortune 500 companies. It encompasses not only carbon dioxide (CO_2) but also methane, nitrous oxide, and hydrofluorocarbons, quantified using global warming potential (GWP) and reported in carbon dioxide equivalents (CO_2e).

As of 2015, the ICT sector was responsible for an estimated 730 million tons of CO_2e, comparable to emissions from the aviation industry. Despite efficiency gains in data centers, the explosive growth of digital services has outpaced these improvements. The sector's complexity and decentralization make precise carbon accounting challenging yet also present unique opportunities due to the availability of granular digital data.

The distinction between on-premises and cloud infrastructure adds further complexity. Cloud adoption often shifts emissions from Scope 1 and 2 (direct and purchased energy use) to Scope 3 (indirect supply chain emissions), which are frequently underreported. Increasingly, organizations are expected to take responsibility for these indirect emissions.

A major obstacle remains the inconsistent reporting of emissions among cloud providers. Disparities in Scope 3 methodologies and limited data granularity hinder the development of standardized and accurate accounting. Without greater transparency and alignment across providers, organizations will struggle to assess and reduce the actual environmental impact of their cloud operations.

18.3 Scope 1, 2, and 3 Emissions

Greenhouse gas (GHG) emissions are categorized into three scopes (as shown in Fig. 18.1) to help organizations comprehensively understand and manage their environmental impact.

- **Scope 1 emissions** refer to direct emissions from sources owned or controlled by the organization, such as those from company vehicles or on-site fuel combustion.
- **Scope 2 emissions** refer to indirect emissions resulting from the generation of electricity, steam, heat, or cooling that an organization purchases or uses to meet

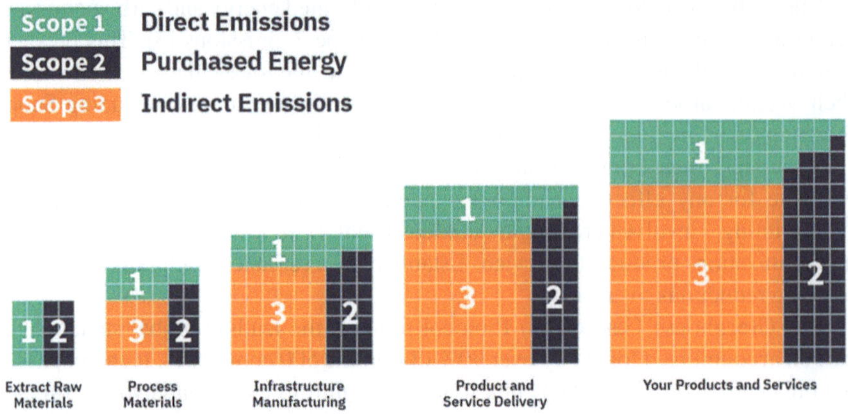

Fig. 18.1 Environmental Protection Agency definition of scopes [3]

its needs. These occur at the facility where the energy is produced but are accounted for in the organization's carbon footprint.

- **Scope 3 emissions** encompass all other indirect emissions across the organization's value chain, including both upstream and downstream activities. This includes supplier emissions, business travel, product use, waste disposal, and cloud computing services. While Scope 3 emissions are often the most significant in scale, they are also the most challenging to measure and manage due to limited visibility and lack of direct control. Addressing all three scopes is essential for a comprehensive and credible sustainability strategy.

Scope 3 emissions are increasingly vital to understand and manage because they typically account for the majority of an organization's total carbon footprint, often exceeding 70% [3]. Unlike Scope 1 (direct emissions) and Scope 2 (indirect emissions from purchased energy), Scope 3 covers all other indirect emissions across a company's value chain, such as manufacturing, transportation, waste, commuting, and cloud services. For cloud customers, emissions typically fall under Scope 3, as providers own the infrastructure. However, customer choices regarding resource efficiency, architecture, and scheduling have a significant impact on these emissions. Thus, organizations can significantly influence Scope 3 emissions despite lacking direct control. Measuring and reducing Scope 3 emissions is vital for achieving net-zero goals, ensuring transparency, and meeting stakeholder and regulatory expectations.

Examples of Scope 3 emissions include:

- Supply chain emissions are from the production and transportation of raw materials and goods.
- Business travel and employee commuting.
- Use of sold products, such as the energy consumed when customers operate electronic devices.
- Waste generated from operations or products.

- Cloud computing and digital services, where emissions arise from third-party data centers.
- Capital goods, such as the embedded emissions in purchased machinery and infrastructure.

By focusing on Scope 3, organizations can identify hidden emissions hotspots, promote sustainable practices within their networks, and make informed procurement and design choices that reduce their long-term environmental impact.

The 2025 FinOps Foundation Report highlights that while sustainability reporting in cloud operations has seen only marginal global growth—a 1% increase over the past year—importance is rising, particularly in Europe, where 53% of organizations now track cloud carbon emissions, up 18% year over year [4].

Based on the report, organizations must integrate sustainability criteria into cloud optimization, strike a balance between environmental efficiency and financial value, and align cloud decisions with their broader organizational sustainability goals. This is increasingly crucial as regulations tighten and as the tech sector's greenhouse gas emissions continue to rival those of the aviation industry, with data centers alone accounting for about 1% of global emissions [4].

Global sustainability regulations are redefining cloud management by requiring organizations to monitor, report, and reduce environmental impact. Mandates on carbon disclosure and energy efficiency are prompting both providers and users to adopt greener practices. This shift is moving cloud strategies beyond cost optimization toward models that balance financial performance with environmental responsibility. Consequently, enterprises are prioritizing energy-efficient architectures, sustainable regions, and enhanced visibility of carbon emissions.

Regulatory Catalysts: A few such regulations [5] from different geographies are described below:

1. European Union—Corporate Sustainability Reporting Directive (CSRD)
    - Prominent companies operating in the EU are required to disclose environmental, social, and governance (ESG) metrics, including carbon emissions and energy usage.
    - Cloud service providers and their customers must track and report emissions from digital infrastructure.
2. United States—SEC Climate Disclosure Rule (Proposed)
    - The US Securities and Exchange Commission is introducing rules that require public companies to disclose climate-related risks, including Scope 1 and 2 emissions, as well as potentially Scope 3 emissions (which includes cloud services).
3. United Kingdom—Streamlined Energy and Carbon Reporting (SECR)
    - UK-based large companies are required to disclose their energy use and carbon emissions in their annual reports, which often include data centers and cloud usage.

4. Singapore—Green Data Centre Standards
   - Singapore has developed strict guidelines under the BCA-IMDA Green Mark for Data Centers to ensure energy-efficient operations in a resource-scarce environment.
5. Japan—GX (Green Transformation) League
   - A public-private initiative promoting climate-conscious business practices, including digital carbon footprint transparency and reduction targets.
6. Australia—Climate Active Certification
   - A voluntary but influential program that helps companies measure, reduce, and offset carbon emissions, including from digital operations, to achieve net-zero certification.

These regulations are accelerating the integration of FinOps and sustainability practices, requiring organizations to adopt tools and processes that enable financial efficiency and environmental compliance in cloud computing.

18.4 Principles and Frameworks

The FinOps Foundation, a part of the Linux Foundation, has evolved its mission beyond managing cloud costs to include the critical priority of cloud sustainability [6]. As enterprises increasingly prioritize environmental responsibility, the Foundation recognizes that cloud usage must be evaluated not only in terms of cost and performance but also in terms of its carbon impact. Cloud sustainability within FinOps involves optimizing cloud resources to minimize financial expenditure and reduce environmental footprint, with a focus on energy consumption and carbon emissions.

According to the Foundation, many practices that lead to cost savings also directly contribute to sustainability goals. Techniques such as rightsizing instances, turning off idle resources, and optimizing workload efficiency reduce spending and minimize energy consumption in data centers. Since cloud providers rely on massive computing infrastructure, any reduction in resource usage has a proportional impact on greenhouse gas emissions, especially when workloads are hosted in regions powered by non-renewable energy.

Research on Australian businesses shows that those adopting cloud-based sustainability practices and integrating FinOps frameworks achieved a 90% decrease in IT-related carbon emissions and a 25–30% reduction in operating costs. These findings highlight the success of merging financial operations with sustainability efforts in cloud settings [1].

The FinOps Foundation emphasizes the significance of a data-driven approach, urging organizations to leverage available telemetry and metrics to inform their sustainability decisions. This includes monitoring usage patterns, utilizing automation to reduce waste, and analyzing reports on energy consumption and emissions generated by cloud providers. As a result, sustainability becomes a measurable and actionable component of cloud governance, embedded into the same workflows used for cost and usage monitoring.

18.4.1 FinOps Framework

The FinOps Framework, as shown in Fig. 18.2, provides the operating model for establishing and excelling in the practice of FinOps.

In the FinOps Framework, Cloud Sustainability aligns closely with the "Optimize Usage & Cost" domain, as reducing environmental impact depends on efficient resource consumption. Wasteful cloud usage—such as overprovisioned instances, idle storage, and unnecessary data transfers—increases both costs and carbon emissions. By optimizing usage, organizations achieve financial savings while lowering their cloud carbon footprint, demonstrating that sustainability and cost efficiency are complementary goals. Incorporating sustainability into cost optimization empowers teams to make informed decisions, such as rightsizing workloads, scheduling tasks during periods of cleaner energy, and choosing low-carbon regions, thereby maximizing business value per cloud dollar.

Cloud sustainability encompasses both the energy required to power and cool data centers, as well as the embodied carbon throughout the cloud service lifecycle, from raw materials acquisition to hardware disposal. Cloud's flexible, on-demand nature offers more optimization opportunities than traditional infrastructure, making Cloud Sustainability teams key drivers of IT carbon reduction.

Fig. 18.2 FinOps Framework as defined by FinOps Foundation [6]

However, sustainability data from cloud providers varies in scope, detail, and reliability. FinOps and Sustainability teams must collaborate to define needed data granularity and adjust provider data for internal reporting. Despite ongoing data quality challenges, organizations should engage vendors to improve data transparency. Importantly, using available—even imperfect—data enables timely decisions on architecture, usage, and costs, driving meaningful sustainability progress without waiting for perfect information.

The FinOps Foundation views sustainability as a key pillar of cloud financial management. Organizations can simultaneously achieve cost control and carbon reduction by extending established FinOps practices to include environmental efficiency, thereby demonstrating responsible cloud stewardship that aligns with broader ESG goals.

18.4.2 Maturity Assessment

The Maturity Assessment of Cloud Sustainability provides a structured framework [7] to evaluate how effectively organizations integrate environmental considerations into their cloud usage and FinOps practices across progressive capability stages: Crawl, Walk, and Run.

1. **Crawl—Foundational Awareness and Initial Efforts**: At this stage, key teams involved in cloud operations understand how cloud computing contributes to greenhouse gas (GHG) emissions. Cloud engineers and operations staff recognize the link between cloud optimization and carbon usage reduction. While there may be a high-level corporate mandate to report or reduce carbon emissions, applying this directive to cloud-specific activities remains underdeveloped. Some carbon emissions data is available, but tends to be fragmented and poorly integrated with cost or usage information. Optimization efforts are primarily reactive and focus on basic elasticity measures, such as shutting down unused resources. Where tradeoffs between cost and carbon arise, they are addressed generally and often relate to already deployed workloads. Enterprise stakeholders, including procurement, finance, and business units, have a limited understanding of how cloud decisions impact emissions.
2. **Walk—Developing Capabilities and Strategic Integration**: In the Walk phase, most engineering teams and other roles engaged in cloud operations are aware of their influence on the organization's broader sustainability objectives. Cloud teams employ diverse strategies to reduce carbon impact through targeted optimization initiatives. Carbon emissions data is more granular and is shared with engineering and product teams though it may still be partially siloed from financial data. Optimization strategies expand to include workload re-architecting and refactoring to improve long-term efficiency and sustainability. Tradeoffs between cost and carbon emissions are assessed more precisely, and such considerations begin to influence decisions earlier in the development lifecycle, such as during

cloud migration planning or architectural design. Collaboration across disciplines becomes more frequent, fostering alignment between technology choices and environmental goals.

3. **Run—Advanced Integration and Proactive Optimization**: At the Run stage, sustainability is embedded into the culture and practices of the entire organization, with a clear recognition of IT's and cloud's roles in the company's environmental footprint. Sustainability considerations are systematically integrated into workload migration, design, and optimization processes. Reporting of carbon emissions is standardized across cloud service providers (CSPs), with data that is highly granular, aligned with cost information, and attributable to individual teams or business units for targeted analysis and action. Cloud workloads are proactively architected with sustainability in mind, and teams use emissions data to inform decisions about where and how to run workloads before deployment. This maturity level reflects a sophisticated, data-driven approach where sustainability and financial optimization mutually reinforce priorities.

18.5 Optimization and Tracking Sustainability

Organizations are increasingly utilizing strategic workload deployment to lower their carbon footprint associated with cloud computing, significantly enhancing energy efficiency and environmental performance. Recent studies on carbon-aware computing have shown that data centers can reduce carbon emissions by 45–55% through intelligent workload distribution and scheduling. Furthermore, the implementation of carbon-aware load balancing algorithms has been shown to lower the consumption of brown energy by up to 31%, all while maintaining required service quality standards [8].

1. **Usage Optimization**

   Usage optimization aligns cloud resource consumption with workload demands, avoiding energy waste and unnecessary emissions. This involves right-sizing instances, removing unused or idle resources, and leveraging elasticity features like autoscaling or serverless architectures. Organizations can significantly reduce their energy usage and associated carbon footprint by tailoring resource allocation to real-time needs while improving cost efficiency. These efforts represent a foundational step in any sustainability-focused cloud strategy.
2. **Geographic Optimization**

   Data centers located in cooler climates or regions with abundant renewable energy sources can significantly mitigate their environmental impact. Research on geographic optimization in cloud computing shows that selecting optimal locations can reduce overall energy consumption by 30–40%. Furthermore, the effective distribution of workloads across varying temperature zones can result in energy savings of up to 25% [1]. This approach makes geographically distributed cloud architectures a compelling strategy for reducing operational costs and minimizing environmental impact. Studies have shown that data centers located in colder environments can improve cooling efficiency by up to 38% compared to those situated in warmer regions.

3. **Architectural Optimization**

   Architectural optimization involves designing or refining applications to enhance efficiency and minimize environmental impact. Cloud-native architectures, such as those built with microservices and containers, are generally more resource-efficient and scalable. Additionally, utilizing managed services, such as databases, queues, and analytics tools provided by cloud suppliers, can further streamline operations, as these services are often optimized for performance and energy efficiency. Organizations can build performant and environmentally responsible systems by adopting sustainable design principles during development and modernization efforts.

4. **Temporal Optimization (Carbon-Aware Scheduling)**

   Temporal optimization, also known as carbon-aware scheduling, focuses on timing workloads to coincide with periods of lower carbon intensity on the electricity grid. Data processing tasks can be scheduled to run when renewable energy is most abundant or during periods of low grid demand. This strategy significantly reduces an organization's Scope 2 emissions, particularly for non-time-sensitive activities like batch processing or analytics. Incorporating time-based energy awareness into scheduling logic promotes a more dynamic and environmentally conscious utilization of cloud resources. Studies show that data centers can reduce their carbon footprint by up to 50% during periods of high renewable energy use by implementing advanced carbon-awareness algorithms [9].

18.5.1 Cloud Sustainability by Cloud Providers

AWS, Azure, and Google Cloud Platform (GCP) each provide customers with tools and dashboards to calculate the carbon footprint of their cloud usage, using methodologies based on the Greenhouse Gas (GHG) Protocol and relevant ISO standards. Here is how each cloud provider approaches carbon footprint calculation

1. **AWS: Customer Carbon Footprint Tool (CCFT)**

   - Methodology:
     - AWS's CCFT estimates the carbon emissions associated with a customer's use of AWS services, following the GHG Protocol Corporate Standard, Product Standard, and related ISO standards (ISO 14040/44, ISO 14067) [10]
     - Scopes Covered:

       Scope 1: Direct emissions from AWS-owned sources (e.g., fuel combustion in backup generators).

Scope 2: Indirect emissions from purchased electricity, using market-based emission factors that reflect regional grid mixes and AWS renewable energy procurement.

- Allocation:
  - Emissions are allocated from AWS data center clusters down to server racks, specific services, and customer accounts based on actual usage. Unused capacity and overhead are also proportionally allocated to all customers, reflecting the actual environmental cost of providing cloud services.
- Granularity:
  - Provides emissions data by AWS region and service, with monthly updates available via dashboard and export.

2. **Azure: Emissions Impact Dashboard (Formerly Sustainability Calculator)**
   - Methodology:
     - Azure calculates emissions using a lifecycle assessment approach, consistent with the GHG Protocol, covering Scope 1, 2, and selected Scope 3 emissions (manufacturing, transportation, use, and end-of-life of data center hardware). [11]
   - Scopes Covered:
     - Scope 1: Direct emissions from Microsoft-owned operations.
     - Scope 2: Indirect emissions from electricity use, factoring in grid emission factors, renewable energy purchases, and data center/server efficiency.
     - Scope 3: Indirect emissions from the supply chain, including hardware manufacturing and disposal.
   - Allocation:
     - Customer emissions are calculated based on their relative usage of Azure services in each data center region, using usage factors that apportion emissions proportionally to each customer.
   - Granularity:
     - Granular emissions data by subscription, resource group, resource, and region.
3. **GCP: Google Cloud Carbon Footprint**
   - Methodology:
     - GCP uses the GHG Protocol and provides both location-based and market-based emissions data. Calculations are based on machine-level power and activity monitoring in Google data centers, allowing for granular allocation to services and customers [12]

- Scopes Covered:
  - Scope 1: Direct emissions from Google-owned sources.
  - Scope 2: Indirect electricity emissions, reported as location-based (actual grid mix) and market-based (reflecting Google's renewable energy purchases).
  - Scope 3: Indirect value chain emissions allocated for customer reporting.
- Allocation:
  - Emissions are allocated to customers based on their specific usage of Google Cloud services, products, and regions, using both hourly (for location-based) and annual (for market-based) emission factors.
- Granularity:
  - Dashboards and BigQuery exports for emissions data by service, project, region, and month (Table 18.1).

18.5.2 Key Sustainability KPIs

As cloud adoption grows, businesses must monitor the relevant sustainability Key Performance Indicators (KPIs). This practice enables them to measure their progress, identify areas for improvement, and align their IT strategies with broader environmental goals. These KPIs offer insights into energy consumption, carbon emissions, resource efficiency, and the effectiveness of green initiatives. By tracking these indicators, businesses can make informed decisions and ensure compliance with changing regulations.

The most important and widely recognized sustainability KPIs include:

- Energy Consumption (kWh):
- Measures the total amount of electrical energy cloud infrastructure consumes over a specific period. Lower energy consumption indicates greater efficiency and a reduced environmental footprint [13]
- Carbon Footprint (kgCO_2e or metric tons CO_2e):

Table 18.1 Cloud sustainability scopes by cloud providers

Cloud provider	Tool/Platform	Scopes covered	Methodology basis	Allocation granularity
AWS	Customer Carbon Footprint Tool	Scope 1 and 2	GHG Protocol, ISO 14040/44	Region, service, customer account
Azure	Emissions Impact Dashboard	Scope 1, 2, 3	GHG Protocol, LCA	Region, resource, subscription
GCP	Cloud Carbon Footprint	Scope 1, 2, 3	GHG Protocol	Region, service, project

- Quantifies total greenhouse gas emissions associated with cloud operations, often expressed as kilograms or metric tons of carbon dioxide equivalent. This KPI considers the energy source, with renewable energy resulting in a lower carbon footprint [14]
- Power Usage Effectiveness (PUE):
- The total facility energy consumption ratio is the energy consumed by IT equipment. A lower PUE (closer to 1.0) means that more energy is used for computing than for overhead, such as cooling or lighting, reflecting higher efficiency.
- Water Usage Effectiveness (WUE):
- Measures the amount of water used for cooling and operations per unit of IT energy consumption. Lower WUE values indicate better water efficiency, which is especially important in regions with water scarcity.
- Carbon Usage Effectiveness (CUE):
- Assesses the carbon emissions associated with data center energy use, helping organizations benchmark and reduce their carbon impact.
- Renewable Energy Utilization/Renewable Energy Factor (REF):
- Tracks the percentage of total energy sourced from renewables. A higher share of renewables directly reduces carbon emissions, demonstrating a commitment to sustainability.
- Electronic Waste (E-Waste) Generation (kg):
- Measures the amount of obsolete or discarded electronic equipment generated by cloud operations. Responsible management and recycling of e-waste are essential to reducing environmental impact.
- The Energy Efficiency Ratio (EER) of cooling systems is a crucial metric, particularly in data centers, where these systems consume significant amounts of energy. The EER measures the effectiveness of cooling systems by comparing the cooling capacity (measured in watts) to the electrical input (also measured in watts) needed to operate the cooling equipment. The EER is calculated by dividing the cooling capacity by the electrical input. A higher EER indicates that the system can remove more heat for each unit of energy consumed, demonstrating superior energy efficiency and a reduced environmental impact [15]

Tracking these KPIs enables organizations to benchmark progress, identify inefficiencies, and continuously improve environmental and operational performance.

18.6 Challenges and Future Outlook

As organizations increasingly adopt cloud computing, integrating FinOps with sustainability goals—often referred to as Sustainable FinOps—has become a critical imperative. This integration aims to strike a balance between optimizing cloud costs and reducing environmental impact, particularly carbon emissions. However, reaching this balance involves several technological, organizational, economic, and regulatory challenges. At the same time, innovations and changing market dynamics present promising opportunities to overcome these obstacles and create a sustainable future for cloud computing.

18.6.1 Challenges in Implementing Sustainable FinOps

1. **Organizational and Cultural Barriers**

   One of the primary challenges in adopting Sustainable FinOps is overcoming organizational silos and cultural resistance. Traditionally, separate teams with distinct priorities have managed cloud financial management and sustainability. FinOps teams focus primarily on cost control, budgeting, and efficiency, while sustainability teams concentrate on reducing carbon footprints and ensuring regulatory compliance. According to the 2024 FinOps Foundation survey, less than 20% of FinOps teams currently collaborate closely with sustainability counterparts though this is expected to increase significantly in the coming years [16]. Sustainability initiatives often reside within environmental, social, and governance (ESG) or corporate responsibility teams, while FinOps functions are embedded in finance or engineering departments. These organizational silos result in misaligned goals, fragmented data ownership, and a lack of shared accountability.

   Lack of integration leads to fragmented decisions and missed optimization opportunities. Without collaboration, sustainability efforts remain isolated from cloud usage practices, which hinders the development of unified strategies and practical solutions. Cultural resistance, unclear accountability, and weak executive support further block the formation of cross-functional teams essential for Sustainable FinOps success.

   Key organizational challenges include:

   - Defining clear ownership and shared KPIs for cost and carbon metrics.
   - Bridging knowledge gaps between finance, IT, and sustainability professionals.
   - Embedding sustainability into FinOps workflows and decision-making processes.

2. **Inconsistent Reporting Standards and Regulatory Uncertainty**

   One of the most fundamental barriers to integrating sustainability into FinOps is the lack of standardized and consistent data across cloud service providers (CSPs). Some hyperscalers, like Microsoft Azure and Google Cloud, have begun offering carbon footprint metrics. However, the methods they use for data collection and reporting differ significantly. This inconsistency in standardization makes benchmarking challenging and complicates efforts to track progress toward sustainability goals.

   For example, AWS, Azure, and Google Cloud each use different algorithms and assumptions to estimate emissions [17]. As a result, FinOps teams struggle to make direct comparisons or consolidate data into enterprise-wide sustainability reports. The inconsistency extends to levels of granularity, with some providers offering only high-level estimates and others offering detailed, service-level data. This patchwork of reporting complicates efforts to establish an accurate baseline or measure the impact of optimization efforts.

While organizations are becoming adept at tracking Scope 1 (direct) and Scope 2 (indirect energy-related) emissions, Scope 3 emissions—encompassing the entire value chain—remain elusive.

Most cloud providers focus on reporting Scope 1 and 2 emissions for their infrastructure, but they provide limited or no visibility into Scope 3 emissions. This lack of transparency creates a blind spot for companies trying to develop a complete picture of their environmental impact. Ignoring Scope 3 emissions, which can constitute up to 80% of a company's total greenhouse gas (GHG) emissions, severely undermines sustainability efforts [18].

The regulatory landscape regarding sustainability is evolving rapidly, creating uncertainty for businesses operating across various jurisdictions. Governments and international organizations are implementing multiple standards and disclosure requirements, including the European Union's Corporate Sustainability Reporting Directive (CSRD) and the US Securities and Exchange Commission's (SEC) proposed climate-related disclosure requirements.

These frameworks are anticipated to pressure organizations to report accurate and verifiable sustainability metrics, including those related to cloud services. However, the lack of clarity and uniformity in regulatory expectations makes it difficult for FinOps teams to prepare adequately. Compliance efforts can become resource-intensive and detract from proactive sustainability initiatives.

3. **Skill Gap and Training Needs**

   Integrating sustainability into FinOps demands combining skills traditionally found in separate domains. Finance teams must understand carbon accounting (Scope 1, 2, 3, Global Warming Potential, or GWP, and embodied carbon), while cloud engineers need to factor environmental impact into design areas that were previously outside their focus. Sustainability professionals often lack technical cloud expertise, creating collaboration gaps that hinder efforts to reduce emissions.

   Current training remains siloed, leaving practitioners unprepared for sustainable cloud operations. There is a growing demand for interdisciplinary roles, such as Sustainable Cloud Engineers, but clear pathways are lacking. Closing this gap requires cross-functional education, upskilling, and cultural change, supported by executive sponsorship and incentives.

   Sustainability literacy will soon be as vital as cost awareness in FinOps, with environmental considerations embedded in onboarding, certifications, and performance metrics to drive sustainable cloud operations.

4. **Conflicting Priorities: Cost Vs. Carbon**

   While FinOps traditionally emphasizes cost optimization, sustainability sometimes demands decisions that may not lead to the lowest financial cost, such as running workloads in regions with higher renewable energy penetration but more expensive computing. This creates a tension between economic and environmental objectives, requiring cultural shifts, new decision frameworks, and clear prioritization strategies.

Cloud providers often offer lower prices in regions where electricity costs are reduced, typically in areas that rely on fossil fuels. This makes such locations appealing for organizations looking to minimize expenses when placing workloads. However, these regions tend to have higher carbon intensities, meaning that focusing solely on the least expensive computing resources could inadvertently elevate an organization's overall carbon footprint. Conversely, deploying workloads in areas powered by renewable energy or during periods of high renewable availability can significantly reduce emissions. Nonetheless, these environmentally friendly options may come at a higher cost or face limited availability, which can directly impact operational budgets and cost-efficiency objectives.

Technical and operational factors further complicate this tension. For example, temporal optimization—scheduling non-critical workloads when renewable energy is most abundant—can minimize emissions but may lead to underutilization of reserved or committed resources, effectively raising the cost per compute unit. Choosing carbon-efficient instance types and implementing advanced cooling and energy management technologies may require upfront investments, which might not always support short-term cost reduction objectives. As a result, organizations face tradeoffs between immediate financial savings and long-term sustainability objectives, especially when the metrics for cost and carbon are not integrated within their decision-making frameworks.

18.7 Future Outlook: Trends Shaping Sustainable FinOps

As cloud computing expands and integrates with all facets of modern business, the intersection of financial operations (FinOps) and sustainability is poised to evolve from a niche concern into a core strategic imperative. Over the next decade, sustainability will not only be a compliance requirement or a reputational advantage—it will become a business-critical function that influences procurement decisions, architectural strategies, and executive key performance indicators (KPIs). The future sustainability outlook in FinOps includes stronger integration, increased accountability, and innovative practices driven by data, technology, and evolving global standards.

1. **Regulatory Momentum and Standardization**

   The global regulatory landscape is evolving rapidly, with new sustainability reporting requirements emerging worldwide. Governments and bodies, such as the EU's CSRD and the US SEC, are demanding greater transparency regarding greenhouse gas emissions, including those associated with cloud usage. Organizations must provide standardized, auditable carbon disclosures, requiring detailed, verifiable sustainability data from cloud providers.

FinOps teams must collaborate closely with legal, compliance, and sustainability departments to ensure data quality, accurate emissions allocation, and alignment with ESG goals. As standards evolve, cloud providers will be compelled to enhance their reporting tools, offering real-time emissions dashboards and forecasting capabilities to support sustainable architecture. Third-party carbon ratings or certifications for cloud services may also emerge.

2. **Evolving Role of FinOps**

   The traditional role of FinOps has focused on cost optimization, resource accountability, and cloud governance. As sustainability becomes embedded within this framework, the role of FinOps professionals will evolve. FinOps practitioners will become enablers of financial efficiency and environmental responsibility. This dual mandate will necessitate the development of new tools, metrics, and reporting capabilities.

   FinOps will be increasingly responsible for identifying opportunities to reduce cost and carbon, highlighting inefficient workloads, recommending greener compute alternatives, and guiding business units on carbon-cost tradeoffs. Just as FinOps helped organizations understand the concept of unit economics (e.g., cost per user, cost per transaction), they will help normalize carbon metrics, such as grams of CO_2e per API call or kilowatt-hour per compute unit.

   With this shift, FinOps maturity models will expand to include sustainability KPIs, and FinOps platforms will integrate carbon calculators, carbon-aware scheduling engines, and predictive analytics for sustainability. The cross-functional collaboration will deepen, with FinOps as the connective tissue between engineering, procurement, finance, and sustainability teams.

3. **Technology Innovation and Automation**

   Technological innovation will be a key driver in advancing sustainability in FinOps. Automation, AI, and machine learning will play a significant role in enabling smarter, greener decision-making. We will see the rise of carbon-aware orchestration engines that dynamically schedule workloads based on the carbon intensity of energy grids or the availability of renewable energy. These intelligent systems will enable organizations to shift workloads to times or regions where the emissions impact is lower without compromising on service-level objectives.

   Sustainability-focused Infrastructure as Code (IaC) frameworks will emerge, where sustainability principles—like energy efficiency, resource rightsizing, or preferred green regions—are embedded into cloud provisioning scripts. Tagging strategies will also evolve to include sustainability attributes, allowing for detailed environmental impact analysis at the workload, team, or product level.

   Additionally, the expansion of smart sensors, IoT devices, and digital twins will improve visibility into carbon-intensive operations. Cloud services will be able to process and analyze this data in near real-time, establishing feedback loops that support immediate optimizations and informed long-term infrastructure planning.

4. **Decarbonization Strategies and Partnerships with Cloud Providers**

   As organizations strengthen their sustainability commitments, FinOps teams will play a pivotal role in executing decarbonization initiatives. This involves minimizing emissions by optimizing workloads and collaborating with cloud providers to access more sustainable services.

   Organizations will begin to prioritize cloud providers based on sustainability performance, including the share of renewable energy in their operations, the carbon intensity of their data centers, and their transparency in emissions reporting. Green SLAs (Service Level Agreements) may become more common, where service uptime is guaranteed alongside sustainability metrics such as a minimum renewable energy threshold or carbon footprint limits.

   Collaborative partnerships between enterprises and cloud service providers will be critical. Joint innovation programs, carbon offset agreements, and co-developed sustainability tools will help elevate industry standards. Some organizations may co-invest in renewable energy projects or green data centers to support long-term cloud needs.
5. **Customer and Market Pressure**

   Customers are becoming increasingly eco-conscious and are holding companies accountable for their sustainability practices. Businesses will face rising pressure to demonstrate that their digital services are cost-effective and environmentally responsible. This will be especially relevant for B2B companies responding to ESG questionnaires or sustainability criteria from procurement teams.

   FinOps will enable the transparent sharing of sustainability reporting with customers and stakeholders. Metrics such as emissions per digital transaction or customer engagement will become standard elements in annual sustainability reports, investor briefings, and product documentation.

   Market differentiation will largely depend on sustainability credentials. Companies that can effectively showcase their low-carbon digital operations will gain a competitive advantage, especially in industries where sustainability is a key value for customers, such as technology, retail, and consumer goods.
6. **Workforce and Organizational Culture**

   Embedding sustainability into FinOps will also require significant cultural and organizational change. A new generation of cloud professionals will expect their work to have a positive environmental impact. Organizations that provide meaningful opportunities to engage in sustainability efforts will be better positioned to attract and retain top talent.

   Sustainability training will become an integral part of FinOps certification programs, engineering boot camps, and corporate learning platforms. Internal sustainability champions will emerge within cloud and FinOps teams, driving grassroots innovation and continuous improvement.

   Moreover, performance incentives and team KPIs will begin to reflect carbon reduction achievements, embedding sustainability goals into day-to-day operations. This cultural shift will redefine success, not just in terms of cost savings but also in environmental stewardship.

7. **Advanced Metrics and KPIs**

   To support this transformation, sustainability metrics will evolve and become more sophisticated. While today's KPIs focus primarily on emissions and energy use, future indicators will incorporate a broader set of values, such as:

   - Renewable energy utilization by region or provider
   - Embodied carbon of infrastructure over time
   - Average carbon reduction per optimization initiative
   - Forecasted vs. actual emissions trends
   - Emissions per unit of business value (e.g., per customer, per revenue dollar)

   These KPIs will be tracked alongside traditional cost metrics, offering a holistic view of performance. Organizations will also benchmark their sustainability maturity against that of their industry peers, leveraging external audits or sustainability scoring models to assess their progress.

18.8 Conclusion: Charting a Sustainable Way Forward for FinOps

As explored throughout this chapter, Sustainable FinOps is no longer a futuristic ideal—it is a present-day imperative. What began as a framework to control cloud costs has transformed into a strategic discipline that unites financial stewardship with environmental accountability. In a world where digital operations are closely tied to energy consumption and carbon emissions, the value of cloud investments must now be evaluated through a dual lens: economic efficiency and ecological impact.

Sustainable FinOps empowers organizations to not only optimize spending but also actively reduce their carbon footprints. Through practices such as rightsizing, carbon-aware scheduling, geographic optimization, and emissions tracking, FinOps teams are redefining what responsible cloud management entails. This shift is supported by cloud providers offering greater transparency through carbon dashboards, region-specific data, and insights into renewable energy.

However, technical solutions alone are insufficient. Embedding sustainability into cloud financial operations requires a cultural shift. Leadership must champion this change, ensuring that sustainability metrics are embedded in key performance indicators (KPIs), procurement policies, and architectural decisions. Cross-functional collaboration and skill development are essential—engineers must be carbon-conscious, FinOps professionals need fluency in sustainability frameworks, and sustainability leaders must understand cloud economics.

The path forward is guided by an evolving maturity model—from gaining visibility into carbon data to implementing predictive, automated optimizations. Tools and frameworks provided by the FinOps Foundation, the Green Software Foundation, and others are helping even small teams take meaningful first steps.

As global regulations, such as the EU's CSRD and the SEC's climate disclosures, gain traction, Sustainable FinOps is becoming not just a best practice but a compliance requirement. Ultimately, it marks a fundamental redefinition of success in the cloud: not just doing more for less but doing it responsibly. Organizations that embrace this mindset will be best positioned to lead in a carbon-conscious digital economy.

References

1. Mohammed, S. & Researcher, Independent, [Online]. Retrieved from https://www.researchgate.net/publication/389673312_CLOUD_SUSTAINABILITY_AND_FINOPS_BALANCING_ENVIRONMENTAL_IMPACT_AND_COST_EFFICIENCY.
2. Gooding, M. *Global data center electricity use to double by 2026—IEA report*. Data Center Dynamics, [Online]. Retrieved from https://www.datacenterdynamics.com/en/news/global-data-center-electricity-use-to-double-by-2026-report/.
3. Sharma, B., et al. *Cloud sustainability and its intersection with FinOps*. [Online]. Retrieved from https://www.finops.org/wg/sustainability/#what-are-scope-1-2%2D%2D3-emissions.
4. FinOps Foundation. *State of FinOps 2025 report*. [Online]. Retrieved from https://data.finops.org/.
5. Connolly, S. *7-global-esg-regulations-and-frameworks*. [Online]. Retrieved from https://blancco.com/resources/blog-7-global-esg-regulations-and-frameworks/.
6. FinOps Foundation. *FinOps framework*. [Online]. Retrieved from https://www.finops.org/framework/.
7. FinOps Foundation. *FinOps framework*. [Online]. Retrieved from https://www.finops.org/framework/capabilities/cloud-sustainability/.
8. Radovanovic, A., et al., Carbon-aware computing for datacenters. Research Gate. *IEEE Transactions* on PP(99):1–1, [Online]. Retrieved from https://www.researchgate.net/publication/360434183_Carbon-Aware_Computing_for_Datacenters.
9. Bhat, M. A., et al. Cloud computing: A solution to geographical information systems (GIS). *International Journal on Computer Science and Engineering (IJCSE)*, *3*(2). [Online]. Retrieved from https://www.researchgate.net/profile/Bashir-Ahmad-14/publication/50247423_Cloud_Computing_A_solution_to_Geographical_Information_Systems_GIS/links/5600038f08aec948c4f9f59a/Cloud-Computing-A-solution-to-Geographical-Information-Systems-GIS.pdf?origin=journalDetail&_tp=eyJwYWdlIjoiam91cm5hbERldGFpbCJ9.
10. O'Toole, M., et al. *Updated carbon methodology for the AWS customer carbon footprint tool*. [Online].
11. Microsoft. [Online]. Retrieved from https://learn.microsoft.com/en-us/industry/sustainability/sustainability-data-solutions-fabric/azure-emissions-insights-calculation-methodology.
12. Google. [Online]. https://cloud.google.com/carbon-footprint?hl=en.
13. Sunbird. *Top 30 data center sustainability metrics*. Top 30 Data Center Sustainability Metrics. [Online]. Retrieved from https://www.sunbirddcim.com/infographic/top-30-data-center-sustainability-metrics.
14. Barlett, S., et al. *Data center facility sustainability metrics*. [Online]. Retrieved from https://www.opencompute.org/documents/dcf-sustainability-metrics-final-r3-docx-pdf.
15. Kanumuri, V. S. Sustainable cloud computing: Leveraging FinOps for environmental responsibility. *Journal of Artificial Intelligence & Cloud Computing*. [Online]. SRC/JAICC-312. https://doi.org/10.47363/JAICC/2023(2)293.

16. Fuller, M. *State of FinOps '24: Top priorities shift to reducing waste and managing commitments*. [Online]. Retrieved from https://www.finops.org/insights/key-priorities-shift-in-2024/.
17. Kini, R. *FinOps and sustainability teams collaborate to optimize carbon*. [Online]. Retrieved from https://www.finops.org/insights/finops-sustainability-collaborate/.
18. Sharma, B., et al. *Cloud sustainability and its intersection with FinOps*. [Online]. Retrieved from https://www.finops.org/wg/sustainability/.

MIX
Papier aus verantwortungsvollen Quellen
Paper from responsible sources
FSC® C105338

If you have any concerns about our products,
you can contact us on
ProductSafety@springernature.com

In case Publisher is established outside the EU,
the EU authorized representative is:
Springer Nature Customer Service Center GmbH
Europaplatz 3, 69115 Heidelberg, Germany

Printed by Libri Plureos GmbH
in Hamburg, Germany